Global Hollywood

Global Hollywood

Toby Miller, Nitin Govil, John McMurria
and Richard Maxwell

 Publishing

First published in 2001 by the
British Film Institute
21 Stephen Street, London W1T 1LN

The British Film Institute promotes greater understanding of,
and access to, film and moving image culture in the UK.

Cover design: Lisa Swerling/Default

Set in by Fakenham Photosetting, Norfolk
Printed in Great Britain by St Edmundsbury Press, Suffolk

British Library Cataloguing-in-Publication Data
A catalogue record for this book is available from the British Library
ISBN 0–85170–845–5 pbk
ISBN 0–85170–846–3 hbk

Contents

Acknowledgments

The authors wish to thank the following for their assistance during this project: Manuel Alvarado, the US Bureau of Labor Statistics, Edward Buscombe, the US Department of Commerce, Glen Creeber, Sean Delaney, James Hay, John Hill, Geoffrey Lawrence, Marie Leger, Andrew Lockett of the BFI (and his co-workers involved in the book), Anna McCarthy, Denise McKenna, Petra and Luke Maxwell, Albert Moran, Julia Nevarez, Colleen Petruzzi, Dana Polan, Deborah Wuliger and George Yúdice. The spirit of Jack Valenti inspired us every step of the way.

Note on Authorship

Global Hollywood has been a collaborative writing project between the four authors, with research, ideas and words proliferating between us. Primary responsibility for writing specific chapters was as follows: Introduction, Chapter One, and Chapter Two (Miller); Chapter Three (McMurria); Chapter Four (Govil); Chapter Five (Maxwell); Chapter Six (Miller and Maxwell); and Conclusion (joint).

Introduction

[T]he Americans have colonized our subconscious.

(Wim Wenders, 1991: 98).

It is a fact, blessedly confirmed, that the American movie is affectionately received by audiences of all races, cultures and creeds on all continents; amid turmoil and stress as well as hope and promise. This isn't happenstance. It is the confluence of creative reach, story telling skill, decision making by top studio executives and the interlocking exertions of distribution and marketing artisans.

(Jack Valenti, 1998a)

Hollywood is a place you can't geographically define. We don't really know where it is.

(John Ford on BBC Television, 1964; quoted in Bordwell *et al.*, 1988: xiii)

We are all experts at understanding Hollywood movies. We have to be, given their presence on most cinema and television screens. Hollywood is an invitation to replication and domination, an invitation both desired and disavowed – one that many of us resist or doubt. What is it about *le défi américain* that makes it hegemonic, yet troubles people so? These questions surpass the arenas of cinema and television. They address our very frameworks of taste and politics.

In the quotations above, we see multiple sides to the screen industries' attitudes to Hollywood's power and the immensity of US popular culture (valued at US$31 billion in 2000) ('Saving Hollywood', 2001). Whereas the pan-European *auteur* Wim Wenders provides a pithy evocation of despair in the face of US cultural domination, Motion Picture Association of America (MPAA) maven Valenti[1] offers a Panglossian account of talent rising to the top. If Wenders represents a supposedly superior aesthetic that would like to anoint Western European civilisation to world cultural leadership, Valenti stands for a human spectre haunting world film and television, the personification of hearty, gum-chewing US populism. Both quips contain grains of truth, albeit running the way of each man's 'wood'. But the élitism of Wenders and the celebrationism of Valenti are as unsatisfying politically as they are analytically. We hope to read against the grain of each.

This book seeks to explain the national and international success of Hollywood. Most contemporary studies of global Hollywood have veered between uncritical celebration (Olson, 1999; Demers, 1999), neo-classical economic conservatism (Hoskins *et al.*, 1997) and apolitical archivism (Thompson, 1985; Jarvie, 1998).[2] They claim that Hollywood's international success results from the 'narrative transparency' of its continuity storytelling, blended with a vast and internally differentiated internal public of immigrants from diverse cultures. This mixture allegedly makes for a universal alchemy of entertainment that attracts foreign consumers – as per a prominent entertainment consultant's claim that '*the human imagination*' best explains US dominance (Wolf, 1999: 296).

But because Hollywood's cultural products travel through time, space and population, their material properties and practices of circulation must be addressed in a way that blends disciplinary perspectives rather than obeying these restricted orders of discourse. So, unlike economic neo-conservatives, we do not assume the primacy of markets in allocating preferences. Unlike market researchers, we do not accept Hollywood's version of itself as a narrator of universal stories. Unlike political economists, we do not assume the centrality of the economy to the exclusion of meaning. Unlike textual reductionists, we do not assume that it is adequate to interpret a film's internal qualities or its supposed 'positioning' of mythic spectators. And unlike the psy-complexes (psychology, psychoanalysis, psychotherapy and psychiatry), we do not seek to divine what is going on inside audiences' heads. Instead, we address global Hollywood both theoretically and empirically, deploying a mixture of methods from screen studies (the left-liberal humanities bent to what are variously termed film, cinema and media studies) and communications (the radical end to social-science approaches), via an admixture of critical political economy and cultural studies. Our aim is to challenge both *laissez-faire* celebrations and *étatiste* denunciations of Hollywood.

Screen texts are commodities whose key appeal lies in their meanings. Socioeconomic analysis is, therefore, a natural ally of representational analysis in seeking to explain global Hollywood. But a certain tendency on both sides has maintained that they are mutually exclusive, on the grounds that one approach is concerned with structures of the economy, and the other with structures of meaning. This need not be the case. Historically, the best critical political economy and the best cultural studies have worked through the imbrication of power and signification at all points on the cultural continuum. Graham Murdock puts the task well:

> Critical political economy is at its strongest in explaining who gets to speak
> to whom and what forms these symbolic encounters take in the major
> spaces of public culture. But cultural studies, at its best, has much of value

to say about ... how discourse and imagery are organised in complex and shifting patterns of meaning and how these meanings are reproduced, negotiated, and struggled over in the flow and flux of everyday life.

(Murdock, 1995: 94)

Ideally, blending the two approaches would heal the divisions between fact and interpretation and between the social sciences and the humanities, under the sign of a principled approach to cultural democracy. To that end, Lawrence Grossberg recommends 'politicizing theory and theorizing politics' to combine abstraction and grounded analysis. This requires a focus on the contradictions of organisational structures, their articulations with everyday living and textuality, and their intrication with the polity and economy, refusing any bifurcation that opposes the study of production and consumption, or fails to address axes of social stratification (Grossberg, 1997: 4–5, 9–10). That focus has animated our work here. It seems the best way to understand the conundrum of our third foundational epigraph, Ford's provocation about Hollywood's 'nowhereness' – that there is no 'there there', or as Robert Park put it sixty years ago, it is 'visible but remote' even to Angelinos (1943: 732). Conservatives of today claim that 'Hollywood has become an aesthetic and is no longer a place in California' because there are now multiple sites of screen power across the world (Olson, 2000). We have a less fanciful answer: Hollywood's 'real' location lies in its division of labour.

Global Hollywood commences with an analysis of the industry's history of globalisation and the dilemmas it poses as a sign of American ideology and a perceived threat to national cultures, as detailed in the discourse of cultural imperialism. We then consider the explanatory power of alternatives to cultural imperialism, such as conventional ideas from the industry itself and neo-classical economics, as well as foregrounding work through the competing concept of a New International Division of Cultural Labour (NICL).[3] After these ground-clearing chapters, the book turns to the nitty-gritty of how Hollywood texts live and die, their existence as commodity chains (Wallerstein, 2000), with chapters addressing co-production, copyright, marketing and audiences. We seek to answer two questions: Is Hollywood global – and in what sense? And what are the implications of that dominance? For the most part, we focus on wealthy nations, as they provide the greatest amount of capital to the US through the trade in screen texts and via foreign ownership, and are crucial in the NICL, though we also attend to issues of significance for less-developed countries.

The Statistical Backdrop
Hollywood owns between 40 per cent and 90 per cent of the movies shown in most parts of the world. This is not to deny the importance of other screen cul-

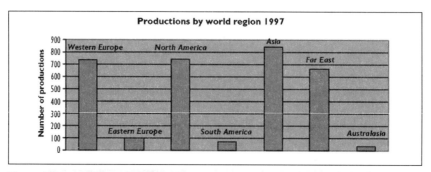

Figure 1(Source: Hancock, 1999)

tures: non-US based people of colour are the majority global filmmakers, with much more diverse ideological projects and patterns of distribution than Hollywood. Yet even with its vast production, strong export trade and extraordinary filmmaking tradition, China's total overseas sales of films between 1996 and 2000 was just US$13.86 million ('Chinese Film Industry', 2001).

But Los Angeles–New York culture and commerce dominate screen entertainment around the globe, either directly or as an implied other, and the dramatic success of US film since the First World War has been a model for the export of North American music, television, advertising, the Internet and sport. Shifts towards a neo-liberal, multinational investment climate over the past decade have reinforced global Hollywood's strategic power over the NICL through the privatisation of media ownership, a unified Western European market, openings in the former Soviet bloc, and the spread of satellite TV, the Web and the VCR, combined with deregulation of national broadcasting in Europe and Latin America (Rockwell, 1994: H1; Shohat and Stam, 1994: 27; Wasko, 1994: 233).

The world market is crucial to the US.[4] In 1998, the major US film studios increased their foreign rentals by one-fifth on 1997; overseas box office of US$6.821 billion virtually equalled the domestic figure of US$6.877 billion. The most popular thirty-nine films across the world in 1998 came from the US, and as that happened, the condition of other major filmmaking countries was declining: the percentage of the box office taken by indigenous films was down to 10 per cent in Germany, 12 per cent in Britain, 26 per cent in France, 12 per cent in Spain, 2 per cent in Canada, 4 per cent in Australia and 5 per cent in Brazil – all dramatic decreases, to record low levels in some cases. These figures were certainly driven in part by the phenomenal impact of *Titanic* (James Cameron, 1997), which made US$1 billion outside the US, but they represented a significant change from the earlier part of the decade, when European audiences for domestic films had increased (*Screen Digest*, August 1997: 177, 183; Foreman *et al.*, 1999). Hollywood's proportion of the world market is double

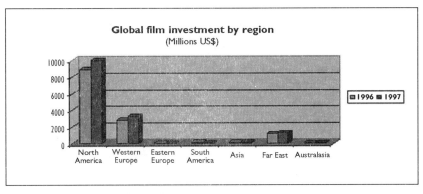

Figure 2 (Source: Hancock, 1998)

what it was in 1990, and the European film industry is one-ninth of the size it was in 1945. Hollywood's overseas receipts were US$6.6 billion in 1999 and US$6.4 billion in 2000 (the reduction was due to foreign exchange depreciation rather than to a drop in admissions [Groves, 2001b]). In 2000, most 'star-driven event films' from Hollywood obtained more revenue overseas than domestically, with eighteen movies accumulating over US$100 million internationally, figures not attained by even one film from any other national cinema (Groves, 2000b). PriceWaterhouseCoopers (PWC) estimates that US companies earn almost US$11 billion by exporting film. PWC predicts that, by 2004, Hollywood will earn close to US$14 billion in export revenue (Winslow, 2001). Europe is a key site for those earnings.

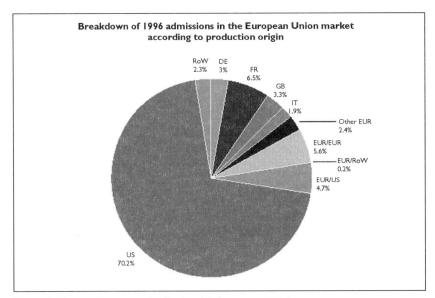

Figure 3 (Source: European Audiovisual Laboratory, 1998)

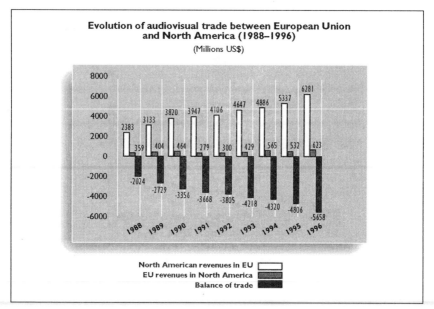

Figure 4 (Source: European Audiovisual Laboratory, 1998)

In 2000, a re-release of *The Exorcist* (William Friedkin, 1973) took more money in Italy than the most successful local title (Dawtrey *et al.*, 2000)! Consider the overall situation in Italy over the last half of the 1990s:

Market Share (%)	1990	1991	1992	1993	1994	1995	1996	1997	1998
National Italian Films	21%	26.8%	24.4%	17.3%	23.7%	21.1%	24.8%	32.9%	24.7%
US Films	70%	58.6%	59.4%	70%	61.4%	63.2%	59.7%	46.7%	63.8%
Films from the RoW	9%	14.6%	16.2%	12.7%	14.9%	15.7%	15.5%	20.4%	11.5%

Figure 5 (Source: Bodo, 2000)

To give an idea of how new this trend is, in 1980 the American film industry relied on exports for one-third of its annual revenue – the same proportion as 1950. So the past decade has seen a truly foundational change. In 2001, the studios demoted their overseas-desk mavens on the basis that global revenues were now *so* crucial that they no longer needed their own management systems or promotional budgets, but could be incorporated in US domestic planning (Dunkley and Harris, 2001). Some have interpreted these changes as signs of hubris by 'domestic distribution czars', a failure to acknowledge difference that will undermine Hollywood dominance (Williams-Jones, 2001; also see Lewis, 2001). Whether or not this 'streamlining' turns out to be a brief fad of managerial warlock-craft, global simultaneity of releases seems assured. Whereas there used to be delays of six months and more between the release of films in the US and overseas, it is now standard to open them everywhere within a month of domestic exhibition, regardless of issues such as climate and local holidays (DiOrio, 2001: 16).

These huge disparities in textual trade show up on the screen, where the large and wealthy domestic US audience for television and video versions of movies is crucial to enabling high budgets for theatrical releases, even though very few films are profitable in cinemas (Waterman and Jayakar, 2000). In 1999, domestic consumers spent US$40.7 billion on filmed entertainment across these sectors, up 5 per cent on 1998 (Veronis Suhler, 2000). When we compare the budgets of Hollywood films to those of other wealthy nations, differences in the amounts of money behind and on the screen become apparent.

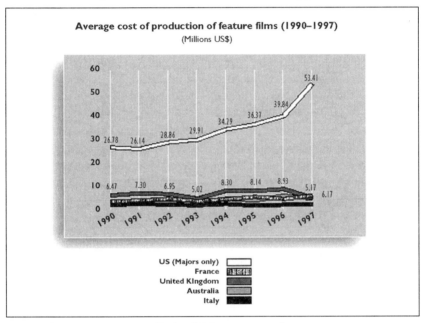

Figure 6 (Source: European Audiovisual Laboratory, 1998)

The trend to US dominance is indubitable. For example, in 1985, 41 per cent of film tickets bought in Western Europe were for Hollywood fare. In 1995, the proportion was 75 per cent. And 70 per cent of films on European television come from the US. Measured in box-office receipts, Europe is Hollywood's most valuable territory. Overall revenue there in 1997 was half the size of the US, but twice that of Asia and four times larger than Latin America. The majors collected over 60 per cent of their box-office revenues from outside the US in the top five European markets, and Hollywood's share of the market in 1996 ranged from 45–55 per cent in France, Italy and Spain to 70–80 per cent in Germany and the UK. Hollywood's proportion of total video revenues mirrored theatrical box office – between 60 and 80 per cent across Europe (*Screen Digest*, September 1999: 232; *Screen Digest*, November 1999: 296; *Screen Digest*, January 2000: 30; De Bens and de Smaele, 2001). In 1997, the balance of film trade between the US and Europe favoured the former by a third (UNESCO, 2000a).

Elsewhere, the percentage of imports from Hollywood showed astonishing growth: US films accounted for 57.4 per cent of screenings in Barbados in 1970 and 97.8 per cent in 1991; 39.7 per cent in Canada in 1970 and 63.9 per cent in 1990; 59.2 per cent in Costa Rica in 1985 and 95.9 per cent in 1995; 8.9 per cent in Cuba in 1970 and 40.9 per cent in 1993. Africa is the largest proportional importer of Hollywood films, which account for 70 per cent of exhibition in Anglophone nations and 40 per cent in Francophone countries. It is easier today to find an African film screened in Europe or the US than on home territory. Following the hyperinflation of the 1970s and 1980s, which decimated film production in Mexico and Argentina, the percentage of Hollywood films exhibited in Latin America has increased dramatically (thanks also to the labours of the MPA-America Latina) ('Home Alone', 1997; Woods, 2000; UNESCO, 2000a; Hayes, 2001; UNESCO, 2000b; Primo, 1999: 190; Amin, 1997: 322–24, 326; Armes, 1987: 49; Mattelart, 1979: 194; Diawara, 1992: 106; Ukadike, 1994: 63; Himpele, 1996: 52; MPA-LA, 2000; O'Regan, 1992: 304). And since the mid-1980s, Japan has been a critical source of Hollywood's revenue. Japan provides 10–20 per cent of worldwide grosses on blockbuster releases (Hayes, 2001).

India and China account for over two-thirds of film screens around the world (Guider, 2000b). Hollywood is optimistic about the market potential of China's 140,000 film theatres, despite severe restrictions on imports since the 1949 revolution. While total US revenues from the PRC are only US$20 million a year on a limit of ten imported films, many expect that a large percentage of its 1.3 billion people, who are used to a steady stream of pirated media product, will become 'conventional' consumers. In January 2001, half of Shanghai's theatrical takings came from five of its 130 venues, and 80 per cent of their screenings came from Hollywood (though the announcement in 2000 that annual imports would increase to twenty films as a quid pro quo for joining the World Trade Organisation was both a minimal change and one seemingly resiled from even as it was made) (Groves, 2001a; 'Chinese Film', 2001). Even in India, where Bollywood and other regional industries dominate the screen, the benchmark for a successful Hollywood release has ballooned almost 1000 per cent over the past seven years, from US$100,000 to US$1 million. By 2015, Asia could be responsible for 60 per cent of Hollywood box-office revenue (Major, 1997).

Of course, theatrical exhibition accounts for barely a quarter of Hollywood's global revenues (29 per cent in 1999). Video provides 25 per cent and television

46 per cent ('Global Media Breakdown', 2001). In 1995, 89 per cent of films screened on Brazil's cable channels were US imports, while in Egypt, the last twenty years have seen Hollywood dominate over Arab national cinemas both theatrically and in video rental. From its earliest days in the 1960s, Malaysian television relied on US films for content. The trend has never let up and dominates prime time. The same is true in Sri Lanka and the Philippines, where local films are rarely seen on television (Duke, 2000; Nain, 1996: 168, 170; Mahendra, 1996: 223; Kenny and Pernia, 1998: 84, 99). Eurodata TV's analysis in 1999 of films on television found that fourteen Hollywood pictures drew the highest audiences in twenty-seven nations across all continents. And television drama in 2000 accounted for almost 50 per cent of worldwide television exchange ('1999: Une Année', 2000; 'Fall 2000', 2001).

Television drama more generally shows the same trend. In 1998, Europe bought US$2 billion a year of US programming. The only sizeable trade the other way was Britain's paltry export figure of US$85 million. Putting together TV, video and theatrical screenings, the proportion of total Hollywood receipts from external sources grew from 35 per cent in the early 1980s to 53 per cent in 1997. The one failure was the decline of US soap opera in the face of indigenous productions that mimic it, and the loss of a domestic audience in prime time. But even the Latin American internal market in *telenovelas* meant that only 6 per cent of imported television was pan-Continental in 1996 – 86 per cent came from the US (Foreman *et al.*, 1999; *Screen Digest*, September 1999: 232; *Screen Digest*, November 1999: 296; *Screen Digest*, January 2000: 30; Durie *et al.*, 2000: 87; Olson, 1999: 1; 'A World View', 1997; European Audiovisual Observatory, 1998; O'Donnell, 1999: 213; Sinclair, 1999: 156).

Yet while its mounting dominance is there for all to see, US governments and businesses continue to assault other countries' attempts to assert rights to national self-determination on-screen via barriers to imports . Washington has the world on notice that it will use the notorious provisions of the 1974 Trade Act against any cultural protectionism it disfavours. Hong Kong, for instance, is often accused of what the US likes to call screen 'piracy'.[5] The European Union (EU) is a particular target because of its wealth and continued insistence on public support for non-US screen alternatives.

In later chapters we seek to understand the climate that generated and sustains global Hollywood, and the policy actions that animate it. This Introduction questions whether the contemporary state of screen studies equips us to address such issues. As noted earlier, mainstream screen studies is a blend of textual analysis, the psy-complexes and bourgeois business history. These tendencies have not enabled us to contribute significantly to public cultural debate. Consider a recent content analysis published by the American Medical Association (AMA). It concerns feature-length animation films made in the US between 1937 and 1997 and the way in which they associate legal but damaging recreational drugs with heroic characters (Goldstein *et al.*, 1999). The study received major public attention via AMA endorsement, a press conference, numerous media stories, and formal replies from Disney. A similar story surrounds the 2001 release of findings that despite the film industry and 'big' tobacco companies having agreed to a voluntary ban on product placement in 1989, since that time, the incidence of stars smoking cigarettes in Hollywood films has increased eleven-fold, mostly to get around the problem of bans on television commercials. This is a truly global marketing issue, again un-addressed and unaffected by screen studies (Laurance, 2001). If one peruses the American Academy of Pediatrics' *Media Matters* programme (2001), notably its advocacy of a letter-writing campaign about cinema and support for the egregious 'TV-Turnoff Week' (see also Mittell, 2000), there is no engagement with screen studies positions, and with good reason – *we* don't engage with dominant discourse. Yet there are examples of cultural studies interventions into policy discourse, such as Stuart Cunningham's work on screen violence. He carefully adumbrates conventional approaches whilst adding theorisation of the state, capital and social movements to the normal science of effects research (Cunningham, 1992: 137–67). Let this be a useful precedent.

On another front, how much academic work on the history and meaning of Hollywood addresses the reach and significance of the publicly-funded US film and television commissions that underwrite this so-called *laissez-faire* industry? In 2000, the number was 205 and growing (Stevens, 2000: 797–804), and their work is a major subsidy. For example, the New York City Office of Film, Theatre and Broadcasting (2000) offers exemption from sales tax on all production consumables, rentals and purchases. The Minnesota Film Board (2000) has a 'Minnesota Film Jobs Fund' that gives a 5 per cent rebate on wages, not to mention paying producers' first-class airfares and providing free accommodation for them and tax-free accommodation for their workers, as well as tax-avoidance schemes. The California Film Commission (2000) reimburses public personnel costs and permit and equipment fees. Hotel and sales tax rebates are almost universal across the country, and such services even extend in some cases to constructing studio sites, as in North Carolina (Rettig, 1998; Ross and Walker, 2000). Now, if most of us were asked to comment on the implications of these agencies for cultural policy, or for the claims that neoclassical economic ideology makes about US cinema, would we have much to offer the public?

The reason for this inability to contribute to debate is screen studies' historical commitment to the formation of taste. Consider the how-to book called *Going to the Cinema*, part of a British series from the 1950s which instructs middle-class readers on how to enjoy culture. It promises 'increased powers of perception' that will develop spectators' pleasure to make them more discriminating. A list of 'Films everyone should see' is even included (Buchanan and Reed, 1957: 13, 155–57). That's remarkably like most contemporary screen studies syllabi and textbooks, albeit with textual politics as the latter-day alibi that displaces a supposedly transcendental taste formation. Both the transcendental and the political projects reiterate long-standing concerns of film theory, from the silent era's faith in what ethical critic Vachel Lindsay called 'the moving picture man as a local social force ... the mere formula of [whose] activities' keeps the public well-tempered (Lindsay, 1970: 243); through 1930s social research into the impact of cinema on American youth via the Payne Fund Studies (Blumer, 1933; Blumer and Hauser, 1933); to post-Second World War anxieties, evident in the anthropology of Hortense Powdermaker and the sociology of J.P. Mayer, about Hollywood's intrication of education and entertainment and the need for counter-knowledge among the population (Powdermaker, 1950: 12–15; Mayer, 1946: 24). That history might have led to the formation of public intellectuals who made major policy and critical contributions to transforming Hollywood. But in hegemonic US–UK screen studies, it has not.

We are sometimes told today that, to quote one recent film theory anthology, there has been 'a general movement in approaches to film from a preoccupation with authorship (broadly defined), through a concentration upon the text and textuality, to an investigation of audiences' (Hollows and Jancovich, 1995: 8); or, to paraphrase the fifth edition of a widely-used anthology, that there has been, consecutively, a pursuit of knowledge about film form, then realism, followed by language, and, finally, cultural politics (Braudy and Cohen, 1999: xv–xvi). Such accounts approximate the history of some humanities-based academic work, but forget the hardy perennials of popular cinema criticism, social-science technique, and cultural policy as applied to the screen via formal analysis of films, identification of directors with movies, studies of the audience through psychology and psychoanalysis, workplace analysis of the industry, and governmental programmes of research and support. All of these have been around, quite doggedly, for almost a century (Worth, 1981: 39), but their remarkable continuity of concerns about audiences is secreted in favour of a heroic, Whiggish narrative of teleological, textualist development that animates the *doxa* of the humanities screen Academy.

The twin tasks of elevation identified in *Going to the Cinema* (see also Manvell, 1950) – addressing spectators and examining texts – have dominated screen studies. To repeat, these tasks focus on audiences and textual ranking. Over time, of course, they both branch out and converge. Audience concerns include psychological, sociological, educational, consumer, criminological and political promises and anxieties. Textual ranking involves authorship, genre, form, style and representational politics. The two tasks cross over in the area of mimesis, with audiences interpreting films against their own worlds of race, gender, class, region, age, religion, language, politics and nation. But screen studies has for the most part failed to articulate these topics against critical political economy and cultural policy concerns.

This is not to gainsay certain useful developments in screen studies. Questions of pleasure and suppression, for example, have become central more recently, as analysts have sought to account for and resist narrative stereotypes and exclusions – to explain, in Richard Dyer's words, 'why socialists and feminists liked things they thought they ought not to' (1992: 4), and why some voices and images have been excluded or systematically distorted. This difficulty over pleasure, presence and absence accounts for film theory being highly critical of prevailing representations, but never reifying itself into the Puritanism alleged by critics of political correctness. The extraordinary diversity of latter-day film anthologies makes the point clear. Contemporary feminist film collections certainly focus on issues of representation and production of common concern to many women, but they also attend, routinely, to differences of race, history, class, sexuality and nation, alongside and as part of theoretical difference (Carson *et al.*, 1994), while black film volumes divide between spectatorial and aesthetic dimensions (Diawara, 1993), and queer ones identify links between social oppression and film and video practice (Gever *et al.*, 1993; Holmlund and Fuchs, 1997).

The implicit and explicit masculinism, Eurocentrism and universalism of earlier theory have been questioned by social movements and Third and Fourth World discourses that highlight exclusions and generate new methods (Shohat and Stam, 1994; Carson and Friedman, 1995). Even here, though, there is a long history of protest at, for example, Hollywood's portrayal of foreigners and minorities, dating back to the African-American print media and many foreign governments during the silent and early sound eras (Vasey, 1997). Concerns about representation and audience are, then, relatively stable across time, but with some distinct changes of focus.

Crucial elements are left out, though, from today's dominant discourse of screen studies – the major journals, book series, conferences and graduate programmes. Our anecdote about the AMA points to a lack of relevance in the output of screen studies to *both* popular *and* policy-driven discussion of films, flowing from a lack of engagement with the sense-making practices of criticism and research conducted outside the textualist and historical side to the humanities. For example, humanities work on stardom seldom addresses the excellent research on that topic in the social sciences.[6] Adding this material to the textual, theoreticist and biographical preferences of humanities critics could offer knowledge of the impact of stars on box office, via regression analysis, and of work practices, via labour studies. This neglect is symptomatic – screen studies frequently fails to engage political and social history and social theory on the human subject, the nation, cultural policy, the law and the economy.

Despite the continuity of textual and audience axes within film theory, for reasons of rent-seeking academic professionalism – on all sides – latter-day lines have been drawn dividing communication, cultural and screen studies. The theorisation of production and spectatorship relations between film and television, for instance, continues to be dogged by the separation of mass communication's interest in economics, technology and policy from film theory's preoccupation with aesthetics and cultural address, although attempts are underway to transform both sides of the divide (Hill and McLoone, n.d.). Of course, much social-science work on the media is leaden-footed positivism that counts and counts while interpreting not a whit and is driven by a dubious media effects methodology that we lay waste to in Chapter 6. On the economics front, a similarly disabling distinction has been drawn between choice as a *means* of action (economics) and a *place* of action (politics). This distinction has precluded a political-economic approach. But the disciplinary division of labour in screen studies that is encouraged by orthodox rent-seeking is also imperiled by the excellent work done on, for instance, race and the media, by the likes of Thomas Nakayama (1994 and 1997; Nakayama and Krizek, 1995; Nakayama and Martin, 1999; Martin and Nakayama, 2000) and Oscar Gandy (1992a, 1992b and 1998; Gandy and Matabane, 1989). These scholars disobey such divides. Second, many college jobs in film now come not from the usual suspect – a literature department in search of a partial make-over – but also from communication and media studies. And third, the influence of globalisation has pushed neo-classical economics and rational-choice political science towards some acknowledgment of the need to allow actually existing social politics and financial transactions to exist and interpenetrate, given that the 'business of government is everywhere increasingly organised along the lines of the government of business' (Higgott, 1999: 29–30; see also Ollman, 2000).

Perhaps the most significant innovation that we need – and it inspires this volume – comes from critical political economy and cultural studies. These areas have witnessed a radical historicisation of context, such that the analysis of textual properties and spectatorial processes must now be supplemented by an account of *occasionality* that details the conditions under which a text is made, circulated, received, interpreted and criticised. The life of any popular or praised film is a passage across space and time, a life remade again and again by institutions, discourses and practices of distribution and reception. Thus to understand texts, we must consider all the shifts and shocks that characterise their existence as cultural commodities, their ongoing renewal as the temporary 'property' of varied, productive workers and publics and the abiding 'property' of businesspeople.

This push for a radical contextualisation of interpretation is aided by a surprising turn – the early history of film as part of a vaudeville bill is being reprised. The moving image is again part of a multi-form network of entertainment, via CD-ROMs, computer games, the Web, DVDs and multiplexes. The brief moment when cinema could be viewed as a fairly unitary phenomenon in terms of exhibition (say, 1920 to 1950) set up the *conceptual* prospect of its textual fetishisation in academia, something that became *technologically feasible* with video-cassette recorders – just when that technology's popularity compromised the very discourse of stable aestheticisation! Now that viewing environments, audiences, technologies and genres are so multiple, the cinema is restored to a mixed-medium mode. The US Federal Government's official classification of screen production (Department of Commerce, 2001: 14, 16 n. 12) includes features, made-for-television films, television series, commercials and music video – and so should screen studies' 'official classification'.

In short, if it is to make an impact on the power and status of global Hollywood, screen studies needs an overhaul. The current orthodoxy is: (i) use of certain limited, seemingly arbitrarily selected, theories of subject-formation; (ii) solitary or classroom textual analysis of 'films' that is actually conducted on a television screen, an analysis that magically stands for other audiences, subjectivities, cultures and occasions of viewing; and (iii) neglect of cultural bureaucrats and industry workers in favour of attention to individuals, collectives or (by magical proxy) social movements, because artists are privileged over governments and unions, and scholarly critics decree themselves able to divine meaning for whole classes of the population, with spectacularity inordinately prized over the mundane. Such readings are interesting things to do, but they are insufficient as political-economic-textual-anthropological accounts, and their politics are all too frequently limited to the Academy.

Instead, we should acknowledge the policy, distributional, promotional and exhibitionary protocols of the screen at each site as much as their textual ones. Enough talk of 'economic reductionism' without also problematising 'textual reductionism'. Enough valorisation of close reading and armchair accounts of human interiority without ethical and political regard for the conditions of global cultural labour and the significance of work, texts and subjectivities within social movements and demographic cohorts. Enough denial of the role of government. Enough teaching classes on animation, for instance, without reference to effects work, content analysis and the international political economy that sees an episode of *The Simpsons* decrying globalisation when the programme has itself been made by non-union animators in South-East Asia. These issues – cultural labour, industry frameworks, audience experiences and cultural policy – should be integral. Institutions do not have to be arid areas of study, and the links to everyday life are real. The remarkable international actions of young people against globalisation as we enter the twenty-first century shows that they can be energised around such topics, notably the world division of labour – so let screen studies 'get' real, too.

We need to view the screen through twin theoretical prisms. On the one hand, it can be understood as the newest component of sovereignty, a twentieth-century cultural addition to ideas of patrimony and rights that sits alongside such traditional topics as territory, language, history and schooling. On the other hand, the screen is a cluster of culture industries. As such, it is subject to exactly the rent-seeking practices and exclusionary representational protocols that characterise liaisons between state and capital. We must ask: Is screen studies serving phantasmatic projections of humanities' critics' narcissism, or does it actively engage social-movement politics? Is Hollywood really giving the people of the world what they want, or does it operate via a brutal form of monopoly-capitalist business practice? And is non-Hollywood, state-supported screen culture expanding the vision and availability of the good life to include the ability of a people to control its representation on screen? Or is that culture merely a free ride for fractions of a comprador, cosmopolitan or social-movement bourgeoisie? To what extent do 'their' national cinemas engage people, and do they spend more time watching imports than their 'own' films? The political audit we make of an audiovisual space should consider its openness, both on- and off-camera, to the demographics of those inhabiting it. No cinema that claims resistance to Hollywood in the name of national or social-movement specificity is worthy of endorsement if it does not actually attend to sexual and racial minorities and women, along with class politics. The ethnographic and political-economy work of Jeffrey Himpele (1996) on Bolivia and Preminda Jacob (1998) on India is exemplary here – but are they, or the AMA's authors, referenced by the hegemons and acolytes of screen studies?

What would it take for screen studies to matter more? We have three proposals: (a) influence over public media discourse on the screen; (b) influence over public policy and not-for-profit and commercial practice; and (c) not reproducing a thing called 'screen studies', but instead doing work that *studies* the screen, regardless of its intellectual provenance. When it comes to key questions of texts and audiences – what gets produced and circulated and how it is read – policy analysis, political economy, ethnography, movement activism and the use of the social-science archive are crucial. We hope, therefore, that this book contributes not only to the debate about global Hollywood, but also to how screen studies goes about its business.

Notes

1   The MPAA is comprised of the major studios in Hollywood. The working definition of 'independent' in the US film industry covers all films made by producers who are not MPAA members and are mostly represented by the American Film Marketing Association (AFMA). Although the two entities are responsible for the release of about the same number of films (more than 200 each annually), MPAA members outspend AFMA members eleven to one (Department of Commerce, 2001: 14).

2   An important, albeit earlier, exception is the work of Thomas Guback (1969, 1974, 1984, 1985 and 1987).

3   We make the acronym NICL rather than NIDCL to offer a homonym for 'nickel', the US five-cent coin.

4   Figures for cinema attendance and receipts are extremely difficult to calculate with confidence. France, Germany, Sweden, Spain and Italy mandate declaration of receipts by theatre owners. Some European countries, such as Portugal, Greece, Iceland, Luxembourg, Russia, Hungary and most of the Third World have no data collection. Others see data promulgated by professional associations (the Netherlands), distributors (Slovakia, Switzerland and the Czech Republic), magazines and private companies (the US, Ireland, the UK, Belgium, France, Spain, Germany and Italy) or governmental statisticians (Finland and Denmark) (*Lumiere*, n. d.).

5   Odd that this concept is never put into dialectical play with the development dictum of the free exchange of ideas and open communication, isn't it?

6   See Simonet, 1980; Rosen, 1981; Adler, 1985; Chung and Cox, 1994; Wallace *et al.*, 1993; Albert, 1998; Peters, 1974; Peters and Cantor, 1982; Levy, 1989; Baker and Faulkner, 1991; De Vany and Walls, 1996 and 1997; Lauzen and Dozier, 1999; Clark, 1995; Marvasti, 2000; Nelson *et al.*, 2001.

Chapter One
Hollywood History, Cultural Imperialism and Globalisation

Cultural imperialism is a perspective that has largely been identified with leftist analysts . . . and is therefore often dismissed . . . [because it allegedly] blots out any capacity of the world's citizens to resist or appropriate in their own fashion the messages of global advertising or US television, and additionally presumes that worries about cultural survival are uniquely provoked by the policies of the major powers, and not equally by nation-states against ethnic minorities within their own frontier.

(John H. Downing, 1996: 223)

We inhabit a moment popularly understood, in Eric Hobsbawm's words, as 'the global triumph of the United States and its way of life' (1998: 1). From a very different perspective, Henry Kissinger (1999) goes so far as to say that 'globalisation is really another name for the dominant role of the United States'. His consulting firm, Kissinger Associates, advises that this era must see the US 'win the battle of the world's information flows, dominating the airwaves as Great Britain once ruled the seas', not least because 'Americans should not deny the fact that of all the nations in the history of the world, theirs is the most just, the most tolerant, the most willing to constantly reassess and improve itself, and the best model for the future' (Rothkopf, 1997: 38, 47). The *Wall Street Journal* trumpets the proclamation loudly: 'the U. S. enters the 21st century in a position of unrivalled dominance that surpasses anything it experienced in the 20th. . . . America's free-market ideology is now the world's ideology; and the nation's Internet and biotechnology businesses are pioneering the technologies of tomorrow' (Murray, 1999). For all the misery internal to the US (in 2000, even as 74 per cent of college students expected to become millionaires, 44 million people had no medical coverage), it has international influence beyond the reach of other regimes, with the military and popular culture a key. And the speed with which culture can spread around the world is accelerating. Whereas radio reached 50 million homes after forty years, it took television thirteen years to do so, and the Internet attained the figure in four years (International

Labour Office, 2000a). With ever-increasing homogenisation of ownership and control and rapidly developing economies of scale, the capacity to dominate the exchange of ideas is strengthened, and global Hollywood is central to that mission.

The source of Hollywood's power extends far beyond the history of cinema, to the cultural-communications complex that has been an integral component of capitalist exchange since the end of the nineteenth century. In the second half of the twentieth century, Third World activists, artists, writers and critical political economists nominated that complex as cultural imperialism. By the late twentieth century, it became fashionable to think of this power in terms of globalisation, a maddeningly euphemistic term laden with desire, fantasy, fear, attraction – and intellectual imprecision about what it is supposed to describe (Jacka, 1992: 5, 2; Jameson, 2000). 'Hollywood' appears in nearly all descriptions of globalisation's effects – left, right and third ways – as a floating signifier, a kind of cultural smoke rising from the economic fires of a successful US-led crusade to convert the world to capitalism. We dispute this thin description of Hollywood as an indexical sign of economic globalisation, because it fails to acknowledge that global Hollywood's imperatives are crucial to the contemporary political economy, both animating and being animated by it. What distinguishes Hollywood from other industries in the present stage of capitalist expansion is its command of the New International Division of Cultural Labour.

We are preparing the way here for a description in subsequent chapters of how Hollywood reproduces and regulates the NICL through its control over cultural labour markets, international co-production, intellectual property, marketing, distribution and exhibition. Our attention to the socio-spatial conditions that have made the NICL (and resistance to it) possible is a departure from the dominant version of Hollywood, which sees it merely as a screen effect of globalisation's 'universal logic of modernity'. Mike Featherstone and Scott Lash argue that this position presumes 'substantial measures of abstraction … disembedding [and] hollowing out … meaning in everyday life'. We resist such temporal biases and their obsession with the ephemera of visual culture in the hope of telling a story that is 'sensitive to the different power potentials of the different players participating in … global struggles' (Featherstone and Lash, 1995: 3). Our goal is to thicken existing theories of global Hollywood's power, and modify current thinking about cultural policies that both enable and resist it.

Early capitalism predated the existence of states, and cultures were usually organised by other points of affinity, such as religion or language. Networks of information and trade connected the Pacific, Asia, the Mediterranean and Africa through the fifteenth century. The slavery, militarism and technology of European imperialism wiped out these routes. Intra-continental communications came to rely on Europe as a conduit, and new ideologies followed, such as racial supremacy and the conversion mission of Christianity (Hamelink, 1990: 223–24). Eurocentric networks circulated the assumptions of social evolutionists, not only in their narcissism, but in their search for a unanimity that would bind humanity in singular directions and forms of development. This discourse enabled its owners to observe themselves in an earlier stage of maturation, by investigating life in the southern Hemisphere, and to police and coordinate what they found there, in keeping with a drive towards uniformity and optimality of human definition, achievement and organisation (Axtmann, 1993: 64-65).

Cultural diffusion has always been international, but the velocity and profundity of its processes seem to be on the increase (Mann, 1993: 119). For this reason, perhaps, theories of globalisation put space and speed at the centre of both analytic and business concerns: social theory links commodification critique to advertising practice in a giddy process akin to the experience of watching an action-adventure film's climactic struggle. Capital moves at high velocity, lighting on areas and countries in a promiscuous way, and the manner in which materials and people are exchanged simultaneously across the globe is profoundly asymmetrical (Sankowski, 1992: 6; Rockwell, 1994: H1; Frow, 1992: 14–15). Put another way, the military domination of empire suffered by First Peoples is now experienced – in milder form – as corporate domination by former colonisers and colonised alike – the 'Americanisation' that Charles Baudelaire referred to as a 'vast cage, a great accounting establishment' (quoted in Grantham, 1998: 60).

One could make the claim that the coordinates for compressing space and time under contemporary globalisation derive from three key events: the Treaty of Tordesillas in 1494 and the Washington and Berlin Conferences of 1884. The Tordesillas Treaty acknowledged the emergence of empire, as the Pope mediated rivalries between Portugal and Spain through a bifurcation of the world – the first recorded conceptualisation of the globe as a site of conquest and exploitation. The Washington Conference standardised Greenwich as the axis of time and cartography, the same year as the imperial division of Africa at the Conference of Berlin. These developments effectively marked out the world as a site of interconnected government and commerce (Schaeffer, 1997: 2, 7, 10–11), with Western Europe and the US as its domineering epicentre.

Capitalism's uneven and unequal development have paralleled the violent cartography of Tordesillas, Washington and Berlin. The mercantilist accumulation and imperialism of 1500 to 1800 were followed by the classical era of capital and its Industrial Revolution, founded on the use of natural resources for manufacturing copper, steel and fuel. Northern industrial development and agrarian change were partnered by European emigration to the Americas (to deal with population overflow) and the division of Africa and Asia (delivering raw materials and enslaved labour) (Amin, 1997: 1, x; Reich, 1999). Cinema technology and narrative emerged around the same time, as the US invented and appropriated a vast array of cultural machines – the airplane, the type-writer, electric light and the telephone. They made it the very image of a mechanical dream or nightmare, depending on where you stood (Grantham, 2000: 13). There were also transformations in colonial politics: the US seized the Philippines and Cuba, the European powers ran Africa, and Native Ameri-can resistance was crushed. And while First People's rights were being trampled, commercial cultural export and sovereign authority were synchronising (with an array of genocidal stories being enacted on-screen). A key economic shift also occurred between 1870 and 1914: average annual global output and exchange increased by more than 3 per cent – an unprecedented figure (Hirst, 1997: 411). Not surprisingly, Bahá'u'lláh coined the phrase 'New World Order' in 1873 (quoted in Calkins and Vézina, 1996: 311).[1] In response to these governmen-tal and business developments, European and US socialists, syndicalists, and anarchists formed large international associations of working people (Herod, 1997: 167).

Up to the Second World War, international trade focused on national capi-tals, controlled by nation-states. The period from 1945 to 1973 represented an 'interregnum between the age of competing imperial powers and the coming of the global economy' (Teeple, 1995: 57), while the international regime fol-lowing the Second World War was based on US military and diplomatic hegemony articulated to the expansionary needs of its corporations. As other economies grew, so did the interdependence between nations, and between companies within nations. After 1950, world trade was dominated by the triad of Europe, Japan and the US, 'each with their immense hinterland of satellite states' (Jameson, 1996: 2). Between 1950 and 1973, total trade increased by almost 10 per cent annually, and output by more than 5 per cent, most of it between the triad (Hirst, 1997: 411). Whereas modern manufacturing tech-niques had been restricted in the nineteenth century to Europe and the north-eastern US, they came to proliferate across the world, as applied intellect and science deterritorialised (Hindley, 1999; Reich, 1999). Politically, the Cold War constructed a polarised world of two totalising ideologies that struggled for control just as empires had done over the previous century. This totality, which obscured other differences, encouraged the view that the future would see the triumph of one pole (Bauman, 1998: 58). Hence today's mavens of lais-sez-faire celebrating the supposed demise of the state – the sense that the United States' anti-Soviet security policy of 'Containment' has been displaced by 'Entertainment', that 'MTV has gone where the CIA could never penetrate' (Gardels, 1998: 2). The US has become an even more significant exporter of services such as popular culture to the other prongs of the triad. In 1999, private sector sales of services to Western Europe amounted to US$85 billion, and US$30 billion to Japan (Office of the US Trade Representative, 2001c).

The back-story to this tripartite division of the world is complex indeed, and it need not have gone the way that it did. Starting in 1945, two historic promises were made by established and emergent governments: to secure (a) the economic welfare of citizens and (b) their political sovereignty. At the end of the Second World War, the promise of economic welfare seemed locally workable, via state-based management of supply and demand and the creation of industries to substitute imports with domestically-produced items. The promise of universal sovereignty required concerted international action to convince the colonial powers (principally Britain, the Netherlands, Belgium, France and Portugal) that the peoples whom they had enslaved should be given the right of self-determination via nationalism. The latter became a powerful ideology of political mobilisation as a supposed precursor to liberation. When this second promise was made good, the resulting postcolonial governments undertook to deliver the first promise. Most followed import-substitution industrialisation (ISI), frequently via state enterprises or on the coat-tails of multinational corporations (MNCs) that established local presences. But Third World states suffered dependent underdevelopment and were unable to grow economically. Their formal *political* postcoloniality rarely became *economic*, apart from some Asian states that pursued Export-Oriented Industrialisation (EOI) and service-based expansion. The ISI of the 1950s and 1960s was progressively problematised and dismantled from the 1970s to today, a tendency that grew in velocity and scope with the erosion of state socialism.

With the crises of the 1970s, even those developed Western states that had a *bourgeoisie* with sufficient capital formation to permit a welfare system found that stagflation had undermined their capacity to hedge employment against inflation. We know the consequences: 'the space of economic management of capital accumulation [no longer] coincided with that of its political and social dimensions' (Amin, 1997: xi). Today, governments are supposed to deliver the two promises to voters via ongoing formal sovereignty and controlled financial markets, but neo-classical orthodoxy and business priorities call for free international capital markets. This amounts to what the *Economist* calls an '[i]mpossible trinity' ('Global Finance', 1999: 4 Survey Global Finance).

In sum, global exchange has been with us for a long time. But since the 1970s, financial and managerial decisions made in one part of the world have taken very rapid effect elsewhere. New international currency markets sprang up at that time following the decline of a fixed exchange rate, matching regulated systems with piratical financial institutions that crossed borders. Speculation brought greater rewards than production, as the trade in securities and debts

Figure 7 (Source: Office of the US Trade Representative, 2001)

outstripped profits from selling cars or building houses. The world circulation of money created the conditions for imposing international creditworthiness tests on all countries. At a policy level, this put an end to ISI and the very legitimacy of national economies, supplanted by EOI and the idea of an international economy. With productive investment less profitable than financial investment and companies rationalising production, the worlds of marketing, labour and administration were reconceived on an international scale, with services, notably entertainment, a crucial category. The US has become an extraordinary trader – to the value of US$3.4 trillion in 2000, a 15 per cent increase in exports from the previous year. Annual expansion in trade between 1970 and 2000 averaged 11.4 per cent, compared to 7.8 per cent yearly growth in Gross Domestic Product (GDP). The US has 86 million private sector jobs in services. They created one dollar in seven of total world production and exported US$295 billion in 2000, producing a US$80 billion surplus in service industry balance of payments (Office of the US Trade Representative 2001a: 1, 10, 15). Media industry merchant bank Veronis Suhler (2000) says that communications was the fastest growing component of the US economy in the five years to 1999 and will continue to be so through 2004.

So the requirement to drop ISI in favour of EOI has clearly favoured the US. But to repeat, the corollary of open markets is that national governments cannot guarantee the economic well-being of their citizens. The loan-granting power of the World Bank and the International Monetary Fund (IMF) has forced a shift away from the local provision of basic needs. It has redirected public investment toward sectors supposedly endowed with comparative advantage. In the domain of the screen, this means that 'if your cultural workers aren't already making movies profitably, don't start or you will be punished'. So

US service exports						
Exports:	**1997**	**1998**	**1999**	**2000***	**99-00***	**90-00***
	Billions of Dollars				*Percent Change*	
Total (BOP basis)	257.2	262.7	271.9	295.0	8.5	99.5
Travel	73.4	71.3	74.9	84.8	13.3	97.2
Passenger Fares	20.9	20.1	19.8	21.3	7.9	39.5
Other Transportation	27.0	25.6	27.0	29.9	10.7	36.0
Royalties and Licensing Fees	33.6	36.2	36.5	37.7	3.3	120.3
Other Private Services	84.5	90.9	96.5	106.0	9.8	163.0
Transfers under U.S. Military Sales Contracts	16.8	17.6	16.3	14.5	-11.5	49.1
U.S. Government Miscellaneous Services	1.0	0.9	0.9	0.8	-4.2	21.1

* Annualized based on January-November 2000 data.

Figure 8 (Source: Office of the US Trade Representative, 2001)

globalisation does not offer an end to centre-periphery inequalities, competition between states or macro-decision-making by corporations; it just cuts the capacity of the state system to control such transactions, and relegates responsibility for the protection and well-being of the cultural workforce to multinational corporate entities and financial institutions (McMichael, 1996: 27–29; Marshall, 1996; Connelly, 1996: 12–13; Wallerstein, 1989: 10–11). In the next section, we examine the micro-screen corollaries to these macro-historical developments.

Hollywood History

[W]hen Saddam Hussein chose Frank Sinatra's globally recognized 'My Way' as the theme song for his 54th birthday party, it wasn't as a result of American Imperialist pressure.

(Michael Eisner, quoted in Costa-Gavras *et al.*, 1995: 10)

In keeping with the conflictual story that flows from an historical perspective on capitalism, we find that the balance of textual trade was not always as it is today: France sold a dozen films a week to the US early in the twentieth century, and in 1914, most movies and much movie-making technology in North America were imported, while Italy and France dominated exhibition in Latin America. On the other hand, the US film production company Vitagraph was producing two negatives for every reel by 1907, one for European and one for domestic use. By 1909, North American companies could rely on the local market to recoup costs, and were tailoring export prices to meet other markets. Legal battles in the US during the early 1900s over motion-picture camera patents, held in monopoly by The Edison Company alongside Biograph's patented device, threatened distribution of overseas film in the US unless foreign companies ceded to the newly formed Motion Picture Patents Company (MPPC). Until it succumbed to US anti-trust legislation in the early teens, the MPPC cartel licensed filmmaking technology to producers and pro- jectors to exhibitors. A few foreign producers were allowed to license from the company. On the surface, it seemed that the cartel was designed to deter upstarts in film technology (it signed an exclusive agreement with Eastman Kodak to sell raw stock to *bona fide* licensees only). In reality, the MPPC sought to stem the tide of foreign film imports that dominated American screens in the first decade of the 1900s (Bowser, 1990: 21–36). This drive towards what Richard Abel (1999) calls, troping Baudelaire, the 'Americanisation' of the domestic market, was aided by the legal codification of film as intellectual prop- erty and mysterious confiscations of French equipment by US customs (Grantham, 2000: 44). Since that time, the US film industry has prospered internationally because it has understood that intellectual property protection is part of the infrastructure that binds otherwise competing companies together, and because it has had a willing servant in the state. By the 1990s, the US supplied over 80 per cent of the world's film stock (Olson, 1999: 60).

Between 1915 and 1916, US exports rose from 36 million feet of film to 159 million feet, while imports fell from 16 million feet before the First World War to 7 million by the mid-1920s. As the feature film took off during those years, Hollywood began to sell to Asia and Latin America, almost wiping out Brazil- ian production, for example, by purchasing local distributors. The State Department set up a motion-picture section in 1916. In 1918, Congress passed the Webb-Pomerene Act, which permitted overseas trusts that were illegal domestically. This enabled an international distribution cartel for the next forty years. Export prices and terms of trade were centrally determined by the Motion Picture Export Association (MPEA), which also worked to ensure blind bidding and block booking. From 1919, overseas receipts were factored into Hollywood budgets. In the 1920s, Hollywood's leading export sites were Britain, Australia, Argentina and Brazil, and the Federal Government institu- tionalised commercial attachés in its embassies – it suited rhetorically non-interventionist Republican administrations of the day to draw on US finance, film and industry to achieve political objectives. By the 1930s, foreign sales provided between one-third and one-half of film industry returns. When sound was standardised, non-English speakers were courted by the musical. Studios set up shop in key countries and created foreign-language versions of domestic hits. The industry also achieved horizontal integration by linking the sale of radios and records to the musical film – US music was often a precur- sor to US film. In 1939, the Department of Commerce estimated that Hollywood supplied 65 per cent of films exhibited worldwide (Balio, 1993:

32–33; Grantham, 2000: 53; de Grazia, 1989: 57; Bjork, 2000; O'Regan, 1992: 313; Litman, 1998: 91; Ulff-Moller, 1999: 182–83; Hoskins *et al.*, 1997: 46–47; King, 1990: 10, 22; Shohat and Stam, 1994: 28; Armes, 1987: 48; Tunstall, 1981: 175, 91; Harley, 1940: 21).

Of course, some of this success resulted from textual appeal. In 1920s and 1930s Italy, for example, Hollywood projected a fabulous modernity that fascinated Mussolini. Beauty, youth and wealth merged under the sign of fun. Local marketing played up the extraordinary pleasures of this world, and its difference from traditional Italian life. At the same time, the local industry was held back by the growth of US-owned distribution, new government taxes and a reliance on importing Hollywood technology (Hay, 1987: 66–71). And the two world wars complicate any notion of narrative transparency, managerial sophistication or global consumer preferences explaining American dominance. The 1914–18 and 1939–45 conflicts left national production across Europe either shut down or slowed. A plenitude of unseen US inventory waited to be unleashed (Italy was sent over 2,000 features in the four years from 1945) while the developing US shipping industry improved transport infrastructure. The MPEA referred to itself as 'the little State Department' in the 1940s, so isomorphic were its methods and ideology with US policy and politics. This was also the era when the industry's self-regulating Production Code appended to its bizarre litany of sexual anxieties something requested by the 'other' State Department: selling the American way of life around the world. Producer Walter Wanger (1950) trumpeted the meshing of what he called 'Donald Duck and Diplomacy' as 'a Marshall Plan for ideas ... a veritable celluloid Athens' (444) that meant the state needed Hollywood 'more than ... the H bomb' (446). The compulsory dismantling of state filmmaking institutions among the Axis Powers complemented Hollywood profit plans with anti-fascist and anti-communist political agendas that ensured the defeated regimes would hold off on protectionist film legislation and take up lost years of Hollywood inventory. For all its rhetoric of pure competition, therefore, the US government has devoted massive resources to generate and sustain its 'private sector' film industry in the interests of ideology and money.

Meanwhile, with profits endangered at home by anti-monopoly laws and the arrival of television, the world market grew in importance for Hollywood during the 1950s. Vertical integration through ownership of production, distribution and exhibition may have been outlawed domestically, but not on a global scale. Britain and Latin America were Hollywood's most lucrative importers until the 1970s. In both cases, economic downturn and the failure to invest in new theatres diminished attendance. As a result, Hollywood turned to new forms of internal commercial exploitation (as in the 1970s 'discovery' of the African-American audience and the emergence of blaxploitation).

Following recapitalisation and the studios' acquisition by conglomerates that could spread risk across different business activities, from mineral extraction to real estate, strategies were developed to regain world audiences. US government and industry set up new cartels to market films everywhere, with special agencies created for Anglophone and Francophone Africa. Hollywood's American Motion Picture Export Company of Africa, for example, dominated cinema sales to former British colonies from the 1960s, when the continent screened about 350 films a year, perhaps half of them American (Armes, 1987: 49; Mattelart, 1979: 194–208; Diawara, 1992: 106; Balio, 1998a: 61; Ukadike, 1994: 63; Sama, 1996: 150).

As early as 1912, Hollywood exporters were aware that where their films travelled, demand was created for other US goods. Commerce Secretary Herbert Hoover praised the industry in the 1920s for putting forward 'intellectual ideas and national ideals', for its trade earnings, 'and as a powerful influence on behalf of American goods'. His support of state aid to industries seeking to export proved crucial. Then-MPAA head Will Hays, who worked closely with Hoover to ensure that the studios operated as an overseas distribution cartel to deal with recalcitrant foreign powers, told the J Walter Thompson advertising agency in 1930 that 'every foot of American film sells $1.00 worth of manufactured products some place in the world'. By the late 1930s, stories of heroic merchandising links between the cinema and sales were legion, such as the ones that told of the new Javanese market for US sewing machines that followed a screening of American factory conditions, Hollywood-style, and the Brazilian taste in the bungalow that mimicked Angelino high life. Wanger even expressed delight at a strike by Paris stenographers in protest at the gap between their conditions and those of office workers in US films, the impact of what he called '120,000 American Ambassadors' (a reference to the number of prints exported each year). US capacities for mass production and marketing transformed values – on the one hand, requiring intense productive discipline; on the other, promising transcendence through equally intense consumption of commodities of pleasure. Such links are encapsulated in two famous scenes involving Clark Gable. In the 1930s, a deputation of Argentinian businessmen protested to the US Embassy about *It Happened One Night* (Frank Capra, 1934) because Gable was seen removing his shirt, revealing no singlet below. This supposedly created an undershirt inventory surplus in their warehouses – overnight! A quarter of a century later, *It Started in Naples* (Melville Shavelson, 1960) found Gable instructing a local boy on how to eat a hamburger, which produced public controversy about compromising Mediterranean cuisine. Thirty years on, the task of tying commodities to films was completed by another kind of envoy, as Disney twinned the release of *Pocahontas* (Mike Gabriel and Erik Goldberg, 1995) with McDonalds' new 'McChief Burger' – early fruit from their ten-year agreement for cross-promotion in 109 countries (Hays, 1931: 15; Hoover quoted in Bjork, 2000 and Grantham, 2000: 53; Grantham, 1998: 62; Wanger, 1939: 50, 45; King, 1990: 32; Sardar, 1998: 26; McChesney, 1999: 108).

The politics of Hollywood images have drawn critical reactions from many sources. Although anxieties about screen stereotypes are often identified with a contemporary liberal sensibility, they have in fact been a long-standing concern of conservatives. Since the 1920s, Hollywood has monitored how representations affect audiences. Mexico placed embargoes on film imports because of this issue in 1922 and was supported by other Latin American countries, Canada, France and Spain (De Los Reyes, 1996: 29–31). And official complaints from Germany, England, France, Italy and Spain over cultural slurs were made during the same decade (Vasey, 1992: 618, 620–21, 624, 627, 631). (To this day, Thailand has banned Hollywood's clumsy representations of its monarchy ['Thailand', 1999].) In 1926, the British Cabinet Office issued a paper to participants at the Imperial Economic Conference warning of the perils implicit in the fact that 'so very large a proportion of the films shown throughout the Empire should present modes of life and forms of conduct which are not typically British'. By the following year, the *Daily Express* newspaper worried that the exposure of British youth to US entertainment was making them 'temporary American citizens' (quoted in de Grazia, 1989: 53). The British Board of Film Classification insisted that Hollywood films released in imperial possessions follow the rule that 'white men may not be shown in a state of degradation amidst native surroundings' (quoted in Barker, 1993: 11). The industry's 1927 list of 'Dont's and Be Carefuls' instructed producers to 'avoid picturizing in an unfavorable light another country's religion, history, institutions, prominent people, and citizenry' and foreigners were hired to vet productions for potential to offend. The British insisted on the unrepresentability of Christ, so he was absent from *The Last Days of Pompeii* (Ernest B. Schoedsack, 1935), while Samuel Goldwyn complained that 'the only villain we dare show today [1936] is a white American' (quoted in Harley, 1940: 23) and Siegfried Kracauer (1949: 56) argued that the industry was perennially afraid of placing overseas revenues in jeopardy through misrepresentation. On the other hand, the Japanese were threatened with narrative stereotyping as criminals in the 1930s if they failed to give access to Hollywood films. Franco's Spain enthusiastically embraced the pro-capitalist side to Hollywood while abjuring its pro-worker, anti-fascist and libertarian films – *The Grapes of Wrath* (John Ford, 1940), *To Be or Not to Be* (Ernst Lubitsch, 1942), *The Great Dictator* (Charles Chaplin, 1940), *Some Like It Hot* (Billy Wilder, 1959) and *How Green Was My Valley* (John Ford, 1941) were too dangerous to be seen there until after Franco's death in 1975, while Orson Welles' International Brigade past was excised from *The Lady from Shanghai* (1948) (Wanger, 1950: 445; Bosch and del Rincón, 2000: 108–9, 111).

The power of Hollywood triggered responses from both left and right. European progressives admired the US for its secular modernity, egalitarianism and change, even as they deplored its racism, monopoly capitalism and class exploitation and their corollaries on camera. The right was disturbed by the *mestizo* qualities of African-American and Jewish contributions to the popular (Wagnleitner and May, 2000: 5–6). After the Second World War, widespread reaction against the discourses of modernisation foregrounded the US capitalist media as crucial components in the formation of commodities, mass culture and economic and political organisation in the Third World. Examples included the export of US screen products and infrastructure as well as American dominance of international communications technology (Nigeria, for example, was first tied to US television through the supply of equipment, which was articulated with the sale of programmes, genres and formats [Owens-Ibie, 2000: 133]). Critics claimed that the rhetoric of development through commercialism was responsible for decelerating economic growth and disenfranchising local culture, with emergent ruling classes in dependent nations exercising local power only at the cost of relying on foreign capital and ideology. In *A Foreign Affair* (Billy Wilder, 1948) a US Congressperson refers to postwar relief efforts in Europe in the following way: 'If you give them food, it's democracy. If you leave the labels on, it's imperialism.' He was right, and the complaints were soon to grow louder.

Cultural Imperialism

> America is not just interested in exporting its films. It is interested in exporting its way of life.
>
> (Gilles Jacob, Cannes Film Festival director, quoted in 'Culture Wars', 1998)

The US was an early-modern exponent of anti-cultural imperialist, pro-nation-building sentiment. Herman Melville expressed strong opposition to the unquestioning devotion by the US literary establishment in the early to mid-nineteenth century to all things English, notably Shakespeare. He questioned the compatibility of this Eurocentrically cringing import culture with efforts to 'carry Republicanism into literature'. Yet his own work tropes Shakespeare (Newcomb, 1996: 94). In the mid-nineteenth century, when the first international copyright treaties were being negotiated on the European continent, the US refused to protect foreign literary works – a belligerent stance that it would today denounce as piratical. As a net importer of books seeking to develop a national literary patrimony of its own – an 'American Literature' – Washington was not interested in extending protection to foreign works that might hinder its own printers, publishers or authors from making a profit. This mix of indebtedness and *ressentiment* characterises the relation of import to export cultures, where taste and domination versus market choice and cultural control are graceless antinomies. It also characterises the dependent relationship of development, a lesson that the US learnt quickly and used to do unto others as had been done to it.

But the US had reached political-economic international domination by the end of the Second World War. The ensuing export of modernisation ignored the way in which the very life of the modern had been defined in colonial and international experience, both by differentiating the metropole from the periphery and by importing ideas, fashions and people back to the core. In the 1950s, modernity was designated as a complex imbrication of industrial, economic, social, cultural and political development, towards which all peoples of the world were progressively headed. The founders and husbands of this discourse were First World political scientists and economists, mostly associated with US universities, research institutes, foundations and corporations, or with international organisations. Among the premises of this modernity were nationalist fellow feeling and individual/state sovereignty as habits of thought. The daily prayer called for a 'modern individual' who would not fall into the temptation of Marxism-Leninism. Development necessitated the displacement of 'the particularistic norms' of tradition by 'more universalistic' blends of the modern, as part of the creation of an 'achievement-oriented' society (Pye, 1965: 19). The successful importation of media technologies and forms of communication from the US were touted as critical components in this replicant figure, as élite sectors of society were trained to be exemplars and leaders for a wider populace that was said to be mired in backward, folkloric forms of thought and lacking the trust in national organisations required for modernisation.

The theory of cultural imperialism comprehensively challenged this implausibly solipsistic model. Apart from the latter's unreconstructed narcissism, its precepts disavowed the existing international division of labour and the success of imperial and commercial powers in annexing states and/or their labour forces. Although diffusionist theorists and others came up with neo-modernisation models that were more locally sensitive to conflicts over wealth, influence and status, they did not measure up to critical theories of dependant development, underdevelopment, unequal exchange, world-systems history, centre-periphery relations and cultural and media imperialism. These radical critiques of capitalist modernisation shared the view that the transfer of technology, politics and economics had become unattainable, because the emergence of MNCs united business and government to regulate cheap labour markets, produce new consumers and guarantee pliant regimes (Reeves, 1993: 24–25, 30). The development of the cultural imperialism thesis during the

1960s argued that the US, as the world's leading screen exporter, was transfer-
ring its dominant value system to others, with a corresponding diminution in
the vitality and standing of local languages and traditions that threatened
national identity.

The last few decades of US cultural hegemony have been attributed to control of news agencies, advertising, market research and public opinion, screen
trade, technology, propaganda, telecommunications and security (Primo, 1999:
183). Inevitably, there have been reactions. US involvement in South-East Asian
wars during the 1960s led to critiques of its military interventions against struggles of national liberation. Such critiques increasingly targeted links between
the military-industrial complex and communications, pointing to the ways that
communications and cultural MNCs bolstered US foreign policy and military
strategy and enabled the more general expansion of multinationals, which were
seen as substantial power brokers in their own right. These anxieties were not
restricted to the Third World. At Mondiacult 1982, the Mexico City world conference on cultural production, the French Minister for Culture Jack Lang made
the following remark:

> We hope that this conference will be an occasion for peoples, through their
> governments, to call for genuine cultural resistance, a real crusade against
> this domination, against – let us call a spade a spade – this financial and
> intellectual imperialism.
>
> (Quoted in Mattelart *et al.*, 1988: 19–20)

While the leftist connotations of this rhetoric were not universally welcome, its
moral fervour resonated widely and profoundly, such that all Western European countries now echo it. The Association of South-East Asian Nations issued
a statement in the 1990s calling for 'a united response to the phenomenon of
cultural globalization in order to protect and advance cherished Asian values
and traditions which are being threatened by the proliferation of Western
media content' (quoted in Chadha and Kavoori, 2000: 417). These states are
caught between the desire to police representations and languages along racial
and religious lines and financial commitments to internationalism (Hamilton,
1992: 82–85, 90; Fitzpatrick, 1993: 22).

From this complex background, major studies deriving from the insights of
the cultural imperialism critique have looked at US control of world media, the
role of international press agencies, television programme flow, village versus
corporate values, the export of US screen products and distribution systems,
and American dominance of international communications technology and
infrastructure. Another major area of work has deconstructed the rhetoric of
development via commercialism, particularly in advertising, which was found

to discourage the allocation of resources to industrialisation (Reeves, 1993: 30–35; Roach, 1997: 47; Mowlana, 1993).

During the 1960s and 1970s, cultural-imperialism discourse found a voice in the Non-Aligned Movement and the United Nations Educational, Scientific and Cultural Organization (UNESCO) (an irony this, as the US had fought so strenuously after the Second World War for the Organization to emphasise the impact of the mass media and information flows [Sewell, 1974: 142–43]). In the 1970s, UNESCO was run by the Frenchman Jean Maheu and the Senegalese Amadou Mahtar M'Bow, who set up the MacBride Commission to investigate cultural and communication issues in North–South flows and power. At the same time, Third World countries lobbied for a New International Information Order or New World Information and Communication Order (NWICO), mirroring calls for a New International Economic Order and a revised North–South dialogue. The MacBride Commission reported in 1980 on the need for equal distribution of the electronic spectrum, reduced postal rates for international texts, protection against satellites crossing borders, and an emphasis on the media as tools of development and democracy rather than commerce. There continue to be annual Roundtables on the MacBride Commission's legacy, but the insistence by the United States on the free-flow paradigm was a successful riposte to NWICO strategies and claims (Mattelart and Mattelart, 1998: 94–97; Roach, 1997: 48; Mowlana, 1993: 61). UNESCO has ceased to be the critical site for NWICO debate. The US and the UK withdrew payment and support from UNESCO in 1985 on the grounds that it was illegitimately politicised, supposedly evidenced by its denunciation of Zionist racism and support for state intervention against private-press hegemony. The past decade has seen UNESCrats distancing themselves from NWICO in the hope of attracting their critics back to the fold. The UN has also downplayed its prior commitment to a New Order (Gerbner, 1994: 112–13; Gerbner *et al.*, 1994: xi–xii).

Not surprisingly, calls for a NWICO have become less influential in both the political and intellectual registers since that time. The NWICO position was vulnerable from all sides for its inadequate theorisation of: capitalism, the postcolonial condition, internal and international class relations, the role of the state and the mediating power of indigenous culture; and for its complex *frottage* – a pluralism that insisted on the relativistic equivalence of all cultures and defied chauvinism, but rubbed up against a distinctively powerful equation of national identity with cultural forms (Schlesinger, 1991: 145). In a telling accommodation, the UN began to sponsor large international conferences in the late 1990s, such as the World Television Forum, to promote partnerships between commercial media managers, entrepreneurs and investors from the US and Europe and their poorer counterparts from Africa, Asia and Latin America. And while UNESCO is a supporter of the 'Screens Without Frontiers'

(2000) initiative, which aims to facilitate a 'readjustment movement of North-South information exchanges' within the rubric of quality and public service, i.e. to encourage First World broadcasters to give away non-commodity-oriented programmes, even this project was endorsed provided it was not paid for from the UNESCO budget (Tricot, 2000)

There were also conceptual limitations to cultural imperialism's analyses of transplanted culture, which tend to concentrate on Hollywood in one market, in isolation from other regions or take a very totalising view that is insufficiently alive to specificities (O'Regan, 1992: 75). The issue of customisation is critical here, as evidenced in the capacity to fuse imported strands of popular culture with indigenous ones (e.g., Nigerian juju and Afro-Beat), to rediscover and remodel a heritage via intersections with imported musical genres. Criticisms have been made of MTV Asia, for example, because of its preponderance of Western material. Management defended this not on price grounds, but via a logic of communication: Saudi and Taiwanese audiences would be alienated by the 'foreignness' of either culture on-screen, but feel familiar with the 'internationalism' of American product. At the same time, when Rupert Murdoch bought the parent STAR TV, he insisted that indigenous programming would be critical to success in China, Indonesia and India (Reeves, 1993: 36, 62; Fitzpatrick, 1993: 22; Heilemann, 1994: Survey 12).

Part of the talent of the cultural commodity form is that it leads a lengthy career and can be retrained to suit new circumstances. As Liberace once put it: 'If I play Tchaikovsky I play his melodies and skip his spiritual struggles. . . . I have to know just how many notes my audience will stand for' (quoted in Hall and Whannell, 1965: 70). Because much that we call culture lays a claim to aesthetic discrimination rather than monetary exchange, culture is simultaneously the key to international textual trade and one of its limiting factors. Ethics, affect, custom and other forms of knowledge both enable and restrict the processes of commodification (Frow, 1992: 18–20). So General Motors, which own Australia's General Motors Holden, translates its 'hot dogs, baseball, apple pie, and Chevrolet' jingle into 'meat pies, football, kangaroos, and Holden cars' for the Australian market. This can be read as an indication of the paradigmatic nature of the national in an era of global companies, or as the requirement to reference the local in a form that is obliged to do something with cultural-economic meeting-grounds. In the end, the sale is always local. On the other hand, the fact that Germany's huge post-production company Das Werk launches a screen production subsidiary in Spain and calls it 42nd Street is signal testimony to this ambivalence and the continuing force of the US as an index of capitalist entertainment, whatever its origin (Hopewell, 2001).

The NWICO version of cultural imperialism also risks cloaking the interests of emergent bourgeoisies that seek to advance their own market power under the sign of advocacy for national cultural self-determination. Such a framework disavows the NICL, displacing it with the problem of national cultural identity. This encouraged cultural imperialism theorists to champion hierarchical and narrow accounts of culture as discrete and super-legitimate phenomena that, they soon discovered, mostly served as a warrant for an asphyxiating parochialism created and policed by culture bureaucrats (Mattelart and Mattelart, 1992: 175–77; Roach, 1997: 49). We also lose sight of the NICL if we automatically identify economic effects of globalisation with cultural ones (Golding and Harris, 1997: 5). Then we perceive only superficial oppositions, like the one that the neo-liberal business columnist 'Lexington' (2000) discerns in the pleasure and gloom of 'Pokémania v Globophobia'.

Instead of limiting our thinking to a choice between false consciousness or polysemy, the worldwide divergence of filmgoers' labours of interpretation and judgment should call our attention to the way the NICL interacts with taste distinctions even as it regulates their reproduction. Indeed, anxieties about local confrontations with the NICL are frequently expressed under the guise of a concern for spurious effects on national or regional cultures or identities that may themselves be repressive or phantasmatic. In the past, opponents of cultural imperialism critique have looked at these anxieties only superficially, arguing that such worries, and the cultural protectionism they inspire, derive from a Puritanism that denies the liberatory aspects of much US entertainment for stifling class structures (Federico Fellini famously equated 'America, democracy . . . Fred Astaire' [quoted in Hay, 1987: 64]). When national cinemas refuse to take a critical distance from Hollywood cinema as some damned other, seeking instead to imitate it – notably the 1980s *Si Boy* cycle in Indonesia, with its youth culture of fast cars and English-speaking servants – they are fusing imported strands of popular culture with indigenous cultural labour. This embrace of imported Hollywood texts might indeed rework cultural identity, as in Irish cinema, or act as buffers against cultural imports that are too close for comfort, as when Pakistanis may prefer the difference of North America to the similarity of India (Sen, 1994: 64, 73, 129–30; Rockett *et al.*, 1988: 147; O'Regan, 1992: 343). Again, thinking narrowly about identity distracts from the normativity of the NICL and the manner in which cultural practices are engendered and reproduced in a way that facilitates the smooth annexation of cultural labour.

Difference and sensitivity to cultural specificity can be one more means towards the homogenisation of cultural production and its incorporation into the NICL. Neo-conservative proselytisers for pluralism often confound logic with their simultaneous claims that the United States' migrant history and contemporaneity make for a unique form of narrative transparency (AKA minimal dialogue complexity) that is universally appealing because its polysemy is available to 'indigenous readings', even as they tell us that these narratives address uniquely universal themes, *and* that the US itself excludes other nations' films because it is entirely Anglo-insular (Olson, 1999).

Against the currently fashionable idea that globalisation eradicates difference in a dialectic of cultural homogeneity/integration versus heterogeneity/fragmentation, Featherstone argues that we must question who is served by globalisation (1990: 1–2). Here we return the emphasis to Hollywood's power over the geographical coordinates of the NICL. As Herbert Schiller expressed it, 'the media-cultural component in a developed, corporate economy supports the economic objectives of the decisive industrial-financial sectors (i.e., the creation and extension of the consumer society)' (1976). This insight should counter such charmingly hyperbolic rhetoric as Masao Miyoshi's assertion that the 'formation of a highly complex web across national borders of industrial production and distribution (transnationalization) largely invalidates disputes over surpluses and deficits in trade' (1993: 745). In bitter response to this imagined *pax munda*, the cultural workers of the world might chortle, 'Yeah, right'.

In one sense, there are now three distinct varieties of cultural-imperialism discourse. First, Africa, the Middle East and Latin America continue a debate about local democratic participation and control. Second, the major economic powers of Western Europe argue about the need to build pan-Europeanism in contrast to the homogenising forces of Americanisation. And third, the former state-socialist polities of Eastern and Central Europe seek to develop independant civil societies with privatised media (Mowlana, 1993: 66–67). There can be no better illustration of the durability of cultural-imperialist analysis. Today, perhaps the greatest force working for cultural imperialism and Hollywood's geographical command over the NICL is the World Trade Organization (WTO), established in 1995 out of the General Agreement on Tariffs and Trade (GATT).

Globalisation – the GATT, the WTO and the Global Business Dialogue

> If the European Commission governments truly care about their citizens' cultural preferences, they would permit them the freedom to see and hear works of their choosing; if they are really concerned about a nation's cultural heritage, they would encourage the distribution of programming reflecting that heritage – Jack Golodner, President of the Department for Professional Employees, American Federation of Labor-Council of Industrial Organizations.
>
> (AFL-CIO, 1994: H6)

From its emergence in the late 1940s as one of several new international financial and trading protocols, the GATT embodied in contractual terms the

First World's rules of economic prosperity: nondiscrimination, codified regulations policed outside the terrain of individual sovereign-states and multilateralism. Born under the logic of North American growth evangelism, whereby standardised industrial methods, vast scales of production and an endless expansion of markets would engineer economic recovery and development for the Western European detritus of the Second World War and preclude any turn to Marxism-Leninism, the GATT helped to restructure capitalism. The General Agreement was a paradoxically bureaucratic voice of neo-classical economics, rejecting parochial national interests and state intervention in favour of free trade. Officials worked like Puritans ordered by intellectual manifest destiny to disrupt trading blocs and restrict distortions to the putatively natural rhythms of supply and demand as determined by consumer sovereignty and comparative advantage.

The US immediately sought coverage of cinema, and later television, without success. An accord signed in 1948, the Beirut Agreement, eliminated duty and licensing costs for educational audiovisual imports, but not for texts designated as cultural or popular (Marvasti, 2000: 108 n. 3), because the Europeans maintained, against the US, that such screen texts were services, not commodities. In any event, US exports increased rapidly. Even in the 1950s, when Britain was the only country with anything like the proportion of television households that the US had, it quickly became a staple customer for US programming. This established a trend of deficit financing for US material based on overseas sales that obliged it to continue to press for 'open' markets (Tunstall and Machin, 1999: 26; Jarvie, 1998: 38–39; McDonald, 1999). Although it briefly had a TV programmes panel in 1961, the GATT was slow to recognise trade in services (TIS – entertainment, finance, health and other unproductive, non-manufacturing, non-subsistence industries). This was in part because the frequently object-free exchanges that characterise the 'human' side to the sector (restaurants, for example) were not especially amenable to conceptualisation and enumeration. But as the Western powers saw capital fly from manufacturing, they sought to become net exporters of services by discovering ways to open the area to bureaucratic invigilation. The Punta del Este Declaration of September 1986 began the seven-year-long Uruguay Round of the GATT. It put TIS at the centre of GATT negotiations for the first time, because of pressure from the US (always the main player in negotiations) in the service of lobbyists for American Express, Citibank, IBM and Hollywood (Loeb, 2000: 308; Sjolander, 1992–3: 54 n. 5; Grey, 1990: 6–9).

A decade later, TIS accounted for 60 per cent of GDP in the industrialised market economies (IMECS) and more than a quarter of world trade. In 1999, total world TIS was valued at US$1350 billion, with the US responsible for 33.8 per cent. Entertainment was a significant sub-sector. After the US failed to have cultural industries incorporated in the 1988 Free Trade Agreement with Canada, its diplomats and trade officials tried to thwart EU plans for import quotas on audiovisual texts. EU law enshrines freedom of expression through media access – the Union's alibi for putting quotas on US screen texts, along with the continuing claim that the screen is not a good but a service. The EU's 'Television Without [intra-Western European] Frontiers' directive (adopted in 1989 and amended in 1997) drew particular ire for an annual limit on texts imported by member nations of 49 per cent of broadcast time (World Trade Organization, 2000; Theiler, 1999: 558; McDonald, 1999). But US attempts to have the GATT's Uruguay Round derail such policies were almost universally opposed in the name of cultural sovereignty, with significant participation from Canada, Japan, Australia, all of Europe and the Third World. This position equated the culture industries with environmental protection or the armed forces, as spheres that exist beyond neo-classicism: their social impact could not be reduced to price. In 1993, thousands of European artists, intellectuals and producers signed a petition in major newspapers calling for culture to be exempted from the GATT's no-holds barred commodification (Van Elteren, 1996a: 47), in what became known as the 'Cola and Zola' debate (Kakabadse, 1995). The 1993 coalition opposed the idea that the GATT ensure open access to screen markets, on the grounds that culture is inalienable (non-commodifiable).

To US critics, however, cultural rights secreted the protection of inefficient industries and outmoded dirigisme (Kessler, 1995; Van Elteren, 1996b; Venturelli, 1998: 61). The US argued from a *laissez-faire* position, maintaining that the revelation of consumer preferences should be the deciding factor as to who has comparative advantage in television and film production – whether Los Angeles or Sydney is the logical place for audiovisual texts to be produced. 'Washwood' claimed there was no room for the public sector in screen production, because it crowded out private investment, which was necessarily more in tune with popular taste. Both the active face of public subvention (national cinemas and broadcasters) and the negative face of public proscription (import barriers to encourage local production) were derided for obstructing market forces. This smokescreen obscured the constitutive nature of the NICL in deciding the Los Angeles versus Sydney question. As always, Washwood's moralism on this question is contingent – it's fine for Israel to exclude certain items and practices from free trade with the US based on cultural specificity (Loeb, 2000: 305). But that conditionality is itself never taken as a precedent for cases involving states that are not fellow rogues of the international system.

The struggle between the EU (against cultural imperialism) and the US (for unhampered market access) saw the screen excluded from the GATT in 1993.

Over forty countries exempted audiovisual sectors from their eventual endorsement of the Agreement – including the US (World Trade Organization, 1998)! But this exclusion has not prevented Hollywood from peddling its wares internationally. As noted in our Introduction, half of Hollywood's revenue comes from overseas. The US supplies three-quarters of the West European market, up from half the market a decade ago. The consolidation of 'wealthy' Europe into one sales site has been a huge boon to Hollywood, along with the deregulation of television. Over the first eight years of 'Television Without Frontiers', net audiovisual trade between the EU and the US saw Europe's annual culture industries deficit rise from US$2 billion to US$5.6 billion. The screen-trade imbalance grew from US$4.8 billion to US$5.65 billion between 1995 and 1996 ('After GATT', 1994: 16; 'Culture Wars', 1998; Van Elteren, 1996b; European Audiovisual Observatory, 1998; Hill, 1994b: 2, 7 n. 4; 'Déjà Vu', 1994: 3). Meanwhile, the studios fretted that their 55 per cent proportion of these other nations' box-office takes was cut by foreign exchange controls and assorted barriers to 42–43 per cent ('You're Not', 1995)!

In January 1995, the WTO replaced the GATT and bought the services of its GATTocrats. The WTO has a legal personality, a secretariat and biennial ministerial conferences. This new machinery makes it easier for MNCs to dominate trade via the diplomatic services of their home governments' representatives. Environmental concerns and other matters of public interest no longer have the entrée that the GATT gave to non-governmental, not-for-profit organisations. Multinationals now find it easier to be regarded as local firms in their host countries, and Third World agricultural production has been further opened up to foreign ownership (Lang and Hines, 1993: 48–50; Dobson, 1993: 573–76).

The WTO's operating protocols stress transparency, most-favoured nation precepts, national treatment (identical policies on imported and local commodities), tariffs in preference to other protective measures, and formal methods of settling disputes. The Organization's initial focus on the service industries highlighted the lucrative telecommunications market, but its oleaginous hand is turning to culture. When Canada and France tried to remove cultural issues from the WTO and place them within the purview of UNESCO, they met with little support (Department of Commerce, 2001: 82). Commodities and knowledges previously excluded from the GATT, such as artworks and international export controls, have been included in the WTO's remit, with extra-economic questions of national sovereignty eluding the written word of trade negotiation, but thoroughly suffusing its implementation and consequences (Zolberg, 1995). In 1997, the WTO made its first major movement into the culture industries, in cases concerning Turkish taxation of US film revenue (WT/DS43 – subsequently settled privately) and the Canadian version of *Sports*

Illustrated magazine. The Organization ruled that Canada could not impose tariffs on the magazine because it was enticing advertisers away from local periodicals. This case is regarded as beginning the WTO's cultural push (World Trade Organization, 2001: 71; Valentine, 1997; Magder, 1998). The new US move is to cluster cultural issues under the catch-all rubric of intellectual property, which saw it bring WTO cases against Greece for allowing the re-broadcast of US television programmes without regard to copyright. This prodded the Greek government to legislate on television copyright and then close down television stations that broke the law (Venturelli, 1998: 62, 66; World Trade Organization, 2001: 51; 'Administration Settles', 2001).[2]

Although the General Agreement on Trade in Services (GATS) (the WTO's protocol on TIS from the Uruguay Round) states that there must be easy market access and no differential treatment of national and foreign service suppliers, it gives room to exempt certain services from these principles. This margin for manoeuvre is utilised, for example, by the EU in setting quotas for films (Hoskins *et al.*, 1997: 5–7). However, since January 2000, the WTO has been conducting GATS 2000, a round of negotiations lasting until the end of 2002 that further addresses the liberalisation of goods and services 'to entrench privatization and deregulation worldwide' (Gould, 2001) and rein in democratic controls over corporations across a broad swathe of business activity (Sinclair, 2000; see also Office of the US Trade Representative, 2001c). One major issue is virtual goods. As audiovisual services are absorbed into concepts such as electronic commerce, information and entertainment, the distinction between goods and services begins to blur. The EU fears that the US will muscle its way into film and television through insisting on free-market access to new communication services, using 'the Internet as a Trojan Horse to undermine the Community's "Television Without Frontiers" directive' (Wheeler, 2000: 258). The US has been like a child with a toy in the WTO, proud that it has filed more complaints than any other country and has prevailed so often (Barshefsky, 1998). And just in case it should fail to destroy cultural policies through international trading institutions, it has lodged the EU on its internal Special 301 'Priority Watch List' for sanctions (USIA, 1997). Again, there is a sense of a child, this time keeping a list of most-hated peers and real or imagined 'meanness'.

Now, despite its high-theory commitment to pure/perfect competition, political pressures mean the GATT at least nodded in the direction of archaeological, artistic and historic exemptions to free-trade totalisations (Chartrand, 1992: 137). Today, culture is not just a problem of political pressure – it is one more category for commodification. In December 2000, Washington sent an official paper to the WTO's Council for Trade in Services on 'Audiovisual and Related Services' that it hoped would give the Organization a framework to assist 'the continued growth of this sector by ensuring an open and predictable environment' that would allegedly enable greater diversity of artistic output. Clearly this was the key to the United States' *laissez-faire* politics. But there was now recognition of a countervailing legitimacy, that this environment must pay heed to 'the preservation and promotion of cultural values and identity', just as nations retain control over local prudential rules for their domestic financial systems (United States, 2000). It remains to be seen whether this is one more invocation of national concerns on behalf of a bourgeoisie, as per the cynical use of culturalism by other countries' media producers in favour of state support for national cinemas and broadcasters.

In addition to setting public servants to work on its behalf at the WTO, the international ruling class also holds its own parties. The Global Business Dialogue on Electronic Commerce, which held its first meeting in September 1999, works with parallel imperatives to the WTO. Cees Hamelink (2001: 15) describes this meeting of '500 top executives from media and IT industries (among them CEOs from Time Warner, Bertelsmann, Nokia, AOL, and Japanese NTT)' in which the cultural MNC leadership 'discussed policy topics such as taxation, data protection, intellectual property rights, tariffs, information security and authentication. ... Basically global business leaders told governments what to do in the governance of CyberSpace'. Of the hundred government representatives present, none were given more than observer treatment. This MNC leadership set up 'a 29-member steering committee with representatives from the private sector only' to shape strategies and policy initiatives. Among the main industry-led policies are lifting Internet taxes, eliminating export restrictions on encryption software as well as 'third party arbitration in e-commerce disputes', and relaxing EU privacy laws, which the Global Business Dialogue rejects as a barrier to global trading.

In the global economic system that has evolved since the mid-1970s, Northern class fractions support a transnational capital that has displaced non-capitalist systems elsewhere (Robinson, 1996: 14–15). Regulatory and other mechanisms have been set in place to liberalise world trade, contain socialism, promote legislation favourable to capitalist expansion and aggregate world markets (for harmonisation of copyright, see Chapter 4). World markets, including the EU and other trade groupings, have been crucial for the promotion of free trade regimes in the 1980s and beyond (though trade since then has not exceeded that of the post-war quarter century [Hirst, 1997: 412]). The growth of corporate power is so strong that corporations can demand the removal of national barriers to trade, such that the spread of foreign capital and currency markets has meant that economic decisions are taken outside the context of the nation-state, in ways that favour the market. And by 1994, half of the one hundred biggest economies in the world 'belonged' not to nation-states, but to MNCs (Donnelly, 1996: 239). Four hundred of the latter accounted for two-thirds of fixed assets and 70 per cent of trade (Robinson, 1996: 20). But the US, Western Europe and Japan are really the only key sites of MNC activity, housing more than two-thirds of MNC sales and assets. Direct foreign investment elsewhere is limited (Hirst, 1997: 418; Kozul-Wright and Rowthorn, 1998). Perhaps one in twenty MNCs actually function globally (Gibson-Graham, 1996–97: 7–8). Multinationals look around for marginal utility and then retreat to what is known and controllable – so the explosion of foreign investment in the three years from 1994 saw an increase of 40 per cent in MNC money flowing into the US, while investment the other way was primarily in Britain, the Netherlands, Canada, France and Australia ('Trade Barriers', 1997).

Viewing the market as a deterritorialising movement does not imply a borderless world, but it does mean a transformation of the state. Through structural adjustment and liberalisation, states adopt policies to manage global, rather than national, economic relations. These policies facilitate global circuits of money and commodities at the expense of social stability and environmental security within the nation-state. At a fundamental level, they do violence to open debate over the direction of national and global cultural policies that promote malevolence and condescension towards any cultural policy that does not facilitate the NICL.

Today's prevailing neo-liberal 'Washington Consensus' has vanquished the key politico-economic questions of the last half-century (there is less need for 'Conferences' now, with the WTO and the Global Business Dialogue). Dominant since the late 1970s, the 'Consensus' favours open trade, comparative advantage, deregulation of financial markets and low inflation. It has, of course, presided over slower worldwide growth and greater worldwide inequality than any time since the Depression. Job security and real wages are down and working hours are up. By the year 2000, Americans were working close to an average of 2,000 hours annually, the only developed country beside Sweden in which obligatory work hours increased (average annual hours fell from 1,809 to 1,656 in France, from 2,121 to 1,889 in Japan, and from 1,512 to 1,399 in Norway) (International Labour Office, 1999: 166). At the same time, the richest 20 per cent of the world's people earned seventy-four times the amount of the world's poorest in 1997, up from sixty times in 1990 and thirty times in 1960 (UNDP, 1999: 3). But despite the manifold catastrophes of the 'Consensus' across the late 1990s – Mexico, South-East Asia, Russia and Brazil – it is still hailed as exemplary policy. Repeated failures are deemed aberrations by apologists, who confidently await 'the long run', when equilibrium will be attained (Palley, 1999: 49; Levinson, 1999: 21; Galbraith, 1999: 13). The 'Consensus' is animated by neo-liberalism's mantra of individual freedom, the marketplace and minimal government involvement in economic matters. This provides the intellectual alibi for a comparatively unimpeded flow of capital across national boundaries, and the rejection of labour, capital and the state managing the economy together.

Certain critics argue that the promiscuous nature of capital has been over-stated, that the nation-state, far from being a series of 'glorified local authorities' (Hirst, 1997: 409) is in fact crucial to the regulation of MNCs, with regional blocs strengthening, rather than weakening, the ability of the state to govern. And people around the world continue to look to the latter for both economic sanction and return (Smith, 1996: 580). While the 'relationship between capitalism and territoriality' has shifted (Robinson, 1996: 18), it remains governed by inter-state bodies, albeit dominated by the G8 (Hirst, 1997: 413; McMichael, 2000a: 177). Capital markets, for example, operate internationally but with national supervision and regulation; all conceivable plans for dealing with their transnational reach still necessitate formal governance ('Global Finance', 1999). A supposedly exemplary open market specimen, the North American Free Trade Agreement/Tratado de Libre Comercio Norteamericano, needs a mere one thousand pages of governmental rules to 'work' (Palley, 1999: 50), while the last GATT amounted to twenty-thousand pages of protocols, weighing 850 kilograms! So far as investment is concerned, this is an international, not a global age – and governments continue to matter. The same applies to Hollywood expenditure.

Conclusion

> The core of globalization is to achieve economic hegemony of a few rich states, the United
> States of America in particular, as well as the hegemony of Western consumer culture, threat-
> ening the peoples' cultures, methods of living and spiritual values.
>
> (Tariq Aziz, Prime Minister of Iraq, quoted in Landers, 2000)

We have reached a point where it is said that 'the state remains a pre-eminent political actor on the global stage', but 'the aggregation of states . . . is no longer in control of the global policy process'. In their place is a fundamentally non-normative system, run by banks, corporations and finance traders (Falk, 1997: 124–25, 129–30). Core and periphery are blurred, the spatial mobility of capital is enhanced, the strategic strength of labour is undermined, and the power of the state is circumscribed by the ability of capital to move across borders. A fundamental shift in the bargaining and power relations between capital and labour has been facilitated by transportation and information technologies and trends towards casualisation, though it continues to display the traces of specific national modes of integration into the NICL. We shall see more of this in Chapter 2 (Ross and Trachte, 1990: 63; Thompson and Smith, 1999: 197; Broad, 1995a).

The demise of the nation-state and the emergence of international sovereignty have been routinely – and mistakenly – predicted over the past century.
More and more states appear, even as the discourse announcing their departure becomes increasingly insistent (Miller, 1981: 16–18). But as we have seen,
the internationalism of new communications technologies and patterns of
ownership and control, and increases in the variety and extent of global dias-
poras, *extend* the significance of the state as a regulatory and stimulatory entity.
The corollary has been a developing need for each state to create a national subjectivity from disparate identities. Internationalisation is perhaps nowhere
better exemplified than in the work done by states to build belonging among
their polyethnic populations, and the labour performed by those populations
to seek new forms of state representation. Clearly, the screen industries are crucial actors in this sphere, not only because of issues of collective identity, but in
the material realm of engendering and reproducing the NICL. The major corporations active in Hollywood follow AOL-Time Warner's specification for
globalisation: horizontal expansion to enter new markets worldwide, vertical
expansion to work with independant producers, and partnership with foreign
investors to spread risks and increase capitalisation (Balio, 1998a: 58).

In this chapter, we have endeavoured to explain global Hollywood's presence
and power. While this commanding position is entangled with the fortunes and
projects of US-led capitalist expansion, such domination is uneven – fraught
with resistance, failure and competition. Other states' notions of cultural sovereignty underpin concerns *vis-à-vis* the US, but so too does support for
monopoly capital (Burgelman and Pauwels, 1992). That the EU must to some
degree shape its cultural labour markets and deliver its cultural workforce to
the NICL only serves to keep the EU culture industries struggling with Hollywood for control of the NICL. This is most obvious in the area of international
co-production, as Chapter 3 will show. Meanwhile, the old notions of state cultural sovereignty that were so crucial to Europe's political traditions are being
attenuated by the twin forces of 'bruxellois centralisation' from outside and sep-
aratist ethnicities from within (Berman, 1992: 1515).

The effects of screen trade are not merely registered in cultural identities, but
on the very bodies and dispositions of cultural workers. As Dana Polan suggests, 'globalism is not an abstraction but a concrete activity whose mode of
being has its effect on the local body. Even if it is represented in abstract terms,
globalism's mode is embodied, and its embodiment occurs locally' (1996: 258).
Global Hollywood is an institution of global capitalism that seeks to render
bodies that are intelligible and responsive to the New International Division of
Cultural Labour.

Notes

1   It took over a century for George Bush Senior to pick up on the idea.
2   Ironically, the first case of this nature (WT/DS160/1) went against the United
    States. The WTO found that American copyright law violated global trade
    rules by permitting large businesses to play recorded versions of music by
    foreign artists without paying royalties (Newman and Phillips, 2000; World
    Trade Organization, 2001: 20).

Chapter Two
The New International Division of Cultural Labour

'Bring Hollywood Back to the U.S.A.'
(Film and Television Action Committee [FTAC] Banner, 2000)

On 9 October 1992, three days prior to the so-called Christopher Columbus Quincentenary, Paramount Pictures released *1492: Conquest of Paradise* in more than 3,000 theatres across thirty countries. French actor Gérard Depardieu played the Italian-born Spanish explorer, under the direction of ex-British television commercials maker Ridley Scott. Co-produced by the venerable French film studio Gaumont on the eve of its own centenary, *1492* was the first in a series of Gaumont English-language features intended to reach the valuable US market, and a worldwide audience, through Hollywood's global distribution cartel. Shot in Spain and Costa Rica, the production hired 170 Indians from Costa Rica (at US$35 per day) and six Waunana Indians from Colombia who had acted in *The Mission* (Roland Joffé, 1986). If Costa Rica provided both the First Peoples and the cheap labour to keep the budget under US$40 million, it was perhaps also chosen at the request of the executive producer's husband, the head of the newly-born Costa Rica Film Commission. An official British-French-Spanish co-production, *1492* qualified for public funding under co-production treaties between the three countries that had been struck to protect national cultural expression and support national culture industries. While the Spanish cultural heritage to this story is clear, the trinational status of the film aligns more closely to industry and labour imperatives than cultural protection: a British director and post-production work, a French actor and production company, and Spanish/ex-Spanish possession locations and crews. The film failed in the US, but topped the European box office (except for Italy, where it did particularly poorly in Genoa, Columbus' birthplace) (Williams, 1994; Berkman, 1992; Jäckel, 1996; Groves, 1992).

If the *year* 1492 reminds us of the colonial legacies that have structured globalisation's long history via the pursuit of gold, commodities and labour (Broad, 1995b), the *film 1492* exemplifies the legacies of 'America's' twentieth-century economic ascendance, including a cultural legacy that finds nation-states around the world vying for expressive space and cultural industrialisation in the face of Hollywood's continued proliferation. Just as the birth of nation-states in the colonised world occurred through struggles for independence from colonial domination, the co-production protocols that brought *1492* to the screen are among more than 135 bilateral and multilateral treaties between over eighty-five countries outside the US. Designed to combat Hollywood's domination of screen culture, they frequently enable the very NICL that ratifies it (Taylor, 1998: 134; see Chapter 3).

Conventional economics explains Hollywood's historical success in terms of 'a flexible managerial culture and an open and innovative financial system' (Acheson and Maule, 1994: 271–73) that have adapted to changing economic and social conditions. On this account, the silent era saw films made for the big American domestic market that could also be sold in other English-speaking countries. Because English was a very international First World language by contrast with those of other wealthy linguistic groups, the coming of sound aided the process, while the diverse ethnic mix of the US population encouraged a universal mode of storytelling. As Terry Ramsaye put it over half a century ago, '[t]he American motion picture born to serve a vast polyglottic patronage was born international in its own home market' (1947: 8). The argument goes that these strengths have been built on since, under the guiding principle of free-enterprise competitiveness, to produce a product that is popular with audiences (Wildman and Siwek, 1993; Dupagne and Waterman, 1998; and, for a spectacularly egregious instance, Noam, 1993). Global corporate media firms are seen as solutions to the market's low productivity and inefficiency – an effective means of delivering consumers what they want, while opening up cultures to change in ways that encourage liberal democracy through new ideas (Demers, 1999: 5). Hollywood's own account of itself intersects with these neo-classical economics *nostra* in claiming that comparative advantage determines the location of globally successful cinema. Hollywood 'wins' because it is set in a melting-pot society and obeys *laissez-faire* protocols (Pollock in Peres and Pollack, 1998).

Conversely, this chapter questions: (a) whether Hollywood is truly a free market based purely on consumer demand; and (b) whether the industry realises the stated aims of public policy based on the tenets of neo-classical economics. We use four tests of worth, outlined below, based on the promises and premises of that discourse.

| Freedom of entry to new starters?
Neo-classical economics says that the degree of real competitiveness in an industry can be gauged by the openness of its markets to new entrants. It is cer-

tainly true that there have been new owners of major Hollywood studios over the past decade, such as Australia's Channei Seven and News Corporation, Canada's Seagrams, France's Canal Plus/Vivendi and Japan's Sony, plus a new domestic venture in Dreamworks, but control of studio output remains in California and New York. What matters spatially is not the company's head-quarters, or its major shareholders' residence, but where its actual product development and management are domiciled. Given that US entertainment anti-trust has been a joke since the 1980s, and the close ties of television to film following deregulation of Federal Communications Commission rules, con-tinued governmental limits of 25 per cent foreign ownership of US radio and television stations permit limited external participation, even as they encour-age domestic oligopoly (Stokes, 1999). So most foreign direct investment in Hollywood is through portfolios (Marvasti, 2000). With large conglomerates owning studios and networks, and Wall Street demanding routine and regular success of industries used to routine failure, there is an increasing tendency for films to be made with this foreign investment (Groves and D'Alessandro, 2001). Nearly 20 per cent of the US$15 billion expended on Hollywood pro-duction in 2000 was, for example, German, and based on tax subsidies (Zwick, 2000; Kirschbaum, 2001). Control of these funds remains firmly in 'American' hands, just as it did during unsuccessful purchases of studios by others over the previous decade.

2 No state subsidies?

Neo-classical reactionaries claim that state subsidies in other countries under-taken in the name of cultural sovereignty impede the free market and disadvantage other nations because, allegedly *ipso facto*, such intervention sti-fles innovation, thereby aiding US dominance (Marvasti, 2000). But this woefully misreads the constitutive nature of US governmental assistance to Hollywood. The local film industry has been aided through decades of tax-credit schemes, State and Commerce Department representation, the Informational Media Guaranty Program's currency assistance (Izod, 1988: 61–63, 82, 118; Guback, 1987: 92–93; Schatz, 1988: 160; Muscio, 2000: 117–19; Powdermaker, 1950: 6; Harley, 1940: 3; Elsaesser, 1989: 10–11), and oligopolis-tic domestic buying and overseas selling practices that keep the primary market essentially closed to imports on the grounds of popular taste (without much good evidence for doing so). The US Department of Commerce continues to produce materials on media globalisation for Congress that run lines about both economic development and ideological influence, problematising claims that Hollywood is pure free enterprise and that the US government is uninter-ested in blending trade with cultural change. The US has a vast array of state, regional and city film commissions, hidden subsidies to the film industry (via

reduced local taxes, free provision of police services, and the blocking of public way-fares), Small Business Administration financing through loans and
support of independants, and State and Commerce Department briefings and
plenipotentiary representation. Negotiations on so-called video piracy have
resulted in PRC offenders being threatened with beheading, even as the US
claims to be watching Chinese human rights as part of most-favoured nation
treatment, while protests by Indonesian filmmakers against Hollywood that
drew the support of their government saw Washington threaten retaliation
against Indonesia via a vast array of industrial sanctions, and the US pressured
South Korea to drop its screen quotas as part of 1998–99 negotiations on a
Bilateral Investment Treaty. Copyright limitations prevent the free flow of
information, and foreign funds have often been raised through overseas tax
shelters (Acheson and Maule, 1991; Guback, 1984, 1985 and 1987; 'Commerce
Secretary', 2001; Robinson, 2000: 51; Kim, 2000: 362). The state also has a long
history of direct participation in production (Hearon, 1938). Finally, the new
hybrid of SiliWood blends Northern Californian technology, Hollywood
methods and military funding, while the Californian State Government offers
a 'Film California First Program' (Hozic, 1999; Directors Guild of America,
2000; 'Americans', 2001). No wonder that *Canadian Business* magazine – archly,
and with a deeply endearing hypocrisy – refers to 'Hollywood's Welfare Bums'
(Chidley, 2000).

3 A relationship between the cost of production and consumption?
Unlike most forms of manufacturing, the production of film drama is dominated by a small number of large companies with limited, individually
differentiated outputs. Most investments are complete failures, a pain that can
only be borne by big firms. The absolute significance of story over cost for audiences – who are accustomed to paying the same amount for all releases – goes
against neo-classical economics' standard assumptions about the role of price
in balancing supply and demand. Because of textual meaning's centrality to
film, again unlike manufactured goods, screen texts have very short product
lives and only minimal opportunities for the reuse of already extant 'parts'.
Instead, films are transformed from services to products and then services again
as they move between theatrical, video, televisual and Internet forms of life
(Litman, 1998: 25, 1). Costs are not reflected in ticket prices or cable fees. They
are amortised through a huge array of venues, so reusable is each full copy of
each text, unlike a car or painting. Although the means of production are standardised, economies of scale are rare when each project is costly and unlikely
to succeed. There is a clear correlation between GDP, public-sector broadcasting, and the purchase of US television in both Asia and Europe – the richer the
nation and the stronger its public media, the less need it has for Hollywood

material (Dupagne and Waterman, 1998). This indicates that economic power exploits poor countries, not that prices are determined by consumer desire.

4 Textual diversity?

Open markets supposedly make for diverse products, permitting extensive freedom of choice for customers. Do we have this on US screens? In the 1960s, imports accounted for 10 per cent of the US film market. In 1986, that figure was 7 per cent. Today, it is 0.75 per cent. Foreign films are essentially excluded from the US, as never before. Neo-classical reactionaries attribute this to US audiences, who are said to be 'unusually insular and intolerant of foreign programming or films, because historically they are exposed to very little' (Hoskins *et al.*, 1997: 45). As a country with huge everyday use of non-English languages and a thriving Spanish-language cultural market, this account of the US is as laughably off the mark as we have come to expect from these ideologues. Minimal screen diversity is due to the corporatisation of cinema exhibition, in combination with increases in promotional and real-estate costs for independant distributors and exhibitors and higher demands from the original producers, who have had to put more and more money 'on the screen' to compete with the Hollywood 'look'. This has reached the point where subtitling and dubbing have become insupportable – the average Hollywood film had US$21 million budgeted for advertising in 1999, an unthinkable figure for European rights-holders (Stanbery, 2001), and overall average film costs have doubled in less than a decade (Walters, 1999), increasing by 6.5 per cent between 1999 and 2000, to US$54.8 million (Valenti, 2001c). In television, the proliferation of channels in the US over the past ten years has required companies to change their drama offerings significantly. In 1990, action-adventure, the most expensive television genre, occupied 20 per cent of prime time on the networks; four years later, the figure was around 1 per cent (Balio, 1998b: 65; Schwab, 1994; Martin, 1995). Reality television, fixed upon by cultural critics who either mourn it as representative of a decline in journalistic standards or celebrate it as the sign of a newly feminised public sphere, should frankly be understood as a cost-cutting measure and an instance of niche marketing. This has not led to significant variety or quality.

In summary, the neo-classical vision of Hollywood asserts that the supposedly neutral mechanism of market competition exchanges materials at costs that ensure the most efficient people are producing, and their customers are content. This model may occasionally describe life in some fruit and vegetable markets today. But as an historical account, it is of no value: the rhythms of supply and demand, operating unfettered by states, religions, unions, superstition and fashion, have never existed as such. Or rather, they have existed as enormously potent prescriptive signs in the rhetoric of international financial organisations, bureaucrats and journalists, at least since economists achieved their hegemony via the Keynesian end to the Great Depression, and then worked to maintain it, despite 1970s stagflation, via their mass conversion from demand- to supply-side doctrines.

There are alternative forms of theorisation to bourgeois economics. Political economy proposes that Hollywood's success has been a coordinated, if sometimes conflictual and chaotic, attempt by capital and the state to establish and maintain a position of market and ideological dominance, in ways that find US governments every bit as crucial as audiences and firms. These radical critiques focus on the division of labour, as derived from its classical origins:

> One man draws out the wire, another straightens it, a third cuts it, a fourth points it, a fifth grinds it at the top for receiving the head; to make the head requires three distinct operations; to put it on is a peculiar business, to whiten the pins is another; it is even a trade by itself to put them into the paper ...
>
> The division of labour ... occasions, in every art, a proportionable increase of the productive powers of labour.
>
> (Smith, 1970: 110)

Today, the expression 'division of labour' is used to describe sectoral differences in an economy, say between fishing and restaurants, or the occupations and skills of a labour force, or the organisation of tasks within a firm. As Émile Durkheim sceptically noted a century ago, economists see the division of labour as a 'higher law of human societies and the condition for progress' (1984: 1). But pushing at its superficial merit of efficiency, we find that the present-day division of labour is organised around eight realities. First, wages increase with age, but at a diminishing rate. Second, levels of unemployment relate to levels of skill. Third, workers in the global South have least control over the means of production. Fourth, young people change jobs most often and are most involved in ongoing training. Fifth, earnings are skewed towards skill levels. Sixth, highly-trained people tend to be those who continue to benefit from ongoing training. Seventh, the market determines the division of labour. And finally, human-capital investments are less predictably valuable than more material investments. These features of the division of labour lead some theorists to endorse an approach based on the value of investing in training for all participants in the economic process (Becker, 1983: 16). For us, this reality leads to an analysis of the political situation of exploitation and the generation of stratified inequality in Hollywood. As the US Department of Commerce put it in a 2001 report:

Since there are no distinct, physical locations for making movies, it is difficult to quantif[y] all the skills, equipment, technology, or even number of workers that contribute to the production of a film or television show. Films and television productions tend to be short-term projects lasting only a few months. Often there are different combinations of crews and workers involved in different projects. Because of these factors, motion picture and television production is less visible than a stationary manufacturing facility, such as an automobile plant. Moreover, in 'floating factories' film workers tend to be relatively fragmented, belonging to literally dozens of professional associations and unions, and lacking a unified national identity akin to workers in the steel or auto industry.

Correspondingly, when production is lost, it neither generates the same tangible, visual image of unemployed workers standing outside the fence of a shuttered physical factory, nor does it elicit a cohesive nationwide industry response. However, the economic impact and job loss are no less real or important to local communities.

(Department of Commerce, 2001: 12)

The conservative British newspaper the *Financial Times* called this 'a whine of a report', noting that Hollywood has 'self-righteous unions' ('Why Hollywood', 2001). That hysterical response signifies that the US Department of Commerce was onto something that hews to a profound historical truth.

Working backwards from the finished product, it is clear that objects and services obtain their surplus value as commodities through exploitation of the value derived from the combined labour generated by different kinds of work. Once these commodities enter circulation with a price, they attain exchange value. The power gained by capitalism through ever-widening exchange includes both surplus value, realised as profit, and authority over the conditions and possibilities of labour. The division of labour is the mechanism for this linkage of productivity, exploitation and social control. As its subdivisions multiply and spread geographically, it acquires a talent for hiding the co-operation of labour that constitutes it (Marx, 1906: 49, 83). But the process is visible to those administering it: some distance from Marxism, the International Monetary Fund (2000) positions the division of labour at the centre of globalisation.

The development of surplus production and the division of labour correspond to four distinct phases of trading history. In the fourteenth and fifteenth centuries, a mercantile system arose from calculations of climate, geography, flora and fauna. Exchanges of goods turned into exchanges of labour. As food commodities made their way around the globe, so did people, often as slaves. When machinery was developed, work split into an industrial mode. Across the sixteenth, seventeenth and eighteenth centuries, cities grew into manufacturing sites, populations urbanised and wages displaced farming as the basis of subsistence (Lang and Hines, 1993: 15). This is the moment of Adam Smith's famous example of pin-making quoted above.

When developed countries moved onto the global stage, new forms of labour were institutionalised in empire. Manufacturing went on at the centre, with food and raw materials imported from the periphery in the eighteenth and nineteenth centuries. Differences of opinion emerged about the significance of the balance of trade to a country's well-being. Mercantilists thought it should be controlled, but free traders wanted market forces to rule, in accordance with factor endowments and an international division of labour. Keynesian responses to the Depression made protectionism a more legitimate position in economic theory, until stagflation emerged from the transnational phase that commenced after the war. By the mid-1980s, the volume of offshore produc- tion by multinationals exceeded the amount of trade between states for the first time. Today, life-cycle models of international products suggest that they are first made and consumed in the centre, in a major industrial economy, then exported to the periphery, and finally produced and consumed 'out there', once technology is standardised and savings can be made on the labour front. Goods and services owned and vended by the periphery rarely make their way into the centre as imports. The global capitalist economy depends on the integration of production processes, even when they are geographically dispersed but gov- erned by states and para-statal institutions in the service of capital accumulation (Strange, 1995b: 293; Keynes, 1957: 333–34; Cohen, 1991: 129, 133–39; Evans, 1979: 27-28; Wallerstein, 1989).

As we have seen, bourgeois economists theorise the combination of high GDP, managerial sophistication, narrative clarity and the *lingua franca* status of English as factor endowments aiding Hollywood's hegemony. Our critique argues instead that Hollywood's hegemony is built upon and sustained by the internal suppression of worker rights, exploitation of a global division of labour, and the impact of colonialism on language – so Hollywood might fancy the not-too-threatening difference of a Pakeha New Zealand director who works in the US (Roger Donaldson) or a Scottish actor/British national resi- dent in Spain who works in the US and avoids British tax by a special deal that he limit his time spent there (Sean Connery) to the ready credentials of a USC alum (Hoskins *et al.*, 1997: 40–43; Tunstall and Machin, 1999: 18).

The neo-classical model fails to explain the inherent violence of exploitation and the stratification of work in global Hollywood. A more adequate analysis of the division of labour would account for how practices and labourers are concentrated in one place and disciplined by their access to local labour markets, while establishing increasingly globalised 'means for co-ordination and control under the despotic authority of the capitalist'. This distant power reacts to competition's 'progressive concentration of activity (until, presumably, all economies of scale are exhausted)' by 'tightening authority structures and control mechanisms within the workplace'. This leads our analysis of the NICL towards a confrontation with processes in global Hollywood that go hand in hand with globalisation of the 'hierarchical organisation and forms of specialisation which stratify the working class and create a social layer of administrators and overseers who rule – in the name of capital – over the day-to-day operations in the workplace' (Harvey 1999: 31).

In seeking a more politicised understanding of work in global Hollywood – how an international division of labour links productivity, exploitation and social control – we deploy the concept of the NICL to account for the differentiation of cultural labour, the globalisation of labour processes, the means by which Hollywood coordinates and defends its authority over cultural labour markets, and the role national governments play in collusion with MNCs. The NICL is designed to cover a variety of workers within the culture industries, whatever their part in the commodity chain. So, it includes janitors, accountants, drivers and tourism commissioners as well as scriptwriters, best boys and radio announcers (Throsby, 2001: 256). The NICL is adapted from the idea of a New International Division of Labour (NIDL): developing markets for labour and sales, and the shift from the spatial *sen*sitivities of electrics to the spatial *in*sensitivities of electronics, pushed businesses beyond treating Third World countries as suppliers of raw materials, to look on them as shadow-setters of the price of work, competing among themselves and with the First World for employment. As production was split across continents, the prior division of the globe into a small number of IMECs and a majority of underdeveloped countries was compromised. Folker Fröbel and his collaborators (1980) christened this trend the NIDL. The upshot has been that any decision by a multinational firm to invest in a particular national formation carries the seeds of insecurity, because companies move on when tax incentives or other factors of production beckon (Allan, 1988: 325–26; Browett and Leaver, 1989: 38; Welch and Luostarinen, 1988; Fröbel *et al.*, 1980: 2–8, 13–15, 45–48).

Because of their mobility, MNCs can discipline both labour and the state, such that the latter is reluctant to impose new taxes, constraints or pro-worker policies in the face of possible declining investment (not to mention settling for spectator status in the Global Business Dialogue). Post-state-socialist labour movements are advised on 'appropriate' forms of life by the AFL-CIO, in keeping with the latter's strong opposition to Marxism-Leninism over many decades (Herod, 1997: 172, 175). The 'uncompetitive' countries of the Arab world and Africa have their labour forces bracketed by MNCs as a reserve army of low-cost potential workers who are imported to the North as required (Amin, 1997: ix), while throughout the world, 'household and informal sector activities' increase 'to sustain global reproduction' (Peterson, 1996: 10). The state under-mines the union movement on behalf of capital through policies designed to 'free' labour from employment laws. In the process, the Keynesian welfare sys-tem, which helped to redistribute funds to the working class, is being dismantled. Ralph Nader refers to this as 'a slow motion *coup d'état*' – the his-toric gains to representative discussion and social welfare made by working people and subaltern groups are displaced by corporate power (1999: 7). Third World peoples experience 'comparative advantage' as exploitation, working long hours for meagre pay on commodities that expose their countries to the flights of fancy and instability of global markets in a form of 'primitive Tay-lorism' (Robles, 1994: 1–2, 136–37). Contemporary international labour recruitment via the Web, for instance, has already instantiated racist and sexist cultural stereotypes (Tyner, 1998).

Although most of the literature on migration focuses on the poor, inter-national skill exchange has accelerated in the past twenty years, with the departure of professionals often a ghastly loss – Ghana saw 60 per cent of its doctors leave in the early 1980s, and the African continent loses 20,000 pro-fessionals annually (Stalker, 2000: 107). Cultural production has also relocated, though largely within English-language IMECs, as factors of production, including state assistance, lure business. This is happening at the level of popu-lar textual production, marketing, information – data-processing everything from airline bookings and customer warranties to the literary canon and pornographic novels – and high-culture, limited-edition work. The UN Devel-opment Programme estimates the value of offshore information and chip-insertion services at US$30–40 billion annually, and growing at twice the rate of the rest of the world economy. The competition for this market fre-quently leads to grotesque working conditions and contingent, 'disposable' labour: the Asian Monitor Resource Center reported in 1999 that Mattel toys were being assembled by workers in China who were required to be on the job seven days a week, ten to sixteen hours a day, while India's dramatic success in undercutting US software wages is constantly at risk from Mexico, Hungary, China, Ireland, the Philippines, Israel and Singapore. Time and space are refor-matted via the exploitation of workers (Greider, 2000: 152–53; Dicken, 1998: 398; 'Technology-Labour', 1999; Burawoy *et al.*, 2000: 175–202).

Labour market slackness, increased profits and developments in global trans-portation and communications technology have diminished the need for co-location of these factors, depressing labour costs and deskilling workers. This has been especially true of cinema and television in the period since 1980, when the compound annual rate of increase of screen production costs has well outstripped inflation. Animation, for example, is frequently undertaken in Southeast Asia by employees for lower pay than US workers (who still do well because there is a supply problem in the wake of the stimulus to cartooning generated by deregulation's creation of dedicated-genre US television networks). There are 239 major producers spread across thirty-nine countries, and 90 per cent of the world's television cartoons are made in Asia, from *The Simpsons* to *Ninja Turtles*. Manila's studios produce half-an-hour for US$120–160,0000, whereas the US cost is US$300,000. China and Vietnam offer still lower pay rates. Even the US Public Broadcasting Service sends cartooning offshore. It is sometimes claimed that high-technology changes to the craft have repatriated work to Southern California, but Southeast-Asian nations are constantly upgrading their equipment and downgrading labour (Vogel, 1998: 72; 'Asia's', 1997; Lent, 1998; 'Animation', 2001; Freeman, 2000: 2, 9; 'Cartoonist', 2000; Scott, 1998a: 147).

The long-term trend in Hollywood is for the US to attract or otherwise exploit talent developed by national cinemas to compete with it. Attempts by the French film industry in the 1980s to bring in Hollywood investment may have the ultimate effect of US studio takeovers (Hayward, 1993: 385). Director Peter Weir's post-production for *The Truman Show* (1998) or *Witness* (1985) might take place in Australia, satisfying off-screen indices of localism in order to obtain state financing, but does that make for a real alternative to the US? What does it mean that Michael Apted, James Bond and *7 Up* series director, can speak with optimism of a 'European-izing of Hollywood', when Gaumont points out that 'a co-production with the Americans . . . usually turns out to be just another U.S. film shot on location', and Guillermo del Toro turns the success of his Mexican film *Cronos* (1995) into a big-budget Hollywood career with *Mimic* (1997) ('Top', 1994; Apted quoted in Dawtrey, 1994: 75; Gaumont quoted in Kessler, 1995: n. 143; López, 2000: 434)?

Newness is endemic to capitalism's propensity for continual disruption of production, a restless expansion-contraction-dispersion dynamic that sees companies move in concert with the revised social conditions they have helped to generate, which ultimately lead to raised worker expectations and hence a need for businesses to move on in order to avoid meeting those expectations. In this sense, rather than a national scale to economic growth, our model is based on three international foundations: first, a world centre; second, intermediate zones nearby of secondary importance; and third, outlying regions of labour subordinate to the centre (Mattelart and Mattelart, 1998: 92). These three foundations could be seen as, respectively, Hollywood; Western Europe, North America and Australia; and the rest of the world.

How did this globalisation of the labour process come about? The standard argument about Hollywood's industrial history is as follows: an artisanal system obtained in New York from the early 1900s until the wholesale shift to California in the 1920s (ironically undertaken in part to elude the powerful

Eastern union movement and because of the West's stature as an anti-union state). Following the stimulus of the New Deal legislation, notably the Wagner Act, the Californian film industry unionised rapidly across the latter half of the 1930s (Milkman, 2000; Ross, 1947: 58). Vertically integrated industrialisation followed, in the form of a studio system that made and distributed films like car manufacturers made and distributed jalopies, that is, through rationalised techniques of mass production. In the 1940s, the system was undermined by governmental trust-busting and processes of televisualisation and suburbani-sation: the state called on Hollywood to divest ownership of theatres, even as the spread of television and housing away from city centres diminished box-office receipts. The studios are said by some to have entered a post-Fordist phase of flexible specialisation at that point, through product differentiation and vertical disintegration that rely on high-end genres and subcontracted independant producers, pre- and post-production companies, and global locations, rather than comprehensive in-house services. There are, for example, literally hundreds of multimedia production houses in Southern California, and most film and distribution businesses there employ fewer than ten workers. They add up to an interconnecting critical mass, a cluster of technology, labour and capital which operates through contracts with and investments from the studios, rather than ownership by them. The system works because of four fac-tors: flexible delivery of services by specialised companies; intense interaction between small units that are part of a dynamic global industrial sector; highly diverse and skilful labour; and institutional infrastructure. The cluster has evolved through the articulation since the mid-1980s of Southern and North-ern California semi-conductor and computer manufacture and systems and software development (a massively military-inflected and –supported industry until after the Cold War) to Hollywood screen content. Disused aircraft-pro-duction hangars were symbolically converted into entertainment sites (Aksoy and Robins, 1992; Scott, 1998b: 31; Porter, 1998; Bureau of Labor Statistics, 2000a: 205; Vogel, 1998: 33; Scott, 1998a; International Labour Office, 2000a; Raco, 1999; Walters, 1999). Despite this splintering, power remains vested in a small number of companies that resemble the very entities that were suppos-edly opened to competition fifty years ago through anti-trust, because they have successfully controlled the gateways to film and television that make real money for minimal outlay – distribution. The fact of this centralised control makes an interrogation of the NICL all the more pressing.

The US film industry has always imported cultural producers, such as the German Expressionists. (Alfred Hitchcock used to reprimand anti-Hollywood Britons with 'There are no Americans. America is full of foreigners' [quoted in Truffaut with Scott, 1967: 54].) During his tenure as Valenti's pre-war prede-cessor, Hays referred to this as 'drawing into the American art industry the talent of other nations in order to make it more truly universal' (quoted in Higson and Maltby, 1999: 5). Hence Antonio Gramsci's reference to the 30,000 Italian women who sent photographs of themselves in bathing suits to Hollywood when *Ben-Hur* (Fred Niblo and Alfred Raboch, 1925) was shot there as would-be 'luxury mammals' (1978: 306). This was mostly one-way traffic during the classical Hollywood era, although as early as 1938, when MGM was establishing an English studio, unions in Los Angeles were expressing concern about job losses overseas, and in 1941, the Federal Government encouraged Disney to go offshore, in part to undermine striking workers. The decade from 1946 saw increased overseas production. Location shooting became a means of differentiating stories, once colour and widescreen formats became fashionable and portable recording technology was available. Studios purchased facilities around the world to utilise cheap, docile labour. By investing in local industry, Hollywood avoided foreign-exchange drawback rules that prevented the expatriation of profits, simultaneously benefiting from host-state subvention of 'local' films. 'Runaway production' is the common journalistic and industry shorthand for the ensuing exodus of Hollywood production. In 1949, there were nineteen runaway productions. Twenty years on, the figure was 183, mostly in Europe, while Japanese animators were drawing US cartoons from the early 1960s. Between 1950 and 1973, just 60 per cent of Hollywood films in production began their lives in the US. Foreign direct investment by the US in offshore production increased by a factor of five between 1977 and 1993. In 1984, 151 of Hollywood's 318 major features were runaways (Townson, 1999: 9; Leff, 2000; Kehr, 1999; Smoodin, 1993: 147; Christopherson and Storper, 1986; Marvasti, 2000).

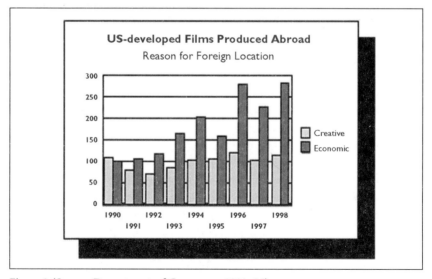

Figure 9 (Source: Department of Commerce 2001: 26)

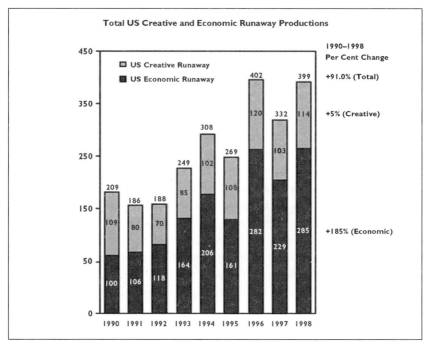

Figure 10 (Source: Monitor, 1999)

Many of the films made were cheap and nasty compared to those shot at home. This aura of second-rate production is thematised in particularly stark form in a 1966 episode of the television programme *I Spy*, starring Robert Culp and Bill Cosby. 'The Trouble with Temple', itself shot offshore in the interests of a cosmopolitan look, is set in Spain, during the production of a down-market Hollywood film. The movie features a producer-star derided by his female counterpart as an 'All-American boy with time snapping at his heels', who later turns out to be a traitor in 'real' life. As we shall see, this sense of runaway producers as disloyal has significant resonance today, when the opposition of creativity and economics continues to characterise reasons for shooting abroad.

For example, driven by the possibilities of syndicating its considerable television library, Sony's Columbia/Tristar is involved in producing a Putonghua version of *Charlie's Angels* for China and historical costume epics for India, two traditionally hostile places for Hollywood's business. And while most Hollywood exports are still only dubbed into German, Italian, Spanish and French, with the rest of the world reading subtitles, there is a trend towards hiring 'local' actors across the thirty largest language groups to dub high-budget films (Orwall, 2000).

Proponents regard the NICL as a sign of successful post-Fordist flexible accumulation, whereby unions work with business and government to operate competitively in a tripartite heaven (Murphy, 1997; Shatilla, 1996). For critics, industries built on policy responses to external cultural domination are simply enabling that domination, as place is governmentalised and commodified as an industrial setting of sites and services. Its stature as a cultural-historical space is obliterated. This de-localisation that permits re-territorialisation in the lens of the foreigner, making Canada, for example, not 'Hollywood North' so much as 'Mexico North' (Gasher, 1995). For the first time, 2000 in Toronto saw more foreign than local production and reduced money going to Canadian firms. Less than 1 per cent of English-language production nationally now goes on Canadian stories (Menon, 2001; Mokhiber and Weissman, 1999). The NICL is also a source of concern for Hollywood workers. The US Federal Govern-ment first investigated runaway production in the 1960s, when some Congresspeople proposed labels that would identify films made in the US. In 1979, US animators went on strike against runaways, achieving a contract clause that Los Angeles-based unionists should be given first option on work. But producers blithely ignored it, regardless of stiff fines (Lent, 1998: 240). Today, it is again a cause for anxiety. Runaway television and film production from the US amounted to US$500 million in 1990 and US$2.8 billion in 1998. By the end of the 1990s, the NICL was allegedly costing Los Angeles US$7.5 billion annually in multiplier effects, plus 20,000 jobs. Hollywood's proportion of overseas productions in the last decade went from 7 per cent of its total to 27 per cent, according to a study undertaken by the Monitor Group for the Directors and Screen Actors Guilds.

Eighty-one per cent of runaways went to Canada, a total of 232 in 1998 com-pared to 63 in 1990, and 10 per cent to Britain and Australia.

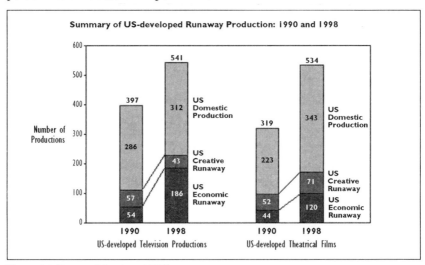

Figure 11 (Source: Monitor, 1999)

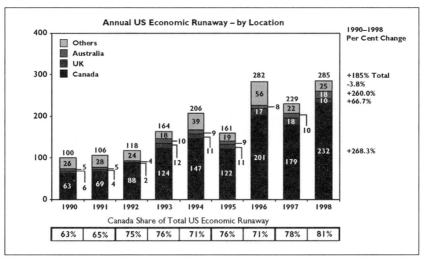

Figure 12 (Source: Monitor, 1999)

Much of this loss was in mini-series and made-for-television films, the key sector in terms of regular production work for cable networks. In 1999, Canada boasted 696 weeks of television film production, California just 152 (Department of Commerce, 2001: 31). The industry is working to develop means of extending its offshore options. For instance, after Valenti's servants in the US Government had required Seoul to minimise its quotas on domestic film exhibition in return for other industrial arrangements, he promised training for Korean filmmakers – in order to enter the NICL (Kim, 2000: 363). Therefore, at the same time as greater access is obtained for releasing films, a new cheap labour force is constructed to produce them.

The number of big-budget pictures made overseas went from none in 1990 to twenty-four in 1998. Toronto has doubled as New York City in over one hundred films, and when it played the role of Chicago for *Blues Brothers 2000* (John Landis, 1998), officials had the nerve to telephone the Chicago Film Commission for pointers, while producers boast their readiness to import trees in refrigeration trucks when there is a need to impersonate California. In television, *Due South*'s use of Toronto as Chicago was estimated to save 40 per cent in costs. The number of made-for-television movies lost to the NICL rose from thirty in 1990 to 139 in 1998, a 363 per cent increase. The US share of movies-of-the-week on US television dropped from 62 per cent in 1994–95 to 41 per cent in 1999–2000, and 45 per cent of the genre was shot in Canada in 1998–99. Opponents are more concerned about this sector than occasional high-profile features made there. Of the 1,075 US-funded fiction films and programmes screened on US television in 1998, 27 per cent were filmed abroad, twice the proportion in 1990 ('Culture Wars', 1998; Masur and Shea, 1999; Weller, 1999

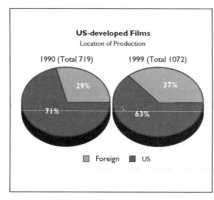
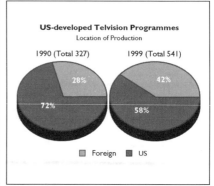

Figure 13 (Source: Department of Commerce, 2001: 24–5)

and 2000; Entertainment Industry Development Corporation, 2001; Gasher, 1995; Grumiau, 2000; Connell, 2000). The first six months of 2000 saw an increase in the value of film production in Toronto of 15.2 per cent on the corresponding period the previous year, to US$352.8 million (Brown, 2000). Several Canadian provinces now have high-technology post-production and editing facilities and tax breaks for this part of filmmaking, so that more and more phases of production can run (Connell, 2000).

While the runaway trend is still a relatively small threat to Hollywood workers when compared to plant closings and jobs moved overseas in sectors like textiles and apparel (Bronfenbrenner, 2000: 25), US entertainment unions have acted out of fear that if the NICL expands, there will be further disemployment in construction, hotels, catering, driving, carpentry and electrical

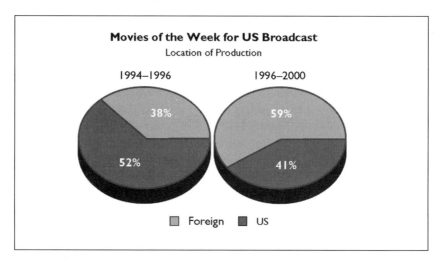

Figure 14 (Source: Department of Commerce, 2001: 24–5)

trades. It is estimated that 270,000 jobs in the US are directly involved in screen production. Many are in these below-the-line sectors, which are easily filled on-site by the NICL (Department of Commerce, 2001: 5, 10).

For all the Clinton administration's boasts that information technology was responsible for a third of US job growth between 1995 and 2000, there has been no credible analysis of job losses in the sector over that period, or the loss of 'good' jobs that have been casualised and proletarianised into freelance employment (Anderson, 2001). The International Labour Office (2000b) suggests that 125,100 jobs were lost to runaway production between 1990 and 1998, mostly by below-the-line workers, and it is common for multimedia firms to supplement a small group of full-time employees with part-timers and freelancers on an *ad hoc* basis (Scott, 1998a: 150–51).

Vancouver and Toronto are the busiest locations for North American screen production after Los Angeles and New York, due to a weak Canadian currency and tax rebates of up to 50 per cent on labour costs, depending on the province. There have been major declines in production since 1995 in several US sites (North Carolina down 36 per cent, Illinois down 20 per cent, Texas down 31 per cent and Washington down 37 per cent). But the two Canadian locations' 1998 production slates, of just under US$1.5 billion, are well behind Califor-

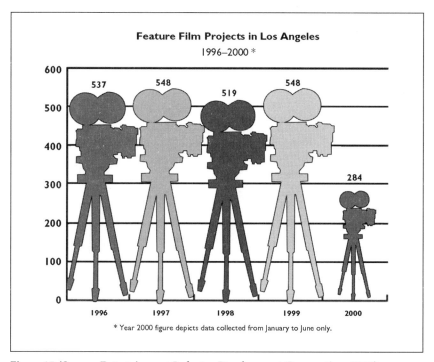

Figure 15 (Source: Entertainment Industry Development Corporation, 2001)

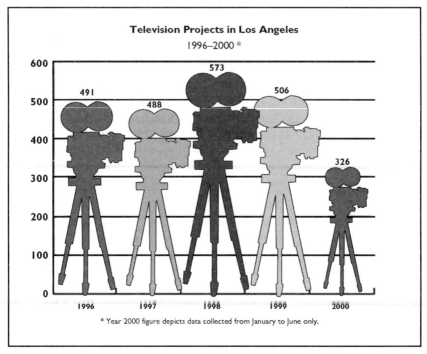

Figure 16 (Source: Entertainment Industry Development Corporation, 2001)

Total US Motion Picture Industry Employment
(000s)

Year	No. of Employees	Yearly Change	2000 Versus
2000 (p)	630.8	3.4%	N/A
1999	609.8	5.9%	3.4%
1998	576.0	4.7%	9.5%
1997	550.4	4.9%	14.6%
1996	524.7	7.6%	20.2%
1995	487.6	10.5%	29.3%
1994	441.2	7.1%	42.9%
1993	412.0	2.8%	53.1%
1992	400.9	-2.4%	57.3%
1991	410.9	0.8%	53.5%
1990	407.7	8.8%	54.7%
1989	374.7	9.9%	68.3%
1988	340.9	--	85.0%

(p) Preliminary estimate

Figure 17 (Source: Motion Picture Association of America, 2001: 24)

nia's total of US$28 billion, which incorporated almost 70 per cent of US film production that year and 60 per cent of national screen employment. Expenditure on screen production in LA County was US$29.4 billion in 1999, and an estimated US$31.2 billion in 2000, with five times the number of shooting days of Toronto. In the twelve years to 1999, the number of culture industry jobs in California rose 137 per cent, while nationwide US employment in entertainment had grown from 114,000 to 240,000 in ten years. And Canadian officials point out that while they represent 10 per cent of the world audience to US texts, only 3 per cent of film production takes place there (Kempster, 2001 and Bates, 2000; Madigan, 2000; Monitor, 1999). In 1999, Canadian unions upped the ante by agreeing to a 13 per cent pay cut (Ryan, 1999; Brinsley, 1999; Madigan, 1999c; Swift, 1999; Brown, 2000; Department of Commerce, 2001: 19; Lowry, 2000).

Hollywood's runaway trend depends on peripheral nations that have the right skills, language, familiarity, business links and foreign exchange rates to suit – what has been called a form of 'peripheral Taylorism,' such that there are highly-developed efficiencies available from a skilled working class in places that nevertheless continue to import what is made on 'their' territory – but never under their control (Robles, 1994: 137, 151). The UK government's decision to float the pound and free the Bank of England from democratic consultation contributed to a situation in 1998 where a strengthening currency raised costs for overseas investors and encouraged locals to spend elsewhere, with severe implications for offshore film funds. The UK, Australian and Canadian currencies declined by between 15 and 23 per cent against the US dollar across the 1990s.

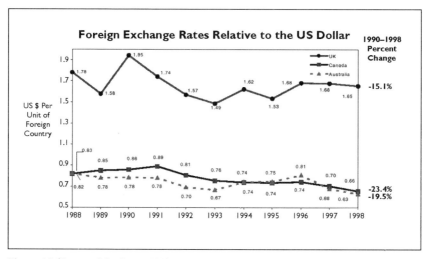

Figure 18 (Source: Monitor, 1999)

Thus the late 1990s offshore production boom in Australia and Canada, driven in part by scenery, infrastructure, language, subsidisation and lower pay levels than the US – but equivalent skill levels – still depended on weak currencies and, in 2000, workers not prepared to support 135,000 striking US actors in a campaign over advertising residuals. These are key issues for nations striving to displace the Anglo white-settler colonies and Britain – RSVP Film Studios advertises the Philippines as 'a non-union town where labor is delightfully inexpensive' and 'filming 16 hour days is not uncommon' (Woods, 1999b; Monitor, 1999; Pendakur, 1998: 229; Brown, 2000; RSVP, n. d.).

Not all Hollywood's exploitation of the NICL is directly associated with screen production, of course. Other key elements include distribution, exhibition, copyright and goods. Disney ensures that it profits from unsuccessful films through merchandising (46 per cent of annual revenue is from such sales). Much of that manufacturing is undertaken in Third World countries by subcontractors who exploit low-paid women workers. *The Hunchback of Notre Dame* (Gary Trousdale and Kirk Wise, 1996) performed poorly at the box office but sensationally in toy stores, with products made in Taiwan, Hong Kong, Mexico, Brazil, El Salvador, Thailand, Malaysia, St. Lucia, Colombia, the Philippines, Honduras, the Dominican Republic, India, Bangladesh, Sri Lanka, China, Haiti, the US, Japan, Denmark and Canada. Disney's labour abuses in China (sixteen-hour days, seven-day weeks, US$0.135-0.36 an hour), uncovered by the Hong Kong Christian Industrial Committee, show how exploitation puts the company into super-profit through 660 Disney retail outlets worldwide waiting to sell the products of exploited workers. Animation is especially appealing as a source of profit from licensing activities because it offers a direct route to children through the original text (McCann, 1998; Madigan 1999a and 1999b; 'Culture Wars', 1998; Tracy, 1999; McChesney, 2000: 94; 'Animation', 2001; 'Disney Labor', 1999).

American financial institutions have also bought foreign theatres and distribution companies, thus sharing risk and profit with local businesses. This is in keeping with the close historic relationship between the film industry and finance capital: as American banks looked overseas for sources of profit through the 1960s, so they endorsed and assisted efforts by Hollywood to spread risk and investment as widely as possible. By the end of the 1980s, overseas firms were crucial suppliers of funds invested in American film or loans against distribution rights in their countries of origin. Joint production arrangements are now well-established between US enterprises and French, British, Swedish, Australian and Italian companies, with connections to television, theme parks, cable, satellite, video and the Internet (Lent, 1998: 243; Wasser, 1995: 424, 431; Monitor, 1999; Buck, 1992: 119, 123; Briller, 1990: 75–78; Wasko, 1994: 33; Miège, 1989: 46; Wasko, 1982: 206–7; Marvasti, 1994;

Kessler, 1995; 'The PolyGram Test', 1998; Wasko, 1998: 180–81; Puttnam with Watson, 1998: 202–5).

The NICL also holds implications for copyright (see Chapter 4). As part of the framework for the NICL, issues of the territory of a text's first publication, its producer's domicile and the location of its owner's corporate headquarters are often crucial in international intellectual property disputes, as when the estates of John Huston and Ben Maddows claimed that, as director and co-screenwriter respectively of *The Asphalt Jungle* (1950), their moral rights had been infringed when a French television station scheduled the broadcast of a colourised version in 1988. Under US law, the heirs would have had little legal recourse, since the Turner Entertainment Company owned the copyright in the film, having bought it from MGM-Loews in 1986 (which had contracted Huston and Maddows as 'workers for hire'). Turner could do whatever it wanted with the film, including colourising it. After an injunction to prevent broadcast on French television, the lower court deemed that, under civil law moral rights, colourisation had not been authorised by those with a perpetual moral right to the film (namely Huston and Maddows). After being upheld on appeal under the rules of national treatment, a higher court reversed the decision by invoking authorial domicile, finding that US law held jurisdiction. Finally, the highest French civil court confirmed the original decision, on the grounds that only natural persons (not corporate entities) could qualify for the authorship associated with copyright by French law. Jane Ginsburg and Pierre Sirinelli (1991) suggest that the Huston ruling will not necessarily result in a flurry of offshore copyright infringement claims from US-based artists suing corporate copyright owners in moral-rights friendly countries. Instead, corporate owners might simply strengthen the contractual language in the 'work-for-hire' agreement that fleshes out the transfer of rights. Such a strengthening of language would, in the case of *The Asphalt Jungle*, align US 'work-for-hire' agreements with France's recognition of a written transfer of exploitation rights. Harmonisation aside, recognition of the subtleties of international legislative difference might inoculate the media owners from international infringement claims. While the moral legitimacy of a national cultural custodianship underlies claims by the directors' descendants that colourisation is a 'conspiracy to degrade our national character', and the American Film Institute's assertion that 'colorization will destroy our national film history' (Grainge, 1999: 627), the internationalisation of film copyright is harmonising the values that underlie domestic cultural polices in keeping with the need for a universal set of rules to facilitate the NICL.

Hollywood producers and networks are also purchasing satellite and broadcast space across Europe, with AOL-Time Warner, Disney-ABC, Viacom, NBC and others jostling their way into the centre of the vast and growing Western

European industry as a site of production and a dumping-ground for old material. The new stations throughout Europe invest in local programming with cost savings from scheduling American filler (Stevenson, 1994: 6). A huge increase in the number of channels and systems of supply and payment is also producing unprecedented concentration of television ownership, horizontal licensing and joint ventures that mirror domestic retailing systems (Schwab, 1994: 14; Roddick, 1994: 30; Markusen, 1995: 170).

Governments see positive as well as negative implications in the NICL, seeking ways to utilise the new internationalism to create or tend their own screen industries and tourism. Between 1990 and 1998, thirty-one national film commissions were set up across the globe, many solely concerned with attracting foreign capital (Guttridge, 1996). We shall now consider some case studies that address the role of the state in facilitating the NICL, concentrating on Australia, Italy, the Czech Republic, Britain and Mexico.

Australia

Kangaroo (Lewis Milestone, 1952) and *The Return of Captain Invincible* (Philippe Mora, 1983) provide chronological and conceptual limit-cases of US screen investment in a film industry. *Kangaroo* was the first of several Hollywood features shot in Australia during the 1950s. 20th-Century-Fox dispatched a crew and most of the cast because its Australian-based capital reserves had been frozen to prevent foreign exchange leaving the country. Shooting took place in Zanuckville, supinely named to honor the studio head. A formulaic Western, the film failed, but then the need to use money lying idle was probably the sole reason for its coming into being. Three decades later, *Captain Invincible* represented another outcome of the state producing conditions for foreign filmmaking. Taxation incentives designed to make Australian cinema more attentive to the private sector saw the local Treasury subsidising Hollywood to make a film set almost 'nowhere'. The text concerns a lapsed US superhero, played by Alan Arkin, who migrates to Australia and dipsomania following McCarthyite persecution, reviving his powers and sobriety to thwart a villainous Christopher Lee. Recut by its producers following difficulties obtaining US distribution, the text was disavowed by its director Philippe Mora and denied certification by the Australian government as insufficiently local by comparison with its original script. A court challenge against this ruling succeeded, but the tax haven designed to boost commercial production was politically and culturally compromised from that point. Governments in Australia have continued to provide risk capital for foreign moguls, but generally at the state level, although the Federal Government has a body named Ausfilm, resident in Los Angeles, which is charged with promoting the NICL (Department of Commerce, 2001: 50).

When Dino de Laurentiis was choosing between Sydney and Queensland's Gold Coast as locations for a joint-venture studio with the Australian company Village Roadshow in 1987, one factor in selecting the latter was the then Queensland Film Corporation patching together an A$7.5 million loan at low interest and attracting A$55 million via a local share-issue. His company collapsed after the stock market crash that year, and the space seemed destined to fail. Touted as a new Disneyland site or a multifunction polis, neither plan succeeded. But in 1988, a 150-day strike by the Writers' Guild of America over creative and residual rights payments led to a chronic shortfall in new programmes. Village Roadshow responded by refinancing its investment via Warner Bros. and seeking foreign business. The first major series shot on the Gold Coast was the television show *Mission: Impossible* in 1988. The Queensland Film Development Office immediately advertised the state to prospective producers like this: 'the production company of a recent American primetime television series found a diverse range of "international locations", from London to the Greek Islands in Queensland'. Village Road-show-Warner Bros. announced a studio expansion in 1989. The state was ready to assist with a construction subsidy that became part of the studios' promotional material. Well might the Queensland Tourist and Travel Corporation refer to itself as the 'last frontier', replete with 'smiling locals'. For Stanley O'Toole, managing director of what later became the studio, Queensland was 'LA without the smog'. The studio is part-owned by Warner Bros. and named Warner Roadshow. The Pacific Film and Television Commission, formed to promote the state to international and Australian filmmakers, offers a revolving fund for low-interest loans secured against guarantees and presales, rebates on payroll tax, and subsidised crewing costs (Miller, 1998a). In its thirteen years of operation, the studio has drawn NICL investment from CBS, Viacom, ABC, Fox TV, Disney TV, Disney Channel, Fox and Warner Bros., aided by Australian Government tax credits on labour of up to 10 per cent. Total run-away production to Australia increased on average by 26 per cent across the 1990s (Hanrahan, 2000; Monitor, 1999).

Of course, not all jurisdictions are so keen to be exploited. The producers of the television series *Baywatch*, then screened in 144 countries, decided to move to Australia in the late 1990s. Beaches are public property there, and residents of Avalon in Sydney protested when their local politicians offered to sign the space over. But Queensland's Gold Coast stood ready to help out ('Baywatch', 1999). Such neediness has seen Hollywood producers refer to Queenslanders as 'Mexicans with mobiles', which has become a sore point with the local Screen Directors' Guild (quoted in 'Australia', 1998; Fitzgerald, 2000). The shooting of high-profile movies like *Mission: Impossible 2* (John Woo, 2000) and *The Matrix* (Andy and Larry Wachowski, 1999) in Australia saw savings on LA prices of up

1999 Costs

	Los Angeles	*Australia*
Soundstage(*)	A$8,000 daily	A$2,000 daily
Make-up van	A$5,000 weekly	A$1,500 weekly
Trailer	A$4,000 weekly	A$1,000 weekly
Supporting actor	A$880 daily	A$300 daily
City shoot	A$15,000 daily	AS10,000 daily

(*) The US generally hires stage managers and crews and lighting costs
Source: Idato, 1999

to 30 per cent – not to mention that US$100 million of the budget was Ger-
man (Waxman, 1999; Zwick, 2000).

Labour costs can be cut by a further 20 per cent by South Africa, Australia's
major regional competitor. One hundred and eighty-two foreign television
commercials were shot there in the year to March 1997, up 40 per cent on the
year before, with major governmental subvention. Once worker expectations
and claims rise, unionisation follows, and it is time to move on again (for
example, to Zimbabwe) (Grumaiu, 1998; Department of Commerce, 1997;
'Africa's', 1997; Guider, 2001; 'Telenovela de Caracol', 2001). Similarly, by the
mid-1990s, Mexico City and Rio de Janeiro had lost their monopoly on dubbing English-language television into Spanish and Portuguese to Los Angeles
and Miami (Sinclair, 1999: 165).

Rich McCallum, co-producer of the *Star Wars* sequels in production in Australia, prefers it to Hollywood, which 'represents everything repugnant ... it's
so unionized'. He and his colleague George Lucas like Australia so much that 'I
made the commitment to two films', a sign that '[t]his isn't rape and pillage'
(quoted in Fitzgerald, 2000).

The skills available in Australia derived from a long-standing domestic cultural policy. Consider the Grundy Organisation. It produced Australian
television drama and game shows from the 1950s that were bought on licence
from the US. Then the company expanded to sell such texts across the world,
operating with a strategy called 'parochial internationalism' that meant leaving
Australia rather than exporting in isolation from relevant industrial, taste and
regulatory frameworks. Following patterns established in the advertising
industry, it bought production houses around the world, making programmes
in local languages based on formats imported from Australia that had originally
drawn on US models. From a base in Bermuda, the organisation produced
about fifty hours of television a week in seventy countries across Europe, Ocea-
nia, Asia and North America, until its sale in 1995 to Pearson for US$280
million. This exemplified the NICL offshore – a company utilising experience

in the Australian commercial reproduction industry to manufacture US palimpsests in countries relatively new to profit-centered television. The benefits to Australia, where a regulatory framework had birthed this expertise by requiring the networks to support such productions as part of cultural protection, are unclear. As Greg Dyke, the Pearson executive responsible for the Grundy purchase and later head of the BBC, proudly put it, the typical Grundy programme *Man O Man* 'has no redeeming social values' (Cunningham and Jacka, 1996: 81-87; Moran, 1998: 41–71; Short, 1996; Stevenson, 1994: 1; Tunstall and Machin, 1999: 30; Dyke quoted in Short, 1996).

In such cases, cultural policy merely underwrites local and international cultural bourgeoisies. And the US learns from these satellites and their development of palimpsestic techniques. The Grundy model has become a Hollywood standard, with Sony, Warners and Disney all producing thousands of hours of television texts in foreign markets each year, designed for local audiences. Similar stories apply to material produced by the Spanish-owned Endemol in the Netherlands, Action Time, Granada and All American Fremantle. Granada, for instance, has customised the British soap opera *Coronation Street* for China (*Joy Luck Street*) and Hollywood finally won over a key segment of the Indian market with a localised *Who Wants to be a Millionaire?*. *Joy Luck Street* is shown on cable for free, with advertising revenue going to Granada. This means that small cable networks can fill airtime and global companies can move easily and cheaply into markets (Landler, 2001; Fry, 2001).

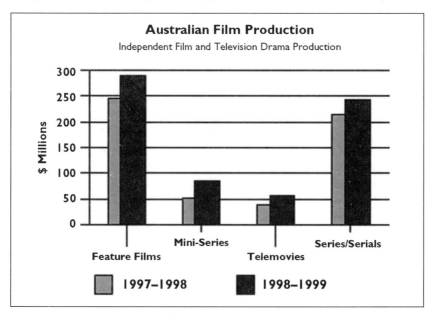

Figure 19 (Source: Department of Commerce, 2001: 50)

Italy

Italy has a long history of runaway production – in the 1920s, several Hollywood studios had post-production facilities there (Nowell-Smith *et al.*, 1996: 2). But Mussolini's gradual turn to anti-US cultural politics diminished business for many years. As part of post-war reconstruction, the government enacted a Cinema Law in 1949 that guaranteed screening time to locally-made films (as had been the case from the 1920s until Allied occupation) but otherwise did little by way of cultural protection. Although this aspect of the legislation was observed more in the breach than the observance, the law also required that revenue from Hollywood releases had to remain in Italy, which encouraged expenditure on plant and production by Hollywood as a substitute for repatriating theatrical profits. The majors invested in Cinecittà and began co-productions, with skilled crews and fresh locations an additional means of sweetening the mandated investment. In the early 1950s, following the making of *Quo Vadis?* (Mervyn LeRoy, 1951), 'Hollywood on the Tiber' was a recognised phenomenon, with the studios drawn both by blocked accounts and docile labour. Stars moved to Italy, independant producers sought new settings and US workers denied employment at home because of their leftist ideology were welcomed: Jules Dassin, John Berry, Michael Wilson, Cy Endfield, Bernard Vorhaus, Joseph Losey and Ben Barzman all worked in Italy, along with Welles, Huston and Robert Rossen. Well-known films with extravagant on- and off-camera narratives included *Alexander the Great* (Robert Rossen, 1956), *Ben-Hur* (William Wyler, 1959), *Lawrence of Arabia* (David Lean, 1962) and *55 Days at Peking* (Nicholas Ray, 1962). In all, twenty-seven Hollywood films were produced in Italy between 1950 and 1965 (Nowell-Smith *et al.*, 1996: 5, 140; Muscio, 2000: 120–21; Bono, 1995). As well as being a haven for radicals who could not be employed in Hollywood, it became a luxury site of excess, as immortalised in Fellini's *La Dolce Vita* (1960). This culminated with *Cleopatra* (Joseph L. Mankiewicz, 1963), which ran so far over budget that it became a legend. Its financial difficulties and parity of labour costs with Hollywood-based productions saw the end of 'Hollywood on the Tiber.' Redemption awaited late 1960s 'Spaghetti Westerns', which used Italy and Spain to resemble Mexico and California and featured US television stars such as Clint Eastwood. They became a way back into the world market until producers were allegedly perturbed by Red Brigade terrorism, then seduced elsewhere by post-state socialist privatisation, while deregulation of television produced a tabloid effect that cut into film production and employment (Weil, 1998; Bodo, 2000). Cinecittà is now mostly a site for television production with a new twist on runaways: Hollywood idols who eschew US television commercials as signs of failure but appear on Italian television promoting products for huge sums and sturdy guarantees of non-broadcast at home. For example Brad Pitt (jewellery),

Kevin Costner (footwear), Harrison Ford and Catherine Zeta Jones (cars), Marlon Brando, Leonardo DiCaprio and Woody Allen (telecommunications), Richard Gere (sweetmeats), and Sharon Stone and George Clooney (alcohol) all made appearances in 2000 (Lyman, 2000), as Italian audiences had huge advertising costs added to the price of their consumables and the money travelled offshore. Cinecittà was restructured in 1997, undergoing partial privatisation – building new sound stages and developing digital imaging. The television commercials stars were not alone in 2000: Martin Scorsese shot *Gangs of New York* and George Lucas filmed parts of the second *Star Wars* prequel at the studio to elude Hollywood union wages and capitalise on the convention that screen workers should labour 50-57 hours a week before overtime, with their pay set in relation to budgets rather than skills and relativities (Hancock, 1999). Meanwhile, Miramax looked for cheap local texts to form a new genre – Miramaxizzazione (Coletti, 2000).

The Czech Republic

In 2001, Wesley Snipes and a cadre of Hollywood above-the-liners arrived in Prague to shoot the action film *Blade 2: Bloodlust* (Guillermo del Toro, 2001). The formerly state-owned Barrandov studio, one of Europe's largest production facilities that employs 500 skilled below-the-liners and has eleven sound stages and on-site laboratories, welcomed the New Line Cinema production and the estimated US$10–15 million they brought to the studio. Prague's weak exchange rate and base of cheap skilled labourers makes shooting there 30 per cent less costly than in the West, and it is the latest destination for Hollywood big-budget filmmaking – six of the seven majors had been there to shoot in 1999–2000. Stillking Films and Milk and Honey Films, two international film production service companies with ties to US and British clients, facilitated an influx of production to Prague, first with commercials in the mid-1990s, then with television -movies, mini-series and feature films. Productions include the mini-series *The Scarlet Pimpernel* (BBC/A&E co-production), *Dune* (Sci-Fi Channel) and *Mists of Avalon* (TNT), and the feature films *Messenger: The Story of Joan of Arc* (Luc Bresson, 1999), *Dungeons and Dragons* (Courtney Solomon, 2000) and *The Bourne Identity* (Doug Liman, 2001) (Meils, 1998, 2000a, 2000b and 2000c). German and Czech studios prepared for English-language production pending possible Hollywood guild strikes in Spring 2001 (Meils, 2000c), and the government prepared to continue its supine welcomes, such as permitting producers to set off fireworks in the downtown area in the middle of the night but diverting air traffic for several hours in the interests of 'quiet on the set' (Krosnar *et al*, 2001).

Here, the NICL facilitates the free movement of screen capital into cheap production locations, contains labour mobility and undermines labour internationalism – all brokered on the exploitation of skills and facilities developed under state socialism. The Czech Republic is an oft-cited instance of privatisation without mass unemployment. But that story hides major declines in labour force participation (Gitter and Scheuer, 1998). Barrandov exemplifies this dubious history. In some ways it represents the 'Washington Consensus' at work on set. The decision by the government to sell 75 per cent of the studios was opposed by the local filmmakers union, who pointed out its illegality – the process was begun in 1991, two years before the passage of a law ending the state monopoly on filmmaking. In 1994, directors who had made films under the previous regimes, and who called for retention of a national cultural policy, were told 'Don't even think about it' by Prime Minister Vaclav Klaus, under whom domestic films dropped to 2 per cent of the studio's output. Such world-renowned artists as Jiri Menzel and Vera Chytilova were excluded from filmmaking (Hames, 2000).

Another story has been told from within by one of the privatisation's architects, Michael Millea (1997), who joyously relates going to Prague with the US Agency for International Development (USAID) to find that: 'the former Czechoslovakia was carpetbagger heaven' (489). He may have been referring to Hollywood filmmakers, but of course he was the carpetbagger wonk in this story. The plan to privatise was predicated by USAID on data about US studios that correlated favourable exchange rates and comparatively low budgets with decisions to shoot offshore. Based on the Agency's projections, the successful purchase offer proposed translating Barrandov from nationally-framed texts to US ones, extending even to converting studio space into shopping centres and hotels for visiting crews. The competitor, a plan drawn up by filmmakers that favoured domestic production, was rejected by the Agency. Millea concludes his essay with the triumphant observation that the shooting of the first *Mission Impossible* (Brian De Palma, 1996) film in Prague indicates 'capitalism has taken firm root in the Czech Republic' (1997: 504).

'Capitalism' immediately led to lay-offs for 85 per cent of the studio's employees. After London, Prague is today Hollywood's 'second centre' in Europe. At 2001 prices, labour was 40 per cent cheaper than in Los Angeles – union painters are paid less than US$3 an hour, for example, while extras 'command' US$15 a day to Hollywood's US$100 ('Hollywood on the Vltava', 2001; 'Hollywood Cashes Runaway Checks', n.d.; Hejma, 2000; Holley, 2000). One studio manager boasted in 2000 of 'one artist working on set-building for the last two months who's been earning about as much in a week as his British counterparts earn in a day and he just happens to be a famous Czech sculptor', while a non-union workforce meant that injuries to locals did not require compensation (quoted in I'Anson-Sparks, 2000). With the Republic due to join the EU in 2004, US filmmakers were already looking to move on and elude the worker protections and expectations of that system (Krosnar, 2001).

The United Kingdom

Post-war runaways began thanks to Britain's 1948 Anglo-American Film Agreement, which required the majors to leave US$40 million a year of their receipts in blocked accounts (Nowell-Smith *et al.*, 1996: 139). This policy invited Hollywood to use the money to make films in Britain, and even after its abandonment, later state incentives continued to encourage runaways. Most major post-Second World War forms of support rewarded successful films made in the UK with state aid, thus *Superman II* (Richard Lester, 1980) and *Flash Gordon* (Mike Hodges, 1980) cashed in on measures that had been designed to encourage local production (Hill, 1999: 36 n. 18, 43). In order to keep British studios going while avoiding such misuse, regulations were promulgated in the mid-1990s that meant films entirely made in Britain counted as British, regardless of theme, setting or stars. This meant that *Judge Dredd* (Danny Cannon, 1995) with Sylvester Stallone was 'British', but *The English Patient* (Anthony Minghella, 1996), whose post-production work was mainly done abroad, did not qualify. Until 1998, 92 per cent of a film had to be created in the UK. At the end of that year, the government reduced this requirement to 75 per cent to encourage American companies to make their films in Britain (Woolf, 1998). A 100 per cent tax write-off is now available for film and television production, provided that most crew members are EU citizens and half the equipment used is owned by UK firms. Failure to qualify under these terms may still mean eligibility for a lease-back scheme, whereby a local company buys the film rights then leases them back to the producer (Department of Commerce, 2001: 72).

The long-term strategy of successive governments in Britain since 1979 has been to break up unions within the media in order to become a Euro-Hollywood by default: the skills generated in a regulated domain of the screen would be retained without the 'inefficiency' of the so-called 'X-factor' – labour. In short, 'flexibility' has supplanted wage stability, non-union negotiations are conducted at a highly individual level, and texts are to be oriented towards export. As a consequence, the UK now has a negative balance of screen trade for the first time in its history. Associated deregulation produced a proliferation of networks and the inevitable search for cheap overseas content (Cornford and Robins, 1998: 207–9; Hancock, 1999; Ursell, 2000).

The British Film Commission (BFC) markets UK production expertise and locations by providing overseas producers with a free service articulating talent, sites and subsidies, and generating a national network of urban and regional film commissions. In 1997, seven Hollywood movies accounted for 54 per cent of expenditure on feature-film production in the UK. The British Government opened a British Film Office in Los Angeles to normalise traffic with Hollywood by offering liaison services to the industry and promoting British locations and crews. Its priority was: 'to attract more overseas film-makers' (Hiscock, 1998; British Film Commission, n. d.). The London Film Commission was also formed, to promote the capital to overseas filmmakers, arrange police permits and negotiate with local residents and businesses. Its defining moment was the first *Mission: Impossible* film, when the Commissioner proudly said of that film's Hollywood producers: 'They came up with all these demands and I just went on insisting that, as long as they gave us notice, we could schedule it' (Jury, 1996). Lest we forget. After all, the trailer for the movie could not be differentiated from Macintosh's 'Mission: Impossible. The Web Adventure' television commercial until their respective punchlines: either 'Expect the Impossible May 22 1996' or 'Your mission, should you choose to accept it, begins at http://www.mission.apple.com'. Commodification undertaken in the name of local culture – how dramatically different from J.M. Keynes' address to the nation as he inaugurated the Arts Council in 1945 with these words: 'Let every part of Merry England be merry in its own way. Death to Hollywood' (quoted in Mayer, 1946: 40)!

Nor is this a purely south-east phenomenon. According to David Bruce:

> Location shooting by overseas companies in 1995 ... [was] at a record level and Scotland would be appearing on screen in its own right, or doubling for somewhere else, all over the world. (Someone said that had there been a 1996 Oscar for 'best supporting country' Scotland would have won.)
>
> (Bruce, 1996: 4)

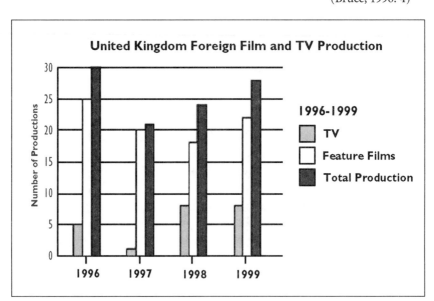

Figure 20 (Source: Department of Commerce, 2001: 49)

Some of this lust for attention becomes quite heinous, as when the Liverpool Film Commission advertises itself internationally as 'a lookalike for ... Nazi Germany, and cities of the Eastern bloc' (Afilm.com, 1998). The looming threat of strikes by actors and writers in Hollywood in 2001 meant that British studios and post-production facilities were heavily booked as offshore union-busting sites. In all, there has been a trebling of offshore US production in Britain during the Labour Government's time in office (since 1997). Utilisation of post-production and special effects as well as studios and film production increased by over 30 per cent in 2000, thanks to US investment (Richard, 2000; Gibbons, 2000; Department of Commerce, 2001: 49; 'Film Production Soars', 2001).

Mexico

The US has been a crucial participant in Mexican filmmaking for sixty years. The '*Época de Oro*' of the 1940s and 1950s was built on Second World War infrastructure provided by the US to encourage anti-Fascist, pro-US propaganda (Robinson, 2000). In the 1960s and 1970s, *auteurs* such as John Huston and Sam Peckinpah filmed in Mexico for the scenery, and Richard Burton, Elizabeth Taylor and their attendant *paparazzi* turned Puerto Vallarta into a tourist destination (Tegel, 2001). Durango was the site for over one-hundred Westerns and genre films in the same decades, because it had non-unionised workers; but runaway productions shifted as other locations vied for studio attention ('Hollywood Heads South', 2000).

The success of *Titanic* saw Mexico again become a key site for offshore production. Restoring Mexico to the Hollywood map gained James Cameron the Order of the Aztec Eagle from a grateful government, which offers Hollywood docile labour, minimal bureaucracy, a weak *peso*, many US-trained technicians, and a new film commission that provides liaison services. It is a screen testimony to NAFTA, which has seen the average number of offshore productions in Mexico per year increase from seven to seventeen as the shipment of film stock and special-effects equipment is facilitated, especially for low-budget productions (LaFranchi, 1999; Riley, 1999). Local workers on *Titanic* in Rosarito, a maquiladora sixty miles south of the border, reported horrific levels of exploitation and mistreatment when the state forced out a leftist union in favour of management stooges. Mexico's new film 'union' even maintains an office in Los Angeles to reassure anxious industry mavens of its cooperativeness and to remain up-to-date on US pay rates – in order to undercut them (Sutter, 1998a and b; Swift, 1999; Bacon, 1999, 2000a and 2000b). US-based Spanish-language television networks frequently produce voice-overs for commercials offshore via high-quality phone lines, to utilise non-union labour (Porter, 2000). *The Mexican* (Gore Verbinski, 2001) was partly shot in Real de Catorce, the first location in San Luis Potosí used by Hollywood. Much was made of the fact that the production invested US$10,000 on new water pipes and to tap a spring in an abandoned mine – doubtless so that its stars Brad Pitt and Julia Roberts would have the best *agua* each morning – and that the local grocer's sales increased 20 per cent during filming. Meanwhile, construction workers were paid US$12 a day to match Pitt and Roberts' US$40 million salaries (Pfister, 2000). In 1999, a union carpenter in Hollywood earned US$275 for eight hours. A union carpenter in Mexico earned US$216 for fifty-five hours. 'Mexico is becoming a "maquiladora" for movies of the week' (Riley, 1999), in the same way that it is a low-cost cross-border site for automobile assembly. It even offers non-*mestizaje* Menonite extras to compensate for the fact that 'the people look different' (Riley, 1999).

Not surprisingly, Rupert Murdoch (1998) cites approvingly the numbers of European workers invisibly employed in the making of *Titanic*: 'this cross-border cultural co-operation is not the result of regulation, but market forces. It's the freedom to move capital, technology and talent around the world that adds value, invigorates ailing markets, creates new ones.' How ironic that the workers submerged at the end of the credits (or not listed at all) should 'owe' their livelihoods to a boat sunk by invisible ice and business *hubris*. And that the ongoing livelihood of people in Popotla has been endangered by *Titanic* – since the production, the local catch of fish has declined by one-third because of Fox's chlorination project (Pfister, 2000). Meanwhile, National Public Radio reported that Rupert's very own Fox company was asking the Mexican Government to offer financial incentives for runaways (broadcast of 24 March 2000), and the privatisation of the film industry during the 1990s had decimated local production (Riley, 1999).

Conclusion

> It may ... be argued that it is less a matter of Hollywood corrupting the world than of the world corrupting Hollywood. The more Hollywood becomes preoccupied by the global market, the more it produces generic blockbusters made to play as well in Pisa as Peoria. Such films are driven by special effects that can be appreciated by people with minimal grasp of English rather than by dialogue and plot.... There is nothing particularly American about boats crashing into icebergs or asteroids that threaten to obliterate human life.
>
> ('Culture Wars', 1998)

As the Ford motor company's credo ('To be a multinational group, it is necessary to be national everywhere') spread to Hollywood cinema in the 1970s, texts were tailored to foreign consumption (Mattelart, 1979: 218). Just as oppositional voices in the US characterise the flight of capital as a reaction to unfair trading that sees state subsidies precluding open competition on the basis of efficiency and effectiveness, there are equivalent culturalist anxieties. The American Film Institute is concerned about any loss of cultural heritage to internationalism. Laments that British costume history crowds out the space for indigenous 'quality' television claim that there was more Australian high-end drama on US television in the 1980s than locally produced material (Quester, 1990: 57). Political economists argue that a newly transnational Hollywood no longer addresses its nominal audience (Wasser, 1995: 433). The *Economist* magazine advises that 'many of America's neo-conservatives (and some liberals) see [US cultural domination] as a perilous solvent acting on the United States itself', because of ethnically specific local marketing and media and a cinema that no longer showcases 'core' Northern European values and subjectivities. The Film and Television Action Committee (FTAC), a Hollywood coalition opposed to runaway production, protests that 'the American motion picture and television industry is a part of our national cultural heritage, not to be surrendered to another nation' – almost a case of cultural-imperialist concerns ('Culture Wars', 1998; Film and Television Action Committee, 1999)! Even the US Government now speaks in these terms as can be seen from the following quotation.

More Than an Economic Issue

Some industry insiders consider the significant increase of American television and film production moving offshore to be more than an economic issue. They point out that, throughout the twentieth century, democratic and free market ideals were the cornerstone of American films successfully produced, exhibited, and distributed throughout the world. In addition to serving as one of our most lucrative exports, the entertainment industry provided the world's population with a clear understanding of a democratic society. America exported stories defining a system of government that could withstand open criticism and still grow stronger (*Mr. Smith Goes to Washington, Gentleman's Agreement*); stories demonstrating that talent and hard work could surpass birth into a social class as determinants of wealth or fame (*Rocky*); stories about one person's ability to make a difference (*Norma Rae*), and to overcome persecution and prejudice (*To Kill a Mockingbird*); stories exploring the impact of American slavery and prejudice and the struggle to transform society into one of equal rights for all (*Roots*). Many of these American films and television programs have helped promote freedom and democratic values, the same values that encouraged throngs of people throughout the world to rise up and challenge repressive governments, contributing to the end of the Cold War, the destruction of the Berlin Wall, and the events in Tiananmen Square before the crackdown. Many foreign incentive programs were initially created to encourage production that reflected the local language and characteristics of that population. However, these incentives, particularly when paired with quotas, often require that the major creators and artists be citizens or hold passports of the country providing the funding, limiting the opportunity for Americans to participate in the production. In addition, these incentive programs bring with them a requirement to consider the creative opinions of the local partner, whether a broadcaster or a governmental entity. Some American storytellers have questioned whether their messages will have to change in order to meet the financial incentives created by foreign interests.

> (Department of Commerce, 2001: 6, adapted from an essay
> by Meryl Marshall, Chairman of the Board and Chief Executive
> Officer of the Academy of Television Arts and Sciences)

Congress considered legislation in 1991 to limit foreign ownership of the culture industries to 50 per cent, a xenophobia that retreated along with the Japanese economy, but returned with Canadian runaways. The House of Representatives contemplated a bill in 2000 to provide subvention to low-budget films, and new production-wage tax investments incentives or research-and-development tax credits are expected to come before the 107th Congress (Steinbock, 1995: 21; Blankstein, 2001; Goldman, 2000; 'Congress to Address', 2001). FTAC and other leftist activist groups doubt the efficacy of additional, local corporate welfare as a counter to foreign corporate welfare, since the media giants that utilised such subsidies are international in their operation. Activists favour rooting out all such policies (Cooper, 2000a) – almost a link to the neo-classical ideal – in the name of saving Hollywood from 'rustbelt' status thanks to NAFTA (Bacon, 1999; see also Talcin, n.d.).

The screen is back where primary and secondary extractive and value-adding industries were in the 1960s, needing to make decisions not just about export, but the site of production. Advances in communications technology permit electronic off-line editing and synchronised special effects and musical scores across the world through digital networks (International Labour Office, 2000b), but also enable special effects, thereby problematising the very need for location shooting:

> Nowadays, once a film is shot, it is transferred to videotape format,
> digitalized, transmitted over the internet, and an editor sitting at any
> location in the world can use powerful computers and sophisticated
> software programs to perform his tasks. The editor can then get feedback
> almost immediately from directors, actors, and others, no matter where

they happen to be, and re-edit the 'film' to produce the final product. Long distances and geographical borders are simply not as important as they once were. This phenomenon holds true for many other specialists involved in film production, particularly those involved in the post-production phase.

(Department of Commerce, 2001: 4)

The coming generation of screen workers are synthespians or vactors – virtual actors. Labour is fetishised as never before when the images of dead stars are reanimated facially onto images of somatotypically similar living actors. The law suggests at this early stage that copyright holders will have greater artistic and financial control over the results than the estates of the deceased, and that residuals will not be payable to the living, since it is not exactly 'their perform-ance' that is on screen (International Labour Office, 2000b).

American late-night talk-show host Jay Leno's mid-1990s promotional spot for NBC's pan-European Super Channel promised 'to ruin your culture just like we ruined our own'. Cultural imperialism discourse is now so commonsensi-cal, given the NICL, that it has become material for stand-up.

In as labour-intensive an industry as the screen, we know that Leno's promised 'ruination' will involve over one million working people in the US alone, most of whom have low weekly earnings. Organised labour has suppos-edly been an endangered species since the 1980s – ready for fossilisation (White, 2001). According to business leeches and their emissaries, high technology has rendered unions anachronistic. In 2000, with Internet workers happy to change employers regularly, and the new technology empowering them to see a future in 'meritocracy' rather than 'seniority', this new flexibility was allegedly a great boon to all – so, down with collective bargaining and job security. Harris Miller, president of the Information Technology Association of America, proudly suggested that 'The philosophy is, Till death us do part – until I get a better offer' (quoted in Dreazen, 2000a: B1). But many people in the high-technology indus-tries saw cracks widen beneath their feet, reading the signs in Federal Reserve Chair Alan Greenspan's blunt remark that European and Japanese domestic investments in the 'New Economy' had not been as profitable as the US, where it is so easy to hire and fire and there is minimal health insurance (Petras, 2000).

Union membership in the US is up as at no point in the past two decades (265,000 new subscriptions in 1999), in part due to mergers that mimic the functions of capital. There are now 16.5 million unionists in the US (Dreazen, 2000b). Managerial high-technology people are organised (but not as unions) into the Association of Internet Professionals (AIP), a quasi-guild that includes executives as well as 'creatives' and freelancers. The Communication Workers of America (CWA) triumphed in 2000 over Verizon, the new Esperantish drag-name of Bell Atlantic, chosen to mark the company's emergence as part of the 'New Economy'. The very week that the drag-name was announced, CWA members compromised the magic by striking – and won their struggle in a fortnight. The CWA is looking to assist workers with Microsoft and Amazon.com as they deal with an employer sleight of hand that categorises them as temporary employees or independant contractors as a means of denying them retirement and health benefits (Dreazen, 2000a). These brutal practices have seen Microsoft face a class-action lawsuit from its 6,000 temps (Greenhouse, 1999a). The Washington Alliance of Technological Workers is fighting for the right of Amazon.com workers to unionise. The company has retaliated by moving part of its customer services to Delhi and areas of the US with lesser conditions than its original Pacific Northwest home, where working life is satirised nightly by veteran ex-employee Mike Daisey, whose one-man comedy show always holds a seat vacant for Amazon emperor Jeff Bezos (McNary, 2001; Gumbel, 2001; Preston, 2001). Meanwhile, the AFL-CIO has a Silicon Valley not-for-profit temp agency that offers healthcare coverage to workers, and has successfully pressed for the highest minimum wage legislation in the country (double what had been paid) (Greenhouse, 1999b).

The major Hollywood screen unions are the American Federation of Television and Radio Artists (AFTRA), the Directors Guild of America (DGA), the International Alliance of Theatrical and Stage Employees (IATSE), the International Brotherhood of Teamsters, the Producers Guild of America (PGA), the Screen Actors Guild (SAG) and the Writers Guild of America (WGA). In December 2000, SAG, AFTRA and DGA obtained Internet jurisdiction for their members. All these groups have important internal divisions between so-called 'talent' and 'craft' and between the heavily unionised (film and broadcast workers) and the non-union workforce (such as less well-paid but increasingly more numerous cable employees). Women and minorities remain proportionally under-represented and stuck in secondary labour markets.

The screen unions' numerical growth and willingness to strike during the dominance of Republican union-busting was a beacon through the 1980s. They stand against virulent anti-union legislation in so-called 'right-to-work' states of the US, the appeal to capital of the NICL, and pressure for Hollywood workers to de-unionise in order to retain employment. (Industry analysts use the terms 'non-union or flexible-union territories outside of Hollywood' to refer to scab labour, noting cost reductions of up to 40 per cent for productions that evade unions.) SAG has 135,000 members across twenty-six national production sites and the WGA represents 11,000 members. This is no labour aristocracy – average 1999 earnings for actors in the film industry were US$26,000, although the hourly wage of US$20.57 compares favourably with private industry's overall average of US$13.44. Adding all directors and producers to actors found a mean 1998 salary of just US$27, 400. Eighty per cent of unionised actors in the US who make television commercials earn less than US$5,000 per year in residuals, for instance, and a struggle over that issue in 2000 saw them link with central labour councils in unprecedented ways that overcame professional-proletarian divisions. Further up the pay scale, the strike over television commercials drew donations to a fund from Britney Spears and 'N Sync (but found Tiger Woods filming Buick advertisements in Canada and Elizabeth Hurley also breaking the picket – although Hurley claimed she was unaware of the protest). The high level of offshore flight to make commercials suggested itself as a long-term union-busting strategy to many observers. SAG puts runaway production 'at the very top of our legislative and organizational agenda' (Gray and Seeber, 1996a: 34; Gray and Seeber, 1996b: 4, 7; Christo-pherson, 1996: 87, 105–6; Lauzen and Dozier, 1999; Wasko, 1998: 179, 184 n. 4, 185–86; Vogel, 1998: 75; Toto, 2000; Screen Actors Guild, 2000; Mallet, 2001; Bureau of Labor Statistics 2000b: 256; Cooper, 2000b; Association of Internet Professionals, 2000; Barrett, 2000; Department of Commerce, 2001: 17; Weller, 1999; Johnson, 2000; SAG quoted in Cooper, 2000a). T-shirts with crossed-out maple leaves and 'how 'bout some work, eh?' proliferate among disemployed workers in the Los Angeles screen sector (Ryan, 1999). FTAC Chair Jack Degovia said of the Canadian government and industry: 'They came after us. They got us. The effects companies in Silicon Valley are next' (quoted in Stroud, 1999). This may be the start of a major backlash against the NICL (Madigan, 1999b; Screen Actors Guild, 2000).

There are also indications of a growing internationalist sentiment among unions, as they start to mirror the globalism of capital: Los Angeles cooks vis-iting Tokyo in a pan-Pacific labour action against a hotel conglomerate, French and German metalworkers organising collaboratively, Mexican farm labourers working with the US Farm Labor Organizing Committee against importation of cut rates at a Mexican tomato paste factory, a Council of Ford Workers rep-resenting Mexican, Canadian and US labour interests – transnational labour networks that are necessary to ensure acceptable levels of worker control and affluence. In May and June 2000, there were six major strikes in India, Argentina, Uruguay and South Africa against globalisation, the WTO and the IMF (Smithsimon, 1999; O'Brien, 2000a; Munck, 2000; Howard, 1995; Brecher *et al.*, 2000: 105; Buckley, 2000; Frundt, 2000; Burbach, 2001: 145; Stevis and Boswell, 1997; O'Brien, 2000b).

Certain film unions in Canada have shown international solidarity ('Soli-darity', 2000; 'Defend', 1999) and the International Federation of Actors seeks parity of pay-scales (Grumiau, 1998), although US unions joined AFMA and MPAA in opposing cultural exemptions to the GATT, letting their brothers and sisters in the European group of the International Federation of Actors down, and they adopted a neutral stance on NAFTA, other than IATSE worrying about a new Mexican studio (Wasko, 1998: 183–87). The North American Agreement on Labor Cooperation was supposed to police infringements of workers' rights under the parent agreement, but has been largely ineffectual – something rued by Hollywood union activists that ultimately led to anti-NAFTA demonstrations, which were the first cross-union political actions in fifty years. But many activists despair of effective union radicalism and point to racial segregation as a problem of closed shops (Bacon, 1999; Everett, 1999; Wuliger, 2000; Malcolm, 2000). In 2000, a Union Network International was formed to bind together world screen workers across as many divisions as possible in order to deal with capital's mobility and government's impotence (International Labour Office, 2000a). The venue for discussion of labour issues at a peak level remains vexed. Other parties to NAFTA would rather work through the ILO, which has stringent contract-labour standards. But embracing internationally agreed and democratic labour standards is, predictably, more than the US Trade Representative can stomach (2001b). The same struggles apply to dealings with the WTO and its links to labour (Hughes and Wilkinson, 1998).

Even as producer Peter Sussman fetishised Canada's workers – 'like any labor pool it keeps cloning and breeding itself' (quoted in Kirkland and Buckley, 2001) – on the last day of the Clinton administration, the US Department of Commerce released a report on offshore filming. Secretary Norman Mineta gravely intoned that 'Runaway film production has affected thousands of workers in industries ranging from computer graphics to construction workers and caterers' (quoted in Gentile, 2001). This is not a labour aristocracy suffering temporary inconvenience.

Clearly, the NICL is uneven. It relies on cultural consanguinity, favourable rates of exchange, supine governments, minimal worker internationalism and high levels of skill equivalency – but it is real. In the next chapter, we investigate the NICL through a specific practice – the co-production – that exemplifies the complexities of transnational culture businesses and their use of public funds supposedly dedicated to preserving and developing national heritage.

Chapter Three
Co-producing Hollywood

We have created a product that by, say, putting the name of Warner Brothers on it is a stamp of credibility. But that could be an Arnon Milchan film, directed by Paul Verhoeven, starring Gérard Depardieu and Anthony Hopkins, and shot in France and Italy, and made with foreign money.

(John Ptak, Creative Artists Agency of Hollywood, quoted in Weinraub, 1993: L24)

As we have noted, screen production is enormously expensive. The average cost of releasing a Hollywood film was US$75.6 million in 1997, a price-tag that Valenti referred to as 'a great shaggy beast prowling the movie forest, a fiscal Godzilla slouching toward our future' (quoted in Fuson, 1998). We now turn to the collaborative efforts of national culture industries to challenge Godzilla. Thus far we have traced the trajectory of Hollywood's ascent within historical patterns of global economic systems that have created hierarchies of labour specialisation across central, intermediate and peripheral geographic trading zones. We argue that this state-sponsored legacy and control over the NICL facilitates Hollywood's continued success rather than the persistent exceptional-birthplace equation: migrant democracies + free markets = textual universalism.

International co-production is a product of, and a response to, the NICL and these increasingly monstrous barriers to entry in the screen industries. The results often surprise: *JFK* (Oliver Stone, 1991) was funded by a Hollywood studio, a French cable network, a German production house and a Dutch financier, while *The Full Monty* (Peter Cattaneo, 1997), supposedly the *ur-*British film of its generation, is of course owned by Fox. Co-production engages the NICL in two ways: via *work*, in that national screen industry and policy provide employment opportunities for residents; and via *culture*, in that it regulates audiovisual modes of expression. At stake are opportunities for media producers and receivers to engage diversely in the world's principal form of collective address. Neo-liberals say human needs are best satisfied when national comparative advantage meets consumer sovereignty (i.e., the US is best at making what we all want to see the most – dinosaurs and sinking ships).

The more than eighty-five countries that have signed co-production treaties register the gross inadequacies of this formula. And claims to comparative advantage fail to account for the accelerated level of equity stakes that non-US media conglomerates have taken in Hollywood in the 1990s – a sign of commercial power rather than national exceptionalism.

In this chapter we consider developments in treaty and equity co-production activities. The former is a strategy by non-US film industries to combat Hollywood's long-time domination of feature-film production and circulation, and the latter an indication of just how multinational Hollywood production became in the 1990s. Treaty co-productions lead us to sites of debate over diversity in cultural expression, a debate constituted through policy initiatives that call for the protection and preservation of national culture. Equity co-productions signal changes in film delivery, where wealthy European pay-TV conglomerates increasingly finance Hollywood motion pictures.

We begin with a sketch of world co-production activity, then focus on government policy and industry transformation in the EU, the most active co-production region, and Hollywood's most valuable intermediate zone in the NICL. We consider the efficacy of funding procedures for treaty co-production and other government provisions in meeting the challenges of combating Hollywood's proliferation, then ask how a NICL-oriented approach might re-conceive policy objectives currently based on supporting individual artists and contouring cultural affiliation via economic trading blocs. As we turn to equity co-production, we trace the rise in economic power of pan-European pay-TV conglomerates, and consider their role in fostering, rather than challenging, the Hollywood NICL. The France-based Canal Plus is our case study, where French money flows through Hollywood independents in Los Angeles and lottery franchises in London. Our conclusion addresses the challenges European media policy faces given the vast imbalances between European investments in Hollywood, and treaty provisions crafted to impede its continued growth.

Although co-production statistics are unevenly reported, according to the industry trade magazine *Screen Digest* (see Table 3.1), at least 35 per cent of all feature films in Europe in 1998 were co-productions. Hong Kong is the most active co-producer in Asia, with 22 per cent co-productions that year, followed by China with 7 per cent (down from 19 per cent in 1996), and just 8 of 249 for Japan. France, Spain and Germany are the co-production centres in Europe, as many smaller film markets seek to tap into these larger European film industries. Although co-productions can fluctuate widely from year to year, between 1994 and 1998, French co-productions averaged 49 per cent of total production, Spanish 28 per cent and German 29 per cent. The UK co-produces with the US and Canada more than with the rest of Europe, and co-production accounted for between 37 and 47 per cent of its total over the 1990s. Argentina co-produced 6 of 23 features in 1998, four of these with Spain and one each with Mexico and Mali (*Screen Digest*, May 1997: 105; *Screen Digest*, June 1999: 129–35; *Screen Digest*, June 2000: 182–83).

Television Business International compiled a database of over 2,000 co-productions from 1978 to 1995 (see Table 3.2). Most co-production activity was concentrated in drama and documentary television, while 21 per cent were feature films. Again, the vast majority of television co-production activity took place in Europe. The most frequent co-producers were the UK and France, which together comprised 32 per cent of all co-productions. The US is a much more active co-producer of television programmes (14 per cent) than feature films (1

Table 3.1 Feature film co-productions

Countries where data available	Feature films produced		Co-Production numbers and percentages			
	1998	1991	1998	%	1991	%
United States	661	583	9	1%	n/a	
Europe:						
France	183	156	81	44%	83	53%
Italy	92	129	13	14%	18	14%
UK	87	46	24	28%	22	48%
Spain	65	64	18	28%	18	28%
Germany	50	72	11	22%	19	26%
Poland	25	25	2	8%	9	36%
Sweden	20	27	7	35%	17	63%
Romania	12	19	8	67%	4	21%
Latin America:						
Mexico	23	32	n/a		1	3%
Argentina	23	21	6	26%	6	29%
Chile	4	n/a	2	50%	n/a	
Asia:						
Japan	249	230	8	3%	n/a	
Hong Kong	92	211	20	22%	4	2%
China	82	100	6	7%	n/a	
Australia	38	27	1	3%	4	15%

Source: Data compiled from *Screen Digest*
(May 1997: 105–6; June 1999: 130–31; June 2000: 182–3).

per cent). This is largely due to the proliferation of cable and satellite channels in the past decade, which has fragmented audiences. International sales are becoming ever-more crucial. Documentary co-productions in the US are found on the public broadcasting networks and on reality-based thematic channels such as the Discovery Channel. Drama co-productions are principally high-pro-file made-for-television movies and mini-series that air on the major broadcast and cable networks, and action-adventure series that air in syndication and on cable networks such as USA and Sci-Fi. Canada (7 per cent) and Australia (4 per cent) are the most frequent co-producers outside Europe and the US, often with each other and the UK. Many of these English-language co-productions seek higher production values to sell into the US market (Brown, 1995: 2.1.1–2.1.3).

The above figures are mostly for 'official' co-productions, meaning that each participant's national government recognised the work as a product of national culture, and accordingly granted subsidies and tax breaks in the name of pro-tecting national culture or fortifying national industry. But the figures also include non-treaty co-productions, where international partners find econ-omic and cultural benefits in sharing resources despite not meeting criteria for treaty provisions. In these cases, partners usually hold equity, which means they take a percentage ownership in a project or production company, rather than just buying territory rights for initial distribution. Equity partners have a voice in the types of projects that are developed, but the level of input into creative decisions can vary considerably. If the audiovisual industries often use the terms co-financing and co-production interchangeably, the conceptual distinc-tion usually hinges on whether there is a shared creative component in the

Table 3.2   Television Business International: Database of TV/Film co-productions, 1978–1995

By country	%	By genre	%
United Kingdom	16	Drama (all)	41
France	16	Documentary	24
USA	14	Feature films	21
Germany	10	Drama: mini-series	8
Canada	7	Drama: TV movies	7
Italy	6	Animation	7
Spain	4	Drama: series	6
Australia	4	Children's (exc. animation)	3
Japan	3	Comedy	1
Switzerland	2		
Belgium	2		

Source: Brown, 1995

planning or execution of a project (Light, 1994: 79–80). It is difficult to plot the market share of co-productions, because nationally gathered statistics tend to claim such texts as their own (*Goldeneye* [Martin Campbell, 1995] is said to be British, for example). As a percentage of total EU box-office admissions, EU co-productions had a slim 5.6 per cent market share in 1996, and less than 3 per cent in 1997. This contrasts with the growing presence of US-European co-productions in which the box-office successes of *The English Patient*, *Tomorrow Never Dies* (Roger Spottiswoode, 1997) and *Evita* (Alan Parker, 1996) contributed to a 4 to 5 per cent share of the European market in 1996, and a 6 per cent share in 1997 (Lange, 1998).

Economies of Scale: Cultures of Cash

> I would argue that ... the entertainment industry of this country is not so much Americanizing the world as planetizing entertainment.
>
> (Michael Eisner in Costa-Gavras *et al.*, 1995: 9)

International co-production in the screen industry asks us to consider the question of culture and national origin. As a practice of international cultural collaboration, co-production destabilises national measures of cultural identity, while also reinscribing them in treaty language that struggles to find national descriptors that will help preserve cultural worth. Co-production marks a site of transformation in cultural scale, from the local and national to the regional and global. As Erik Swyngedouw has argued, 'scale becomes the arena and moment, both discursively and materially, where sociospatial power relations are contested and compromises are negotiated and regulated' (1997: 140). The sections below on treaty and equity co-production address various points of transformation across such scales of cultural production. Because 'theoretical and political priority ... never resides in a particular geographical scale, but rather in the process through which particular scales become (re)constituted' (Swyngedouw, 1997: 141), we seek to identify the institutions, from culture ministries to corporate conglomerates, that reconstitute the scale-politics of audiovisual co-production.

Treaty and equity co-productions intersect scales of political modernity (the super- and supra-national), vertical industrial scales (production, distribution and exhibition), and horizontal industrial scales (conglomeration and synergies). Neo-classical economists tend to sever the relations between these scales when they argue that audiovisual products follow unique economic laws that pertain to 'joint-consumption' goods, those with high initial costs and low reproduction expenses. These laws are said to explain 'the high volume of [audiovisual] trade', because production costs are 'largely unaffected by the number of viewers', with the US enjoying an economic advantage in film and television trade given the wealth of the English-language market, and a competitive advantage born in a vigorous domestic free market where 'sophisticated and demanding' film and television buyers must cater to a 'polyglot' US audience, resulting in the 'new universal art form' that is Hollywood. Yet America's 'melting-pot' viewers are also 'unusually insular and intolerant of foreign programming or films'. Even as these micro-economists recognise Hollywood's cartel control over world film distribution, their methodological focus on segmented economic units and industry behaviour leads to these glaring contradictions in ascribing Hollywood's success (Hoskins *et al.*, 1997: 31–36, 44–45, 51–67).

As we saw in Chapter 2, a consideration of the political economy of scale in the audiovisual industries leads us to an opposite conclusion, that historical patterns of ownership and control over distribution have largely determined the scales of production. Asu Aksoy and Kevin Robins argue that 'the Hollywood studios owe their long-standing position in the film industry to their strategy of controlling the critical hubs in the film business, that is distribution and finance', and history has revealed that the key to securing the latter is control over the former (1992: 15). Thus, the key to the high volume of audiovisual trade is not cheap reproduction costs, but the vast infrastructures of distribution that secure financing for production. And as marketing expenditures increase as a percentage of production costs, they are unaffected by the cost of reproduction altogether (see Chapter 5).

We also find neo-classical economic indicators of cultural difference, such as the stilted concept of 'cultural discount' which quantifies the imperceptibility of imported programming, to codify rigid national cultural indices by predominantly measuring cultural value in vulgar national economic chunks (Hoskins *et al.*, 1997: 32–33, 40). Rather we turn to what John Frow describes as a 'regimes of value' approach, which considers the institutional contexts that produce sets of criteria, the degree to which these criteria are open to a diversity of participants, and the effectivity of policy decisions made on the basis of these criteria (1995: 144–45). This approach, which blends political economic concerns for structure with a cultural approach to institutional analysis, will better account for the complexities of co-production contexts.

Treaty Co-productions and Hollywood

> Critics of protectionism question the reality of ... European culture, asking whether Spain actually has more in common culturally with Sweden than with Argentina ... noting that a great deal of England's cultural content, including its language, is more like that in the United States than in Greece.
>
> (Edwin C. Baker, 2000: 1373)

Co-production treaties are agreements between two or more national governments that create rules for collaborative projects to qualify for subsidies and
fulfil quota restrictions in each country. As clear legacies of nation-state for-
mations under modernity, treaties measure cultural specificity by way of
national borders, a demarcation that necessitates folding intra-national cultural diversity under an exclusionary sign of unity, failing to gauge
supra-national cultural affiliations across borders. So although national audiovisual industries have turned to international co-production to stall Hollywood
dominance by pooling resources to create audiovisual products with greater
international appeal, international co-production treaties also inscribe boundaries that distinguish a product of national cultural expression from one that
is not. Such treaties institutionalise normative and static conceptions of
national culture in the very process of international collaboration.

Multilateral treaties seek to harmonise international treaty provisions along
the axes of economic trading blocs or regional language markets. The Confer-
encia de Autoridades de Ibero-América encompasses the countries of Latin
America, and the Pacific Rim Consortium for Public Broadcasting (PACRIM)
facilitates transpacific co-productions (Taylor, 1995). In the European context,
the Council of Europe (COE) set out to harmonise co-production rules to make
access to funds easier for producers by creating the pan-European co-production fund Eurimages in 1989, and convening a European Convention on
Cinematographic Co-production in 1992 to establish common criteria for eli-
gibility. These pan-European cultural initiatives have their roots in Europe's
desires to form a common market, beginning with the formation of the COE
in 1949, and the European Community (EC), founded by the Treaty of Rome
in 1957. While the EC sought economic unity for Europe, the COE was equally
concerned with the cultural mission of 'safeguarding and realising the ideals
and principles which are their common heritage'. The cinema was considered
an important medium for giving expression to 'European identity'. And when
the 1992 Maastricht Treaty folded the EC into the EU (European Union), culture was addressed in article 128: 'The Community shall contribute to the
flowering of the cultures of the Member States, while respecting their national
and regional diversity and at the same time bringing their common cultural
heritage to the fore.' The audiovisual policies of the COE and the EU have set
out to meet the economic imperatives of unification through cultural imperatives, to foster what has been widely championed as 'unity in diversity'
(Hainsworth, 1994: 13–15, 29).

Eurimages' stated goal is to 'promote the European film industry'. It has support programmes for the distribution and exhibition of film, but allocates most
money to co-productions. Designed to augment existing bilateral treaties
between member countries, Eurimages initially only funded co-productions

with three or more participating countries, but in 1997 began accepting bilateral co-productions. The majority of total financing on projects must come from Eurimages members, no more than 30 per cent can come from outside Europe, and no partner can exceed 80 per cent participation. In 2001 the Fund had twenty-five member States in Western, Central and Eastern Europe. France provides half of the budget and has been a co-producer of half the projects funded so far. The UK did not sign-on until 1993, and left the Fund in 1995. The co-production budget decreased from 22 million Euros in 1994 to 20 million Euros in 1999, and although all funding is repayable from net box-office receipts, no more than 1 million Euros have been returned to the fund in any given year. The Fund has awarded co-production assistance to such internationally known directors as Lars Von Trier (*Europa*, 1991), Chantal Akerman (*Nuit et jour*, 1991), Krzysztof Kieślowski (*Bleu*, 1993), Emir Kusturica (*Underground*, 1996), Theo Angelopoulous (*Eternity and a Day*, 1998) and Peter Greenaway (*Eight and a Half Women*, 2000) (Jäckel, 1999: 187–88; Taylor, 1998: 137; *Screen Digest*, July 1999; Council of Europe, 2000a: 9–18).

Eurimages is run by a board of management with one representative from each member state. To determine that each project meets a sufficient level of 'European Character', the board follows a point system established in the European Convention of Cinematographic Co-production, which weights the value of individual cultural labourers according to their production assignments. Projects must have a director with European resident status. The director, scriptwriter and leading actor all receive three points on a nineteen-point scale. Two points are awarded for supporting actor roles, and one point each for craft labourers such as camera operator, sound recordist, editor and art director. One point each is awarded for studio or shooting location and post-production location. A total of fifteen points is required for a screen text to qualify as 'European' (Council of Europe, 2000a: 6–8; Council of Europe, 1992).

This scheme sets out to regulate the NICL along two axes, of work ('to promote the European film industry') and culture (to foster 'European character'), by way of labour residency. 'Culture' is given expressive weight in the labour of a few above-the-line culture workers (director, writer and leading actors), a point-system that would qualify the 'Hollywood' blockbuster *The Fifth Element* (Luc Besson, 1997) as European. Board members also bring their own cultural preferences and those of their representative nations to bear when making decisions. But the Fund's policies privilege bureaucratic élites making decisions based on authorial measures of cultural value. That is, the locus of cultural expression is found in the transcendental and creative potential of 'artists', a notion which is given weight by the Western concept of subjectivity that valorises the individual as producer of cultural value through personal expression (Crofts, 1998: 310–13). This cultural measure has had a long history in Europe, from the influential French critics/filmmakers of the 1950s affiliated with *Cahiers du cinéma*, who measured the cultural worth of motion pictures via the expressive signature of the director or *auteur*, to the internationally recognised art-house cinema of North Asian and Western and Eastern European film-makers. Often privileging personal vision over plot, formal experimentation over generic forms, and nuanced character studies rather than causal narra-tives, the art-house and *auteur* cinema have secured only limited distribution, and been unable to finance competitive marketing. They have rarely had popu-lar appeal among European audiences (Nowell-Smith, 1998: 6).

In part to address these issues, Eurimages implemented reforms in 2000 that split funding between two schemes. The first awards money on the basis of 'cir-culation potential' and the second on the basis of 'artistic value'. The first scheme assesses the commercial viability of a project based on 'pre-sales and sales estimates, the number and quality of distribution commitments, the per-centage of market financing confirmed and the experience of the producers and the director' (Council of Europe, 2000b: 12). The second scheme funds lower budget 'arthouse films with strong artistic potential, and films that are more innovative in their form and subject' (Council of Europe, 2000a: 9). Decisions regarding the potential for wider audience engagement are not based on con-tent criteria, but are deferred to marketplace gatekeepers, suggesting that if these élite committees are more qualified and intent on gauging artistic poten-tial, they have no criteria for gauging popular appeal outside existing market mechanisms.

This screen policy blatantly omits consideration of cultural labourers who fall between art and markets – or, in industry-speak, those that labour 'below-the-line'. This vast majority of screen workers receive a maximum of two points for their indirect association with production and/or post-production location. Anchored in the physical plant of production infrastructures, these skilled workers are held hostage to the fiscal vicissitudes of national currency markets and runaway production. The typically well-compensated above-the-line tal-ent is guaranteed a free ride to the production location *du jour*. Screen policy needs to address this fundamental imbalance between labour and capital mobility in the NICL. As European screen production is subject to the vicissi-tudes of currency markets (as we saw in the UK in Chapter 2), tax incentives (as with the Dutch scheme below), and least-cost production facilities (as we saw with Prague in Chapter 2), international labour standards should be a fun-damental aspect to pan-European screen policy.

The COE's Eurimages has worked in tandem with the more economically-minded EU, which initiated two principal audiovisual policies to create a unified European market. First, as we have seen, the 'Television Without Fron-tiers' directive sought to form a single European television market by liberalising broadcast trade between members and setting content quotas for European television. The directive has been criticised for fostering the expansion of commercial channels faster than the European revenue base and production infrastructure could fill. This led to an influx of cheap imported programmes from the US unimpeded by the weak language of the quota provision (Collins, 1999: 200–2). Of course the policy provisions are not without frontiers. Border defining parameters have simply shifted from the national to the European (a cultural descriptor as yet to be defined in any policy document or successfully exemplified in programming formulae). After six years of trying to bring together the public television stations of Europe to create a deliberately European drama series, producers continue to encounter difficulties with notions of discrete national dramaturgies and fears of creating the ultimate blandness of *'un Euro-pudding'* that works so hard to include multiple linguistic, audience and production norms that it loses form. The resounding failure of the Joseph Conrad *Nostromo* adaptation is a classic example of this – funded by three European public broadcasters (the BBC, Italy's RAI and Spain's TVE), and with British and Italian stars. These failed attempts at compiling a European television text have given birth to a policy initiative with the best acronym ever: BABEL – Broadcasting Across the Barriers of European Languages (Ungureit, 1991: 16; McDonald, 1999: 2004; Field, 2000: 100; Theiler, 1999: 570). Sony Entertainment published a report in mid-1994 that argued against quotas as inimical to the very producers they were designed to assist, with many commercial television networks failing to observe national production quotas (Stern, 1994a; Zecchinelli, 1994; Stern, 1994b: 1).

Second, the MEDIA programmes have funded the distribution and exhibition of European motion pictures and have strengthened the Community's audiovisual technological capacity. Initiated in 1990, it was designed to 'encourage market liberalization whilst avoiding cultural uniformity', but has been under-funded, and created conflict between France, which supported it, and the UK, which did not. In 1995, MEDIA II allocated 265 million Euros over five years, a 55 per cent increase over MEDIA I, but still just 0.5 per cent of the total European audiovisual sector. MEDIA II had three priorities: 'vocational training, development of projects and businesses, transnational distribution of films and audiovisual programmes'. As of 1998, forty projects were completed or underway, including *Elizabeth* (Shekahar Kapur, 1998) and *The Million Dollar Hotel* (Wim Wenders, 2000). The latter fused the unlikely combination of an art-house director with the ex-Australian resident, Hollywood star and co-producer Mel Gibson, who called the film 'as boring as a dog's ass' (quoted in Mackenzie, 2000). One hundred and ten films labelled 'difficult works' were awarded 2.3 million Euros for distribution outside their country of origin, including *Breaking the Waves* (Lars Von Trier, 1996), *Carne Tremula* (Petro Almodóvar, 1997) and *Secrets and Lies* (Mike Leigh, 1996). The programme includes an automatic system for re-investment which channels loan repayments back into the industry. In two years, the programme helped European films find 75 million filmgoers outside their national territory, and through these admissions, reinvested 19 million Euros back into the programme (Hainsworth, 1994: 19; 'Commission', 1999: 2, 8–10). European co-productions peaked in 1995 at 50.2 per cent and dropped to 36 per cent in 1998 (*Screen Digest*, May 1997: 105; *Screen Digest*, June 1999).

The extremely limited resources of programmes like MEDIA and Eurimages, mean that local film provision has been swimming against a tide of European-financed Hollywood films, as we shall see. And just as the total 1999 domestic take of national productions in the five largest European markets struggled to retain market shares, so cinemas rooted in national cultural contexts have struggled to circulate across borders. Reasons for this include limited pan-European distribution, small marketing budgets, or limited audience appeal. For example, German and Spanish films took no more than 0.3 per cent of the national box office in any of the five core European markets outside their own, and French films comprised no more than 1.5 per cent of box office in any country. British films fare better in other European countries, ranging from 4 to 6 per cent of the box-office in each. Italian films comprised 4 per cent of the Spanish market, but no more than 1.2 per cent elsewhere. However, European co-productions do much better in perspective markets, achieving near parity with domestic market shares in France, Germany and Spain. Accordingly, European co-productions hold a certain promise for regional economic sustainability in Europe, perhaps as the place where trans-border identifications and pan-European popular cultural expressions can take place outside what appears to be an otherwise fragmented European film industry (*Screen Digest*, June 2000: 189).

However successful the MEDIA II programme has been in circulating films throughout the EU, the scale of provision is dwarfed by competing national tax incentives, such as a 1999 Dutch scheme of write-offs and depreciation that injected an estimated US$150 million into the local industry. It is telling that one of the first projects to receive assistance was *Hollywood Sign* (Sönke Wortmann, 2000), starring Rod Steiger and Burt Reynolds. As negotiations for MEDIA II's successor, MEDIA Plus, got underway, the Dutch government lobbied to decrease the budget because of its newfound source of film financing (Edmunds, 2000a and b). From an industry standpoint, the MEDIA programmes, with proportionally small budgets, are largely ineffective at combating a US audiovisual trade deficit that reached US$8 billion in 1998 ('Commission', 1999: 1).

Genre, Scale and Cultural Provision

> If Europeans were producing better movies instead of intellectual bull ... people would flock
> to see them.
>
> (Jean-Paul Vignon, Hollywood Association of French Actors,
> quoted in Agence France Presse, 1998)

On 3 February 1999, a different kind of European blockbuster opened in a record 764 theatres across Europe. *Astérix and Obélix vs. Caesar* (Claude Zidi) was shot in French for US$45 million, and grossed over US$111 million in world-wide box-office receipts, less than US$1 million of which came from the US market (Rawsthorn, 1997; Frater, 2000; D'Alessandro, 2000). A French (51 per cent), German (33 per cent) and Italian (16 per cent) co-production that qualified for Eurimages funding, *Astérix* is based on popular French comic-book characters who defend Gaul against invading Romans in 50 BC (Elley, 1999). The comic book has sold over 280 million copies since 1959, mainly in France and Germany, but also throughout Britain and the Commonwealth. It has had only limited release in the US since 1994 (Riding, 1999). The successful Disneyesque Parc Astérix was built outside Paris in 1989, and an Astérix videogame went into production in 2000 (Cox, 2000).

Do these marauding cartoon figures represent the promise of an economically self-generating pan-European expressive screen culture to combat Hollywood's domination? The French newspaper *Le Monde* seemed to think so when it hailed *Astérix* as 'the image of resistance to American cinematographic imperialism' (quoted in Riding, 1999: 2). With over sixty actors, 1,500 extras and pricey special effects, *Astérix* borrows Hollywood's own tactics, creating spectacular action-adventure formulae for international markets. But does this mean *Astérix* represents a future European cinema that mimics Hollywood at the expense of a diverse alternative cinema of smaller budgets and local expressivity? John Hill has suggested that strategies to build a big-budget pan-European cinema are not economically feasible or culturally desirable. He argues that Hollywood represents a type of film that is not so anchored in any particular quality of American culture that has universal appeal, but is more of a 'global event' based on a long history of control over global distribution, resulting in widespread familiarity with Hollywood forms of cultural address. And pan-European policies based on notions of a common heritage or European identity are suspect given their heritage of 'whiteness, colonialism, Christianity, and High Culture'. Because the countries of Europe, unlike the US, share no popular sensibilities or traditions except those emanating from Hollywood itself, Hill and others have advocated that rather than sponsor big-budget international film making in Europe, 'it is through the mobilization of transnational resources in support of national and regional cinemas rooted in specific cultures that the cause of a genuinely European cinema would be most successfully advanced' (Hill *et al.* 1994: 1–7; Hill, 1994a: 59–68).

Given these important concerns, is it worth considering *Astérix* as an example, though exceptional, of a big-budget film based on non-US pan-European popular cultural currents. As Tom Ryall has noted, 'it is an irony that the critical acceptance of Hollywood cinema was initially achieved through its extensive mapping, by the critics of *Cahiers du cinéma*, in terms of authorial oeuvres rather than in terms of the genres that, along with the stars, have defined its image for the moviegoing public' (1998: 327). If the *auteur* and textual traditions cited above measure diversity by way of knowing artists and readers, genre criticism has located cultural meaning within broader social contexts, where cultural forms and textuality are born at the intersection of culture industries and lived publics. Genre is a cultural referencing system that provides pleasures for filmgoers as well as pre-sold forms for risk-averse industries. Generic cultural forms are products of modernity where technologies of mass production and distribution privilege formal standardisation. These industrial imperatives regulate cultural production within historical contexts that engage with widespread public recognition and consent. In this sense, genres both shape and are shaped by cultural specificities at particular moments and across various geographical scales. Verisimilitude and variation are equally important to genre, as viewers find pleasure in recognising stylistic and thematic protocols, and in experiencing novelty and difference (Neale, 1995). Hollywood genres such as the Western, musical, horror, romantic comedy or action film are said to be variants of the broader genre of the Hollywood narrative film, which is composed of core characteristics such as quickly paced linear story-lines, goal-oriented central protagonists, stars and narrative closure, with bigger-budget films deploying increasing use of special effects and spectacular action sequences (Ryall, 1998: 332). As we have seen, it has also been argued that this particular narrative form, tried and tested in the competitive market and diverse cultures of the US has universal appeal across the world. The narrative and generic codings of *Astérix* serve as an interesting test-case, as the film attained huge popularity in Europe but not the US.

Astérix is a product of three generic coding systems: the Astérix comic strip, the popular Greco-Roman era muscle-man epics of post-war Europe, and the Hollywood narrative film. Similar to the recent slate of Hollywood films based on comic series (*Batman* [Tim Burton, 1989], *Dick Tracy* [Warren Beatty, 1990] and *X-men* [Bryan Singer, 2000]), *Astérix* creates generic verisimilitude through reproducing the *mise-en-scène* of the comic strip with elaborate sets and costuming, and of course through basing the story on the main characters in the strip. In 50 BC, Astérix, Obélix and a group of misfits prevent Caesar from reaching the English Channel through the aid of a magic Druid potion that turns them into superior warriors. *Astérix* is also reminiscent of the *peplum* film, a popular genre set in the Greco-Roman era that sees a peasant strongman standing up for the people against corrupt politicians. The *peplum* emerged in Italy in the silent era, but in the post-war years became popular throughout Europe. As production costs and international audiences grew, most *peplum* films were co-produced with other European countries (Lagny, 1992).

If *Astérix* shares generic Hollywood traits in its fast-pace linear narrative, goal-oriented characters featuring star actors (Christian Clavier, Gérard Depardieu and Roberto Benigni) and spectacular special effects and action sequences, it also shares with Hollywood a populist address. Just as Hollywood adaptations of cartoon strips contain heroes who are typically underdogs or outcasts with special powers to fight various institutional forces of oppression, *Astérix* and the *peplum* invest their everyday heroes with the strength to resist larger forces – a narrative that one reviewer of *Astérix* described as a 'cheeky underdog getting the better of a mightier foe' (Elley, 1999). These are not uncommon themes in Hollywood, and indeed they proliferate in other leading film export industries such as Hindi and Hong Kong cinema. Popular films which register these power relations might rather suggest that universality resides in lived social injustice rather than in Hollywood narrative transparency. This populist address, however, is most often couched in an ideology of liberal humanism where individuals are empowered to stand up to oppression through their own perseverance, rather than through any unified struggle against systemic power and domination.

So what can these generic measures of textual production and circulation tell us about the relationship between budgetary scale and cultural diversity within the contexts of pan-European audiovisual policy? The unprecedented box-office success of *Astérix* throughout Europe is in part the result of tapping into pan-European popular generic cultural registers (the cartoon strip, the *peplum* and Hollywood) that cannot be said to simply mimic Hollywood's global narrative formula. After all, regardless of *Astérix*'s close match to Hollywood narrative characteristics, the film only obtained an extremely limited release in the US, and is proof that big-budget European films can succeed without catering to US popular cultural sensibilities. This is also evidence that while the rise and fall of US art-house theatre circuits correlate closely with the volume of highbrow European imports, populist European films have been locked out of Hollywood controlled US distribution.

Astérix stands as a sharp corrective to claims that the competitive and polyglot US market is an exceptional breeding ground for textual universalism. Quickly paced narratives, stars and action sequences are no less culturally specific and diverse than art-house, auteurist personal visions. Small budgets and high cultural measures should not be bureaucratic litmus tests for European cultural diversity, just as generic pleasures, star affiliation and populist themes should not be left to Hollywood. It is doubtful that the populist cartoon slapstick of *Astérix* is what the framers of EU cultural policy had in mind in bringing Europe's 'common cultural heritage to the fore', yet it is hard to find a more exacting example of such. It is also hard to find a more fitting example of how deregulation and horizontal integration in the European media context have given birth to synergistic commodity forms geared for lives across media (comic books, film, videogames) and beyond (theme parks). This process seeks to colonise the widest possible audience in crowded media environments through attempts to be everywhere all the time. It follows the twin logics of a commercial industry: textual standardisation (genre, sequels, series, serials, remakes, reruns and media synergies) and differentiation (spectacle, stars, post-production and high-concept marketability) – not the desired prescription for diversifying European cinema under a banner of Hollywood defence.

Under the stated goal of promoting a pan-European audiovisual marketplace, the COE and EU media policies set into play two opposing regimes of value, best represented by MEDIA's goal to 'embrace liberalization without uniformity' and Eurimages' splitting appropriations for works with 'circulation potential' from those with 'artistic value'. Though this language reveals a tacit recognition that liberalisation favours the dominant GDP markets and cheap US imports, cultural value is found in supporting 'difficult' experimental works of artists while the more commercial forms of cinema are valued more for their economic potential than cultural worth. This value hierarchy splits cultural decision making in the hands of a few *dirigistes* who judge artistic worth and cultural heritage, and gatekeeping market financiers and distributors who calculate reduced risk and increased efficiency and marketability. In this split regime, there is little space outside market mechanisms for policy that engages the generic pleasures which have roots in collective histories, memory and popular culture and offer the visceral pleasures of spectacle and action, or the populist sentiments that provide spaces for imagining the empowerment of the everyday. And while pan-European film policy largely ignores popular cultural currents, liberalisation has fostered the growth of European transnational media conglomerates that have placed their bets on Hollywood's hold on pan-European cultural expression through investing in Hollywood itself – as the case of equity co-productions will attest.

Equity Co-production

Hollywood movies move; European ones linger; Asian ones sit and contemplate.

('Not the Last', 1995)

In January 1998, Paramount released *Hard Rain* (Mikael Salomon) in 2,100 theatres in the US. The film was a high-concept generic hybrid that mixed the Western conventions of a stagecoach heist with the disaster film and found its inspiration in the 1993 summer floods across the US Midwest. Armoured-car security guard Christian Slater faced-off with outlaw Morgan Freeman and his henchman over bank spoils against the backdrop of a major flood, while the English actress Minnie Driver sported a Midwestern accent and the Danish director Salomon signed-on with water-picture credentials (camera work on *The Abyss* [James Cameron, 1989]). *Hard Rain* was firmly a product of the Los Angeles talent pool. Orchestrated by the independent Mutual Film Company, 500 cast, crew, and other key personnel were assembled by way of informal personal networks that characterise the flexibility of post-studio Hollywood NICL production practices (Bates, 1998; London Economics, 1992).

Mutual finances its projects through an international consortium that gives equity positions to six distribution giants from Europe and Japan. European financing for *Hard Rain* came from Union Générale Cinématographique (UGC), France's largest cinema chain, Britain's public broadcaster, the BBC, the formerly Dutch-owned French film distributor Polygram Film Entertainment, the German television rights distributor Telemunchen (TMG), and the Danish studio Nordisk Film. Financing from Japan came from the Marubeni Corporation, a video and television rights distributor, and the film distributor Toho-Towa Company ('Paramount', 1996; Hindes, 1998a; Herskovitz, 1998). Although US independents have sought financing from abroad for decades, including DeLaurentiis in the 1970s, Cannon in the 1980s and Carolco in the 1990s, Mutual's projects give an equity stake to its partners, rather than just territory rights. In other words, Mutual's partners have a say in the kinds of projects that are developed, and offer creative input as to the types of projects that will attract audiences in their respective regions. For example, Toho-Towa opted not to invest in *Blues Bros. 2000*, but decided to back Mike Nichols' *Primary Colors* (1998). As a Toho executive said, 'If you just see [*Primary Colours*] as a political satire, that's a problem. But we see it as a well-crafted human drama, directed by a great, famous director' (quoted in Hindes, 1998a). Mutual's consortium has produced big-budget films including *12 Monkeys* (Terry Gilliam, 1995), *The Jackal* (Michael Caton-Jones, 1997), *The Relic* (Peter

Hyams, 1997) and *Virus* (John Bruno, 1999), as well as the medium-budget pictures *A Simple Plan* (Sam Raimi, 1998), *Wonder Boys* (Curtis Hanson, 2000) and *Man on the Moon* (Milos Forman, 1999). But certain Mutual projects have been less risky, and perhaps too American, to obtain international money predicated on difference. Mutual developed *Saving Private Ryan* (1998) before Spielberg became interested. Subsequently, Mutual lost all equity in the picture, and co-produced for a fee with Dreamworks and Paramount (Eller, 1998). The same happened with *The Patriot* (Roland Emmerich, 2000), which Mutual co-produced with Sony. Since then, Mutual, TMG, Toho-Towa and the BBC have created a three-year, US$200 million revolving credit to finance films outside the studios (Guider, 2000b).

The Mutual consortium is just one example of how highly capitalised theatrical and television distributors in Hollywood's largest export markets of Europe and Japan have become integral players in facilitating rather than challenging the Hollywood NICL. Twenty integrated media conglomerates in Japan and Europe have pushed foreign financing for big-budget Hollywood films to 70 per cent (Groves and D'Alessandro, 2001). The most recent influx of funding has come from Germany's Neuer Markt, the Frankfurt-based new media and technology stock exchange. In 1999 and 2000, thirteen German film licensing companies raised Euros 1.9 billion on the Neuer Markt, 1.3 billion of which flowed into big-budget Hollywood films (Harding, 2000). With the collapse of the market in 2001, many of these rights-holders (Senator, Kinowelt, Helkon) are considered ripe for takeover by European and Hollywood conglomerates, as the Kirsh Group's February 2001 acquisition of EM.TV exemplified (Dawtrey and Foreman, 2001).

This emerging source of funding from new media (cable, satellite and the Internet) has shifted the foreign financial base for Hollywood from banking to rights-seeking electronic distributors. Revenue streams for Hollywood feature films have increasingly moved away from theatrical and video to free and pay-TV, particularly in Europe. While a heavily marketed theatrical release serves to promote a film's life throughout all windows, and is actually a measure of value for non-theatrical distribution rights, European television buyers have created such a steady source of income for Hollywood in the late 1990s that they are now central to the surge in equity co-productions with Hollywood majors and a new generation of Hollywood independents. As equity co-production arrangements between Hollywood and these growing European media conglomerates dwarf the provisions for treaty co-production, a survey of this growth is warranted to challenge the efficacy of European media policy's embrace of liberalisation as a means of fortifying European cultural expression.

European Conglomerates and Hollywood

> Trade is much more than goods and services. It's an exchange of ideas. Ideas go where armies cannot venture. The result of idea exchange as well as trade is always the collapse of barriers between nations.
>
> (Jack Valenti, 2000)

For over a decade now, viewers in Europe have spent more to consume film via video than in the theatre. In 1998, they paid US$4.8 billion at the box office and US$7.2 billion either buying or renting videos (*Screen Digest*, November 1999: 296). But the key new mode of film spending worldwide has been pay-TV, which increased at a rate of 23 per cent in the last five years of the 1990s (*Screen Digest*, August 1999: 2). For the EU, pay-TV spending as a percentage of total film expenditure grew from 14 per cent in 1988 to 34 per cent in 1996, while video spending dropped from 45 per cent to 35 per cent, and box-office receipts fell from 41 per cent to 31 per cent. Of the five largest European film markets, pay-TV as a percentage of movie spending is considerably larger in France and the UK than in Spain, Italy and Germany. In France, pay-TV as of 1996 accounted for 48 per cent of movie spending, the box office received 27 per cent, and video 25 per cent, while in the UK, pay-TV accounted for 42 per cent, video 39 per cent and box office 19 per cent (*Screen Digest*, January 1997: 11, 13). Of the estimated US$9 billion Western European pay-TV market in 1999, 68 per cent came from France and the UK (*Screen Digest*, November 1999: 301).

This shift in motion-picture revenue from theatre and video to pay-TV has implications for Hollywood distribution and finance. For while Hollywood has maintained cartel-like control over the world theatrical distribution of motion pictures, it lacks dominance in television distribution. The regulatory structures of television in Europe, and indeed in the US, have their origins in national broadcasting as a means of protecting and augmenting the public interest, a policy logic that has restricted foreign ownership and fostered the regulation of state and private national broadcasting monopolies (Negrine and Papathanassopoulos, 1990: 15–24). For example, Hollywood's theatrical distribution cartel UIP, a joint venture that originally included Paramount Pictures, Universal Studios and MGM, lobbied the competition directorate of the EU for five years to extend its anti-trust exemption status, finally winning an extension through 2004 (*Variety*, 20–26 September 1999: 30). When in 1997 the EU ordered UIP's pay-TV division to disband, this had little effect on UIP's member studios, given that most of their contracts with broadcasters in Europe and around the world had been conducted individually outside the cartel – a sign of broadcasting's historical commitment to national cultural expression (*Daily Variety*, 14 March 1997: 50).

Deregulation, commercialisation and the rise of cable and satellite across Europe have transformed this culture of state-regulated national public television, and regulatory patterns have facilitated the growth of national and pan-European audiovisual conglomerates such as Leo Kirsch in Germany, Mediaset and Telipiu in Italy, Canal Plus in France and Murdoch's BSkyB in the UK. These media giants, with ownership positions in free and pay-TV, are becoming increasingly important sources of financing for Hollywood, and have signed valuable multi-year contracts for European television rights to Hollywood films. For example, in 1996 Kirsch signed contracts with Hollywood majors worth over a billion dollars for movie rights extending up to ten years, and paid a reported US$30 million for the German-language rights to *Jurassic Park* (Steven Spielberg, 1993) and *Schindler's List* (Steven Spielberg, 1993) (*Screen Digest*, July 1997). To consider the place of these emerging pan-European broadcasters, and their relationship to Hollywood co-production and financing, we will turn to the case of Canal Plus, Europe's largest pay-TV service.

Canal Plus is owned by Vivendi, which in 2000 acquired Seagram/Universal for US$33 billion, the third time in the past decade that the Hollywood major has been owned by a foreign conglomerate. The Japanese electronics company Matsushita, then the Canadian spirits company Seagram, held ownership, only to give way to the French water/energy utility and real-estate conglomerate. While this is not the first time the French have invested in Hollywood, the coupling makes for strange bedfellows as metaphors of war have been widely used to describe Franco-American cinema relations: beginning with Pathé and Edison's battle over patents in the silent era, through the contested Blum-Byrnes Agreement in 1946 that set the stage for a state-centred French film policy based on quotas and production subsidies, to the exclusion of services from the Uruguay round of the GATT in the name of cultural protection, as we saw in Chapter 1 (Jeancolas, 1998; Miller, 1996). *Variety*'s long-time editor Peter Bart ironically yet bitterly complained that the Vivendi offer represented reverse 'cultural imperialism', reflecting the Los Angeles-based trade weekly's commitment to Hollywood boosterism, and echoing the widespread xenophobic response to Japanese investments in Hollywood in the 1980s. At the same time, French filmmakers protested the merger for fear that the station was 'being dissolved into a global, Americanized behemoth'. Canal Plus President Pierre Lescure said that this would in fact be a successful move into Hollywood, unlike foreign ownership of MGM, which he described as 'run by an exotic and sulphurous Italian' (quoted in Tartaglione, 2000).

Since its launch as a government-backed French terrestrial pay-TV channel in 1984, Canal Plus has grown to become Europe's largest pay-TV service, with 14 million subscribers throughout Belgium (since 1989), Germany (1989),

Spain (1990), French-speaking North Africa (1991), Poland (1995), Italy (1997), the Netherlands (1997) and Scandinavia (1997). The French subscription channel remains the corporate cash crop. It attracts half the total European-wide subscribers and garners 63 per cent of corporate revenues. Movies and sports make up most of the programming schedule, with 400 movies aired per year, 300 of which are first-run (Canal Plus 1999, *Annual Report*).

In the late 1980s, Canal Plus began creating cable/satellite thematic channels, including Planète, Canal Jimmy, Ciné Cinémas, Ciné Classics and Canal Seasons, a nature and outdoor sporting channel. Canal Plus used these channels to launch an analogue satellite service in 1992 and a digital package in 1996. As of 2000 Canal Plus owned stakes in twenty-five themed channels in fourteen countries throughout Europe (Canal Plus 30 per cent, Vivendi 30 per cent and Liberty Media 30 per cent). Canal Satellite organises its thirty-nine basic service into nine themes (Sport, Discovery, Entertainment, Music, Youth, News, General Interest, Services and Games), and offers up to 200 pay-per-view and interactive services, including home banking, home betting, local news, job search, classified ads and e-mail services. Much of Canal Plus' success across Europe stems from its control over interactive decoding and encryption technologies, and Canal Plus has contracts for its digital access system and interactive software technologies with major media service providers in the US (MediaOne), India (Zee TV) and Japan (Pioneer) (Canal Plus 1999, *Annual Report*).

Canal Plus' ascent to pan-European preeminence in television and Internet delivery is not simply the outcome of the liberalisation and privatisation of state monopoly broadcasting across Europe. It is beholden to the French system of broadcast regulation that some have referred to as 'land-owning capitalism'. Here, the government awards licences on the basis of the political affiliations and discretion of government bureaucrats rather than through a venture-capitalist approach based on competitive bidding. For example, state monopoly control of broadcasting in France ended when François Mitterand and his Socialist government awarded the first commercial licence to Canal Plus in 1984. Mitterand then appointed his Chief of Staff André Rousselet as Chairman and Managing Director. Canal Plus was also granted a ten-year license extension in 1994 without a new call for competitive bids (Regourd, 1999: 35–36). Yet both the venture-capitalist and land-owning capitalist routes to deregulation and privatisation in Europe have created proprietary concentration through conglomeration. In the late 1990s, Canal Plus lost its *de facto* monopoly in pay-TV in France when a competing bouquet of satellite channels (TPS) was launched through an alliance of French public and private television channels (France Television TF 1), a public utility company, France

Telecom, and the German media giant Bertelsmann (Palmer, 1999: 153–54).

But this integral relationship between the state and capital in France has benefitted European film production as well as Canal Plus' pan-European expansion. Under a special agreement with the Conseil Supérieur de L'Audio-visuel, Canal Plus was granted the right to show recent films one year after their theatrical release, and one to two years before other channels had access to air them. In exchange, Canal Plus must dedicate 60 per cent of film rights spending on European works, 45 per cent of which must be French-language films. And although Canal Plus agreed not to use advertising in exchange for this special access to recent films, in 1985 it was allotted a portion of the prime-time schedule for unscrambled advertising sponsored programming, a combination which provided a valuable promotional widow for Canal Plus to pitch its scrambled pay-service programming (Jäckel, 1999: 180; Palmer, 1999: 149).

Canal Plus is involved in financing 80 per cent of all current French films, and has manoeuvred to establish a major European movie studio and theatrical distribution network. Le Studio Canal Plus produces medium-budget French-language films with co-production partners or independant producers, and Canal Plus funds leading internationally known filmmakers such as Italy's Nanni Moretti, Spain's Alejandro Amenabar and Germany's Tom Tykwer. Le Studio Canal also co-produces and funds US independant films such as *Ghost Dog: The Way of the Samurai* (Jim Jarmusch, 1999) and *The Straight Story* (David Lynch, 1999), and has the European rights to films from Francis Ford Coppola's Zoetrope studio through 2011 (Williams, 1999).

Canal Plus' state-facilitated ascent to the largest pan-European pay-TV network, a majority financier of French-language cinema, and a production and distribution infrastructure has provided a foundation of support for European cinema. But Canal Plus has been Hollywood's most substantial source of European funding, including two phases of equity co-production in the 1990s. The first in the early 1990s consisted of three co-production and co-financing agreements with Hollywood independents and majors, and a later phase involved a series of deals with newborn independents. In May 1990, Canal Plus paid US$30 million for a 5 per cent stake in Carolco Pictures, producer of the successful Rambo franchise and one of a number of independent Hollywood film companies in the late 1980s and early 1990s that packaged high-budget, star-driven special effects films financed by pre-sales of foreign distribution rights to European and Japanese buyers. Carolco was widely credited with this shift to ultra-high-budget films and the escalation of star fees such as the reported US$12 million paid to Michael Douglas for his role in *Basic Instinct* (Paul Verhoeven, 1992). Despite the success of *Basic Instinct* and *Terminator II: Judgment Day* (James Cameron, 1991), Carolco lost US$353 million in 1991 and 1992. In

October 1993, Canal Plus raised its share in Carolco to 17 per cent and invested in individual films in need of further funds. With bank creditors pressing for forced bankruptcy in 1994, Carolco hastily pushed forward its final picture, the pirate film *Cutthroat Island* (Renny Harlin, 1995), which lost its star Michael Douglas and became the largest flop in film history to date, losing over US$100 million. While the Carolco executives received multi-million dollar minimum fees to bring the film to market, and thus had nothing to lose given that everyone understood this was Carolco's final film, foreign backers like Canal Plus lost a great deal of money banking on big-budget Hollywood movies – and this despite the figures that Carolco's twenty-three films averaged US$115 million at the box office. Carolco was sold in 1995 to 20th Century Fox for US$50 million, and Canal Plus purchased the Carolco library in 1996 (Eller, 2000b; Balio, 1998a; Willman and Citron, 1992; Sterngold, 1996; Parkes, 1995; 'Canal', 1999).

Canal Plus entered an equity partnership in January 1991 with Warner Bros. and Germany's pay-TV group Scriba & Deyhle to produce twenty films through independent producer Arnon Milchan's Regency International Pictures. Warner Bros. offered US$400 million to cover marketing costs in exchange for domestic rights and US$600 million came from Canal Plus and Scriba, which received theatrical and pay-TV rights in their territories and access to Warners' theatrical European distribution network. Because all rights return to the joint venture after initial distribution, the partners have equity stake in the library of films produced by Milchan, an important asset for the European television distributors. And on the eve of the EU's 'Television Without Frontiers', Warner Bros. benefitted from contracts with leading European pay-TV companies. As then Warner Studios president Terry Semel stated, 'if there are new regulations in 1992, we'll have strong partners on our side' (quoted in Nussbaum, 1991).

The Carolco-Canal Plus co-production deal represented an aspect of Hollywood globalisation that meant a turn to star-driven, high-budget pictures, action-centred and special effects spectacles that constituted a widely marketable global event. Canal Plus' affiliation with Milchan presents a different trajectory, a global Hollywood that finds new European media giants investing less in global event projects than in a select group of producers who have demonstrated skills in attracting creative talent and packaging deals. Milchan came to Hollywood from Israel, where he amassed a fortune in chemical and plastics manufacturing companies, and gained notoriety for becoming Israel's largest arms dealer. By the early 1990s, he had built a reputation for producing the films of such prestigious directors as Martin Scorsese (*King of Comedy*, 1983) and Sergio Leone (*Once Upon a Time in America*, 1984), as well as the successful medium-budget films *War of the Roses* (Danny DeVito, 1989) and *Pretty Woman* (Garry Marshall, 1990). Canal Plus' involvement in the consortium was short lived, for although in two years the group had box-office successes such as *JFK* and *Under Siege* (Andrew Davis, 1992), a string of flops such as *Memoirs of an Invisible Man* (John Carpenter, 1992), *The Power of One* (John G. Avildsen, 1992) and *Mambo Kings* (Arne Glimcher, 1992) led to heavy losses (Bardach, 2000; Bates, 1993). Canal Plus' third co-production arrangement was with Universal, and gave each side the freedom to choose which projects to participate in. The first co-production was Robert De Niro's directorial debut, *A Bronx Tale* (1993), but the arrangement was short-lived, perhaps because of the heavy commitments Canal Plus made with Carolco and Regency ('Principal', 1992; West, 1991).

Canal Plus' early foray into the Hollywood equity business showed the risks and costs of betting millions on a handful of aesthetic products that carry little guarantee of engaging and pleasing audiences, even those with high-concepts, wide distribution and large marketing budgets, or medium budgets and star producers. Many in the industry faulted Canal Plus' early 1990s deals for giving too much for too little by agreeing to limited French theatrical and pay-TV rights for its 17 per cent investment over five years. But by the mid-1990s, Canal Plus expanded its pay-TV operations across Europe, and had distribution interests far beyond the French rights it had held in the early 1990s.

Meanwhile, a new generation of Hollywood independants emerged that had risk-sharing ties to the studios and thus more stable and leveraged projects than Carolco, plus additional sources of capital through the emerging European and Japanese media conglomerates. In 1998, Canal Plus signed equity agreements with three such independents: Bel Air Entertainment (Warner Bros.), Mandalay (Paramount) and Spyglass (Disney). Each was run by prominent producers or ex-studio heads: Steven Reuther (New Regency), Peter Guber (Sony) and Gary Barber and Robert Birnbaum (20th Century Fox). The deals run from a fifty-fifty partnership between Canal Plus and Warner Bros. for Bel Air pictures, including *Message in a Bottle* (Luis Mandoki, 1999) and Keanu Reeves' *The Replacements* (Howard Deutch, 2000), a twelve-picture deal with Mandalay that included *Sleepy Hollow* (Tim Burton, 1999) and Jean-Jacques Annaud's Stalingrad war film *Enemy at the Gates* (2001), and a fifteen-picture deal with Spyglass that has produced *The Sixth Sense* (M. Night Shyamalan, 1999) and Jackie Chan's *Shanghai Noon* (Tom Dey, 2000). In July 2000, Canal Plus signed a US$900 million deal with Michael Ovitz' new production company for fifteen films over three years, continuing a trend of foreign money financing known producers through newly emerging independant companies (Carver, 1999; Hindes, 1998b; Eller, 2000a; James, 2000).

The emergence of these and other Hollywood independents like Mutual (see above), Franchise, Hyde Park, LakeShore and Beacon Pictures is in part due to cost-cutting measures by the studios at the behest of conglomerate heads. For example, Sumner Redstone of Viacom reduced Paramount's motion picture

budget from US$600 million to US$300 million in two years, and Disney's Eisner cut US$200 million from feature-film budgets. The studios also began
co-producing large budget films such as Paramount and Buenavista's *Runaway
Bride* (Garry Marshall, 1999) and Warner Bros. and Paramount's *Payback*
(Brian Helgeland, 1999) and *Southpark: Bigger, Longer and Uncut* (Trey Parker,
1999) (Eller, 2000b; Carver, 1999b; 'Canal', 1999; Williams, 1999; Brodesser and
Lyons, 2000).

While Canal Plus signed equity co-production packs with LA-based independants, they also emerged as a Gaelic hub for English-language films
intended for the international market. In 1998, Canal Plus entered a fifty-fifty
partnership with Universal Pictures to co-finance Working Title, the London-
based producer of *Four Weddings and a Funeral* (Mike Newell, 1994), *Bean*
(Mel Smith, 1997), *Elizabeth* (Shekhar Kapur, 1998) and *Notting Hill* (Roger
Michell, 1999). The five-year contract gave Canal Plus continental television
rights to all Working Title films for an investment of between US$100 and 150
million annually. The first film under the deal was the Coen brothers' *O
Brother, Where Art Thou?* (2000), a story of escaped convicts in rural Missis-
sippi, and a clear indication that this French-British film pact set its sights on
the US market (Carver, 1998; Cox, 1998; Rawsthorn, 1999; Dawtrey, 1999; Fry,
1998; Williams, 1999).

More controversial has been Canal Plus' involvement with publicly funded
projects. In May 1997, the Arts Council of Britain changed its policy of funding film on a per-project basis to allocating lottery money to three production
consortia in an effort to build more stable production and distribution groups,
à la mini-Hollywood studios. The Arts Council awarded three franchises access
to US$153 million in lottery funds to produce British films over six years, with
the idea that these groups would be self-sustaining studios after that time.
Canal Plus financed the Pathé Pictures franchise, which was awarded access to
US$55 million for thirty-five films over the six years. Pathé, the long-established
French production and exhibition company, has had a presence in British film
production through its London-based Pathé Productions. Pathé and Canal Plus
have had an ongoing relationship with Canal Plus through its 20 per cent ownership of Canal Satellite and a joint venture signed in May 1997 that established
a pan-European film distribution network throughout France, the UK, Germany and Spain (Dawtrey, 1998; Williams, 1997).

The British press widely criticised the Arts Council for subsidising a US$1.4
billion media conglomerate run by a 'family of French multimillionaires' and a
company that had a 17 per cent stake in Murdoch's profitable BSkyB (Purnell,
1999; Walker, 1999; Norman, 2000). As of January 2001, only one of the fourteen films financed by the three lottery franchises had made money – Pathé's
star-driven *An Ideal Husband* (Oliver Parker I, 1999) (Stringer, 2001). This pol-

icy shift toward franchise sponsorship set off industry squabbles that pitted the 'Dinosaurs' who 'have labored for decades to create a genuinely indigenous industry' and a younger generation admonished as 'Trashtafarians', whose sensibilities are said to be 'hip, cool, youthful and commercial' (Walker, 2000). These invectives belie a racist policing of Britishness and the failure to build a successful Eurowood. The British Film Council (BFC) emerged in this context in May 2000. The BFC consolidated British film provision under a new mission to produce popular films for audiences home and away. The council's budget allocations emphasise script development (£5 million) new talent training (£5 million), and bigger-budget international films (£10 million). As the BFC claims to produce a range of films from *Orlando* (Sally Potter, 1992) to *Gladiator* (Ridley Scott, 2000), and commits 20 per cent of its budget to European co-productions, yet has no distribution or exhibition strategy, critics worry whether commercial *or* creative successes will emerge (James, 2001). These equity co-productions suggest new powerful pan-European pay-TV giants are gaining leverage, but that they remain partners rather than adversaries to Hollywood's continued proliferation.

Conclusion

> The countries of Europe, encumbered as they are with all sorts of historic, linguistic and sociological barriers, were more or less impervious to each other, while the European market – unified – existed only for the Americans.
>
> (Jack Lang, quoted in Collins, 1999: 200–1)

Co-production marks an important axis of sociospatial transformation in the audiovisual industries, a space where border-erasing free-trade economics meet border-defining cultural initiatives under the unstable sign of the nation. Co-production works through the NICL to facilitate a transatlantic investment highway traversed westbound by European pay-TV giants and eastbound by Hollywood producers enticed by tax incentives and cheap labour. This dwarfed European treaty, subsidy and quota provisions meant to create alternatives to Hollywood's domination. The central tenets of this defence called for economic liberalisation to create a unified pan-European audiovisual space, fortified culturally by the embrace of a common European heritage, weak quota provisions and subsidies for the artistic expression of a few above-the-line European residents. We find this formula to be inadequate to challenging the regulatory supremacy of the NICL for the following reasons.

First, the tax incentives, currency imbalances and labour bargains that lure Hollywood to European soil provide financial incentives that far exceed treaty, subsidy and quota provisions in support of European audiovisual expression.

Our survey of ties between pan-European television distributors and Hollywood reveals that European audiovisual liberalisation largely fuels rather than challenges core aspects of the Hollywood NICL. While the expansion of cable/satellite technologies has shifted distribution leverage away from Hollywood-controlled theatrical distribution to European-owned pay-TV conglomerates, these rights-buyers have stepped-up their equity positions in Hollywood, fuelling a NICL that places product development in the hands of a few Los Angeles-based former studio heads and star producers. Why shouldn't we entrust these exceptional gatekeepers to look after the diversity of our needs? One marketing executive for 20th Century Fox International admitted that Europe is indeed not a homogeneous market, because Germans favour comedies while the Latin countries prefer romantic stories (Field, 2000: 100). While studios operate according to these vulgar pronouncements of cultural difference, below-the-line labourers continue to struggle under capital regimes of wage, currency and tax fluctuations. A first-step approach to any supranational cultural policy would be to open up cultural policy fora to the collective bodies that represent the majority of culture industry workers. This would not only elevate the crucial issues of equitable working conditions, job stability and fair compensation, but bring a diversity of cultural affiliations to the exclusionary and taste-rigid bureaucratic boards which have dominated cultural policy decision-making. Empowering a wider area of cultural workers to make policy decisions would also better tap into the popular cultural references that circulate through generic registers, stars and narratives of populist address.

Second, screen policy should not square cultural affiliation via the nation or the regional borders of economic trading blocs. The global patterns and histories of empire, trade and migration detailed in Chapter 1 speak to the implausibility and undesirability of confining co-production relations and quotas to the territorial boundaries of EU members. In his assessment of European co-production, Murdock comments that 'the simple dichotomy between market solutions and subsidies' does not account for the many linguistic and historical alliances with territories outside Europe. He calls for policies that 'consider more fluid relationships' (Murdock, 1996: 114). Existing quota provisions have revealed equally inflexible results. 'Television Without Frontiers' kept TNT and the Cartoon Channel off cable as well as channels in Arabic and Turkish (Sergeant, 1999: 109). Multicultural citizenship groups, rather than residency-based point systems, should be considered in determining screen subsidy. Pan-European co-production policy could augment rather than forbid arrangements between France and North Africa, or between Spain/Portugal and Latin America. More initiatives like the ones by BFC and Scottish Screen that supported Love Love Love (*Pyar Ishq aur Mohabbat*, Rajiv Rai, 2000), the first Hindi-language film to be shot entirely in the UK, point in this direction ('Full', 2001).

The case study of Canal Plus demonstrates the relevancy of the state as a critical sponsor of local cinema and a facilitator of transnational pay-TV expansions. It is our third point that this integral role of the state not get lost in the frenzied and irresponsible *laissez-faire* discourse of liberalisation's unbounded promise. As cable and satellite replace analogue broadcasting infrastructures, there is an imperative to re-inflect notions of the public airwaves into our digital futures. These delivery conduits are the critical hubs that will channel our collective screen experience, and decisions regarding access to these public passageways must open up to a diversity of participants. As pan-European cable systems fall under the control of conglomerates like Canal Plus and United Global Communications, each with vertical ties to content owners, the state will be an important arbiter to ensure access for local and national content producers (Fabrikant, 2001). The MEDIA programmes have had success in distributing national films outside their country of origin, but to a limited extent, given restricted distribution and financing. Television distributors – whether through cable, satellite, broadcast or the Internet – should continue to be considered custodians of the public air(cable)waves, and thus the key sources for ensuring that cultural productions receive distribution and finance across the scales of the local, national and regional.

Throughout the co-production side to the NICL, the law is a complex player, via binding treaties, quotas, subventions, and patterns and systems of ownership. In Chapter 4, we interrogate perhaps the most important legal foundation to the NICL – copyright. Hollywood's harmonisation of diverse national regimes of rights via diplomatic and economic muscle is best understood within the contexts of the history of intellectual property protection and the production and distribution technologies it engenders. Along the way, we find that statutory issues of piracy and other forms of innappropriate appropriation have a lot to tell us about the labours of creators and users, and the narrowing divide between the two in the age of digital reproduction.

Chapter Four
Hollywood's Global Rights

'The law, my boy, puts us in everything.' (Al Pacino in *The Devil's Advocate*)

Cut to a Chinese wholesale market at the turn of the twenty-first century – say the US$3 billion-per-year Yiwu market, which attracts 200,000 visitors a day. Yiwu's 33,000 stalls and shops offer shrink-wrapped tributes to brand fetishism: Rolex watches, Gillette razor blades, Sony TVs, American Standard toilets, Beanie Babies, Viagra pills (even Viagra soup), Suzuki motorcycles, Evian bottled water, Duracell batteries, Timberland boots, Levi jeans, Marlboro cigarettes and Microsoft Windows. As regular shoppers know – indeed this is the reason why many of them come in the first place – an estimated 80 per cent of goods sold at Yiwu are fakes. Testifying to the international desire for forgeries, Yiwu distributors have opened branches in Brazil and South Africa, with further plans to expand in Nigeria, Pakistan and Thailand. The flag of Hollywood flies prominently aboard this pirate ship: *Titanic*, pirated a few days after its US release and nine months before its projected video release in China, is widely available on the streets for the equivalent of between US$2–4; *Gladiator* and *Shanghai Noon* for US$2. *Mission Impossible 2*, released in the US on 24 May 2000, was in China by 27 May, with quick subtitling courtesy of stolen scripts that might travel ancient heroin smuggling routes; fully 90 per cent of the video disks are illegal copies. In Beijing, pirate Hollywood is just around the corner from the American Embassy at Xiushui Street (better known to foreign tourists as Silk Alley), a huge counterfeit apparel and electronics market. Though one can easily find the pirated version of a Communist Party-sponsored anti-corruption film called *Life and Death Choice*, the script for counterfeit Hollywood is not so full of dramatic irony. Flaunting conventional neo-liberal wisdom linking the protection of intellectual property to strong economies, piracy sells. The whole world is buying (Behar, 2000; Long, 1998; Smith, 2000: 13).

Struggling to keep up with ever-developing technologies, negotiating national legislative difference, encouraging the development of local consumer education groups on the civic evils of copyright infringement, coordinating among various customs and excise departments in piracy hotspots such as

Indonesia, Singapore, Hong Kong, Macao, the Middle East and Eastern Europe, the ever proprietary Motion Picture Association (MPA) has mounted an aggressive campaign to combat its hefty share of an estimated US$3.5 billion in earnings that Hollywood lost to piracy in 2000. Of course, it is especially difficult to measure the international trade in audiovisual products because of its involvement with both goods (films that are materialised by certain forms of carriage such as a film print, videotape or DVD) and services (for example, rights to licensing or broadcast). Since the passage of audio, video and digital signals is rarely impeded by borders and customs checkpoints, forecasting lost revenues is an enterprise prone to fancy; nevertheless, numerical estimates play an important rhetorical role in securing enforcement budgets (see Acheson and Maule, 1989).

Locating new legal imperatives within the history and philosophy of copyright law, and outlining tensions between audience and corporate ownership rights, this chapter shows how Hollywood uses intellectual property (IP) law to facilitate its international profile. The advent of new delivery and screen duplication technologies presents IP challenges and risks at the same time that Hollywood strives to extend its market into new digital distributional arenas like the Internet. IP protection is especially important now, because the copyright industries are the fastest growing sectors of the US economy. These industries – which include film, sound recording, software and books – gather foreign sales and exports of over US$60 billion per year, exceeding automobile export and even aerospace, which had held the number one ranking for many years (Stern, 1998). The export of US copyright material is now 'America's grandest trade prize', what Valenti calls the 'crown jewel in America's trade crown' ('Protecting America's Grandest', 1998; 'MPAA Identifies', 2000).

Hollywood's global rights intersect with the NICL in complicated ways. The US and the EU recently derailed a World IP Conference by disagreeing over performers' movie royalties in audiovisual trade. The thorny issue was the transfer of performers' rights (which state that a performer has the right to 'object to any distortion, mutilation or other modification of his performances that would be prejudicial to his reputation') from the protection-rich and creative labour-friendly terrain of European copyright law to the litigation-heavy and producer-friendly landscape of the US (McClintock, 2000). Clearly, the US negotiation team was frustrated in its desire to extend domestic copyright provisions to other places, in order to bring the NICL to the lowest common denominator of legal protection. Differences in the territorial protection of performers' rights can result in such intricate stories of international litigation as the *Asphalt Jungle* colourisation controversy described in Chapter 2.

On the other hand, the NICL's tendency to aggregate investment data at the level of *production* runs the risk of inadequately theorising the slippery distributional terrain that matters most in an industry with almost *no* production costs: media piracy. Remember that IP issues in film history have always been tied to distribution, and as the patent wars that enveloped the early American film industry indicate, securing monopoly rights over new technologies were designed to pave the way for distributional hegemony. Distribution is key when it comes to modern media piracy, which circumvents national citizenship protections, labour rights and state subvention – precisely those national arenas where differences are needed in order to be exploited by the NICL – and whose *negligible* production costs run on the model of small-scale manufacture. Of course, counterfeiting has different economies of scale. The worldwide trade in counterfeit apparel shadows the NICL through the massive efforts of low-paid workers in huge underground Chinese factories. But entry into the pirate video disk market simply needs a certain degree of entrepreneurial and computer savvy, a few duplication machines, a small air-conditioned space in which to do business, and a table on which to fill out the mail orders that distribute your product to vendors and consumers. Media piracy, more fully and flexibly than any other form of manufacture, takes full advantage of its commodity's infinite reproducibility. It has never been as easy or as cheap – thanks to the digital – to book passage on the pirate ship. There is a reason why most copyright enforcement materialises at the retail level: it is much harder to capture pirates at the moment of production because manufacture is so dispersed, operations so small, and distribution pipelines so informal. At the same time, there are international circuits involved in illegal production of media goods, and piracy is as embedded in localities as are traditional forms of cultural labour: recording the film in a US theatre, sending the tapes to China for dubbing and photo enhancement, stamping the disks in Taiwan, and retailing them in Latin America. National differences in the protection of IP law most often dictate where pirate production occurs, and pirate distribution is concentrated in sectors which are last in line for hard-top theatrical exhibition (which is why Hollywood's major anti-piracy tactic is worldwide simultaneous film release).

As a theory, the NICL might strain to explain the black-market and grey-ware allure of those alternative, informal and illegal distributional networks through which Hollywood flows into its most problematic – and increasingly most important – markets. Whether or not these distributional agendas are shadow-setters for the way Hollywood goes about its legitimate business is a complexity that this chapter only begins to engage (perhaps, like Hollywood itself, you must await a sequel). On the other hand, in addition to explaining the exploitation of uneven development in the terrain of international labour that facilitates the spooling of Hollywood around the world, the NICL has a lot to tell us about the nationally specific system of IP provisions exploited by the copyright-owners of media product. Finally, copyright fundamentally addresses an issue at the heart of the NICL: what do culture and ownership have to do with one another?

This issue of cultural ownership motivates a number of non-Western nations to undermine international legislative homogeneity (especially the notion of equal national treatment). They correctly diagnose Western initiatives on copyright internationalisation as a thinly veiled recapitulation of traditional dependency, and seek to prevent foreign monopolisation of cultural ownership or the flight of foreign exchange. While some economists understand that stronger IP protection in less developed countries rises as foreign direct investment from the more developed nations increases (Lai, 1998; Seyoum, 1996), Iran, for example, has new laws that protect *domestic* software producers, not US software. Indeed, the disavowal of copyright can be captured as a camera obscura snapshot of Hollywood's self-perception as top of the NICL food chain: after his film was pulled from a 1998 New York Film Festival for its alleged resemblance to JD Salinger's *Franny and Zooey*, Iranian director Dariush Mehruji said, 'in our country we don't have copyrights, we feel free to read and do whatever we like' (quoted in 'IP Watch', 1999).

Since film is a collaborative art, securing it as a form of IP (based on notions of *singular* authorship) seems counter-intuitive. But Hollywood is also a commercial, corporate and industrial enterprise, and these are constituencies that have always had the most to gain from copyright controls. The old Motion Picture Association mantra about Hollywood is that its international success is predicated on talent and markets. Hence the ubiquity of copyright, which establishes the parameters of creativity as well as the terrain of distribution. Copyright and the control of IP have underwritten Hollywood's internationalism because they stabilise the market and render it predictable, a crucial factor given the tremendous costs of feature film production.

The economies of scale involved in the film industry, where duplication costs are negligible in comparison to huge initial production outlays, confer commodity status on media forms of knowledge. Mass media products have the characteristics of a *public* good in that their value does not diminish as the number of users rise. Media commodities are also intangible goods; while they are embodied in material products such as videotape, new delivery technologies such as satellite and the Internet engage with media as *immaterial* forms of service, as signal (Duarte and Cavusgil, 1996). As the complexities of distinctions between content and carriage suggest, media owners have trouble anticipating the usages of immaterial goods except retroactively, that is, in terms of the contexts of their use (Frow, 1997: 188). This is precisely why control of delivery is of utmost importance to the MPA, which brokers media product through IP protection and permits access to cultural knowledges only via an elaborate system of generating scarcity by *renting* consumers access. As Frow notes, media ownership continually struggles with the dual 'problems of defining and enforcing exclusive property rights in something intangible' and 'attaching exchange value to an entity which has almost limitless use-value'. There are, of course, infrastructures that provide for the scarcity of media via copyright, the control of distribution channels, obsolescence, state subsidy and the 'institution of authorship, which remains the single most important channel for the creation of textual desire and the minimization of market scarcity' (Frow, 1997: 188–90). Ultimately, though, emergent media technologies remind us of the fundamental contradictions at the heart of copyright law itself. Copyright law is predicated on securing and individuating the fruits of artistic labour to encourage and diversify creative innovation. However, copyright's historical implementation only highlights the tendency towards monopoly control and privatisation of IP by a shrinking number of multinational media conglomerates. In addition, IP's transformation of knowledge into property traditionally prioritises ownership over use, creators over audiences, and production practices over reception.

The internationalisation of film copyright has a turbulent history. In some countries the screenplay writer was most closely associated with copyright protection, with films considered adaptations of the literary work embodied in screenplays. The 1908 Berlin revision to the Berne Convention for the Protection of Literary and Artistic Works folded cinema under the rubric of adaptation and did not recognise film as an independent category until its 1948 revision in Brussels. In its 1967 Stockholm revision, the Convention inserted a new article which attempted to resolve the issue of film authorship by shifting protection away from the author towards the work, thus blunting the issue of individual 'moral rights' in favour of those who own the work, that is, towards corporate ownership. After noting that 'ownership of copyright in a cinematographic work shall be a matter for legislation in the country where protection is claimed', Section 2b of the Berne Convention's new Article 14bis states:

> However, in the countries of the Union, which, by legislation include
> among the owners of copyright in a cinematographic work authors who
> have brought contributions to the making of the work, such authors, if
> they have undertaken to bring such contributions, may not, in the absence
> of any contrary or special stipulation, object to the reproduction,
> distribution, public performance, communication to the public by wire,
> broadcasting or any other communication to the public, or to the
> subtitling or dubbing of texts, of the work.

The Stockholm revision also considered whether to extend copyright protection to film in its *unfixed* transmission, for example over live television, and decided to leave the matter to national discretion although coverage was available under the revision. The crucial policy change was expressed in a subtle language shift: the 1948 revision protected 'reproduction or production *obtained* by any other process analogous to cinematography; the 1967 revision protected works *expressed* by a process analogous to cinematography' (Salokannel, 1997: 66–67). Such distinctions are part of the semantic gymnastics of international trade policy, with linguistic contortions struggling to steady the (ever-narrowing) bar between the extension of legal protection and its denial.

Hollywood has always articulated its copyright initiatives with a forked tongue. American-based IP owners have characterised infringements of their rights as trade barriers for well over half a century. We often hear that these barriers restrict the free flow of US motion picture and television entertainment around the world. In fact, as Ronald Bettig notes, 'new communications technologies have caused this programming to flow *too freely*' (Bettig, 1990: 65): digital reproduction and the distributive capabilities of the Internet break through a number of geographic and legal restrictions. While Hollywood's early international history consists of a series of attempts to remove those barriers that impeded the free flow of its media forms, the proliferation of new media and reprographic technologies is a challenge precisely because of their *excessive* distributional freedom. Clearly, the discourse of the '*free* flow of information and entertainment never meant "without charge!" In practice, "free flow" has always been a rhetorical device for justifying US government and multinational corporate efforts to pry foreign markets open' for US copyright-related export (Bettig, 1990: 65). Thus, the rhetorical lifting of restrictions takes a backseat when ownership and trade are confronted by the relatively borderless data flows in piracy's shadow politics of distribution.

Copyright concerns more than ownership, however. The law itself is normative; outside the statutory sphere, copyright permeates our everyday assumptions about the uses of culture. Copyright conditions our ideas of authenticity and originality and draws boundary lines that divide the winners from the losers in cultural production; it systematises the 'semiotic affluence' of reception practices through the enumeration, governance and disciplining of audiences (Hartley, 1996: 66). Since its inception, copyright has fragmented the semiosphere of media consumption into public and private terrain, often with convoluted results. For example, while eighteenth-century English law withheld copyright protection (which allows for dissemination to a paying public) from printed works deemed pornographic, the result of such a lack of protection ensured a work's place in the public domain. Hence the public that is to be served by a copyright's commercial imperatives (rewarding legitimate creators with an economic incentive) and ostensibly protected from the immorality of 'obscene' literature, is the very same constituency that can pirate the pornography for both private and public free use (see Saunders, 1990). Copyright's characteristic equations of the commercial with the public have often resulted in proactive protections of privacy. In the US, cases on the legality of private copying, whether it be photocopying or videotaping, affirm the majority of US copyright decisions of the last two centuries, which generally understand copyright to be a law of 'public places and commercial interests'. This means that only public performances can constitute infringement. Non-commercial use is more likely to be protected under fair-use clauses than commercial use, where economic detriment can be demonstrated (Goldstein, 1994: 131). By putting the issue of cultural ownership into play, copyright legitimises certain forms of media consumption and prohibits others. While art historian Otto Kurz notes that forgeries 'translate the work into present-day language', that fakes 'serve the same purpose as translations and modernizations in literature' (1967: 320), copyright traditionally refuses to grant legitimacy to the pirated product as a form of social good. For Frow, 'the tension between free public provision and the pressures to treat information as a commodity with a price is ... an aspect of the aporia that organizes liberal and neo-liberal theories of the market' (1997: 209). Through the construction of consumption and prohibition in the public sphere, copyright law has played an important institutional role in the historical formation of audiences and practices of reception. This is primarily due to the fact that 'the law is never a simple reflection or instrument of socioeconomic processes [and therefore] can register with ... detailed exactitude the slow historical transformation of social categories' (Frow, 1997: 132). The most significant outcome of continuing pressures put upon extant copyright law is to question social forms of privacy, public interest, access and economic gain.

Political economy theories of copyright protection have been instrumental in recognising the historical conditions that led to the protection of cultural products as forms of intellectual and private property. Yet, economic imperatives and an analysis of state intervention alone cannot explain the complexities of Hollywood's engagement with copyright. On the one hand, Hollywood engages the proprietary logic of ownership to buttress its mechanics of distribution. On the other hand, Hollywood strategically espouses a freedom of dissemination which recognises that piracy plays an enormous role in creating audiences and demand for media products. Indeed, these *cultures of anticipation* account in large part for both Hollywood's popularity and the successes of its marketing strategies around the world.

By engaging the discourse of media copyright in its institutional form, this chapter recognises the proliferate status of cultural ownership, the transitory, palimpsestic and permeable nature of categories of producer and consumer, and the ways in which legal, public and cultural policy has engaged the audi-

ence as a fictive, yet constitutive marker of social difference, action and mobilisation. While we are clearly interested in the disciplinary shifts towards
institutional and policy analysis in cultural studies, we don't want simply to
reinscribe Tony Bennett's rather rigid provocation that the 'network of relations
that fall under the *properly* theoretical understanding of policy have a substan-
tive priority over the semiotic properties of such practices' (1992: 28). If this
prescription results from his interests in '*severing* the connection between
philosophical aesthetics and Marxist socio-economic analyses' (Bennett, 1990:
117–90), the distinctions between textuality and policy are untenable when one
works on copyright and IP. The semiotics of image and content analysis are
absolutely critical in policy determinations of duplication, the legal determination of what constitutes fair use and juridical notions of substantial similarity
that turn on *textual* resemblance. In addition, by arguing for a productive
relation between poststructuralist literary theory and law, some have suggested
that copyright's evocation of the singular work might be shifted to a conception of a depropertised, dynamic textuality that recognises the fundamentally
incomplete nature of all forms of cultural production and reimagines the audience as co-creators of textual forms (see Rotstein, 1992 and Aoki, 1993b). This
chapter argues for a hybrid methodology that approaches policy and institutions as they are imbricated in both the political economy of cultural
enumeration and the tremendous signifying power of ownership in the everyday life of culture.

Copyright: 'Reading Within the Length of the Chain'?

> The Internet marauders argue that copyright is old-fashioned, a decaying relic of a non-
> Internet world. But suppose some genius invented a magic key that could open the front
> door of every home in America and wanted to make the keys available to everyone under a
> canopy sign that read, 'It's a new world – take what you want'.
>
> (Valenti, 2000b)

Even before the statutory 'invention' of copyright in the eighteenth century mid-
wifed the birth of the author as a significant legal category of person, owners of
texts devised ways to control the dissemination of the printed word. Monaster-
ies, for example, where most transcription and copying of scripture took place
(free from legal servitude to an originary scribe), took advantage of their geographical remoteness and instituted complex lending procedures to track a
book's whereabouts. Later, European university libraries would take a page from
the protection strategies of their ancient predecessors, securing books in a series
to each other and then finally to chest-high lecterns by means of a chain, such
that the books' removal required the complex and cumbersome detachment of

rings and rods. Indeed, 'reading within the length of the chain' remains an apt metaphor for copyright's central imperatives to this day (Petroski, 1999: 60).

Copyright is, literally, the right to make copies of a given work while preventing others from making copies without permission. The historical origins of copyright as a legal determination are intimately linked to the industrial development of duplication technologies, beginning with the printing press. Copyright is a form of IP law that protects these often intangible products of the human mind; IP is a form of 'fugitive' property, since it resists legal circumscription. The spatial metaphors are apt, because copyright law is enacted territorially, based on the place in which the infringement occurs. Therefore, a Hollywood studio that charges a New Zealander/Aotearoan with copyright infringement for pirating videocassettes will have to plead the case under New Zealand/Aotearoan law rather than American law. Such territorial differences have increased copyright-owners' desires for international harmonisation of domestic copyright provisions. In addition to the articulation of space under regimes such as copyright protection, complex changes are taking place with the advent and proliferation of digital technology, because the Internet fractures the traditional spatial infrastructure of IIS. While simultaneity is the general condition of any service – where the production of the service and its consumption are coterminous – innovation in the field of information technology produces trans-border data flows that reconfigure the spatial parameters of trade between consumer and producer that were perhaps more 'concrete' in traditional forms of trade in service such as tourism, labour migration, sport and the postal system (Nayyar, 1988).

Copyright, which is essentially a law of authorship, is only one of the three traditional forms of IP. The remaining terrain is covered by patent law, which deals with technological invention and protects the intellectual labour involved in creating new products, and trademark law, which polices marketing and advertising and protects symbols that identify a single product or product source. Put simply, copyright covers laws of duplication, patents are laws of invention, and trademarks are laws of recognition and discrimination (Goldstein, 1994). Only patents protect ideas – trademarks and copyrights locate protection only in the *material expression* of ideas. The distinctions between content and carriage are, however, often provisional markers of protectability rather than firm classificatory boundaries.

Information commodities have the qualities of a public good in that each act of use fails to diminish the quality of the object being consumed; unlike a hamburger that decreases in value once shared among five people, in the simplest sense a film does not decrease in value when screened for an audience. In the legal arena, the commodity imperative overrides the public good criterion, and ownership of copyrighted materials is conferred as an economic incentive to be creative. The problematic position of the public good – which reveals the tensions between public and private property – is generative of copyright's crucial distinction between idea and expression (Boyle, 1996: 57–58): ideas are not subject to copyright protection, but their material instantiation is. IP laws endeavour to draw boundary lines between private property and the public domain and deal with the essential contradictions between freedom of expression and the capitalist imperative of a free market. Indeed, in recent years, alongside the privatisation of the public domain – which 'turns the information superhighway into a toll road' (Venturelli, 1997: 69) – copyright infringement claims have been evoked because information has become 'too free'. However, questions of legal propriety turn not only on *where* and *how* to draw boundary lines, but *why* to draw them at all?

To merit copyright, an expression must be 'fixed' as a work, leading to the exclusion of works in oral traditions. Since copyright extends only to 'original' works, it denies protection to folklore and other items of cultural heritage. At the same time, the intensity of protection extended to productions that qualify as works of authorship tend to bar their use for new creative purposes, making outlaws of those who draw on such works for their raw material. Since it is derived from Western, especially Continental, author's rights principles, the international copyright regime that governs relations between developed and developing nations has huge problems. It is a structural feature of the NICL that, while the traditional, folkloric and collaborative productions of these countries circulate internationally, becoming subject to appropriation by the culture industries of the developed world, for the most part they go unprotected by both national laws in their countries and the international copyright system (see Jaszi and Woodmansee, 1996; see also Brush and Stabinsky, 1996 for key pharmacological IP issues). As James Boyle astutely summarises, the 'author concept' is a

> gate that tends disproportionately to favor the developed countries'
> contribution to world science and culture. Curare, batik, myths, and the
> dance 'lambada' flow out of developing countries, unprotected by IP rights,
> while Prozac, Levis, Grisham and the movie *Lambada!* flow in – protected
> by a suite of IP laws, which in turn are backed by the threat of trade
> sanctions.
>
> (Boyle, 1996: 124–28)

The primary marker of protection in textual dissemination constitutes the author as a privileged frame or node and the temporal and spatial considerations of authorship and policy are crucial in the production of juridical knowledges. While reproduction has different valencies, formal and differential taxonomies of repetition and replication, copyright law engages reproduction as a social *practice*. As Celia Lury notes, reproduction is regulated 'through specific regimes of rights of copying' which, while *juridically* determined, are the 'outcome of economic, political and cultural struggles between participants in cycles of cultural reproduction'. Imbricated in the constitution of particular types of cultural work as IP, such regimes 'define the terms under which such property may be copied and distributed for reception' (Lury, 1993: 4). Under the definitional rubrics of 'originality', 'innovation' and 'novelty', copyright law:

> adjudicates between the need to secure the free circulation of ideas, a
> process which is commonly accepted to be integral to the functioning of
> the democratic public sphere, and the commercial demand for monopoly
> rights in copying and the associated creation of markets in cultural
> commodities. ... Regimes of copying rights can thus be considered in
> terms of both the possibilities and constraints they offer cultural producers
> in the organization of the processes of internalization, and the actual
> constraints that they offer for reactivation.
>
> (Lury, 1993: 8)

Both legal *possibilities* and *constraints* constitute the field of cultural consumption as well as internalised notions of audience (in the sense that copyright law adjudicates the realm of acceptable behaviour in cultural consumption). The central assumption on which copyright systems are based is that creators of intellectual works need an economic incentive to be creative. Economic reward is implied in the exclusive right to exploit copyrighted work and is meant to supply motivation for intellectual and artistic activity and to ensure a source of income. The argument goes that if the copyright system functions in this way, it functions for the social good, because it stimulates creativity. That is not to say that duplication is an issue restricted to the courtroom. Forms of cultural quotation and recycling such as genre are also ways of dealing with difference and repetition. Genre makes clear the cultural delimitations of textuality and obligation alongside the more juridical parameters of ownership and use.

Generic forms emerge, in part, from the works that precede them. This is why Rick Altman jokes that 'in the genre world, every day is *Jurassic Park* day' (1998: 24). Genres are recombinatory forms, playing on historical antecedents (though not wholly circumvented by evolutionary origins). Genre as a historical mode is caught up within duplication technologies such as the printing press, which along with the emergence of utilitarianism (which supported copyright in its nascent form) engendered the rise of the novel, and the videocassette recorder, which continues to influence the cut-up editing style of much television programming. In addition, genre is indebted to a legal conception of the public domain which understands creativity as a collective process. As early as 1845, US courts recognised that 'every book in literature, science and art, borrows, and must necessarily borrow, and use much which was well known and used before' (quoted in Cohen, 1996: 1006). Many copyright decisions of the early twentieth century understood that the textual stuff of genre – 'plots, titles, characters, ideas, situations and style' – were part of the public domain, as were textual similarities among works that could be counted as elements of the social *lingua franca*: as trite, common, idiomatic or cliché (Litman, 1990: 986–93).

In a speech made in 2000 outlining corporate strategy in the new digital environment, Disney CEO and head Mouseketeer Eisner gave a visual presentation that demonstrated *Dinosaur*'s (Eric Leighton and Ralph Zondag, 2000) allegiance to the films that preceded it: *The Lost World* (Harry O. Hoyt, 1925), *King Kong* (Merian C. Cooper and Ernest B. Schoedsack, 1933), *Godzilla* (Roland Emmerich, 1998) and *Jurassic Park*. Noting that Disney had obtained copyright clearance to show clips from most of these films (except *Jurassic Park*), Eisner explained that IP law provided both the economic and the moral framework for the incentive to create works of cinematic art. He neglected to mention the loopholes in patent law that allow film studios to reverse-engineer the software code in patented high-tech special effects technologies and save valuable research/development time and money. He also failed to note the way in which genre takes advantage of cultural competencies that are generated over time, habituations that give viewers a common language through which to appreciate and connect films. While all art is in a sense derivative, terms like originality, skill and labour have complex valencies when legal ownership is to be decided (see Van Camp, 1994). And the big corporate owners are often on the other side of the litigation fence: Disney has itself been sued for copyright violation (albeit mostly unsuccessfully) – accused of stealing the idea for a sports complex, stealing the 'tinkerbell' trademark from a perfume company, stealing screen treatments, stealing children's magazine formats, and stealing the concepts behind *The Lion King* (Roger Allers and Rob Minkoff, 1994). Of course, Disney's zealousness about its own IP is not a new issue; in 1989, the House of Mouse sniffed out three South Florida pre-schools that had painted some Disney characters on their outside walls and pursued retribution in the courts (Verrier, 2000).

Eisner's five-point plan for copyright protection – avoid extending compulsory licensing (which requires, for example, broadcasters to make their signal available to cable companies), coordinate global legal efforts, foster civic education, erect technological firewalls, and lobby for fair pricing – has both a moral and an economic prerogative. It brings into sharp relief the demarcations between commerce and art that are established in IP law. The central and (to stay within Disney's purview) animating question is this: who will set prices and establish the logic of distribution – workers who invest their intellectual labour and creativity in the manufacture of an art object, corporations that finance and invest in the material production of these objects, or the consuming public? And how are lines to be drawn around these fields?

The success of most copyright infringement suits turn on the key relationship between economics and use. Section 107 of the US Copyright Act of 1976 excludes certain forms of use from the category of infringement. These forms of 'fair use' allow copying for a limited range of activities (teaching and scholarship, social criticism and commentary, news reporting) so long as these activities do not cause economic detriment to the copyright holder. The section on statutory fair use in the Copyright Act outlines four factors in considering whether usage constitutes infringement: the purpose and character of the use (whether it is of a commercial nature or for not-for-profit educational purposes); the nature of the copyrighted work; the amount/substantiality of the portion used relative to the copyrighted work as a whole; and the effect of use on the potential market for the value of the copyrighted work. In the historical evocation of Section 107, the key element separating fair use from infringement has often been the last issue – commerciality. Since the statute makes clear that there are forms of use that are public and forms that are private, the major problem for corporate copyright owners like the Hollywood studios is how to substantiate the key category of 'detrimental effect': can the corporate owners of copyrighted material like songs and films delineate the amount of money lost because of the proliferation of a new duplication technology? Once the potential effect on the market is substantiated by the copyright owner, however, it has been very difficult to overturn the commercial limitations on fair use.

In *Universal City Studios, Inc. v. Sony Corp of America* (1979), the corporate owners of copyrighted images claimed 'contributory infringement' and sought to impose liability on consumer electronic manufacturers of VCRs. The court decided that the majority of uses of VCRs, such as time shifting or the accumulation of private libraries, was protected under fair use. Upon appeal in 1981, the decision was reversed in favour of Universal (joined by Disney). As the case reached final arbitration in the Supreme Court, the MPAA suggested the imposition of a fixed royalty on VCRs and blank videotapes in order to compensate for its purported losses. In early 1983, Sony's final appeal in *Sony v. Universal* was heard in the US Supreme Court. The key issue, again, was private copying and time shifting, and the court decided that these were non-infringing uses and granted (5–4) Sony's appeal. In other words, although VCR hardware could be used for infringing purposes, the fair uses of the technology outweighed any contributory infringement possibly engendered by them. The Sony case lives on in current debates about the encryption of digital television transmissions to prevent the possible taping of 'superpremium' pay-TV programming and the control of other forms of digital content. Recent cases regarding digital multimedia have sought the legal protection of 'transformative use' – i.e, that the use significantly changes the dimensions of the original and that multimedia developers are authors too (see Goldberg, 1995). The consumer electronics industry is again locked in a struggle with the corporate owners of copyrighted materials, and fair use will determine the outcome (Goldstein, 1994).

Although film directors protest when 'their' work is altered for video, television and airline exhibition, most infringement suits are brought by the corporate owners of film copyright, since the directors essentially lack authorial rights – they are considered 'workers for hire' under US law. The notion of corporate citizenship, where corporations have similar legal status to individuals, has been crucial in ongoing copyright battles, especially the recording industry. The recording companies themselves initiated infringement actions against Napster.com, an Internet clearing house for sharing digital music files, despite the high-profile involvement of musical acts like Metallica (who are one of the rare groups to own their songs). Internet services such as Scour, iMesh, Gnutella and the cleverly-named Metallicster and Wrapster allow users to locate and download digital material from others' hard drives. These companies also learned the lessons that Napster put into play – that some form of cooperation with the corporate owners of copyright materials is the best way to navigate the legal terrain. Even as Scour fights a copyright infringement suit brought against it by the Hollywood majors and a number of record companies, it is negotiating licences with Miramax (named as a plaintiff in the suit). Miramax is also allowing Sightsound.com to distribute a number of its titles over the Internet. Where jurisprudence has had trouble in the anti-Napster cases, the MPA has found a wellspring of anti-piracy rhetoric. As Valenti (2000) recently put it, 'a number of new movies, the ones now in theaters, have already been put on the Internet by pilfering zealots eager to unfold films in the same embrace now choking the music world'.

Copyright controls allow film studios to coordinate and maximise returns from a film's release schedule across a number of different venues and exhibition platforms: domestic exhibition in the US is followed by an (increasingly smaller) delay in international exhibition, followed by video and DVD release, pay-per-view, cable and then network television (see Chapter 5). Alongside coordinating exhibition schedules, copyright plays a part in new Hollywood initiatives to do away with prints distributed to individual theatres in favour of direct-to-theatre satellite and/or Internet distribution. Digital distribution would shave over US$10 million dollars in domestic post-production print manufacturing costs for a Hollywood budget for a film like *Godzilla* (Natale, 2000). If the 39,000 screens in North America were to switch to digital projection today, film studios would save the US$800 million they spend annually on making, insuring and shipping film prints (Sabin, 2000).

Copyright is a strange and contradictory beast. On the one hand, it addresses the need to secure the free circulation of ideas, a process that is commonly accepted as integral to the democratic public sphere. At the same time, copyright manufactures the commercial demand for monopoly rights in copying and the associated creation of markets in cultural commodities. In the US, for example, copyright promises innovators that their ideas can be returned to the wellspring of the public domain, for example, fifty years after their initial publication or after their author's death. This is a materialisation of the recognition that drawing on previous works motivates creative labour. Jane Gaines has called this duality within copyright doctrine 'the double movement of circulation and restriction' (1991: 9). In practice, however, copyright law has actually resulted in a tendency towards the granting of monopoly control to the corporate owners of information.

Commenting on agricultural law in eighteenth-century Britain, E.P. Thompson (1975) notes that the law is so imbricated in production relations that it is indistinguishable from the mode of production. This tenet of legal realism might also be applied to Hollywood: IP law guarantees the consolidation of textual control on behalf of corporate owners of the screen image. Hollywood's fervent interaction with new international governing bodies (like the WTO) convened to organise disparate national copyright regimes is thus clearly an extension of this domestic strategy. But is it that simple? After all, 'doing nothing' is one of the many legitimate strategies that corporate owners have when it comes to IP protection. When dealing with counterfeit cultural products in a low legal export area, Hollywood might be better off (even in terms of a simple cost-benefit analysis) to avoid bad publicity and take the opportunity for free promotion for a product that will be supplanted by many others down the line. Maybe copyright infringement is simply an unofficial tax for doing business in, say, China or India. Backing off on copyright protection might help imbue a type of aspiration that contributes to the cultures of anticipation that buttress Hollywood's ancillary merchandising markets so that affinities for pirated brand images 'can be converted to authentic products when the market becomes more developed' (Schultz and Saporito, 1996: 22). New directions for Hollywood as it endeavours to come to terms with markets where IP protection is scant (notably China) may include forfeiting an iron-clad grip over media property, in favour of stabilising the infrastructure of a smoothly running distributional system. This is what Thomas Streeter calls 'systems consciousness', the 'bureaucratic coordination of flows of programs and profits with an eye to maintaining the system overall' (1996: 273). In 2001, with China about to double its quota of Hollywood films (to twenty) after years of trade battles with the US, hardware piracy is not significantly addressed in a Sino-American trade agreement passed by the US Senate in 2000, although copyright is. Hollywood knows that, to play its copyrighted software, you need the hardware – counterfeit or not.

The subtle shift away from total IP protection is mirrored by recent legal scholarship, which contends that there is a marked shift from copyright law to trademark law as films, blockbusters in particular, have increasingly come to be judged in terms of their capacity to act as logos or have a distinct product image. In these cases, the film itself is not the only commodity that can be sold through its circulation – it is also used to sell records, clothes, toys, video games, books, magazines, drinks and food. Here, trademark is related to the product-image around a film. This intentional shift in legislative practice since the 1940s, from a conception of textual ownership as copyrightable to a codification of its value as a trademark, is designed to engage textuality in its most immediate iconic modality, rather than through an engagement of material practice – in other words, to systematise regulation through the recognition of symbols rather than through readerly semiosis. While trademark law's earlier claims to civic management had a 'deference to context, convention and genre' in attempting to prevent consumer confusion between commercial products, the lodging of the trademark owners property-like rights in a mark (accreted over time by statutory decisions) has 'frequently trumped free speech concerns in several US state law anti-dilution cases which have ruled against "recodings", or subsequent unauthorized uses of marks, even in the absence of consumer confusion' (Aoki, 1993b: 832; see also Denicola 1999). The recent enactment of Trade Related IP (TRIPs) agreements at the international level attests to the great overarching reach of trademark provision:

> Any sign, or combination of signs, capable of distinguishing the goods or services of one undertaking from those of other undertakings, shall be capable of constituting a trademark. Such signs, in particular words including personal names, letters, numerals, figurative elements and combinations of colours as well as any combination of such signs, shall be eligible for registration as trademarks. Where signs are not inherently capable of distinguishing the relevant good or services, Members may make registrability depend on distinctiveness acquired through use. Members may require, as a condition of registration, that signs be visually perceptible.
>
> (Article 15 of TRIPs)

Such a sweeping definition begs a clear question: what exactly *isn't* covered under trademark?

The inevitable shift from copyright to trademark as the legal infrastructure for dealing with digital reproduction may be lodged in the older notion of trademark as a form of goodwill branding, a mark of differentiation that guarantees a quality product at the same time as it sets the terms for the evaluation of quality. Indeed, product education has been a part of Hollywood's new international anti-piracy initiatives, with *caveat emptor* the rallying cry of an MPA. Even in the Internet bootleg film market, 'trademarked' copies of *The Phantom Menace* (George Lucas 1999) serve as signs of quality.

Valenti's effort to educate audiences around the world on the inferior quality of pirated Hollywood product redeploys trademark law's nineteenth-century rationale which, as Keith Aoki puts it, 'prevented consumer confusion over competing marketing goods', in the service of a more modern focus that protected the corporate owners of IP from 'dilution and appropriation of a set of positive meanings which have been created by the trademark owner's investment' (1993a: 4). The assimilation of authorial legitimacy and consumer protection within the discourse of civil restraint is part of trademark law's history of signalling quality assurance and consistency in the field of commodity purchase. As the film industry continues to deal with digital transactions, the reputations of sellers will become ever more important as distributors (both legal and otherwise) proliferate – the key will be not over-protection, but the maximisation of product differentiation, making sure that people realise that YOU put out a superior, quality product (YOU get to define the criteria of superiority, naturally). New technologies of digital watermarking are predicated on much the same principles as the embedding of trademarks within the scenes of early silent film. The founder of Digimarc, a digital watermarking firm, is a former physicist who developed a process to clean up digital images of outer space. Worried that his doctored images might be considered public property, he added an almost imperceptible ownership mark to the photographs. This led to the development of both watermarking techniques (which are now themselves patented) and sophisticated search engines that can scour the Internet for copyrighted material (Golden, 1998). This is not unprecedented in film history: the French cinema company Pathé once stamped its red rooster trademark on silent film inter-title cards – not specifically to deter copyright (Pathé never sought copyright protection for its films in the US and the American Copyright Act of 1790 automatically relegated foreign works into the public domain) but to circulate them 'as a recurring symbol of goodwill that, in guaranteeing the quality of its product's performance on stage or screen, incited increased consumer demand' (Abel, 1999: 18–19). Might Hollywood be taking a lesson from the film giant it successfully banished from its domestic shores well before the introduction of sound.

Fundamentally then, copyright establishes relations between textuality, ownership and use. It provides a mechanism for differentiating among texts and articulating relations between the labour of textual production as a form of property and restrictions placed upon the terms of textual reception. Securing reception nodes becomes important precisely because of the indeterminacy of the information commodity's *use*. Establishing scarcity through exclusivity is one of the enduring aims of copyright protection. The information commodity relies on its circulation as a protected form of legal property that can serve as a subsidy for the enormous costs of its production. Distribution (and predictability) become key in the corporate control of IP, deflecting the law (at least in its American invocation) away from authorship towards ownership.

The Complex Logic of the Same: Piracy and Hollywood's International Imperatives

Who can be blind today to the threat of a world gradually invaded by an identical culture, Anglo-Saxon culture, under the cover of economic liberalism?

(François Mitterand, quoted in Brooks, 1994: 35)

There's no free Hollywood.

(Jack Valenti, quoted in Streif, 2000)

The Motion Picture Association (MPA) is a US-based non-governmental trade association which represents its members in international trade. The studio members of the MPA are Buena Vista International (Disney), Columbia Tristar Film Distributors, 20th Century Fox International, Metro-Goldwyn-Mayer, Paramount Pictures, Universal International Films and Warner Bros. International Theatrical Distribution. The MPA was originally formed to combat the growing tide of restrictions and barriers to audiovisual entertainment that targeted American motion picture export after the Second World War (see Guback, 1984 and 1985). Designed to strengthen extant copyright protection, coordinate efforts among local governments and agencies, and provide logistical, technical and legislative support during and after litigation, the MPA's anti-piracy push now has coordinated operations in over seventy countries. Large-scale video anti-piracy efforts and sting operations have been conducted in Malaysia, Mexico, Poland, Italy, Israel, Germany, Peru, Panama, Brazil and Greece and new MPA initiatives since 1997 have targeted Russia, China and Ireland. In 1999, MPA liaisons with government agencies resulted in large cable crackdowns in Pakistan, where copyright laws were relatively lax, and the MPA played a prominent role in a New Delhi ruling prosecuting the two largest

Indian cable providers for the illegal transmission of films. In China, a piracy hotspot because of the proliferation of video discs imported from production plants in Hong Kong and Macao, tightening copyright regulation is understood as a necessary corollary to its fourteen-year ascent to the WTO, as it was for Taiwan. In addition, the MPA coordinates legislative efforts around the world, increasing the penalties for copyright crime in, for example, Mexico, where, under close supervision by the Office of the US Trade Representative and the MPA, the criminal code recently upgraded a piracy conviction from a misdemeanour to a felony, expedited search warrant request criteria, and severely restricted bail and pre-trial release for piracy arrests.

In its all-too-common evocation as an 'epochal totality', globalisation 'projects a lateral knitting together of space/time across an entirely interconnected geopolitical network' alongside a 'vertical isomorphism of economic, political, and cultural levels' (Frow, 2000: 174). In order to secure its interests in making Hollywood a global form, however, the MPA knows that it has to be more fluid than such commonplace evocations of spatial metaphor and focus on the geographic and politico-territorial referents which abound in US statutory language on copyright, trademark and patents (Aoki, 1996: 1300). In addition to its espousal of rights that homestead the notion of cultural production – fix it through marks of authenticity and ownership in a specified time and space – the MPA engages a simultaneous spatial flexibility. The Motion Picture Export Association of America changed its name to the Motion Picture Association in 1994 in order to 'more accurately represent the global nature of audiovisual entertainment in today's global media marketplace' (quoted at www.mpaa.org/about/content.html). However, the dropping of the territorial moniker 'America' suggests more the priority of the international market for Hollywood. While 'America' may have dropped out of the acronym, territoriality and national specificity still guarantee the MPA's litigation infrastructure. For example, in Malaysia, media pirates have been, as in many other places, charged under Trade Descriptions Acts which prosecute cases based on fraudulent 'Made in USA' labels. Given the NICL's characterisation of Hollywood product as dispersed throughout the world, the desire to *fix* national authenticity through a distinguishing mark is part of the protocols of American distinction. Similar restrictions also apply domestically. 'True Name and Address' statutes, which form the backbone of the MPAA's domestic anti-video piracy litigation, impose 'criminal penalties for the rental and sale of videocassettes that do not bear the true name and address of the manufacturer'.

While it may be increasingly difficult to specify the national origins of manufactured goods given the NICL's dispersion of production, national concerns over balanced trade still carry heavy weight. Hollywood still frets at China's import restrictions that keep over 90 per cent of MPA feature product from entering the legal channels of exhibition under the guise of maintaining 'national character'. Notions of national coherency are routinely evoked in the language of the comprador élite who sit at the WTO. Complicating all of this is the fact that even though Hollywood calls for the rationalisation of IP protection – to 'equalise' global legal imperatives in line with US corporate interest – such 'homogenisation' is a strategy based on productively engaging the terrain of national difference. In other words, the spatialisation of uneven development in the international trade in goods and services articulates forms of national *difference* as well as engineering those forms of 'cultural synchronisation' loosely theorised as the checkmate in globalisation's game. Hollywood's unitary conception of IP protection, therefore, is *based* on territorial boundaries in order to 'produce not only the conceptual, but also the actual physical spaces of the information age' (Aoki 1996: 1297). As Kevin Cox puts it, spatial *organisation* – not its traditional annihilation theorised by many discourses of media globalisation – 'becomes a productive force rather than a discrete set of exchange opportunities and offers capital with competitive advantages. Accordingly, capital can become impeded in particular localities and dependent upon their reproduction' (1997: 131).

The US legislature has certainly helped Hollywood in this regard. US government support of the US film industry in its anti-piracy war can be linked to the larger role the government plays in helping US capital exploit foreign markets. For additional intelligence in this struggle over piracy, the US Copyright Office calls on US embassies to systematise the collection of data from foreign countries about such matters as levels of local copyright, patent and trademark activity and infrastructures for the publication, distribution and performance of protected works. US advisers are training foreign lawyers, police and customs officials to handle the enforcement aspects of copyright protection. Under Section 301 of the 1988 Trade Act, the Office of the US Trade Representative has the authority to put foreign nations on a watchdog list for up to two years, after which the President is required to take some form of retaliatory action, ranging from termination of trade agreements to suspension of any trade benefits that had been granted to the importing nation. Often, the rationales behind IP protection and the threat of US sanction are more than symbolic Marshall planning: they are part and parcel of American international diplomacy. For example, as India, along with China, was targeted for Section 301 investigation in the late 1980s, the piracy of US products was related to Cold War concerns over imported supercomputers and the proliferation of atomic technologies. So, pursuing the US$66 million that the MPA lost to Indian piracy in 1997 is part of a diplomatic heritage that includes nuclear non-proliferation and new entry for US banking and insurance sectors alongside lifting restrictions and quotas on Hollywood in the Indian market (Thomas,

1999: 281, 284). And sometimes securing IP protection in a country like China is prioritised over purported concerns about the sale of nuclear technology and human rights abuses.

In mid-1996, the US Trade Representative threatened China with US$2 billion in trade sanctions, citing its poor record on IP enforcement and the wide-scale piracy of US-owned copyrighted material to the tune of US$2.3 billion (Atkinson, 1997b). The threat of sanction was pulled after the Chinese Propaganda Department and Press and Publications Administration cracked down on new pirate CD factories and the Public Security Bureau promised to strengthen IP monitoring in Chinese piracy hotspots like Guangdong. Trade talks also resulted in the loosening of Hollywood's import quotas in China. Since the US absorbs almost a third of China's imports, it is no wonder that equivalence is the name of the trade game (Crock *et al.*, 1997). As Hollywood negotiated in frenetic twelfth-hour lobbying sessions for the normalisation of trade relations with China in early summer 2000, labour unions in the US and many Southern California Congressional representatives protested the possibility of simply opening another source of cheap labour for US manufacturing. While some in the film industry are opposed to trade normalisation – actress Goldie Hawn is a common figure on the protest front – the studio heads, led by Eisner, see trade normalisation as the natural result of beefed-up IP protection (Hook, 2000: A1). In addition, IP is the major concern of the MPA these days; as Valenti puts it, in his characteristic alignment of culture and diplomacy, 'the prospect of piracy is terrorizing' (quoted in Machan, 1997). It is characteristic of the MPA's historical amnesia that Valenti never admits where the US stood on the pirating of foreign (particularly early French) film. And in true NICL fashion, Hollywood studios still record film soundtracks outside the US in order to save royalty payments to US artists.

In addition, the US routinely demands the elimination of trade barriers to American audiovisual export for countries seeking to join the WTO. While Valenti has claimed that it is a defunct 'delusion' that governments know how best to build a thriving cinema industry (quoted in 'Clarity', 1999), during his tenure as head of the American film industry's major lobbying group, he has engineered tax write-offs for films made in the US and tax-shelters for studios to defer taxes on half their overseas profit. Because IP rights are really 'privileges granted by the State through a form of statutory subsidy' (Raghavan, 1990: 116), government intervention in the sphere of IP law has been crucial to Hollywood. One of the MPA's most important lobbying efforts of the 1990s culminated in the 1998 Congressional extension of the US copyright term by twenty years (to seventy-five). This prevented, for example, Disney's first *Mickey Mouse* cartoon from entering the public domain in 2003. Caught between the three conflicting pressures of expansion, stability and political legitimacy (Streeter, 1996: 264), Hollywood studios have poured donations into the campaign coffers of politicians who support copyright extensions, ratification of the World IP Organization Treaty, and anti-piracy technologies. The entertainment industry has doubled its contributions to Federal political campaigns since the 1995–96 election cycle, with over US$17.5 million in donations made through July 2000 (Boliek, 2000).

After the Second World War, the US became a net exporter of copyrighted materials and, since the containment rhetoric of the Marshall Plan carried with it definite cultural prerogatives, proposed an international copyright treaty, the Universal Copyright Convention. Prior to the Uruguay round of GATT and the formation of the WTO, international copyright agreements such as the Berne Convention and the Universal Copyright Convention contained no real enforcement procedures. IP rights have only become subject to international trade negotiation and harmonisation at the regional (e.g., the EU) as well as the global level in the last decade. The international copyright conventions which preceded the GATT and the WTO did not require a universal harmonisation of property rights, merely that nations offer no greater protection to foreign works than their own. For a long time, refusal to recognise or enforce IP rights was a deliberate policy on the part of many non-US or non-Western European countries, who were concerned to prevent foreign monopoly ownership of culture and the outflow of foreign exchange. Recent moves towards IP harmonisation differentiate national traditions and consumption practices, ranging from commercial commodities that imply individual creative genius to community production and shared use (Chartrand, 1996).

International piracy, counterfeiting and other unauthorised expropriations of US IP came to the forefront of US trade policy concerns in the early 1980s once it became conventional wisdom that the future of US-led global entertainment was predicated upon the production, ownership and marketing of IP-based goods and services. Accordingly, state efforts to advance the copyright interests of the film entertainment industry were part of a much larger effort to institute the international legal infrastructure to support IP-based industries. As US IP-based industries sought to secure their rights in foreign markets, they were able to forge alliances with foreign capitalists concerned with the same goal. Added to the GATT under the primary support of the US, Europe and Japan, the TRIPs agreement extends hitherto ambiguous coverage of ownership to natural *and* legal persons; that is, both single authors and corporate owners. It does not specifically address the moral rights component of the Berne Convention. And when the US finally signed the Convention in the late 1980s, the moral rights distinction that had held up its signature for a century was effectively nullified, since Berne gave the author of a work a moral right, while in the US, ownership was synonymous with authorship. Accordingly, the

Berne Convention Implementation Act allowed for the continuation of Federal and State-mandated rights that were in contradistinction to its own, relatively strong, language of moral rights. Yet continued US compliance with Berne may well be contingent on its extension of moral rights to authors (Chinni, 1997). How might this take place in the environment of digital reproduction? The extension of moral rights will not suffice as a panacea for copyright's problems; the distributional apparatus of film makes it difficult for an authorial maverick to hold out under the protective umbrella of moral rights. As director Marcel Ophuls once put it, 'if we were to cling to the notion of moral rights we wouldn't work at all' (quoted in Puttnam with Watson, 1998: 242).

Coming into effect at the beginning of 1995, TRIPs establishes minimum standards for protection (defining the object to be protected, the rights that accompany its ownership, exceptions and minimum duration of protection), enforcement (civil and administrative procedures, prosecutions and penalties), and dispute settlement. Failure to uphold IP provisions now subjects the offending nation to retaliatory sanction under unfair trade provisions. The 'Copyright and Related Rights' section of TRIPs (the others deal with 'Trademarks', 'Geographical Destinations' and 'Patents') incorporates the 1971 Berne Convention, whose Article 10 provided for protection of computer programs (in source or object code) as literary works – the culmination of a decade-long effort by Western software manufacturers. In addition, TRIPs affords protection to the field of neighbouring or related rights, such as sound recordings and broadcast signals.

Given capital's voracious appetite for new markets, it is perhaps inevitable that existing and emerging forms of human artistic and intellectual creativity would be integrated into the global marketing system. So the pressure on national governments for greater copyright protection comes from both locally-based oligopolistic media industries and multinational media companies. Media multinationals operating within the US have come to expect the US government to apply this pressure from the outside – and the idea that the protection and recognition of IP rights is a necessary precondition of modernity and the functioning of a capitalist state holds powerful sway around the world. Sometimes the US has paid a price for internationalism. For example, as part of the implementation infrastructure of both NAFTA and GATT, the US gave retroactive copyright protection to foreign works that had gone into the US public domain due to foreign ignorance of certain bureaucratic formalities or the lack of a bilateral agreement between the US and the foreign country. Of course, the US fully expects such restorative copyright protection for its own works in foreign countries (Sobel, 1995). The US government has pursued three strategies to eradicate piracy in foreign markets: bilateral trade-leveraging against countries where piracy was rampant; free trade agreements with selected partners that incorporate IP protection into their frameworks; and multilateral efforts such as the GATT.

By far the most prominent region in Hollywood's new internationalism has been Asia – and the key issue here has been IP. India alone has between 40,000 and 70,000 cable operators, with over 2,000 in Delhi alone, largely unregulated and without firm licensing procedures for film exhibition (Lall, 1999). Malaysia's Johor Baru is home to a number of pirate VCD outfits, and Hollywood is deeply worried about a recent Malay court decision that copyright owners must be present to execute affidavits of ownership in infringement suits, rather than submit them via local company representatives. The International IP Alliance, which represents the key US copyright industries, reports that Malaysia is a major supplier of pirated product throughout Asia and even as far as Latin America, and the MPA finds Malaysia second only to China in projected piracy losses (at about US$40 million in 1998) (Oh, 2000). The MPA estimates that video piracy cost the US studios over US$550 million in lost revenues in Asia in 2000 and that 90 per cent of the video industry was illegally controlled in China and Indonesia, 85 per cent in Malaysia, 52 per cent in Thailand and 25 per cent in Singapore (Groves, 2000b). A significant feature of the 1996 Asia-Pacific Economic Cooperation Forum was the extension of free trade agreements like NAFTA and GATT to the region. The MPA asserts that free trade depends on loosening protective national barriers and securing IP provisions. Recent measures to court US support for China's introduction to the WTO have licensed patented DVD technologies and trademarked logos to new Chinese DVD manufacturers, and, perhaps most important, offered 49 per cent foreign ownership (probably loosely regulated) of cinemas, which might initiate yet another Hollywood multiplexing construction frenzy (Groves, 2000a and b). Nevertheless, after Bill Clinton's visit to China in 1998, the street pirates who had been removed in the major urban centres during his visit renewed their normal locations.

Hollywood is not the only cinema pursuing piracy regulation. Though most countries are net importers of media programming, those few other regions that have relative industrial self-sufficiency, such as the Hong Kong and the Bombay-based Hindi film industry, have their own significant stakes in copyright protection. Both industries recently staged stoppages to protest against domestic piracy of their films. Even in Thailand, where Hollywood takes 85 per cent of film revenue, the domestic movie industry, which is scheduling the release of seven major films in 2001, has set up a 3 million baht fund to battle copyright violations ('B3m Fund Will fight Piracy', 2000). But with bootleg tapes of *Titanic* earning more than US$2 million before legitimate videos went on sale in Russia, and the commonplace striking of digital video disc copies and the quick turnaround time of high-quality subtitling and dubbing techniques of pirated film buttressing a significant financial threat, Hollywood has the

highest stakes in international copyright protection, and it pursues an unprecedented strategy of legislative standardisation to make sure its products are
protected overseas as they are domestically.

The Work of Hollywood in the Age of Digital Reproduction

copy protection n.
A class of methods for preventing incompetent pirates from stealing software and legitimate
customers from using it. Considered silly.

> (*The New Hacker's Dictionary*, http://www.tuxedo.org/~esr/jargon/jargon.html)

I love film, but it's a 19th Century invention. The century of film has passed.

> (George Lucas, quoted in Sabin, 2000)

Following experiments in digital video compression, patents on software systems designed to broadcast movies on the Internet were issued in the US in the
early 1990s. Hollywood has been relatively slow to take note, until a recent spate
of Internet piracy has made over sixty films, including *Armageddon* (Michael
Bay, 1998), *Godzilla*, *The Matrix*, *Entrapment* (Jon Amiel, 1999), *Saving Private
Ryan* and *The Phantom Menace*, available for public download. The MPAA estimates that, on an average day, 275,000 pirated movies are downloaded, with the
number expected to increase to 1 million by 2002 (Graham, 2001a: 3D). While
the Internet has been notoriously difficult to police, the MPAA has recently
created its own Internet investigative unit. Recalling the imagery of medieval
chastity belts, Valenti calls this unit 'a technological armor plate that guards our
movies from being hauled out in a profligate manner by everybody with a computer'. The development of new encryption models and 'invisible
watermarking' technologies, which carry rights information, reflects Hollywood's acknowledgment of widespread Internet piracy in the recording and
publishing industries. Buttressing their own ever-increasing cadre of legal staff
and enlisting the aid of the Federal Bureau of Investigation (as Lucasfilm has
recently done), Hollywood and its studios have mobilised a whole new set of
relations among different national police forces and local governments to control the relatively borderless dissemination of pirated material over the
Internet. How has Hollywood handled the three factors that contribute to the
proliferate status of the digital form: fidelity, compression and malleability
(Goldstein, 1994: 197)?

Hollywood seems to fear and loathe the Internet. One film industry executive referred to the computer as 'our nemesis' (Alexander, 2000). The Academy
of Motion Picture Arts and Sciences has ruled that films shown on the Internet
prior to theatrical release are ineligible for Oscar consideration. Blockbuster

Video plans to stream video in order to bypass the Internet altogether in favour of a private network provided by an alliance with phone companies. In the face of the massive strike by Hollywood talent that was anticipated after contract negotiations in 2001, members of the Directors Guild of America, Writers Guild of America, Cartoonist Union Local 839 and the Screen Actors Guild signed agreements with Internet content producers that were not yet fully amalgamated into the Alliance of Motion Picture and Television Producers (Swanson, 2000).

Not surprisingly however, Hollywood's take on the digital is, well, a binary one. Fear and loathing aside, the Internet is powerfully attractive for Hollywood. Plans are well underway for Internet sites that trade in film industry and profit speculation as well as selling production 'shares' that give virtual small-time executive producers credit in DVD releases of Hollywood films (Whitaker, 2000: 2). In addition to being a powerful market research tool (see Chapter 6), the Internet facilitates both management oversight (there's nothing like email to keep track of employees and the bottom line) and the sharing of daily digitised rushes as the NICL moves production around the world. Studios can send digitally compressed trailers all over the world and coordinate international releases with even more precision. The MPA recently announced at a meeting of the International Trademark Association that studios will begin distributing films over the Internet by mid-2001 (Soriano, 2001: 1D). This is the most powerful future for Hollywood and the Internet. Seeking to duplicate its successes in the international multichannel television market (which followed the deregulation of the European television industry and the proliferation of new pay-TV systems in the late 1980s), Hollywood studios may launch their own pay-per-view Internet channels. Satellite, digital television, broadband, video-on-demand and other technologies of digital distribution (like the table-top hybrid of television and the PC, forecast by techno-futurists and studio heads alike) allow the studios to cut out the middle people who facilitate Hollywood distribution in foreign countries. Sony Pictures, successful in the multichannel television market with thirty-three networks around the world (which earn about US$150 million in advertising revenue, 80 per cent from Asia) and a huge programme-syndication business, formed Sony Pictures Digital Entertainment to leverage Sony's programming in the digital environment (Galetto and Dallas, 2000). Sony also has an online video-on-demand service called Moviefly, which is designed to replace the pay-per-view cable and satellite business that fell below early speculation that it would be a platform for the premiere of films (Graham, 2001b: 3D). Driven by the need to maximise the value of their content, Hollywood studios look to the Internet and companies like iBeam and CinemaNow – major players in Internet distribution of film (Winslow, 2001; 'iBeam and CinemaNow Partner', 2000). And with hundreds of millions of consumers online and 95 per cent of major media companies broadcasting on the

Internet, e-commerce is a game with a lot at stake and few rules (Pham, 2000).

In 1987, the Motion Picture Experts Group (MPEG) of the Geneva-based International Organization for Standardization began looking into ways to compress digital video, resulting in the 1992 MPEG format, whose Layer-3 version gives it the well-known MP3 moniker. So, even though patents on software systems designed to broadcast movies on the Internet were issued in the US in the early 1990s (like Scott Sander and Arthur Hair's 'Method for Transmitting a Desired Digital Video or Audio Signal' that became the basis for their sight-sound.com Website), Hollywood only took serious note as a recent spate of Internet piracy put over sixty films, including *The Phantom Menace*, online. May and June 1999 were busy months for Lucasfilm Ltd and their new partners at the FBI and Justice. With the additional cooperation of the MPA, Lucasfilm shut down more than 300 Internet sites offering pirated copies of its latest *Star Wars* instalment. Counterfeit versions of the film were available in Malaysia two days after its 19 May 1999 release in America, a few days later in Hong Kong with Chinese-language jackets (for the equivalent of less than US$3) courtesy of one of four CD printing machines in Hong Kong capable of producing 20,000 discs per day *each* (Michael, 1999). Filmed with a camcorder in a US theatre, this version was quickly supplanted by copies made from a film print stolen from a Wisconsin theatre. Digital piracy's shadow politics of distribution honoured *The Phantom Menace* as the first feature to be downloaded illegally in the UK from servers in Eastern Europe.

The hiring of a former digital scanning and imaging company executive to the post of Chief Technology Officer reflects the MPA's mandate for 'creating technical standards for the digital transmission and distribution of films' and safeguarding against digital piracy ('MPA Appoints', 1999). In creating its own Internet investigative unit, the MPA enforces Valenti's recent mandate that the 'defeat of earthbound and cyberspace thieves is my highest priority in the 21st Century' ('Clarity', 1999). The development of new encryption models and invisible watermarking reflects Hollywood's acknowledgment of the proliferation of Internet piracy in ancillary industries.

Following strong lobbying by the MPA and the Consumer Electronics Manufacturers Association for a digital anti-copying bill to protect the 'sanctity of copyright', Congress began to take a number of measures. After passing the No Electronic Theft Act in 1997, it passed the Digital Millennium Copyright Act (DMCA) in summer 1998, which more fully implements the provisions of The World IP Organization Treaties signed in Geneva in late 1996. The DMCA is a special copyright law, outside the main Federal Copyright Act, designed to provide legal coverage for new digital technologies. It contains an 'anti-circumvention provision' that prohibits the distribution of devices that crack copyright encryption, the exoneration of on-line service providers for copyright infractions committed on their system by subscribers, and a codification of penalties and prison terms for convicted infringers. The anti-circumvention statute was designed by the US Congress to ban the distribution of 'black boxes' that might promote piracy of copyright works. But as Pamela Samuelson suggests, 'the ban is far broader than this and threatens to bring about a flood of litigation challenging a broad range of technologies, even where there is no proof that the technologies have or realistically would be widely used to enable piracy' (1999: 563–64). At the most basic level, the DMCA gives the keys to corporate tracking technologies to open the door to your PC in attempts to ascertain whether or not an infringing use is taking place.

Making new law in the digital environment is difficult. Updating older forms of IP protection to cover new technologies is even harder. Hollywood's acknowledgment of this difficulty has resulted in some curious policy initiatives. The MPAA's take on digital piracy debates in the US Congress is to create provisions that might form the basis for infringement claims rather than go after enforcement immediately. As Valenti puts it, 'we're saying that the two issues – copyright protection and copyright enforcement – shouldn't be umbilically attached' (quoted in Machan, 1997). The divergent forms of address manifest the difficulty in 'signifying' the Internet, which has so many possible uses for Hollywood. The Internet is simultaneously a delivery conduit and an exhibition site, a distribution philosophy, a content gathering and talent differentiating device, an advertising platform, and a globally linked network of copying machines. Even the act of downloading visual media can mean a number of different, simultaneous money-making schemes for Hollywood, from being a sale (the Internet as a point-of-purchase) to a broadcast (the Internet as transmitter technology) to a mechanical copy (the Internet as a copy-clearance centre) (see Mann, 2000).

The MPA's digital initiatives stress the economic eradication of geographic space alongside its reterritorialisation. Valenti notes that 'the fury of the future is already upon us. The explosion of channel capacity, the hurling to homes by direct satellite, the multiplicity of optic fiber, among other magic, are the new centurions of the digital age, marching over continents and across geographic borders, breaking down artificial government barriers, the most powerful audiovisual armies ever known' ('Quo Vadis?', 1996). However, in calling copyright officials 'guardians at the gates', who 'build barricades tight and strong to defend the sanctity of copyright',[1] Valenti seems to engage characteristically contradictory forms of institutional address ('With a Wild', 1996). The Internet is a spatial force that is both *centripetal*, in that it preserves gates and barriers, and *centrifugal*, in that it hurls us into new relations between producers and consumers. The MPA has been able to resolve the centrifugal and centripetal spatialisations of digital technology by engaging the historicity of 'authorial genius' that is *morally* free from being bound to a national site. The author as a legal/economic hybrid, what David Saunders and Ian Hunter call a 'monstrous contingency', has its roots in the very formation of copyright law (1991: 485; see also Foucault, 1977). In another instance of his mytho-poetic rhetoric, Valenti (1998) notes that 'IP which leaps full blown and imagined from the brain pan of creative talent is antagonistic to artificial barriers, defies regulation, and resists official definition'. This articulation of authorship – a rhetorical swipe at the division of cultural labour – has been invoked for the past two hundred years or so whenever geographic fragmentation offered a conduit for flexible accumulation.

Driven by the exigencies of establishing an international market for literary works and redefining the dimensions of book publishing, the nineteenth-century internationalisation of copyright was part of the drive to create a world market by overcoming spatial and temporal barriers that might impede the turnover of publishing capital (Feltes, 1994). In addition to the regulation of international publishing, by the late nineteenth century, the 'creation of indigenous national producers seemed to have acquired importance as an exportable product and the source of cultural legitimacy', the economic incentive of a national literary patrimony (a 'national literature') that could be legitimated through its export to other states (Saunders, 1992: 171). Nations differed in their respective domestic articulations of authorial domicile. Some used territoriality as the threshold definition of authorial rights, others adopted a citizenship criterion. But the primary motivations behind internationalisation were curtailing literary property piracy and codifying a universalist notion of authorship. Consider, for example, the Swiss government's boosterist invitation to 'all civilised nations' to join a new international copyright convention in 1883, and recall Valenti's rhetoric above: 'It is, in fact, in the nature of things that the work of man's genius, once it has seen the light, can no longer be restricted to one country and to one nationality. If it possesses any value, it is not long in spreading itself in all countries, under forms which may vary more or less, but which, however, leave in its essence and its principal manifestations the creative idea' (Ricketson, 1987: 54).[2]

If this history shows that that 'genius' is free to roam in the supranational, it benefits also from spatial restriction. Copyright's historical roots in the reconceptualisation of land as 'the paradigm of alienable, marketable property' in the eighteenth century make the relationship between land and author clear. The first English copyright statutes take advantage of the 'transformation of land into the model against which other types of interests were analogized or compared to assess market value' (Aoki, 1996: 1327). Referring to what he calls 'the invasion of the copyright snatchers', Valenti admits that digital piracy takes advantage of a redefined 'IP landscape where there are no protective signs that warn intruders: "THIS IS PRIVATE COPYRIGHTED PROPERTY" ' (quoted in 'Protecting America's', 1998).

The courts in the US have circumscribed the protective materiality of digital data. Through a number of cases dating back to 1993, the courts have affirmed that the right of reproduction contained in copyright law is subject to infringement when a digital copy is stored in a computer's memory (Sullivan, 1996). Anticipating the direct digital distribution of films over the Internet or on digital television set-top boxes, Hollywood has recently teamed up with computer manufacturers like IBM to develop rights-protection technology that uses unique serial numbers on recordable media to create single encryption keys, ensuring that downloaded material can only be saved to a single source. In a troubling gesture that sends shivers down the spine of free-software and privacy advocates alike, the MPAA's current technical officer maintains that this technology will extend to hard drives, so that 'copy-once protection technology goes beyond just a pay-per-view business model to a pay-per-copy business model' (Chmielewski, 2000). Thus Hollywood is revisiting the sealed-set hardware innovation of commercial radio that made the medium a technology of reception rather than relay.

As distribution begins to acknowledge the ever-increasing curve of duplication technology, IP in film will take on issues more traditionally associated with software law. However, the legal terrain in software protection is harrowing indeed. Do computer games, for example, meet the criteria for 'aesthetic representation' maintained by a number of countries; does interactivity render obsolete the traditional notion of an authorial right? In France, a bastion of support for authorial rights, new software provisions in national copyright law resemble the 'work for hire' doctrine of US copyright law, where the employer gains 'all the rights' of an 'author' working under their contract (McColley, 1997). Some countries have drawn up 'composite work' criteria, with different aspects of the same media object protected under a number of IP provisions (which means that the musical score and still images in a video game are protected under separate criteria). The accreting logic of legal protection is designed, of course, to limit access to the design playing-field. Furthermore, the countries which Hollywood pursues for IP harmonisation are also high on the software piracy list; for example, China is accused by the Software Publishers Association of selling US$1.5 billion in pirated business software in 1997 via 'compilation CD-ROMS' (which contain tens of thousands of dollars of retail business software) selling for under US$10. In the Philippines, an estimated 80 per cent of business software is pirated, with government offices the major culprits (Tanzer, 1998).

Studying the contexts of legal and cultural history can help us understand these forms of image duplication and the audiences that are constituted by them. For example, a case in the US in the late 1960s (*Williams and Wilkins Co. v. The United States*) was brought on by the use of the new Xerox copying technology that allowed libraries to keep photocopies of journals in their collection without compensating the publisher. The subsequent development of copyright clearance houses and the establishment of small licensing fees for photocopies may set the precedent for digital film downloading and transformations after the model of fair use, since such copying technologies allow for the creation of derivative works. Copying and creativity would converge as forms of digital use. Barring this radical redefinition of reception – which begins with a foundational acceptance of fair use rather than its invocation as a pothole in the road to full commercial exploitation of the work – Hollywood might borrow the blanket licensing models of the American Society of Composers, Authors and Publishers in order to generate and track royalty revenue for each download. Integrated digital systems designed for on-line transactions and the generation of customer databases for profiling purposes are also a means of implementing technological and price restrictions on uses of copyrighted works (Cohen, 1996: 984).

'Trusted system' technology, designed to track a work via the implementation of digital property rights language, is in development at places like IBM and Xerox. Forms of trusted system hardware might look and feel like a normal duplication platform (e.g., a printer, a VCR, a stereo) but would have the capability to implement a copyright holder's restrictions over usage in a number of arenas: rendering (to play, print or export media via the translation of digital code to a usable form); transportation (to copy, transfer or lend digital works among other trusted systems); and derivation (to extract, edit or embed a copyrighted work in a derivative usage). Along with the implementation of digital watermarking technologies, trusted system technology allows a tremendous level of control over the use of digital works (Gimbel, 1998: 1677–1680). While it was once commonly understood that the information commodity 'can never be endowed with real scarcity, since its most important quality is its inexhaustible reproducibility' (Frow, 1997: 188), the techno-bureaucratic management of film via pro-scarcity measures threatens and imposition of complex methods utopian visions of democracy.

When Norwegian teenager Jon Johansen and two other friends wrote a program that descrambled the anti-piracy Contents Scrambling System (CSS), which Hollywood encrypts on DVDs, and posted it on the Internet, they incurred the MPAA's wrath. And after the Web magazine *2600: The Hacker Quarterly* posted the descrambling software (called DeCSS) on its Website, Hollywood sued under new DMCA guidelines. Interestingly, those same issues of creativity and originality came to bear when a computer scientist claimed on the witness stand that 'if the court upholds this injunction, what would happen is that certain uses of computer language – my preferred means of expression – would be illegal' (Harmon, 2000). Copyright and the US Constitution's First Amendment guarantees of free speech come together when computer code is deemed a form of personal expression. In the DeCSS case, a US District Court judge denied the protection of computer code as a form of speech, noting that 'computer code is not purely expressive any more than the assassination of a political leader is purely a political statement'. How are such forms of expression to be weighed against more traditional forms of IP, such as copyright, which secure the expressive content of the owner? Cognisant of shifts in determinations of expressivity, the MPA's Director of Legal Affairs notes that 'this case is not about infringement of copyright, but about the illegal tracking in the device (code) that makes illegal copies' (Alexander, 2000). Nevertheless, copies of DeCSS are available from Internet sites based in the Czech Republic, Finland, Russia, Slovenia, Israel, Greece and Mexico (VerSteeg 2000: 12A).

In an effort to address the commercial possibilities of digital distribution with the attendant forms of high-fidelity piracy, the MPA along with the US government is attempting to extend TRIPS-related protections while the ink is barely dry on its signatory pages. At the 1996 World IP Conference in Geneva, US negotiators outlined a possible future for copyright in the global information society. Although its most strongly worded policy suggestions were derailed (the WIPO has always been aligned with relatively Third World friendly organisations like UNESCO and UNCTAD), the negotiators worked towards draft language that would find powerful proponents in both the US copyright industries and within the government (and possibly for future WTO/GATS accords, which are much more closely aligned to the IMF and the World Bank). Arguing for the protection for temporary reproductions of copyrighted works in a private PC's random access memory (therefore treating digital *transmissions* as distribution *copies*), the US team upheld President Clinton's Information Infrastructure Task Force's 1995 White Paper which 'deprived the public of the "first sale rights" it had long enjoyed in the print world . . . [and conceived of] electronic forwarding as a violation of both the reproduction and distribution rights of copyright law' (Samuelson, 1996: 136). The 'first-sale' statute, guaranteed by Section 109(a) of the US Copyright Act of 1976, reaffirmed that the purchaser of a particular work is entitled, without the permission of the copyright owner, 'to sell or otherwise dispose of the possession of that copy'; while copyright owners had struggled against the statute for years, it nevertheless prevented movie studios from claiming a royalty on video rentals, or book/record owners from claiming a royalty on copies loaned from a public library. In conceptualising the distribution of digital works as inherently a form of copying, the US WIPO team subtly sidestepped the first-sale restrictions. The drafters of copyright's digital initiatives could therefore argue for an elimination of fair-use rights wherever a licensed use was possible as well as buttress their demands for encrypted tracking software designed to police the use of digital media (Samuelson, 1996: 136).

The US characterises digital transmission as the distribution of copies because it is necessary to copy a digital work in order to reproduce it. This makes such transfers amenable to copyright protection. It is part of a larger agenda at the WIPO to limit user rights and curtail 'fair use and kindred privileges under which private or personal copying of protected works has often found shelter' (Samuelson, 1997: 398). This stance has effectively rolled back fair-use precepts upheld by US courts that allowed private videotaping of audiovisual programming in the early 1980s. Here we find the savvy corporate owners of copyright using the distinctive technology of the digital against itself, since one must copy a text in order to read it (i.e., materialise in some new way, even as signals in RAM). Conveniently, 'copyright's legal threshold of originality is a simple requirement of creation *without* any copying' (Litman, 1990: 1000). Infringement is assimilable to every act of reception – the 'transient reproduction in use' addressed by the US at the WIPO. Every act of digital reading is, therefore, an act of copying. As the President of the US Consumer Electronics Association recently put it, 'if the content industry has its way, the "play" button will become the "pay" button' (Snider, 2001: 1D). For example, say you watch a movie (accessed *legally* from a studio Website) on your computer. While it plays, parts of it are stored within your PC's random access memory, and because a copy (of sorts) is being created, the studio has the right to make sure that you are not circumventing its encrypted rights management software, something that it can only do by entering the domain of your PC. Privacy evaporates in a puff of logic. While such scenarios are the stuff of Internet activists, making sure that digital media receive *greater* protection than traditional forms of media is the heady stuff of neo-liberal policy advocates. The current GATS negotiations are designed to outmanoeuvre European cultural exemptions through liberalisation of on-line services. Under liberalisation, the MPA is fully poised to enter the European new communications services markets and will 'challenge the EC's freedom to maneuver and regulate emerging services due to their massive economic potential' (Wheeler, 2000: 258). In a globalised digital environment, where the WTO guarantees that customs duties will not be levied on electronic transmissions, and the US leads the way in 'the creation of a market-driven policy architecture for this new digital economy' (US Government, 1998: 30), the danger looms that the neo-classical tenets of copyright (fundamental to the prioritisation of IP's economic imperative) will overwhelm protections of the public domain and free use.

Conclusion

As the Internet and forms of digital duplication technology continue to disarticulate the geographic sensitivities of the MPA, regulation and enforcement policies recapitulate the spatial imperative of corporate capital. Clifford Schultz and Bill Saporito (1996) suggest that there are a number of available strategies for IP protection, which proceed in a hierarchical scale (i.e., try the first, and with its gains, move to the second); 'grin and bear it' and trust in the mythic levelling 'even hand' of capitalism; co-opt offenders and offer them legitimate business opportunities; educate the public; eradicate demand for piracy through advertising; erect investigative and surveillance procedures; engineer high-tech labelling and embedded anti-piracy technologies; create a constantly evolving product; lobby for IP legislation; build coalitions with international organisations, foreign governments and local enforcement agencies; then cede certain sectors of the industry. The priority of IP control is manifested in the recent proliferation of alliances and mergers in the media trade (e.g., the link of Dreamworks to Microsoft and the formation of AOL-Time Warner). These transformations allow content producers to gain access to digital information pipelines without compromising their IP (see Bettig, 1997). How this will live alongside Hollywood's attempt to enter hitherto hostile digital IP terrain is unclear, but such NICL-influenced convergence strategies for the consolidation of creative workforces – rationalised through the 'vertical integration of new production with inventory management of owned information' (Benkler, 1999: 401) – move in the inexorable direction of the further privatisation and enclosure of information production.

At the beginning of this chapter, we raised the thorny question of whether Hollywood should acknowledge piracy as a viable form of film distribution. In the Conclusion, we maintain that cultural policy should reformulate traditional forms of IP ownership in recognition of the proliferate status of media *readerships*. This means that, along with fracturing the singularity of authors, policy should recognise the multiplicity of readers. As John Hartley notes, reading is not a 'solitary, individualist, consumptive, supplementary act of silent subjection to a series of imperial graphic impressions'. Contrary to such an epiphenomenal delineation, reading is 'a social, communal, productive, act of writing, a dialogic process which is so fundamental to (and may even *be*) popular culture' (Hartley, 1996: 51). There is little doubt that the sheer proliferation of digital replication ensures that the MPA make use of piracy's powerfully signifying vernacular – culture everywhere just wants to be free. At the same time, as it tries to extend its markets into places where it has traditionally played as a minority culture – and coincidentally markets that house almost a half of the globe – Hollywood will have to be more innovative about disentangling media from proprietary ownership and understand the differences in these new markets. Borrowing from observations made during the aforementioned Sony case, Hollywood might recognise that piracy has forms of fair use in areas where traditional forms of distribution/exhibition result in market failure. In markets such as India and China, where structural and socio-economic factors impede the 'legitimate' distribution of Hollywood, provisional fair use might be extended to piracy for three reasons: market flaws are present; transfer of use is socially and economically desirable (it creates the cultures of anticipation that buttress Hollywood's merchandising markets); and substantial economic injury is not really a factor (Gordon, 1982: 1614). Of course, Hollywood and its representatives in the USTA would be the first to 'Yank' such provisional fair-use privileges once the market became profitable. With the advent of new digital technologies, international IP law and attendant public policy might structure textual ownership across a more variegated terrain rather than yoking it to antiquated and dubious notions of singular authorial genius. For example, taxation and licensing schemes, horizontal private law and centralised purchasing relationships 'might be preferable to a strong interference from the state in the shape of the vertical relationships' established by traditional copyright (Van der Merwe, 1999: 313). Ultimately though, something much stronger and more fundamental must take place. With the explosive interrelation of convergence and diversification engendered by new forms of distribution and duplication technology, *ordinary consumers' rights* are going to have to be taken more seriously – with their reception practices recognised as forms of creative labour: 'moves in a conversation rather than as endpoints for the delivery of product' (Benkler, 2000: 564). We address this in greater detail in our conclusion. For now, we note that cultural policy might even begin by asking people what *they* want out of the audiovisual media. Of course, Hollywood has been doing that for a while. The next two chapters show how.

Notes

1   Carey Heckman, co-director of the Stanford Law and Technology Policy Center, compares the new Internet copyright issues to the barbed wiring that attended new property rights on open territory in the Wild West at the turn of the nineteenth century. See Jonathan Rabinovitz, 'Internet Becomes New Frontier in Copyright Battles', *San Jose Mercury News* (7 Nov. 1999). Indeed, Westerns provide the gun-slinging with a lingua franca, since the MPA offers a whistle-blowing reward programme called 'The Bounty for Pirates Program', which allows those concerned with combating the civic evils of copyright violation – a 'cancer that cheats the consumer, as Valenti puts it – to pursue temporary deputation under the legal aegis of the MPAA (quoted in MPAA press release, 'Almost 18,000 Pirate Videos Seized Nationwide', 8 February 1995). Piracy is a form of contagion in the rhetoric of the MPAA, a

'cancer', illegal video disc plants in China are 'the cancerous core of piracy problems', producing 'poisoned product'; piracy is the 'cancer in the belly of global business', a 'toxin for which there is no known cure' except stronger legislation, penalties and national resolve (MPAA press releases: 'Valenti Announces Enhanced MPAA/VSDA Anti-Piracy Hotline', 21 May 1995; 'Valenti Testimony Before the Senate Subcommittee on East Asian and Pacific Affairs', 29 Nov. 1995; 'Quo Vadis', 23 May 1996).

2   International copyright law originates in the years immediately following the French revolution, when French national law made no distinctions between French and foreign authors and freely granted French copyright to foreign works. Such reciprocity, it was hoped, might engender similar protection of French works in other nations. But underlying this reciprocity was the idealism of a burgeoning modernism, deployed in the push towards unilaterality. A universal law of copyright would *transcend* nationality and territoriality, and would, as Sam Ricketson notes: 'accord directly with the conception of the author's natural right of property in his work, existing independently of, and prior to, the formal rules and sanctions of positive law and admitting no artificial restrictions such as a limited term or protection or national boundaries' (1987: 40).

Chapter Five
Distribution, Marketing and Exhibition

FBI + CIA = TWA + Pan Am
> (Graffito written by Eve Democracy in Jean-Luc Godard's *One + One*)

Commodities elicit desire by wooing consumers, smelling, sounding, tasting or looking nice in ways that are borrowed from romantic love but then reverse that relationship: people learn about correct forms of romantic love *from* the commodities themselves (Haug, 1986: 14, 17, 19). The term 'commodity aesthetics' covers the division between what commodities promise (pleasure) and what animates them (profit) (Haug, 1986: 35). At the 1913 meeting of the US National Association of Advertisers, an electric sign emblazoned 'TRUTH' in letters ten-feet high – a provocation in an industry built on mendacity in labelling. The meeting produced the 'Baltimore Truth Declaration', a code of conduct that specified and denounced misleading advertising. This commitment to truth as a productive force and a banner for the industries of persuasion was two-sided. It combined an internal uncertainty – what was 'true' in a rapidly changing world characterised by competing definitions of need and agency – with an external anxiety: the state might intervene in the Association's business via unwelcome regulation (Lears, 1983: 20). That shift, between self-governance and public governance of the popular, is the key to Hollywood marketing as it has emerged from this most North American of industries.

As we have seen, many reasons are advanced for the supremacy of Hollywood cinema worldwide: superior production values, cartel conduct, cultural imperialism manufacturing the transfer of taste rather than technology or investment, and American sign-value as the epicentre of transcendental modernity – fixing social and individual problems via love, sex and commodities.

Pace Godard and the quotation that begins this chapter, we have avoided simple equations that explain Hollywood's power and instead have endeavoured to rethink this power as contingent on Hollywood's contestable control of the NICL, which is sustained via the exploitation of national cultural labour markets, replication through international co-production of a business culture benefit Hollywood, and the application and enforcement of intellectual property rights as a coercive strategy in pro-Hollywood screen trade. In this chapter, we address the fourth and most prosaic set of processes and practices that have enabled Hollywood to exert control over the conditions and possibilities of cultural labour – selling.

Hollywood has experienced four phases of ownership and concentration in marketing, distribution and exhibition. In the period to 1948, there was intense integration of the exhibition business with production and distribution. US theatres were mostly located in lucrative urban markets and showed whatever their studios made, so there was less need for the organised and aggressive promotion of films we see today. This was followed by a decade of divestiture as per a consent decree with anti-trust Federal forces. Distribution became the locus of industry power, and film marketing began its inexorable move to the centre of industry activities. Television arrived to compete for film audiences, and technical innovations including widescreen, 3-D and other gimmicks surfaced as marketing ploys. Increasing consolidation occurred from that point until the 1980s, since which time deregulation has led to reintegration (Steinbock, 1995: 109–10).

Except for a brief period in the 1960s when the majors flirted with experimentation and director-driven films, an ethos of risk aversion turned them towards such strategies as repeated use of formulae, sequels, the event film, and 'bankable' stars, directors and writers (Litman, 1998: 26; Wyatt, 1994: 69–94). These risk reduction strategies did not eliminate risk; they were merely symptoms of the growing frenzy that 'demand uncertainty' had created in the Hollywood business culture (Litman and Ahn, 1998: 173). Nevertheless, structural uncertainty began to draw increased investment in marketing and audience research in the 1970s. Hollywood had become 'an industry town dominated by media conglomerates more comfortable with MBAs than with movie moguls. The new breed of studio executive already spoke the language of market research. Several marketing firms moved to Hollywood to take advantage of what promised to be a booming business opportunity' ('Lerner', 1999: 18). Marketing took firm hold of global Hollywood in the Reaganite 1980s. By then, marketers had spread throughout the industry in 'bureaucratic layers' of the distribution sector (Litman, 1998: 24), which already formed dense occupational sediment within the NICL comprised of 'accountants, sales personnel, warehouse managers and others' (Moran, 1996: 2). As Albert Moran (1996) observes, distribution workers are 'low on glamour' and invisible to the public, even though they labour everywhere in global Hollywood, from national to global distribution in theatrical and subsidiary markets for pay cable, pay-per-view, commercial television and home video.

The US studios operate vertically integrated networks of distribution, utilising the massive domestic television market to ensure fast returns on investment, even from its multiple failures in hard-top exhibition. Each major studio and most big so-called independents have output arrangements with associated distributors that mean one-third of production costs will be returned no matter what. United International Pictures (UIP), Fox, Warner Bros., Buena Vista (Disney) and Columbia (Sony) all operate in this manner. In the US, distribution is basically an oligopoly, whereas the rest of the world is somewhat splintered (World Trade Organization, 1998). Warner Bros., Fox and Columbia TriStar have their own international distribution networks. Other studios operate joint ventures. UIP, which has been subject to cartel investigations by the EU, released for MGM, Paramount and Universal until MGM left for Fox International. In Canada, distributors collude to assist multinational multiplex owners, while in Spain there is not a single national distributor that is not a subsidiary of a Hollywood major (Durie *et al.*, 2000: 87; Short, 1997; Moerk, 2000; 'Canada Probes', 2000). Both domestically and abroad, distribution is massively concentrated (Litman, 1998: 22–23).

A good example of this concentrated power over a nation's cultural curriculum comes from the notable British film *Riff-Raff* (Ken Loach, 1990), which was doing a roaring trade locally until the exhibitor was required by a distributor to displace it with *Backdraft* (Ron Howard, 1991), which was already a spectacular failure in the US and continued that way elsewhere. Angus Finney (1996: 70, 140–41, 145) reports that *Damage* (Louis Malle, 1993) was removed from a theatre in Britain after a week, having broken all box-office records, in favour of pre-booked US material. And consider *The Full Monty*, which posted phenomenal sales figures and was nominated for an Academy Award for Best Picture. Is its success attributable to the fact that the British suddenly, magically, made a commercial film? No, all this depended on Fox's decision to release the picture. The holy grail of worldwide release by a US distributor guaranteed an audience and fair play for the appeal of the text. In the UK, *The Full Monty* was the kind of film – an account of bleak post-industrial Northern disemployment – that people would generally have to travel fifty miles to see. But the multiplex exposure brought by Fox amounted to hundreds of screens across the country. The film's producer, Uberto Pasolini, puts it like this:

> Distribution, distribution, distribution – that's the issue . . . the whole business of people saying to European producers that you just need to make films audiences want to see is complete crap. There are American movies that should not be in 100 theatres, ghastly movies with terrible reviews that no one cares about, but because a major has the muscle they get them onto those screens.   (Pasolini, quoted in Dawtrey, 1997: 9)

Distribution is similarly important in the video market, which has undergone tremendous consolidation since the end of the 1990s. Here, majors purchase rights to video distribution and vend tapes to retailers, mostly rental stores. For example, Universal is the wholesale distributor in the US video market for DreamWorks, Lion's Gate and Playboy. Artisan distributes Hallmark Entertainment, Trimark, Family Home Video and others. Warner distributes New Line and is scheduled to take its turn as Dreamworks' distributor in 2002. MGM distributes its own video products, but uses Warner's shipping facilities. Whereas home video distributors are wholesalers, theatrical distributors become, in effect, producers once 'their' product has entered the video stage of its life, at which point, they are magically transformed into manufacturers and suppliers with rights to the title that formerly belonged to producers (Wasko, 1994: 138, 140). Smaller producers benefit from selling a percentage of their film to major video distributors via overall savings on distribution costs and the boost their products receive from the majors' scale economy in manufacturing, shipping, marketing, sales force, trademark advantage and, in the case of selling to major retailers, being bundled with 'A' titles in order to capture shelf space.[1] But even that level of distinction between the creative production process and the middle-person mundanity of distribution is misleading. For very early on in the life of a film, it may obtain financing through a pre-sale, whereby distributors are sufficiently taken with a proposal that they guarantee to pass it on via exhibition deals already struck or likely to be so.

With the advent of Internet distribution, or so-called video on demand, the major studios will probably distribute films through in-house servers in order to avoid piracy, to reduce costs while achieving a direct link to audiences for surveillance purposes (see Chapter 6), and to defend their position as principal distributors in home entertainment against competing pay-TV and video rental services (Peers, 2001; Mathews, 2001). By 2001, Sony, Disney and Warner Bros. had begun video on demand projects, and experiments were underway at hardware firms (as we saw in Chapter 4) and at Miramax and several US Internet companies, using encryption technology that made pay-per-download films uncopyable and, after twenty-four hours, unplayable. They were designed to prohibit downloading in countries with distribution restrictions (Arthur, 2001). Such experiments suggest that Internet distribution will supersede pay-TV and video, as happened in the pornography industry, though theatrical distribution should survive this technology shift, just as it weathered the impact of television and video recorders (Moore, 2000: 202–5).

The Conditions of Film Marketing

Viacom boss Sumner Redstone recently told Bill Kartozian, president of the National Association of Theatre Owners, that he had a special formula for reducing film production spending. 'We're not going to make any more bad movies,' he said.

('Hollywood's Incredible Turkey Machine', 1999)

International theatrical distribution is very expensive, due to the cost of prints, advertisements and labour – the multiple media and sites necessitate a huge bureaucracy. Yet as production costs continue to rise for Hollywood films, the relative cost of the physical distribution cycle (both legal and illegal) is declining. This is specially the case for the highly capitalised and integrated entertainment conglomerates that own Hollywood studios, because they are structured to cross-subsidise failures and risks from various media businesses and ensure cash flow, and can coordinate marketing across territories in order to cut the cost of market research and promotional activities (Durie *et al.*, 2000: 89–90; Litman, 1998: 24). At the same time, the cost of distribution spent on marketing films has been spiralling, to the point of becoming a 'drain on profits' (Litman, 1998: 59). The film industry invests on average nearly twice as much money in marketing activities as do other comparable industries. According to *Advertising Age*, if major film studios, including Dreamworks and MGM/UA, were lumped together as a single brand category, their 1999 advertising expenditure of US$2.55 billion would have placed them third in cost after the automotive and retail industries (Endicott, 2000: S12). Hollywood's average costs of promotion increased from US$19.8 million in 1996 to US$22.2 million in 1997 as a means of differentiation from other industries and national cinemas (European Audiovisual Observatory, 1998).

Initially, marketing expenditures on film promotion grow because price competition is not a factor in the business of gaining market share, as in the case of the first-run US theatrical film market. Under these circumstances, rival firms compete through marketing campaigns to differentiate their films from their competitors. Marketing costs escalate when an oligopoly of five or six firms controls the film distribution market using expensive marketing campaigns to beat their rivals and hold back new competitors, as they collectively build and maintain what economists call a 'product differentiation barrier to entry' (Litman, 1998: 277, 59). A product differentiation barrier to entry can be understood as the accumulation over time of consumer preferences (Hoskins *et al.*, 1997: 61). The so-called 'accumulative preference' of consumers builds on such advertising clichés as 'from the creative genius of Walt Disney', or 'from the producers of *Titanic*'. This gives the majors a hypothetical monopoly of filmgoer awareness. But 'accumulative preference' alone does not sustain Hollywood's hegemony or justify the cost of marketing.

First, the risk-reduction strategy of the slate finds the studios making vast numbers of pictures, predicated on the correct assumption that they know absolutely nothing about audience tastes and that approximately 95 per cent of films will fail abysmally. No other filmmaking economy has sufficient capital formation to embark on such a high-risk strategy. This scale economy creates a barrier of entry for competition in distribution, which makes it possible to force foreign exhibitors to engage in block-booking – you only get the Spiel-berg film if you take the Jean-Claude Van Damme movie. Second, scale necessitates a large multifaceted marketing structure to ensure that product dif-ferentiation is ongoing and systematic. This involves a massive sales effort for particular films, using the conventional tools of marketing: advertising, pro-motions, retailing logistics/distribution, innovation and product design. But it also entails expanded tasks of advocacy (corporate advertising, public relations and political lobbying – see below) and, because they know nothing about audi-ences, extensive surveillance (consumer 'behaviour' and audience and market research – see Chapter 6). Finally, it helps to remember that imminent market failure is not a dirty little secret known only to economists; it is fundamental to the dominant business philosophy in Hollywood. The scale of anxiety involved in the filmmaking business provokes an extraordinary need for the rit-ualised use of marketing in all phases of a film's life. Barry Litman and Hoekyuhn Ahn (1998: 173) have suggested that the fear of making a movie without market knowledge is akin to the fear of building a skyscraper only to find out on the day it opened that nobody liked it. With the stakes so high, it is no surprise that, as one former marketing executive put it, a 'marketing cam-paign is tackled with the same zeal and methodical planning as a general preparing an invasion' (Lukk, 1997: ix).

Vast sums of money thus channel into film marketing for reasons (and irra-tionalities) that go beyond the conventional promotional work of building 'accumulative preference' for major distributors: it consoles movie executives who live with the risk of box-office failure; it systematises the competitive prod-uct differentiation barrier under conditions of oligopoly; it regulates populations of moviegoers using consumer surveillance operations; and, through its advocacy work, it promotes positive associations with the Holly-wood distribution cartel generally. Fundamentally, the persistent and growing investment in marketing reinforces the majors' existing scale economy barrier to the entry of new competitors in film distribution worldwide (cf. Hoskins *et al.*, 1997: 61–62).

On a structural level, then, increasingly costly film marketing safeguards the major distributors' market power and Hollywood's hegemony. Only in theory can any number of smaller specialty and B-movie distributors use marketing to challenge the majors. In practice, competitive marketing now requires investments on a scale beyond the reach of smaller distributors everywhere. In fact, chipping away at the majors' 75 to 85 per cent market share in the US alone can mean spending more on *marketing* than *making* a movie. That is why Gramercy Pictures paid twice the production costs of *Four Weddings and a Funeral* to market that film in the US (Lukk, 1997). Of course, Gramercy was a joint venture of Polygram Film Entertainment and Universal Pictures, which kept the reassuring jingle of deep pockets within earshot of this specialty distributor. Finally, with the accelerated capitalisation and organisational reach of film marketing, marketers have scaled up the authorship ladder to occupy a strategic position inside global Hollywood's screen machine.

Textual Gatekeepers: Positioning, Playability, Marketability

> British filmmakers need to learn that great quality doesn't guarantee box-office success. [T]hey should add a dash of focus group and polling, and be prepared to change their product if necessary – just as the major Hollywood studios do. Either that, or keep their integrity and stay poor.
>
> (Darius Sanai, 1999: 12)

For anybody thinking about going to the movies, promotional marketing first appears as a service. Every advertisement, film review and publicity event provides information upon which to make a decision about what to see. In a sense, marketing information appears to reduce everyday risks associated with spending money. After all, you cannot try out a film before paying to see it, as you would with a pullover in a department store. So you might say that film marketing is an informational gift that helps you to make a rational ticket purchase under circumstances that actually force you to do something very irrational – namely, to buy a product sight unseen. Yet it should be obvious by now that marketing is not in the business of consumer protection. Marketers do not work for you, and their clients certainly do not wish you to make an independent decision about how to spend your money. Marketers and marketing executives play a strategic, gate-keeping role for Hollywood, blessing only those film projects with commercial potential and marketability and making sure those films get to the advertisements and theatres nearest you.

The biggest barriers to entry that filmmakers from outside the US face today in global Hollywood are marketers (Lukk, 1997: x-xi). Marketers read stories and watch movies differently from most people. They scan screen and page for elements called positioning and playability, which give them a way to make sense of a film project's US commercial potential. Positioning is not about a film's setting or exhibition, but what marketers want to 'do to the mind of the prospect'. That is, they 'position the product in the mind of the prospect' (Ries and Trout, 1981: 2). The inventors of the positioning concept tell us that its 'basic approach ... is not to create something new and different, but to manipulate what's already up there in the mind, to retie the connections that already exist' (Ries and Trout, 1981: 5). The mind of an audience, as a sales prospect, is conceived as an organ seeking simple answers in a cluttered information-entertainment market. 'The only defense a person has in our over-communicated society,' say Al Ries and Jack Trout (1981: 6), 'is an oversimplified mind.' Positioning a film to the oversimplified mind of the audience means finding story elements of a film that are easily communicated in simple terms. These are its selling points. Marketers mine stories and films for selling points that make positioning possible.

The marketing executives at Gramercy Pictures, for example, positioned *Four Weddings and a Funeral* in a variety of ways. For one probable audience, it was a story of 'two people who belong together but may never be'; to another, it was a story about friends going to humorous weddings and the funny things that happen to them. Positioning gets further simplified with the narrowing of these probable audiences into what marketers call segments. Segmentation sorts audiences into demographic pools for different positionings of the same film. *Four Weddings* was positioned for an 18- to 24-year-old segment as 'a comical look at the perils of being single', while the 25- to 34-year-old segment would see the film as 'an English-humor romantic comedy, a high concept expressed as Monty Python meets *Sleepless in Seattle*', and the 35 plus segment would come to 'a non-Shakespearean *Much Ado About Nothing*' (Lukk, 1997: 5). In similar fashion, each US film is allotted a hundred generic descriptions for use in specific markets. *Dances with Wolves* (Kevin Costner, 1990) was sold in France as a documentary-style dramatisation of Native American life, and *Malcolm X* (Spike Lee, 1991) was promoted there with posters of the Stars and Stripes aflame (Danan, 1995: 131–32, 137). Gérard Depardieu made it into *102 Dalmatians* (Kevin Dima, 2000), Michelle Yeoh into *Tomorrow Never Dies* and Tcheky Karyo into *The Patriot* to boost the films' appeal outside the US (Martin, 2000). International co-productions also cross-breed cultural preferences in order to position films on multiple national screens.

The arbitrary interpretations of positioning simplify the meanings of a film in order to appeal to the imaginary, simple impulses of distinct national audiences. If a film lacks selling points, positioning is still imperiously applied. Preview audiences either loved or walked out of *Pulp Fiction* (Quentin Tarantino, 1994). Those who said they liked it belonged to no clear marketing segment, which only meant one thing to the marketing geniuses at Miramax: 'it was different' and 'had something for everyone' ('Lerner', 1999: 18; Lukk, 1997: 22). For those executives, numerous positionings of *Pulp Fiction* (those who hated it were not counted) would be randomly assigned to the audience in upmarket, blue-collar and ethnic categories, each of which was subdivided further into geographical and age segments.

Obviously, such random guesswork can make a lot of blunders. Disney's Spanish-language version of *The Emperor's New Groove* (Mark Dindal, 2000) failed with Spanish-speaking audiences in the US, who went to see the English version instead. This unsuccessful attempt to cultivate a Latino audience (75 per cent of Latinos in the US do not go to the movies) via an apparently fail-safe positioning strategy was especially embarrassing for marketers in Los Angeles, where nearly half of all potential movie-goers are Latino/a. As a reporter for the Spanish news agency EFE noted, 'Hollywood just doesn't know how to address itself to this bilingual audience' ('Fracasa el Estreno Ultimo', 2001). *Waiting to Exhale* (Forest Whitaker, 1995) was first broadly positioned as a 'chick flick' (*sic*), but when that audience didn't show up it was retroactively repositioned for the segment that did, as 'an African-American chick-flick' (Lukk, 1997: 39). This 'discovery' had more to do with defending marketing's weak techniques than it did with identifying the mind of the middle-class US black filmgoer, for whom Hollywood began positioning one or two films per year.

Whereas positioning is about finding the right place to put a film in an audience's collective mind, playability is about predicting how satisfied that audience will be with the positioning. When it comes to determining a film's playability, marketers stop looking at the film and start conducting surveys, choosing to question people whose outward characteristics match those of an audience they suspect will be predisposed to like the movie or movie idea as positioned. This is where pre-tests, test screenings and tracking are important (for more on this, see Chapter 6). Test screenings and tracking are often used to gauge what marketers call the 'the overcome' and 'the want-to-see'. The overcome is a noun describing an obstacle in the way of clear positioning (Lukk, 1997: 85), as in 'we had a very difficult overcome with the audience for *Meshes in the Afternoon*' (Maya Deren and Alexander Hammid, 1943). Often pronounced 'the wannasee', this noun refers to the level of awareness and desire surrounding a particular movie, as in '*Titanic* had great wannasee' (Lukk, 1997: 8–9). The test of *Pulp Fiction*'s playability, which 'scored' well among US 'urban' and 'ethnic' audience segments, helped marketers build the movie's want-to-see. As one executive commented, the 'audience just went wild' when the trailer came on with the volume 'really pumped up' on the song 'Jungle Boogie' (quoted in Lukk, 1997: 26). He was referring to a trailer carrying an R-rating, itself a sign that is thought to position a film in the minds of audiences to action-adventure and thriller movies. The trailer also sought a position in baby-boomers' children's minds by combining clips of action sequences, always highly marketable elements, with a retro 1970s music track. Other ways of creating the want-to-see have surfaced in e-promotions that publicise new film releases via the Internet, which is thought to offer its own strong positioning capabilities. For example, the fantasy adventure *Lord of the Rings: The Fellowship of the Ring* (Peter Jackson, forthcoming) had the biggest one-day download of an Internet film promotion, with 1.6 million downloads, beating *Phantom Menace*'s previous record of 1 million ('New Line Cinema Verifies', 2000).

Marketability differs from a film's commercial potential (positioning and playability) because it is based on a marketer's calculation of all the elements of the film that can be used in promotion and advertising through trailers, posters, television, radio, magazines and the Internet. It is also based on a film's pre-sold fit with special cross-promotions involving retailers, fast-food restaurants and other entertainment media, especially recorded music. The larger the number of advertising-friendly elements – including a film's imagery, storyline, music, genre and stylisation – the greater the marketability (Wyatt, 1994; Lukk, 1997). From a marketer's perspective, a film might have high playability and great commercial potential but still lack marketability, a problem that confronted marketers of the documentary film *Hoop Dreams* (Steve James, 1994) (Lukk, 1997: 97).

Thus far we have seen how the appraisal of commercial potential (positioning and playability) and marketability is based on restrictive market criteria, and also how this process fosters a technical jargon that lends credibility, or at least a professional aura, to marketers' judgement and interpretation of a movie's value. Marketing's influence is not confined to post-production and release phases, however. Commercial potential and marketability are assessed *and* manipulated in a film's textual elements during pre-production and production, effectively merging distribution into production and blurring the old scalar and spatial divisions of this labour process.

Pre-production calculation and manipulation of marketability are done with an eye on both the level of interest in a film while it is still in production and the future tie-ins and cross-promotions of recorded music, fast food, video games, toys and other merchandising features that can be rendered into the production elements of a film's visual design. Often at this stage, the movie is no more than a title. For example, Disney's *Armageddon* was the name of a marketing concept for a film that had yet to be written (McChesney, 1999: 39). Even marketers have an ironic awareness of this trend in Hollywood. A recent television commercial for a soft drink famously mocked this process by portraying marketing executives designing every icky advertising and merchandising detail for a movie about a giant man-eating slug. The only thing left to do was make the actual film (Lowe & Partners, Sprite brand).

One well-known result of pre-planned marketability involves product placement (Wasko, 1994). Major distributors employ placement specialists and independent placement companies to ensure that 'Virtually everything you see [in a film], other than background stuff, is a negotiated deal' (Herman, 2000: 48). Some directors even try to get their favourite products into movies. There are about thirty-five product placement companies in the US. Retailers and consumer goods producers pay placement companies annual retainer fees of US$50,000 or more to scan hundreds of film scripts a year for scenes in which to place their brand names. One placement company director boasted that product placement is 'legitimately the only way to pay one time for an "ad" that appears forever' (Herman, 2000: 48).

Cross-promotions and merchandising tie-ins, whether planned during production or distribution phases, draw on a film's marketable elements to raise awareness of the film across media and non-media publicity channels. For example, marketing executives at Gramercy came up with an idea to cross-promote *Four Weddings and a Funeral* with a 'Just Say I Do' vacation sweepstakes. They formed a partnership with a French airline and a travel agency to offer winners a free honeymoon vacation to Tahiti. The promotion was also sold through Starbucks coffee shops, a national dating service, bridal shops and florists. Gramercy arranged promotional screenings with the same US dating service and mail-order florist and found television stations willing to promote the film by holding contests for the best wedding video (Lukk, 1997: 15). More famously, perhaps, global marketing tie-ins have promoted recent films from the James Bond franchise in advertisements for vodka, fast cars, cell phones, lotions, credit cards and beer (McChesney, 1999: 39). For another espionage fantasy, *Spy Kids* (Robert Rodriguez 2001), marketable film elements were tied to a bundle of high-tech spy toys from Compaq, RCA, Sprint and other gadget makers and promoted in advertisements for the electronics retailer Radio Shack.

Of course, the goal of cross-promotions and merchandising tie-ins is to sell both the movie and the products associated with it. Sony Signatures, the consumer products division of Sony Pictures Entertainment, arranged for the director and stars of *Stuart Little* (Rob Minkoff, 1999) to appear at a major trade fair for toys because the 'character of Stuart lends itself to a world of licensing and merchandising possibilities' for cross-promotion partners Hasbro (general toys), HarperCollins (publishing) and Learning Curve (specialty toys) ('Columbia Pictures' 'Stuart Little", 1999). They orchestrated similar tie-ins for the 'brands' *Godzilla, Men in Black* (Barry Sonenfeld, 1997), *The Mask of Zorro* (Martin Campbell, 1998), 'Godzilla: The Series', 'Men In Black: The Series', *Dawson's Creek* and 'Extreme Ghostbusters'. Similarly, the Burger King Corporation spent an estimated US$40 million in advertising and themed meals, toys and packaging based on the story and characters in *Chicken Run* (Peter Lord and Nick Park, 2000). Children could hear Mel Gibson's voice on television asking them to save the chickens by eating Burger King's 'Whoppers'. According to a Burger King press release, young consumers were encouraged at the company's fast-food restaurants to 'reenact escape scenes from the movie by making airplane shaped Chicken Tenders part of their meal'. British Airways also invested in *Chicken Run* with a 'Fly the coop to London' campaign. In total, Dreamworks attained US$100 million worth of promotional partnerships, that also included Chevron petroleum, Clorox Co., Gold Circle Farms and a California supermarket chain (Friedman, 2000a: 3).

Lucas is the undisputed leader in merchandising tie-ins and cross-promotions. Weeks before LucasFilm Ltd's blockbuster, *The Phantom Menace* was released, licensed merchandise 'flooded toy stores, Web sites, fast-food restaurants, computer stores, music stores, supermarkets, bookstores and newsstands'. Hasbro Toys, which guaranteed Lucas US$500 million in royalties from *Phantom Menace* dolls, 'light sabers' and toy 'podracers', has even created a special office for 'an executive vice president for Star Wars' (Elliot, 1999: 1). The Pepsi-Cola Company, a unit of Pepsi-Co, spent US$2 billion to sponsor *The Phantom Menace* and sequels. Not surprisingly, *The Phantom Menace*'s relatively small advertising budget of US$20 million (it ended up spending only US$14 million) benefited from the marketing campaigns of its licensees, merchandisers and retailers. Moreover, having turned this event film into an event of film marketing, LucasFilm attracted an unprecedented amount of media publicity, garnering cover articles in *Entertainment Weekly*, *GQ*, *Newsweek*, *Premiere*, *Time*, *Vanity Fair*, *Wired*, *Popular Mechanics* ('The Machines of "Star Wars"'), *Vogue* ('"Star Wars" Couture') and *TV Guide*. As one trade magazine described the *Star Wars* phenomenon, 'the marketing of an entertainment property is becoming the story instead of the property itself' (Elliot, 1999: 1).

So whether or not you finally buy a ticket to the movies, marketing executives have already decided that an audience exists for a film with the right combination of high playability, clear positioning and abundant marketability. If marketers fail to sense the presence of this trinity, they may not bless a film project, though they are more likely to propose changes that normalise the project's commercial content and value. An important effect of marketing's textual gatekeeping is the multiplication of corporate partnerships that result from cross-promotion and merchandising deals. The potential links to retail marketers can be indexed to the level of marketability found in a film project. Greater marketability not only means more film elements congenial to advertising, but also entails more partnerships with consumer goods and services corporations. And when corporate interests proliferate, the slightest sign of box-office failure sends 'shudders down Wall Street' (McChesney, 1999: 39), threatening marketing's credibility among its most important patrons. But after all is said and done, projects that still lack the marketer's endorsement may be made anyway if the film finds a studio executive or big investor to shepherd it through the system. Also, exhibitionary outlets for Hollywood are very numerous, and the majors can always depend on the market muscle of block-booking and blind bidding, the safety net of oligopoly, such that even 'unsuccessful' films may eventually produce a profit.

In addition to the selective filter that the marketing bureaucracy uses to determine which kind of movies get made and what content will endow the screen with marketability, marketing executives also decide when and where a movie will be exhibited. They come up with a rough sixty-day estimate for a film's release date, which they calculate after learning the date they will receive a final print, the earliest date they can screen the print for the media, and how long it will take for the media to start publicising the film. Once this is done, they look at the competition coming out at the same time and make whatever scheduling adjustments are needed before deciding on the first release date for domestic exhibition (Lukk, 1997: 3).

Before a film's release, marketers flood public space with trailers, posters, television and print advertisements – all of which cut up a film's main visual selling points and condense them into simple images that will be used to lure people to the theatre as well as all subsequent exhibition windows (Wyatt, 1994: 131). The Friday and Sunday editions of the *New York Times* are showcases for theatrical releases in the US, largely because marketers believe that this is 'a national paper that can position a film for regional audiences as well as critics' (Lukk, 1997: 27). Print advertisements in general circulation and specialty magazines also draw on the visual attributes of a film. In 2001, major distributors planned to reduce investment in print advertising, which took up about US$900 million in annual newspaper advertising alone (Friedman, 2001: 1), while expanding television advertising and promotion, already the dominant channel for most film marketing. This was largely due to growth in national cable channels and the overlap of national network advertising in local markets, where newspaper advertising was seen as redundant. Cable has especially enhanced marketers' ability to pick and choose their target audiences, especially music television, which offers tremendous flexibility for positioning films among marketers' key segment of 14- to 24-year-old males (Wyatt, 1994: 44–52). It has also become axiomatic for film marketers to buy network television time on Thursday evenings. According to marketers, this is the weeknight when the largest potential film audience congregates in front of the television, and when the most susceptible group for marketability (young, single men) decide on a first-choice film for the weekend (Lukk, 1997; Litman, 1998: 41).

Decisions about the number of prints are also important during the final promotional effort for exhibition. Combined with the advertising budget, prints often raise marketing costs to 50 per cent of a feature film's total value. From a marketing perspective, the investment is justified because more prints mean more opportunities for poster displays and for the film's title to occupy available marquee space, much like a billboard announcing the arrival of a new

product. Release strategies, therefore, usually include consideration of an opti-
mal volume of prints as part of a single marketing event with advertising and
other promotions. Major distributors usually opt for wide release with 1,000
to 2,000 prints, involving '100 theaters in Los Angeles and eighty theaters in
New York'. Wide releases have come to 'represent about three-quarters of total
box office revenue' (Lukk, 1997: 6–7). In contrast, specialty distributors use a
method called platforming, that is, releasing prints to three to five key theaters
in Los Angeles and New York to build awareness and then 'platform' their films
to other cities (Lukk, 1997: 6; Wyatt, 1994: 110). One of the main strategies in
bringing unmarketable movies to market is film-print saturation to ensure that
a film can 'make as much money as possible before [the proverbial] word-of-
mouth kills the film at the box office' (Lukk, 1997: 7), permitting faster
recouping of production costs (Balio, 1998a: 59). Obviously, saturation is a
bald exercise of a major distributor's control over what's offered and what's
chosen.

After the date of first domestic release, US feature-fiction films have at least
nine opportunities to bring in revenue: US theatres, for four months from US
release; foreign theatres (4–18 months); US video (6–30 months); foreign video
(9–24 months); US cable television (12–36 months); US broadcast television
(36–60 months); foreign broadcasters (48–60 months); second US cable television (66–72 months); and US syndication (72 months) (Gershon, 1997: 40).
This efflorescence of formats and sites has been a bonanza for Hollywood. As
recently as a quarter of a century ago, direct consumer purchase in the EU and
the US was only an option through theatrical attendance. In the late 1990s, that
accounted for just 31.3 per cent of spending, with pay-TV at 34 per cent, video
purchase at 20.4 per cent, and video rental at 14.2 per cent. As measured across
all these outlets, for example, British expenditure on films increased 750 per cent
between 1981 and 1997. Theatrical exhibition revenues are a tiny fraction when
considered against video sales and rentals (Durie et al., 2000: 15–17; Hettrick,
2001).

The exhibition system has been modernised during the 1990s with the globalisation of the multiplex, itself a subset of developments in fast-food franchises
and merchandise agglomeration via the growth of the shopping mall, where
local shops often subsidise theatres. This convergence of space with other retail
sectors also applies at the level of managerial systems, with chain ownership
displacing independence and the return of Hollywood producer-distributors to
theatrical interests (Litman, 1998: 18, 33; Blackstone and Bowman, 1999). Up
to the 1990s, Western Europe, still the crown jewel for Hollywood in terms of
international revenues, had seen a decline in the number of screens and
admissions. Theatre numbers fell by 60 per cent between 1960 and 1990, while
total Western European admissions fell from 2.9 billion to 564 million as

alternative leisure-time activities and ways of watching 'films' multiplied. The trend was not reversed until 1997, when EU admissions rose to 758.5 million (Durie *et al.*, 2000: 10–11). This reversal was fuelled in part by the US$1.65 billion construction of new venues in the UK alone, most of which was bankrolled by the US firms, United Cinemas International (a joint venture of MCA and Paramount), Warner Bros., and AMC. Rather than offering sufficient screens to permit diverse selections from around the world (or even the country of domicile) multiplexes have encouraged distributors to seek multiple slots for each film within the one complex. Minor exceptions can be found: the thirty screens in Birmingham's Star City included six dedicated to Bollywood (Durie *et al.*, 2000: 10–11, 153; Younge, 2000). In the US, where, as Sony Pictures Classics president Michael Barker put it, 'once the French were the big thing, now it's the Latin American', 400 screens are allotted to Spanish-language films ('España Promocionará', 2000).

International audiences typically used to wait six months for US films to screen, but that became four weeks during the 1990s – creating further pressure on space for local material (Short, 1997). Often derided in Europe as 'fronts for the American blockbusters' that have undermined independent outlets (European Audiovisual Observatory, 1998), Valenti refers to multiplexes as 'comfortable, clean' (1993: 148). Marketers' interest in what actually goes on inside these 'comfortable fronts' provides our topic in Chapter 6.

Advocacy Marketing and its Others

> Mr. Valenti himself rarely sees the inside of a theatre. As the major studios' chief lobbyist, he spends much of his time hounding his own and foreign governments for more action to staunch the drain on Hollywood revenues from film pirates. He is off again later this month with a bunch of business dignitaries trailing U.S. Commerce Secretary William Daley to Asia, a hotbed of counterfeiting and copyright thievery.
>
> ('Hollywood's Incredible Turkey Machine', 1999)

The constant din of advocacy marketing surrounds the power and profit centres of distribution, marketing and exhibition. Advocacy marketing is closely related to the sales effort and so amplifies during cyclical saturation releases. It is also devoted to polishing the corporate image, especially in response to the occasional headline about Hollywood cartel abuses of children and women, the latest mega-merger, or the threat of a labour strike. To some extent, all movie executives, trade magazines, most film critics, many film scholars and the news media are advocates for the film industry. Still, apart from Valenti's singular role as the conqueror of cultures, advocacy is left largely to professional marketers, lobbyists and public relations firms to promote awareness and acclamation of the industry and its activities. Advocacy aims to build positive brand awareness, popular acclaim and formal political support for the major Hollywood distributors. The brand or trademark is a form of symbolic equity that can be accumulated through regular advocacy, giving major distributors a 'trademark advantage' over newcomers. A studio's brand equity is also bolstered by each film's publicity and advertising campaign, by stars appearing on television, trailers, billboards, posters and theatre displays, and product tie-ins (Litman, 1998: 32–33). The kind of advocacy best known for generating popular acclaim occurs in publicity, promotion and media coverage of trade shows (that is, film festivals) and awards ceremonies. The most celebrated awards ceremony, the Oscars, is sponsored yearly by the Academy of Motion Picture Arts and Sciences. Important annual trade shows include Santa Monica, Cannes, Monte Carlo, Berlin, San Sebastian, Sundance, Toronto, Telluride and the Hamptons. Throughout the year, these marketing festivals spotlight new releases and offer a venue for producers and distributors to mingle and close any unfinished deals. Similar advocacy activities include the Film Information Council's awards for 'Best Marketed Movie of the Month'.

Advocacy takes a more disciplinary turn when powerful trade organisations like the AFMA and the MPAA conduct political lobbying, contribute millions of dollars to influence major political parties, and carry out international relations through cooperative as well as imperious trade efforts, most notably in the transnational corporate fight against piracy (see Chapter 4). The AFMA works for independent motion picture and television companies that make and distribute English-language films around the world. The AFMA represents 150 companies in twenty countries, including New Line, Miramax, Polygram, King World, Saban Pictures International, HBO Enterprises, NBC Enterprises, Endemol, Capitol Films, Intermedia and Kushner-Locke. As we have seen, the most important trade organisation is the MPAA. Most people in the US know the MPAA only for its rating system, which is also a form of advocacy marketing. As a marketing feature of film packaging, a rating conveys something about a film's content, but its core advocacy function is to reinforce the idea that the industry is capable of self-regulation. The MPAA rating system invites people to think that the industry has ethical codes and follows noble ideals, such as protecting children from harmful influences.

While advocacy activities strengthen both popular praise and formal political support for Hollywood's domestic and international hegemony, rival national and pan-regional campaigns have been mounting in support of promotion and distribution systems designed to control the NICL. For example, the National Screen Institute of Canada joined with Toronto-based Cultural Enterprises International to launch the 'Going To Market' programme, aimed at 'increasing the marketing and deal-making savvy of Canadian producers

[and] to set Canadian writers, directors and producers above the crowd at international markets ... through specific, festival-related intelligence' (Binning,
1999a: 2). In Europe, as the 1990s saw decreased export figures and the already
closed US market shrank further (Finney, 1996: 145, 140), national cinemas
sought policies to bolster distribution and marketing in their countries of origin. France, the United States' perennial foe in the GATT and the WTO over
cultural protection, currently offers distributors financial and tax incentives to
purchase local films and facilitate their release, provided that full liability is
taken and the funds actually go to ensure circulation within a specified time. It
has a quarter of the domestic market share, thanks to a range of strategies, but
is still dominated by Hollywood, because the top ten distributors are all US-
owned. Germany offers interest-free loans to aid financing, distributing,
copying and advertising, and there are also municipal mechanisms in place.
Italy provides 'soft loans' to assist local distribution and overseas penetration
(KPMG, 1996: 68–69, 87, 138; Finney, 1996: 146). Britain, which has not had
as much assistance as other European countries, faced a situation where half
the sixty-nine films produced there in 1994 had still never been screened two
years later. The Spanish government has begun a number of initiatives with an
eye toward the elimination of the EU exhibition quota system, including a programme of subsidies to Spanish filmmakers and another to promote Spanish
and Latin American co-productions. The plan for the Audiovisual Development and Promotion of Cinematography rewards partnerships with
commercially oriented projects like Ibermedia, a fund created by Iberomeri-
cana de Chile to support the development of co-productions across the
Spanish-speaking world ('España Promocionará', 2000).

  Titanic drew attention to a phenomenon that had been quietly developing
over a decade – a coalition of two studios, Paramount and Fox, to split national
and global distribution (European Audiovisual Observatory, 1998). Regional
alliances have thus formed to offer a number of advocacy marketing programmes and funding to develop pan-European distribution. European Film
Promotion (EFP), for example, was founded in 1997 to help sell European cinema in the international audiovisual market. It comprises twenty promotion
and export organisations from eighteen European countries,[2] with headquarters in Hamburg, a site paid for by the German Federal Government
Commissioner for Cultural Affairs and the Media. Its major activity so far has
been a road show called 'Shooting Stars', in which new directors and actors
from member countries travel to international film festivals, from Berlin to
Pusan, to show off the diversity of film production across Europe and promote
their own work and careers through exposure to the international press and
buyers.

  Backing the EFP alliance is the MEDIA programme, which was launched during the early 1990s with the aim of making European film production regionally cohesive in the interests of profitability whilst also being responsive to local cultures – an attempt to blend commerce and culture through the exchange of media within the EU through new forms of distribution, rather than via international co-production. The first five years saw annual funding below the production costs of a Hollywood blockbuster. The more substantial MEDIA II (US$405 million) ran from 1995 to 2000, adding a particular focus on distribution, development and training plus the global circulation of European texts. As per the first MEDIA, highbrow production was privileged and successful films tended only to travel within their linguistic community of origin, unlike their Hollywood rivals. MEDIA III (MEDIA PLUS) aimed at similar interventions. Its US$355 million budget is predicated on assisting in the creation of 300,000 new jobs in the EU audiovisual sector between 2001 and 2005 through a link between market success and public subvention, alongside e-Europe, an Internet initiative (Theiler, 1999: 570–71, 576; 'European Commissioner', 1999; Stern, 1999 and 1999–2000).

In Asia, a regional alliance with a different structure but similar goals has formed through the work of the foundation, Network for the Promotion of Asia-Pacific Cinema (NETPAC).[3] NETPAC (www.pacific.net.sg/siff and www.asianfilms.org) was founded in 1994 and includes critics, filmmakers, festival organisers and curators, distributors and exhibitors, and film educators. NETPAC focuses on helping newer directors promote their work in the international audiovisual market. It began as a series of conferences supported in part by UNESCO, which helped build its network of participants and establish Asian Film Centres around the world. Its presence is growing with its participation at Asian Film Festivals and the conferences it has held in conjunction with these in India, Japan, Hawaii, Rotterdam, Singapore, the Philippines and Korea. While NETPAC designs educational materials and coordinates non-commercial international exchange to raise awareness of pan-Asian work (in effect, a counter-curriculum to global Hollywood's), it also conducts promotional and advocacy marketing through such programmes as 'The Asian Film Discovery Selection', which markets packages of Asian films using a single topic or theme (e.g. Asian women directors, Asian documentaries and Asian young cinema).

All the above efforts to sustain state-sponsored, public service or commercial (but non-profit), programmes have offered themselves as sources of funding distribution outside Hollywood's distribution oligopoly, primarily targeting financial aid and low-cost technical aid to small domestic producers. However, as neo-liberal policy menaces the world of public funding, the traditional political safeguards for production and distribution of undercapitalised film projects are disappearing, marking a shift to dependence on private funds from investment capitalists. When financial capital takes over the book-keeping, as in Hollywood, this tends to elevate the power of large commercial distributors. That is because banks see distributors who offer a slate of films as better bets than the small film producer who comes with a one-off project (the reverse order of traditional state and public funding criteria). When the money that used to come from public programmes begins to evaporate, the textual power shifts to the distributors who, as we have seen, translate the banks' press-ure to meet the numbers into market criteria for funding films. As one Canadian investor put it: 'distributors are the cash cows, they pay the loans' (Binning, 1999: 23). Independent projects, already undercapitalised and equity-less, lose out.

Hence, the abiding logic of the EU's audiovisual policy is now commercial and profit-oriented: it clearly favours existing large concerns that can be built upon further. For EU policy-makers, the reasons for embracing market criteria were unambiguous: in 1999, EU theatres were still filled with Hollywood films, which occupied 80 per cent of programming. Of the other 20 per cent, just 5 per cent were imported from other European countries. Viviane Reding, the key European Commissioner, proclaimed that MEDIA PLUS would ensure Euro-pean audiovisual production which no longer relies on its inventiveness and originality, reflecting our cultural diversity, but sets out resolutely to win over European audiences and the rest of the world'. The tactic was clearly a concen-tration on film distribution and marketing rather than production (Theiler, 1999: 570–71, 576; 'European Commissioner', 1999; Reding quoted in 'Circu-lation', 1999; Stern, 1999 and 1999–2000). This push to displace, or at least synchronise public sector investment-distribution with large-scale commercial projects has several EU member states, such as Spain (where domestic films in 2000 made up about 9 per cent of theatrical exhibition), hopping on the band-wagon to win a greater share of private investment for domestic cinema and international co-production. The trade group Federación de Asociaciones de Productores Audiovisuales de España (FAPAE) and the multinational telecom-munication and entertainment conglomerate Telefónica have formed alliances with representatives from over one hundred media businesses from Latin America and Spain to carry out trade talks on Iberoamerican audiovisual co-production, where a major goal is finding strategies to reach Spanish speakers living in the US. The orientation of this group was reflected in a Brazilian mar-keter's comment: 'we must not end up as we always do, by attacking the major Hollywood distributors. It's better to learn from them, not attack them' (quoted in 'Distribuidores Apuntan', 2000).

Screen Studies' Response

For U.S., audiences, the mean, green title character in Universal Pictures' new film 'Dr Seuss' How the Grinch Stole Christmas' needs no introduction. But outside the U.S., mention of the Grinch often elicits a 'Who?' – and they're not talking about the residents of Whoville.

(Bruce Orwall, 2000: B1)

We have raised a number of questions that should be historicised, interpreted and criticised by screen studies as a core part of its labours. Yet there is only a fragmentary screen studies address of the expansion of marketing in global Hollywood and the synchronisation of distribution strategies worldwide. Of course, you hardly need a film scholar to tell you that marketing has made a big impact on the movies – it is abundantly clear when you see Meg Ryan and Tom Hanks drinking coffee at Starbucks or using AOL email to fall in love. It was funny to watch Mike Myer's Dr. Evil plot Austin Powers' destruction over a cup of Starbucks coffee, and hard to ignore when John Travolta bellied up to the Krispy Kreme counter in *Primary Colors* and mumbled that he 'shouldn't eat so many of the glazed treats', only to hear Danny, a Krispy Kremer, tell him: 'Well, you know, you gotta eat something' (Herman, 2000: 48). This list goes on: the cast of *The Faculty* (Robert Rodriguez, 1998) costumed by Tommy Hilfiger, Columbia's *Big Daddy* (Dennis Dugan, 1999) furnished with enough Sony audiovisual equipment to start a small retail electronics store, Matt Damon and Ben Affleck sharing Dunkin' Donuts in *Good Will Hunting* (Gus Van Sant, 1997), Tom Cruise 'racing' a packet of Sweet 'n' Low along Nicole Kidman's thigh in *Days of Thunder* (Tony Scott, 1990), E.T. washing Reese's pieces down with Coors beer. And you certainly don't need anyone to point out that movie characters and storylines populate toy stores, big-box discount stores, specialty retail shops, bookstores, music stores and theme parks. Beyond the obvious, what can screen studies say about marketing's effect on its primary object of interest, the film text?

One author who has taken up this question is Justin Wyatt (1994). He endeavoured to reconcile the history of marketing's incursion into filmmaking with a humanist narrative that preserves both an authorial presence for individual filmmakers and an aesthetic experience for filmgoers. This econo-aesthetic comprehension of film marketing offered a unique starting point from which to record marketing's textual effects as well as its historical significance. Wyatt represents 'high concept' as a distinct film aesthetic engendered during the 'post-classical' period of motion picture history. This was the moment when a new product differentiation orthodoxy gave filmmakers more opportunities to make individual films with varying quality and different looks, even as the oligopoly of major distributors encouraged the homogenisation of product lines (Wyatt, 1994: 104). Wyatt reinscribes concentration and con-glomeration as conditions, rather than obstructions, of aesthetic possibility. From this historical perspective, he perceives the ascendancy of 'industrial expressivity', that is, the self-conscious use of marketing conventions over the 'authorial expressivity' that characterises art-cinema conventions (1994: 60–64). The mutual infiltration of these expressive modes became a general condition of filmmaking after the 1960s.

Of all the formulae to emerge from this aesthetic alchemy, 'high concept' was the one marked with the most 'coherent and repeated structuring of ... its elements around the marketing possibilities in the project' (Wyatt, 1994: 64). Marketing's 'industrial expressivity' made its mark on a film as formal 'excess' motivated by sheer commercial interest. This mark of 'excess' stands out when-ever there is a 'gap in the [artistic] motivation of the work' (Wyatt, 1994: 28), that is, whenever there is a preponderance of a film's elements that are unnec-essary for advancing the story or establishing a style suitable to the story. Wyatt is careful to separate this type of commercially motivated excess from melo-drama's narrative excesses (1994: 34). When 'excess' is used for commercial ends, it aestheticises elements needed to improve the marketability of the film – for example, exaggerated decoration, high-tech settings, or any special effects that disturb an otherwise consistent and coherent set of formal and narrative elements (Wyatt, 1994: 24). Stars are another commonly used component of commercial excess, in particular when their presence in a film is determined more by their 'bankability' than by non-commercial narrative or stylistic con-siderations. The makers of 'high-concept' films allow the logic of the marketplace to dictate these stylistic choices. As he puts it: 'Since the excess rep-resented in the high concept films is not driven by a personal vision, the logic of the marketplace is clearly the author of the style.' 'Excess' is, in short, the sig-nature of corporate authorship (Wyatt, 1994: 34, 36).

This mode of 'industrial expressivity' would be useless for marketing if the marketable elements in a film, its 'excesses', were intractable for film advertis-ing and associated merchandising. Wyatt details the numerous ways in which marketable film content flows from film texts to marketing texts via a variety of commercial venues. For example, music and image can be extracted from a film and repackaged in modules 'separate from the narrative', then moved to television as a music video promoting the film (1994: 40–44). Modular 'excesses' reappear in other media and promotional forms as well, including radio, trailers, poster art, the Internet, print advertisements, cross-promotions and tie-ins. As these marketing modules become widely disseminated through domestic and global distribution, they begin to form what Gary Hoppenstand (1998: 232) calls a 'film environment' outside the film. The externalisation of these modules of 'excess' is an integral part of 'high concept' and film marketing generally. However, the modules serve more than an economic function, for when these marketable elements penetrate public space, they also affect the aesthetic experience of filmgoing. By maximising 'points of contact with the film' they multiply 'the possible meanings' one might derive 'from the film narrative' (Wyatt, 1994: 46; see also Hoppenstand, 1998: 232). Wyatt suggests that this process not only pluralises textual possibilities but that it actually has the potential to enhance people's enjoyment of movies. He argues that marketing, in particular the promotional music video, creates a number of inter-textual influences that, as Barbara Klinger says, 'cannot be settled within the textual system', but spill over into a zone of competing interpretations outside the film narrative (quoted in Wyatt, 1994: 44–45).

The econo-aesthetic method fosters greater appreciation for the textual complexity of 'high-concept' films, and argues for their worthiness as objects of study. In this account, marketing enlarges the experience of filmgoing as well as related experiences of popular music, eating out, child care, education, wearing branded clothing and so on. Wyatt's account of the industrial and corporate imperatives that drive marketing 'excesses' into the movies and into other areas of cultural consumption also invites us to see the movies, and related intertextual encounters, as sites of intertextual wrangling over meanings.

By focusing on the aesthetic dimensions of film marketing, this approach restrains criticism of marketing's textual predilections (is it really a matter of taste or pleasurably ambiguous meanings?) and diverts attention from marketing's role in defending the distribution cartel. Further, the econo-aesthetic method foregrounds textual production within narrowly defined film-industrial conditions, overlooking the coordinated efforts of large entertainment-information conglomerates to annex cultural consumption and elevate market criteria over other ways of interpreting culture's value (Schiller, 1974 and 1989; Miller, 1987; Maxwell, 2001). Finally, in elaborating his econo-aesthetic method, Wyatt criticises the industry's audience research methodology on technical grounds but does not question the fundamental problem of surveillance in marketing research's attention to feelings, desires, memory, tastes, dislikes and other behavioural features associated with the movie-going experience (Litman and Ahn, 1998: 180; De Silva, 1998: 145). Litman and Ahn have also criticised Wyatt's linking of economic concepts to aesthetic and marketing approaches, which, they argue, installed highly questionable presumptions about the filmgoer into an otherwise useful economic model. Style might be identifiable in film content, but its allure cannot be measured. If the impact and significance of the textual elements 'seem to lie in the viewer's mind', as Litman and Ahn put it, then such factors do not belong with the objective criteria that will predict a film's success at the box office. After all, a film's success is about how many tickets are sold, not the quality of film perceived as a statistical projection of audience taste or thought. There is no empirical test for this gamble on quality, only unreliable predictors such as stars, directors and critics (Austin, 1989).

Conclusion

> 'High risk is only in the minds of people. Everybody covers investment by selling. And when you hit the bull's eye, profits can be as high as 500 per cent,' says Sanjay Bhattacharya, vice-president, UTV Motion Pictures [Bollywood]. ... If Bollywood can manage that, multi-billion dollar Hollywood may yet find true and tough competition.
>
> (Shankar Aiyer, 2000: 78)

The distribution oligopoly has carved out an occupational growth area for marketers in global Hollywood. Marketers labour for huge sums of money to tell their clients what a probable audience wants in a film, desires in association with it, and thinks about it and its stars, director, special effects, studio, genre and so on. Part of the growing investment in marketing seeks to find out whether marketers did their job – getting people to their clients' movies. It has even become a common feature of infotainment journalism to analyse or second-guess a distributor's marketing strategy, going so far as to treat a movie's successes and failures as news itself. Of course, the entertainment media have a hard time representing the immanent failure of their own industry without deepening a romantic myth perpetuated by the film industry itself: taking risks makes them come across as glamorous and daring. Confusion in screen studies helps the myth persist: Wyatt (1994) thinks marketing works and marvels at the derring-do of marketing wizards; Litman does not, endorsing only a popular adage about advertising: it works half the time, but nobody knows which half (cf. Litman and Ahn, 1998: 180; De Silva, 1998: 145). This myth is further perpetuated by the secretive way that the industry's own research on marketing's efficacy is guarded as proprietary information, which is publicly disseminated via journalistic reports of widespread, constant monitoring of marketing activities and their routinely urgent modification, indicating a universal lack of confidence in the power of any particular marketing idea. This is echoed in the executive mantra, 'marketing is just a tool'.

The tool showed that Scorsese's *Cape Fear* (1991) tested badly in previews, but the film ended up being his most profitable movie; and research was negative on *Stuart Little*, though it 'did huge business' (Willens, 2000: 20). The most notorious blunder, according to industry lore, was the prediction that Spielberg's *E.T the Extra-Terrestrial* (1982) would not interest anyone over the age of four. Market researchers at Columbia proposed that production on the film be scrapped (Andrews, 1998: 1). And, of course, there is the celebrated failure of New Coke, which still generates enough inward embarrassment and outward *schadenfreude* to keep marketers from making final decisions in any industry.

When marketers are wrong, and, arguably, they are wrong most of the time, the shaky foundation under market knowledge is clearly shown. Marketers have tried 'everything short of hooking up an audience to a machine' (Klady, 1998: 9). They know that 'respondents' are not candid; that they are silent about viewing pleasures that embarrass them; and that the non-response rate – that is, outright resistance to film audience surveys – is too high to make authoritative statistical findings. As one researcher put it, predicting a film's success is like 'sending a rocket to a distant planet. If you're off by half a degree, you wind up in another galaxy' (Klady, 1998: 9). In response, marketing executives keep a favourite scapegoat at hand in the sovereign consumer – who by 'word of mouth' rebelliously makes or breaks a film. Of course, there is a problem with this vision of the audience as a power-broker. Movie executives decide what gets made and what is exhibited, not audiences, and there is not a single executive in Hollywood who, under pressure from the parent firm and financiers, would make a movie that lacks elements congenial with the ability to market, advertise, promote and so on. In sum, the faith in marketing – even if its research is persistently wrong and advertising only works half the proverbial time – has real effects: on the screen, on the manner in which Hollywood production advances, on the dispositions guiding the work within the distribution sector of the NICL, and on the bureaucratic rationalisation of what Todd Gitlin (1983) has called the science of the second-guess.

Marketing's social presence has also stirred up trouble for screen studies: writers who still envision a formal wall between film art and commerce are rendered unintelligible; those who treat production and distribution as autonomous realms of labour (one side 'creative' the other 'business') are baffled by the infiltration of distribution's economic pressures and marketers' selective perception in the production phase. Marketing assails these assumptions by installing a high regard for what Oliver Stone calls the 'product oriented business' up front in the 'creative' pre-production and production parts of filmmaking. To be sure, there has always been tension between the 'creatives' and the marketing people (Wyatt, 1994: 157), but this hardly matters more than the ritual disputes between advertising 'creatives' and market researchers. Commercialisation is questioned only rhetorically, while the real fight is over whose ideas work best for creating marketability, commercial success and getting the banks' approval. The perceived or wishfully hoped for independence of culture from the political economy is further smashed by marketing's growing presence in the contemporary storytelling process.

This chapter has shown how solidarity around commercial interests is cultivated and reproduced through the ongoing and extensive business relations of consumer goods and service companies, the distribution oligopoly, and a myriad of marketing operations. This relation is so robust that it creates a value system of its own, in which the quality of a film, apart from technical questions, is determined by commercial potential and marketability, what Wyatt (1994) calls the 'look, hook, and book'. This value system is carried through the nexus of pre-production, production, distribution and exhibition. The distribution oligopoly necessitates the enrichment and legitimacy of marketing and extends the marketing bureaucracy throughout the NICL. It ensures a preponderance of commercialised texts in the cultural curriculum and exposure to commercial signs in the social space produced around the film-marketing environment. In dim contrast, people's preferences in global Hollywood, whether popular or intellectual interpretations of a film's value, barely influence what gets screened (less what gets made) via the figure of the audience, a construct built from, and known through, the institutional discourses of the state, the academy and the film industry. We now turn to the spectral presence of that audience.

Notes

1   Thanks to Colleen Petruzzi, Senior Account Executive at Universal Music and Video Distribution, for these insights.

2   EFP member organisations are the Austrian Film Commission, British Council, Danish Film Institute, Export-Union des Deutschen Films, Film Fund Luxembourg, Finnish Film Foundation, Flanders Image, Greek Film Centre, Holland Film, Icelandic Film Fund, Instituto de Cine (ICAA) Spain, Instituto do Cinema, Audiovisual E Multimédia (ICAM) Portugal, Irish Film Board, Italia Cinema-Italian Cinema Promotion Agency, Norwegian Film Institute, Swedish Film Institute, Swiss Film Center, Unifrance Film International, and Wallonie-Bruxelles Images.

3   NETPAC include the following participants: Alpha Film (Turkey), Asia Pacific Media Center-Annenberg Center at the University of Southern California, Asian Film Centre (Sri Lanka), China Film Import & Export Corporation, Choijiv Nergui (Mongolia), Cinemaya: The Asian Film Quarterly, New Delhi, Daily News Newspaper (Thailand), Export & Film Promotion (Pakistan), Films from the South Film Festival (Norway), Fribourg International Film Festival (Switzerland), Hong Kong Arts Center, International Film Festival Rotterdam, International Forum for New Cinema (Germany), Japan Film Library Council, Kelab Seni Filem Malaysia, Korean Motion Picture Corporation, Melbourne International Film Festival, Mowelfund Film Institute (Manila), Protishabda Alternative Communication Center (Bangladesh), Pusan International Film Festival (South Korea), Singapore International Film Festival, Sub-Commission on the Arts (Philippines), Taiwan Film Center, The Japan Foundation ASEAN Cultural Center, Vietnam Cinema Association, and the Vietnam Cinema Department.

Chapter Six
Audiences

Entertainment is one of the purest marketplaces in the world. If people don't like a movie or record they won't see it or buy it. The fact that the American entertainment industry has been so successful on a worldwide basis speaks to the quality and attractiveness of what we're creating.

(Robert Shaye, Chair of New Line Pictures, quoted in Weinraub, 1993: L24)

We have travelled from the initial problem of cultural imperialism, through the labour that gives films meaning and value, the laws that police them, and the marketing that promotes them. In this chapter, we look at the target of these processes – viewers – through three lenses: first, as they are construed in critical discourse; second, as divided between citizens and consumers; and third, as the object of surveillance. Our three lenses are turned on the three primary sites for defining the film audience: the industry, the state and criticism.

Our starting point is the provocation that the audience is artificial, a creature of these various agencies that proceed to act upon their creation. Many discussions of the audience are signs of anxiety: laments for a bountiful path to profits that regret the turn towards cable and the Internet away from broadcast television, or laments for civic culture in the US that correlate heavy film viewing with increased violence and declining membership of Parent-Teacher Associations. Such fears are as live today as when the Payne Fund Studies of the 1930s inaugurated mass social-science panic about young people. Those panics were driven, then as now, by academic, religious and familial iconophobia in the face of large groups of people engaged by popular culture and seemingly beyond the control of the state and the ruling class. Before even that, films were connected to gambling and horse racing in various forms of social criticism and were lunged for as raw material by the emergent discipline of psychology, where obsessions with eyesight and the cinema gave professors something to do. At the same time, social reformers looked to film as a potential forum for moral uplift; if the screen could drive the young to madness, it might also provoke social responsibility (Austin, 1989: 33–35).

Today, the screen industries, the state and critics work with similar empirical data, but to very different ends. When we read that the average US resident
spent 9.3 hours of each day in 1999 using the various entertainment media,
that this is projected to rise to 10.4 per day in 2004 (Veronis Suhler, 2000),
and that theatrical revenues have risen by nearly 60 per cent since 1990
(Valenti, 2001c) these are not simple numbers. They are indices and auguries
of opportunity, triviality, docility, violence and bigotry, depending on our
reading position.

This complex trajectory can lead to some difficult decisions for an industry
that always wants to regulate its own conduct while using the state to regulate
others. Consider Valenti's censorship dilemmas:

> Violence is harder to catalog than sensuality. There either is copulation or
> there isn't. There is writhing or there isn't. But it's hard to measure
> gradations of violence. John Wayne hitting the beaches at Iwo Jima and
> mowing down 2,000 people – how do you equate that with a fellow being
> fellated? It's pretty difficult.
>
> (Valenti quoted in Svetkey, 1994: 32)

There is a reason for all this censorious activity: the cultural audience is not
so much a specifiable group *within* the social order as the principal site *of* that
order. Audiences participate in the most global (but local) communal (yet individual) and time-consuming practice of making meaning in world history. The
concept and the occasion of being an audience are textual links between society
and person, for viewing involves solitary interpretation as well as collective
behaviour. Production executives invoke the audience to measure success and
claim knowledge of what people want. But this focus on the audience is not
theirs alone. Regulators do the same in order to administer, psychologists to
produce proofs, and lobby groups to change content. Hence the link to panics
about education, violence and apathy supposedly engendered by the screen and
routinely investigated by the state, psychology, Marxism, neo-conservatism, the
Church, liberal feminism and others.

These groups consider the audience as consumers, students, felons, voters
and idiots. Such approaches fix on what Harold Garfinkel in 1964 called the
'cultural dope,' a mythic figure 'who produces the stable features of the society
by acting in compliance with pre-established and legitimate alternatives of
action that the common culture provides'. The 'common sense rationalities ...
of here and now situations' that people use are obscured by this condescend-
ing categorisation (Garfinkel, 1992: 68). When the audience is invoked as a
category by the industry or its critics and regulators, it immediately becomes
such a 'dope'. Consider the history of *Crocodile Dundee* (Peter Faiman, 1986),

the most popular imported film in US history. Paramount, the US distributor, worked with a particular view of US spectators when it cut five minutes from the Australian version to increase the film's pace, removing scenic segments, altering the sound mix to foreground dialogue, and concentrating on the heterosexual couple (Crofts, 1989: 129, 137, 141). The changes were based on a patronising view of the US audience. Conversely, the Australian Government's promotion of the film had been based on showcasing this ultimately excluded scenery to potential tourists. Clearly, different conceptions of the audience produce radically divergent versions of a film.

Much non-Hollywood-oriented film is charged with turning audience dopes into a public of thinkers beyond the home – civic-minded participants in a political and social system as well as an economy of purchasing. National cinemas in Europe, Asia, the Pacific, Latin America and Africa are expected to win viewers and train them in a way that complements the profit-driven sector. The entertainment function is secondary to providing what the commercial market does not 'naturally' deliver. Audiences are encouraged not just to watch and consume, but to act differently, to be 'better' people than their 'dope' status as Hollywood viewers.

What happens when the audience receives the product? One hundred and fifty years ago, it was taken as read that audiences were active, given their unruly and overtly engaged conduct at cultural events. But the spread of public education in the West in the nineteenth century, allied to the emergence of literary criticism and psychology, shifted critical rhetoric about audiences (Butsch, 2000: 3) towards Garfinkel's 'dope'. Ever since the advent of the mass media, much energy has been devoted to evaluating the active versus passive sides to media audiences. This is because popular-culture texts are 'symbols for time' (Hartley, 1987: 133). The alleged misuse of time has become integral to the desire to police everyday life. Communitarian philosophy and sociology rail against rampant individualism, secular selfishness and the absence of civic responsibility. An allegedly active public is contrasted with a putatively inactive screen audience:

> we are not happy when we are watching television, even though most of us spend many hours a week doing so, because we feel we are 'on hold' rather than really living during that time. We are happiest when we are successfully meeting challenges at work, in our private lives, and in our communities.
>
> (Robert Bellah *et al.*, 1992: 49)

Sometimes the criticisms are about particular genres (e.g., action-adventure cinema is mindless and talk shows trivialise current affairs, whereas character-driven drama builds moral fibre in the audience and 'real' journalism informs the electorate). This is often a gendered critique, as Michèle Mattelart explains:

> in the everyday time of domestic life ... the fundamental discrimination of sex roles is expressed. ... The hierarchy of values finds expression through the positive value attached to masculine time (defined by action, change and history) and the negative value attached to feminine time which, for all its potential richness, is implicitly discriminated against in our society, interiorized and lived through as the time of banal everyday life, repetition and monotony.
>
> (Mattelart, 1986: 65)

Melodramas, soap operas and talk shows are deemed inferior because they are associated (contradictorily) with both passivity and high emotion. These criticisms have supporters on both left and right, across both the social sciences and the humanities.

In opposition to these *données*, an active audience tradition picks up on Garfinkel's cultural-dope insight. Instead of issuing jeremiads, it claims that audiences are so clever and able that they outwit the institutions of the state, academia and capitalism that seek to control and measure them and their interpretations. In one sense, this position has a venerable tradition, through literary theorists like old Nazism man Hans Robert Jauss' (1982) aesthetics of reception and old Marxism man Jean-Paul Sartre's (1990) philosophy of the mutual intrication of writer and reader in making meaning (Mattelart and Mattelart, 1998: 119–20, 123). In screen culture, the idea really spread with Umberto Eco's mid-1960s development of a notion of encoding-decoding, open texts and aberrant readings (1972). This was picked up by sociologists Frank Parkin (1971) and Stuart Hall (1980), on the left, and on the right by uses-and-gratifications functionalist Elihu Katz (1990).

This counter-critique attacks criticisms of the screen for failing to allot the people's machine its due as a populist apparatus that subverts patriarchy, capitalism and other forms of oppression (or diminishes the tension of social divisions, depending on your politics). The screen is held to be subversive/relieving because, almost regardless of content, its output is decoded by audiences in keeping with their own social situation (Seiter, 1999). The active audience is said to be weak at the level of cultural production, but strong as an interpretative community. Consider the special skills of cultish fans. They construct para-social, imagined connections to celebrities or actants, who fulfil friendship functions or serve as spaces for projecting and evaluating schemas that make sense of human interaction. In addition to adoring the text, cult audiences domesticate the characters, removing them from the overall story and quoting their escapades and proclivities as part of a fan's world that is opened up to others through quizzes and rankings. References to favourite scenes, the behaviour of actants, or the qualities of stars, catalyse memories. Sequences and tendencies are disarticulated from screen time, reshaped and redisposed to contrast with one's own social circumstances (Leets *et al.*, 1995: 102–4; Harrington and Bielby, 1995: 102–4, 110; Eco, 1987: 198). In addition, the despised genres listed earlier are recuperated: Hong Kong action becomes carnivalesque, and talk shows address hitherto suppressed topics of public debate.

The mediation of Hollywood's output by indigenous cultures has been particularly important in qualifying the cultural imperialism thesis. Michel Foucault's story (1989: 193) of a white psychologist visiting Africa is instructive in its detail of differing aesthetic systems: when the academic asks local viewers to recount a narrative he has screened, they focus on 'the passage of light and shadows through the trees' in preference to his interest in character and plot. A television survey by the *Economist* in 1994 remarks that cultural politics is always so localised in its first and last instances that the 'electronic bonds' of exported drama are 'threadbare' (Heilemann, 1994: SURVEY 4). In their study of the reception of the television soap opera *Dallas* in Israel, Japan and the US, conservative functionalists Tamar Liebes and Katz (1990: 3–4,v) establish three prerequisites for the successful communication of US ideology: the text contains information designed to assist the US overseas, it is decoded as it was encrypted, and it enters the receiving culture as a norm. They 'found only very few innocent minds' across the different cultural groups that discussed the programme; instead, a variety of interpretative frames led to a multiplicity of readings. We need, then, to avoid any sense that the transmission of US material is straight out of a US textbook on sender-message-receiver communications theory. Accommodation always already involves transformation by a local culture, and an increasing awareness of the heterogeneous and conflictual nature of US culture itself (Schou, 1992: 143–45).

Today, this active audience position may be the most visible aspect of cultural studies. In 1999, Virginia Postrel wrote an op-ed piece for the right-wing US financial newspaper the *Wall Street Journal* welcoming active audience research, describing it as 'deeply threatening to traditional leftist views of commerce' because notions of active media consumption by fans were so close to the sovereign consumer beloved of the right. Postrel writes that 'The cultural-studies mavens are betraying the leftist cause, lending support to the corporate enemy and even training graduate students who wind up doing market research' (Postrel, 1999). Gitlin argues that some sectors of cultural studies are indeed in synch with neo-classical economics and the right: 'What the group wants, buys, demands is *ipso facto* the voice of the people. Supply has meshed with demand' (1997: 32). As Herbert Schiller puts it, the direct opposition that is frequently drawn between political economy (production matters) and active audience theory (interpretation matters) assumes that the fragmentation of audience niches and responses nullifies the concentration and reach of economic power in mass culture – that pluralism ensures diversity (1989: 147–48, 153). But is this credible? Perhaps a 'shared interest in [a TV] show is an end in itself and seldom leads to some action beyond that interest, some larger political purpose' (Butsch, 2000: 291).

Screen studies tells us of men identifying with women in melodramas, women identifying with male action heroes, Native Americans identifying with Western pioneers – in short, the theatre as a site of carnival as much as machine, where viewers transcend the dross of their ordinary social and psychological lives (Stam, 1989: 224). The crucial link between theories of the text and spectatorship – one that abjures the extremes of the dope and its opposite – may come from a specification of occasionality, that moment when a spectator moves from being 'the hypothetical point of address of filmic discourse' to membership in 'a plural, social audience'; for that moment can produce surprises (Hansen, 1994: 2). Jacqueline Bobo's analysis of black women viewers of *The Color Purple* (Steven Spielberg, 1985) shows how watching the film and discussing it drew them back to Alice Walker's novel and invoked their historical experience in ways quite unparalleled in dominant culture – a far cry from the dismissal of the film by critics. These women 'sifted through the incongruent parts of the film and reacted favorably to elements with which they could identify' (Bobo, 1995: 3). Similarly, gay Asian-Caribbean-Canadian videomaker Richard Fung (1991) talks about searching for Asian genitals in the much-demonised genre of pornography; an account not available in conventional denunciations of porn and its impact on minorities. And when JoEllen Shively (1992) returned as a researcher to the reservation where she had grown up, she found that her fellow Native Americans had continued their practice of reading the Western genre in an actantial rather than political way, cheering for the 'cowboys' over the 'Indians' because of narrative position, not race. Should we regard this as false consciousness, or the capacity to interpret films through their story worlds as well as via the horizon of personal life?

Neither answer will do. As we argued in Chapter 1, the worldwide divergence of filmgoers' labours of interpretation and judgement is not reducible to a choice between false consciousness or polysemy. Historicised specificity is a valuable antidote to any purely textual or symptomatic reading – it alerts us to encounters of divergent tastes, even as the NICL regulates distinctions in the fusion of imported strands of popular culture with indigenous cultural labour.

Meaghan Morris glosses, enacts and criticises the dilemma of this position in her account of *The Lucille Ball Show* as seen on 1950s Australian television.

This isolated image of women evading patriarchal control had dramatic effects on the Morris household – mother and daughter revelled in the show while father absented himself. But the programme was also a sign of political economy and diplomacy: it represented the re-siting of Australian geopolitical culture away from Britain and towards the US. The screen is certainly amenable to notions of localism, resistance and feminism, working via the 'subversive pleasure of the female spectators' to produce an active engagement with both the text and the family. But this can become a critic's alibi for social speculation. Our suspicions should be aroused when academic theory cites 'the people' as demotic supports for its own preoccupations, because when 'the people' become one more text to be read and interpreted, they stand for the critic's own practice of reading. Far from being sources of information, they have been transmogrified into delegates that endow the critic's *own* account with a populist ring (Morris, 1990: 15–16, 21–23). Aberrant decoding by fans becomes a means of making the output of the culture industries isomorphic with a professor's anti-capitalist, anti-patriarchal, anti-racist politics.

In reaction to both the cultural dope and active audience models, Alec McHoul and Tom O'Regan (1992) criticise the idea that 'local instances' of people 'embracing' or 'refusing' the dominant interpretations preferred by global producers 'guarantee any general statement about textual meaning'. Instead, they propose a 'discursive analysis of particular actor networks, technologies of textual exchange, circuits of communicational and textual effectivity, traditions of exegesis, commentary and critical practice'. In other words, the specific 'uptake' of a text by a community should be our focus; but not because this reveals something essential to the properties of screen texts or their likely uptake anywhere else or at any other time. We can only discern a 'general outline' of 'interests', applied to specific cases 'upon a piecemeal and local inspection' (McHoul and O'Regan, 1992: 5–6, 8–9). The screen is an instrument of instruction and response that varies with place, time, genre and audience (O'Shea, 1989: 376–77). As Justin Lewis says, 'viewing is a cultural practice, and like all cultural practices, it involves not only "doing it" but "ways of doing it"' (1991: 49).

For those of us schooled in pub-talk or Leavisite talk, whether about sport, art, politics, literature, friends or television, there is nothing necessarily new or socially subversive about evaluations by fans. None of which is to say that, on the other side, the anti-populists are correct in their infantalisation of audiences. As Pierre Bourdieu suggests, 'paternalistic-pedagogical television' is 'no less opposed to a truly democratic use of the means of mass circulation than populist spontaneism and demagogic capitulation to popular tastes' (1998: 48). Dan Schiller (1996: 194) proposes a way beyond such graceless antinomies. Screen production need not be thought of in opposition to consumption, with one practice 'productive' and the other not, or one side trumping the other. Instead, the work of screen employees is one moment of labouring activity, and the work of screen audiences is another. Rather than embarking on *either* active interpretation *or* passive reception, audience members' labour includes self-understanding – but that labour cannot and should not be conceptualised in isolation from their day-jobs, or the work of others in bringing television to them, or, as we discuss later in this chapter (see 'Surveillance'), the manner in which such labour can be exploited through the consumer surveillance networks of market research (see also Maxwell, 2001).

The Citsumer

> The customer knows precisely what is attractive and valuable.... It is the local citizenry casting their own votes, not the American film industry.
>
> (Valenti, 1993: 147, 149)

Jack Valenti is finding it hard to distinguish here between citizens and consumers. This section of our book is designed to help him sort out this complex difference. It leads us to the heart of the *laissez-faire* bifurcation between Hollywood and its others, between audiences as citizens and consumers. We do not provide a comprehensive account of how the terms 'citizen' and 'consumer' have been used historically, but we do spell out certain rationalities that mobilise these terms in transnational cultural battles, challenging assertions made in their name while recognising their necessity.

There is a complicated relationship between the citizen and its logocentric double, the consumer. The citizen is a wizened figure from the ancient past. The consumer, by contrast, is naïve, essentially a creature of the nineteenth century. Each shadows the other, the *national* subject versus (or is it *as*?) the *rational* subject. We all know the popularity of the consumer with neo-classical economists and policy wonks: the market is said to operate in response to this ratiocinative agent, who, endowed with perfect knowledge, negotiates between alternative suppliers and his or her own demands, such that an appropriate price is paid for desired commodities. The consumer has become the sexless, ageless, unprincipled, magical agent of social value in a multitude of discourses and institutions since that time. Unmarked in this rationality by national origins, consumers are runaways from national culture, animated by individual preferences.

What of the other side to our couplet, the citizen, currently invoked in Europe against US demands for a free market? The citizen has also undergone a major revival in the last decade. Social theorists and policymakers have nominated it as a magical agent of historical change. More easily identified than class, and more easily mobilised as a justification for state action, citizenship has become a site of hope for a left that has lost its actually existing alternative to international capital. We now address the utility of this move in the context of film and television.

Two accounts of screen citizenship are dominant in academia, public policy and social activism. In their different ways, each is an effects model, in that they both assume the screen *does* things *to* people, with the citizen understood as an audience member that can be a 'dope', abjuring both interpersonal responsibility and national culture. The first model, dominant in the US and exported around the world, derives from the social sciences and is typically applied without consideration of place. We call this the *domestic* effects model, or DEM. It is universalist and psychological. The DEM offers analysis and critique of such crucial citizenship questions as education and civic order. It views the screen as a machine that can either pervert or direct the citizen-consumer. Entering young minds osmotically, it both enables and imperils learning. And it also drives the citizen to violence through aggressive and misogynistic images and narratives. The DEM is found in a variety of sites, including laboratories, clinics, prisons, schools, newspapers, psychology journals, television network and film studio research and publicity departments, everyday talk, programme-classification regulations, conference papers, parliamentary debates and state-of-our-youth or state-of-our-civil-society moral panics (see Buckingham, 1997 and Hartley, 1996). The DEM is embodied in the nation-wide US media theatrics that ensued after the Columbine high school shootings, questioning the role of violent images (not firearms or straight white masculinity) in creating violent citizens. It is also evident in panics about the impact of television advertisements on the environment or politics.

The second way of thinking about screen citizenship is a *global* effects model, or GEM. The GEM, primarily utilised in non-US discourse, is specific and political rather than universalist and psychological. Whereas the DEM focuses on the cognition and emotion of individual human subjects via replicable experimentation, the GEM looks to the knowledge of custom and patriotic feeling exhibited by collective human subjects, the grout of national culture. In place of psychology, it is concerned with politics. The screen does not make you a well- or an ill-educated person, a wild or a self-controlled one. Rather, it makes you a knowledgable and loyal national subject or a duped viewer who lacks an appreciation of local custom and history. Cultural belonging, not psychic wholeness, is the touchstone of the global effects model. Instead of measuring responses electronically or behaviourally, as its domestic counterpart does, the GEM looks to the national origin of screen texts and the themes and styles they embody, with particular attention to the putatively nation-building genres of drama, news, sport and current affairs. GEM adherents hold that local citizens should control local broadcast networks because they alone can be relied upon to be loyal reporters in the event of war, while in the case of fiction, only locally sensitised producers make narratives that are true to tradition and custom. This model is found in the discourses of cultural imperialism, everyday talk, broadcast and telecommunications policy, international organisations, newspapers, heritage, cultural diplomacy, post-industrial service-sector planning and national cinemas. The enumeration of national authenticity in screen texts through fractional ownership has been a common practice in countries concerned to protect their national cultural economies from foreign imports. The GEM favours 'creativity, not consumerism', as UNESCO's 'Screens Without Frontiers' initiative puts it (Tricot, 2000).

Let us run through the problems with these models. The DEM suffers from all the disadvantages of ideal-typical psychological reasoning. Each massively costly laboratory test of media effects, based on, as the refrain goes, 'a large university in the mid-West,' is countered by a similar experiment, with conflicting results. As politicians, grant-givers and jeremiad-wielding pundits call for more and more research to prove that the screen makes you stupid, violent and apathetic – or the opposite – academics line up at the trough to indulge their contempt for popular culture and ordinary life and their rent-seeking urge for public money. As for the GEM, its concentration on national culture: (i) denies the potentially liberatory and pleasurable nature of different takes on the popular; (ii) forgets the internal differentiation of viewing publics; (iii) valorises frequently oppressive and/or unrepresentative local bourgeoisies in the name of national culture's maintenance and development; and (iv) ignores the demographic realities of its 'own' terrain.

Once we add some history, spatiality and politics to the DEM/GEM, they become more complicated. Consumption and citizenship have a dynamic relationship to left and right discourse. Citizen-consumers are said to be both constructed and corrupted through popular culture. On one side of the debate, the exercise of choice through purchase is supposed to guarantee the democratic workings of a market-driven society, because the culture industries are simply providing what the consuming public desires. It is also supposed to effect social change – for example, Denny's restaurant chain is boycotted by some leftists in the United States because of racist hiring practices. Many such activists also use the Working Assets long-distance telephone service because it donates a portion of its proceeds to left-wing causes. At certain moments, those on the left who resist authoritarian politics may embrace ideologies of liberal individualism and free choice, whereas at other times they may foreground questions of labour rather than consumption in a struggle for collective justice. Nation-building eras see a similar slippage between citizen and consumer, depending on the historical moment and geographical location. For example, state-based modernisation projects in Latin America between the 1930s and the 1960s utilised the mass media – song in Brazil, radio in Argentina and cinema in Mexico – to turn the masses, newly migrated to the cities, into citizens (Martín-Barbero, 1993). Conversely, the 1990s brought a wave of deregulation in the mass media, generally because of the 'Washington Consensus' and partly as a reaction to the clientelism and *dirigisme* of the authoritarian states of earlier decades. In lieu of citizen-building, the new logic of the culture industries is the construction of consumers. Néstor García-Canclini notes that this shift in emphasis from citizen to consumer is sometimes linked to the change in Latin America's dependency from Europe to the US: 'We Latin Americans presumably learned to be citizens through our relationship to Europe; our relationship to the United States will, however, reduce us to consumers' (2001: 1). And in the name of the consumer, ideas of the national popular are eschewed – consumer choice becomes an alibi for structural adjustment policies imposed by international lending institutions that call for privatisation of the media. Of course, the consumer is also figured into Hollywood's calculations and is subject to intense scrutiny, as our next section explains.

Surveillance

> Mr. Louden, who is directing an effort with the behavioral science unit of the FBI to create empirical records on serial killers, rapists and other criminal types, said that the McDermott film list could be useful as part of a psychological reconstruction. 'You have to look at the totality,' he said. 'And someone's movie preferences, when laid out at such length, would be helpful.' [Louden is referring to the Amazon.com video-DVD 'wish-list' of a man arrested for shooting seven people to death in a suburban Boston office.]
>
> (Pamela O'Connor, 2001: C4)

The industry's interest in audiences has seen another, seemingly conflictual paradigm emerging, under the sign of Foucault, that considers the contemporary moment as an electronic transformation of a long history of surveillance under modernity, from the panoptic prison designs of Jeremy Bentham to the all-seeing gaze and internalisation of today's mall security and virtual home cinema (Denzin, 1995).

The guiding ethos of immanent/imminent failure has a curious side-effect on Hollywood's vision of audiences. Filmgoers are at once perceived as the ultimate arbiter of a movie's success. Bad or good, films are judged at the box office. Yet, as we saw in Chapter 5, film marketing research treats filmgoers as potential threats – to be controlled rather than respected. Audiences are, after all, the causes of demand uncertainty; they are responsible for a certain Hollywood frenzy. In this sense, marketing scapegoats filmgoers for the industry's failure while providing apparent solutions for controlling them. This perception of audiences motivated early filmmakers and opinion pollsters to develop some rudimentary forms of audience research: silent movie comedians tested films for laughs (comedies still undergo more tests than most genres), studios collected audience opinions on 'idiot cards', and George Gallup monitored audience opinions with tele-voting machines while a movie played ('Lerner', 1999). Today, the presumption that audiences are an untamed labour force that must be domesticated for consumption justifies film marketing's ever deepening surveillance of people's feelings, opinions, loves and hates in a much more intense, even righteous, quest for knowledge of the film-going experience.

While there are excellent studies of film audience research, very little has been written on how these activities form part of a wider system of surveillance. That is perhaps a result of focusing too narrowly on the form and results of pre- and post-production surveys, focus groups, and consumer panels, pre-release test screening, and audience or box-office tracking. Wyatt's (1994) econo-aesthetic interpretation of high concept, for instance, relies on the same unexamined presumptions about the film-going experience as the film marketers themselves. He assumes that an audience must perceive marketing's mark of a film's difference in order for it to stand out as a 'differentiated product'; yet the audience must also perceive marketing's mark of a film's *likeness* to other films in order to minimise the uncertainty of box-office sales. Nestled in the unstable foundation of this paradoxical presumption is surveillance. The probability of an audience perceiving difference and/or sameness can only be guessed at after inquiring into people's tastes, preferences and abilities to articulate opinions about variety and quality.

Litman and Ahn (1998: 193) confirm that most research used by the film industry is based on 'uncertainty about audience preferences', which 'necessitates the development of an often vague "audience image" that governs much of the decision-making in the economic stages of the movie business'. Thus, in addition to surveillance, the assessment of audiences relies on a pre-scripted interpretation of the collective character of a probable audience (that is, actions that only make sense as marketplace behaviours in a story of economic rationality). So marketers conduct surevillance not to discover something new and wonderful about people's boundless diversity, identifications and creativity, but to sort people into predetermined marketplace identities with propensities to like certain kinds of movies or movie components and to buy certain kinds of goods and services. The best that marketers can do under these conditions is match film elements to those probable consumption habits – that is, after all, what banks and assorted investors who want their brands inscribed in film narratives in product placement pay for – selling the film and the associated merchandise in an integrated marketing concept.

Nevertheless, in doing this, professional marketers profess a better way to judge and sell a film than by intuition, strong feelings for a pet project, or outright saturation of theatres. Marketers' confidence derives from their use of survey research to endow their decisions and recommendations with an aura of pseudo-science. Most studio executives who use marketing research today find utility in such *hubris*, since it gives marketing the immediate disciplinary function of bending the ears of uncooperative directors and producers to make them 'hear something' from the test audiences that 'they don't want to hear from us' (Willens, 2000: 20). If a major distributor wants to change a movie, it wields the marketing research to the point of manipulating it in support of its point of view. As director Andrew Bergman puts it, 'if the test is bad, the studio panics', and the Hollywood frenzy crashes down on the director. But, adds Bergman, 'If it goes well they say, "It doesn't mean anything" and the studio heatedly demands changes anyway' (quoted in Willens, 2000: 20). With the hammer of marketing research behind them, says John Frankenheimer, 'they have the power' to put 'terrible pressure' on the director 'to make the movie they want' (quoted in Willens, 2000: 11). Here are signs pointing to common ground between filmgoers and filmmakers opposed to consumer surveillance, a place we revisit in the Conclusion. For now, we note that there is deep discord among many directors and producers. They see any surveillance designed to fine tune their film as 'part of the dumbing down of the business'. For a few dissenters, like Stone or Coppola, who do not mind the basic principle of giving a film a final test run in front of audiences, the problem is, as Stone puts it, when testing threatens to reduce filmmaking to 'a product-oriented business' that ruins a film's integrity and makes the director a mere 'cog in the machine' (quoted in Willens, 2000: 20). Nevertheless, there are as many if not more cogs in the machine who, in exchange for an aggressive and well-financed sales and promotion effort from distributors, happily surrender their movie to the scrutiny of audience research and the distributor's demands.

Many small firms handle subcontracting surveillance work for a distributor's marketing division. For instance, marketing executives at Gramercy hired thirty separate advertising agencies to promote *Four Weddings and a Funeral*. Each agency drew on files from databases in which they had independently stored volumes of consumer information collected for previous jobs. Their goal was to identify other advertisers whose customer base matched Gramercy's idea of *Four Weddings'* probable audience (Lukk, 1997). By cross-matching information drawn from previous consumer surveillance efforts, these agencies found retailers with whom Gramercy formed alliances to promote each other's products (florists, travel agents, airlines, specialty coffee shops, bridal stores).

The sales effort may involve dozens of firms, but there is only one large audience research company devoted entirely to studying the film audience. The

National Research Group (NRG) effectively dominates this sector of the industry, holding exclusive contracts with all major distributors and most of the prominent second-tier companies. As Mark Horowitz (1997), producer of *Kindergarten Cop* (Ivan Reitman, 1990) and *The Nutty Professor* (Tom Shadyac, 1996), said of the NRG's research, 'everybody in the industry, the ones who are really in the game, looks at this stuff'.

The NRG's offices are located in Hollywood in 'purposefully anonymous quarters with claustrophobic corridors, lots of opaque glass and all the personality of a CIA front' ('Lerner', 1999: 18). The NRG provides tracking studies that gauge awareness of upcoming releases, preview screenings and post-viewing focus groups, overseas market analysis, and testing for a film's appeal in terms that it can apply to video sales and other exhibition windows. It also tests the appeal of film titles and how television spots and print advertising for films are working (Klady, 1998: 9). Prices for these services range from US$15,000 per test screening up to US$500,000 charged to big-budget movies for full service market research. The NRG was founded during the late 1970s boom in marketing research. After making a big impression on its first client, Coppola, for testing *Apocalypse Now* (1979), the NRG became best known for the tests of *Fatal Attraction* (Adrian Lyne, 1987) that caused Warner Bros. to change the ending for US audiences. The NRG has amassed a proprietary consumer database that links audience attendance to 'every major motion picture released since 1982, cross-referenced by actor, director, box office, genre, studio, country and just about any other index imaginable' ('Lerner', 1999: 18).

About 2,000 people work full-time for the NRG in the US, but the bulk of the surveillance legwork is carried out by unskilled, part-time interviewers. Writer Preston Lerner ('Lerner', 1999) followed these 'recruiters' around to detail their labour. He found them roaming 'suburban malls and multiplexes with ever-present clipboards' looking for prospective interview subjects. The recruiters were instructed to gather a group that best matched the test film's broadest probable audience. This statistically correct test audience was supposed to be 'plucked', as Lerner aptly put it, 'from the heartland of the bell curve'. But because these young workers' wages depended on the number of people they delivered, they were 'notoriously and understandably reluctant to reject test-screening candidates'. This seriously compromised the statistical protocols they were expected to follow. To help ensure that the 550 people waiting to be interviewed shared attributes with the presumed audience for the film, the recruiters were told to make sure that the recruits were between 17 and 49 years of age, did not work in the entertainment-information industry, and had seen at least two of the following movies: *Scream* (Wes Craven, 1996), *Scream II* (Wes Craven, 1997), *Wild Things* (John McNaughton, 1998), *Mimic* (Guillermo Del Toro, 1997), *An American Werewolf in Paris* (John Landis, 1997), *I Know What*

You Did Last Summer (Jim Gillespie, 1997) and *Alien Resurrection* (Jean-Pierre Jeunet, 1997). Apparently, these films were analogous in some way with the test film. By associating them with the test film, perhaps the NRG could better assess the film's positioning. A flyer handed to recruits said the film was called *The Whole Nine Yards* (Jonathan Lynn, 2000), and described it as 'an outrageous dark comedy' starring Bruce Willis in 'a life-and-death struggle with disastrous but hilarious consequences'. At the end of the movie, the work of the recruits began. Interviewers distributed two-page questionnaires to the people they had corralled into the theatre, which asked: 'How would you rate the performances? Which scenes did you like? What do you think of the ending? and Where were you confused?' Later a smaller focus group was formed from this sample audience to work clarifying the survey answers (Lerner, 1999: 18). In addition to these special test screenings, the NRG conducts phone interviews with about 400 people across the US three times a week to assess film awareness and first-choice options (Klady, 1996: 3).

Today, the NRG helps to plan marketing for almost all major Hollywood films in the US and Europe. The only significant challenges to the NRG's dominance in the field of motion picture audience research have come from outside the traditional market research business – Lieberman Research tried and failed to win business away from the NRG in the mid-1990s, and even the venerable Gallup Organization could not compete with the NRG, though it re-launched its Motion Picture Research Division in 1994 after forty years (Klady, 1994: 1).

One new challenger in the audience surveillance field is MovieFone, a consumer spy operation owned by AOL-Time Warner that is disguised as a phone service offering movie times, locations and bookings. In pursuit of its goal to sell box-office revenue predictions, MovieFone has been amassing a huge database on filmgoers' preferences and spending habits from the over two million weekly calls it gets in twenty-eight US metropolitan areas. One MovieFone executive couldn't sugarcoat his spying disposition: 'We know who our callers are,' he said, 'and have set up tests to monitor their preferences' (quoted in Klady, 1996: 3). The number of inquiry calls received on this service mirrors later ticket sales, and so it has become a surveillance device for predicting audience moves (Sreenivasan, 1997; for a benign interpretation, see Orwall, 2001).

Other challengers are in the Internet consumer surveillance business, where the NRG has already begun to develop research with sister companies Nielsen Media and NetRatings. One is the Hollywood Stock Exchange (HSX). As of 2000, HSX had 570,000 registered users, mostly affluent young men, who trade stocks of movies and bonds of stars. Every movie or star traded on the site has a value in fake H-dollars. Music groups are also traded. HSX makes up initial prices based on past performances and sales, then lets trading determine price fluctuations, which it tracks as if it were a Wall Street exchange. Reports in

Advertising Age described ersatz trading on HSX: Piper Perabo's 'StarBond' was 'trending upwards' above H$1,100, while *Coyote Ugly* (David McNally, 2000), a film in which Perabo appears, was trading stock in the H$30 range, far below *Space Cowboys*' (Clint Eastwood, 2000) stock, in the high US$50s; Winona Ryder's StarBond hovers above Eastwood's, while neither star has reached Kevin Bacon's H$2,218 high; and so on (Friedman, 2000b: 24). 'HSX was conceived as a game to take advantage of the public's obsession with box-office numbers', said one of the founders, but HSX's real plan is to sell forecasts based on 'information it has collected on the folks who frequent the site' (Bates, 2000: C1). HSX's success in predicting such otherwise unpredictable successes as *The Blair Witch Project* (Daniel Myrick and Eduardo Sánchez, 1999) has not yet convinced major distributors to rely on its services. A major source of doubt is the statistical profile of its users, who are mostly 20-something male movie fans, with average household incomes of more than US$53,000. Nevertheless, some movie executives are interested. As one *Los Angeles Times* reporter wondered, 'maybe it's true: rich young guys do rule pop culture' (Bates, 2000: C1).

The irony that flows from the film industry's problem of how to 'know' audiences might help attenuate worries about the surveillance activities taking place in global Hollywood. At this point, however, it is important to recall that the main users of marketing information and labour are large entertainment conglomerates. The gamble of predicting the whereabouts and desires of the audience, while generating many amusing stories of blunders and missteps, is no joke to them. They demand from all who work for them the defence of their marketing assets, whether these are built upon a product differentiation barrier to entry, a lucrative marketing unit, or some other highly capitalised venture involving marketing and marketing research. This creates constant pressure on marketing executives and marketing researchers to refine their techniques, to build better methods of data collection and bigger databases. In short, marketers encounter two structural challenges at once. They must strive to overcome film marketing's fragile reputation and at the same time satisfy unyielding corporate demand for more, and more accurate, information on people's lives. These structural pressures drive marketing research inexorably into ever more extensive and invasive areas of surveillance.

Marketing firms have opted for a few different strategies to advance information gathering and analysis. The computer industry offers new tracking devices that have surpassed traditional marketing strategies for their invasiveness and mendacity. For example, new spy techniques have emerged from Silicon Valley concealed within a gadget that eliminates television advertisements and automatically records television shows that viewers want to see. The catch is that the devices are hooked up to the Internet to allow the service providers, TiVo and ReplayTV, to collect information on every choice, channel change and skipped commercial. In addition to amassing a huge database of consumer information, this particular surveillance device is capable of pinpointing the identities and actions of individual television viewers (Lewis, 2001: 40; Rose, 2001b). Like HSX and MovieFone, these surveillance operations conceal their spying activities by offering what looks like a free or low-cost gift – a game, a directory service or a way to enhance television viewing. Each exchange appears to favour consumer needs, but in actuality is merely a lure to get users to generate personal information, which the company then transforms into proprietary market research. In effect, they create an involuntary informational labour market from which they can surreptitiously exploit the effort that gives value to their enterprise. Whenever the Internet and digital technology are involved, the entertainment media will always get more from you than you get from them (Raphael, 2001). The Personal Video Recorder, initially hated by television networks anxious about their ratings, has been transmogrified by them into a source of consumer information with which to seduce advertisers (Rose, 2001b).

The established, larger marketing firms have long exploited this informational labour. The NRG, of course, offers free previews of Hollywood features in exchange for viewer data and opinions. Like other traditional market research firms, it has sought to advance this surveillance technique by sticking largely to a business strategy, conservative by comparison to Internet enterprises, that focuses on updating existing tracking hardware and analytical software to add value to its already engorged databases. It has also sought to build strategic alliances and cross-licensing agreements to help its cause, perhaps even investing in non-traditional ventures, as the NRG's parent firm has.

None of these schemes measure up to the scale and scope of changes that have followed concentration and conglomeration strategies in the consumer surveillance industry. As large marketing firms reach a limit point for internal innovation and growth, they have begun purchasing competitors and merging databases, software and licensing deals into even bigger corporations. By getting bigger, marketing firms hope to get better surveillance results. This strategy corresponds with a thirty-year pattern of intense concentration in the global entertainment-information industry. Concentration in the consumer research business creates global surveillance services on a sufficiently large scale and with enough variety to meet the demands of transnational corporations, whose businesses encompass interlocking interests in media, entertainment and retail industries. The globalisation of consumer surveillance has resulted in unprecedented levels of capitalisation in proprietary market research, with one multinational conglomerate rising to dominate this area in the 1990s. That the multinational corporation happens to be the parent firm of the NRG.

The NRG exemplifies the NICL's surveillance sector, and not merely for its

singular role in testing and tracking film audience preferences. More import-
antly, the NRG forms part of a much larger surveillance network owned by the
Dutch firm Verenigde Nederlandse Uitgeversbedrijven (VNU), or United
Dutch Publishers. In fact, the NRG is just one of seventeen market research sub-
sidiaries operated by VNU USA's Marketing Information Services Group
(MIS). VNU has long been an important business information provider
through professional newsletters, trade magazines, directories and trade shows
and a publisher of telephone directories and consumer magazines in Europe,
Japan, South Africa and Puerto Rico. It owns several financial data services, a
film distributor in the Netherlands, where it is building a chain of television
stations, and the largest consumer magazine publisher in the Czech Republic.
Its marketing research operations span North America and Europe, and it holds
85 per cent of ORG-MARG, the leading market research company in India. Its
most prominent magazines include *Editor & Publisher Magazine* and those
published by VNU USA's subsidiary, BPI Communications, *Hollywood
Reporter, Adweek* and *Billboard* magazines, among others. BPI also manages the
Clio Awards, which celebrate and promote good will toward the advertising
industry ('VNU', 2000; 'VNU NV', 2000).

By 2000, VNU USA had become one of the leading business information
and service providers in the world, largely through its control over the principal commercial and consumer surveillance companies in North America.
VNU USA's 1997 acquisition of NRG from Saatchi & Saatchi was followed in
1999 by its US$2.5 billion purchase from Dun & Bradstreet of both Nielsen
Media Research (television and Internet audience measurement) and a
majority share of Nielsen NetRatings (Internet user measurement), giving it
leading audience and consumer tracking companies for film, television and
the Internet. In 2000, as part of an anti-trust settlement following the Nielsen
purchases, VNU sold Competitive Media Reporting – the biggest advertising
tracking service in the US and the leader in Internet usage surveillance – to
the world's fourth-largest market research company, Taylor Nelson Sofres,
which already dominates media tracking in Europe, in particular through its
UK Tellex and French TNS Secodip operations (Tomkins, 2000: 24). Soon
thereafter, VNU completed its absorption of the old Nielsen empire with the
US$2.3 billion purchase of A.C. Nielsen Corporation, the world leader in con-
sumer behaviour surveillance and analysis (Elliot, 2000: C7). Among VNU's
remaining holdings in surveillance are Claritas, Scarborough, Spectra, and
National Decision Systems. Finally, as a symbol of its growing wealth, VNU
USA signed the largest lease for New York City property in 1999 to house its
headquarters in a former department store in the East Village, a deal that incidentally 'came with about US$9 million in tax incentives from the city and
state' (Kanter, 1999: 1).

VNU USA subsidiaries:

- A.C. Nielsen Corporation
- Bill Communications Inc.
- BPI Communications Inc.
- NetRatings Inc (54 per cent)
- Nielsen Media Research Inc.

VNU USA's products and services:

A.C. Nielsen Corp. – survey and analysis of sales and consumer behaviour.

Adman/AMS – accounting services and software for advertising agencies.

Aircheck International Ltd – online forum for radio industry advocacy, Ireland.

Bill Communications Inc. – conglomerate (food, beverage, business travel services, conference services, retail, sporting goods).

BPI Communications Inc. – film and music magazine publisher (e.g., *Billboard, Hollywood Reporter, Adweek*), administers Clio Awards.

Broadcast Data Systems (BDS): Operations/Sales and Marketing – monitors radio station airplay.

Claritas Inc. – Marketing research (geo-demographics).

Competitive Media Reporting (Sold to Taylor Nelson Sofres PLC in 2000) – media planning and buying; advertising expenditure tracking.

Entertainment Marketing Information Services – point of sale promotions: retail entertainment products (through EMS) and POS tracking of video, music, and books (through VideoScan, SoundScan, SoundData, and BookScan).

HCIA-Sachs – healthcare market research.

Interactive Market Systems (IMS/MRP) – media planning and buying; advertising expenditure tracking; MRP markets, IMS products; UK, Canada and US firms.

Intermedia Advertising Solutions (IAS) – Internet advertising expenditure tracking.

MediaPlan – server technology for media and marketing planners.

National Decision Systems – geo-demographic market research.

National Research Group Inc. – film audience research; consulting.

NetRatings Inc. (54 per cent) – Internet user research.

Nielsen Media Research Inc. – television market research and information.

PERQ/HCI Research Corporation – media planning/buying; tracking healthcare advertising expenditure.

Retail Marketing Systems (RMS) – geo-demographic market segmentation
   research.

Scarborough Research – syndicated custom and panel consumer behaviour
   research.

Spectra Marketing Systems Inc. – geo-demographic research.

SRDS – print and electronic media market information.

Trade Dimensions/NRB – geo-demographic research.

Video Monitoring Services of America/VMS – abstracts of local and network
   television programme content.

VNU Consumer Research Services – Syndicated custom and panel consumer
   behaviour research.

In a trend that is sure to continue, VNU established a strategic alliance with
Equifax in 2000, a move that extended its surveillance network into new areas.
Equifax is a credit reporting agency that gathers personal information related
to individual debt, income and purchasing throughout the Americas and in
Europe. The company determines hundreds of millions of people's creditworthiness for credit card transactions, loans, cheques and insurance. The
relationship with Equifax began when VNU purchased National Decision Systems from them in 1996. This partnership in marketing and cross-licensing of
consumer surveillance products not only gave VNU 'one of the most robust
databases in the industry', as the then president of VNU MIS put it. It made
VNU one of the few firms to offer a single source for predicting 'demographic,
lifestyle and financial behaviour of consumers' ('Equifax', 2000).

Prior to purchasing the A.C. Nielsen Corp., VNU had already struck a deal
with the company to help VNU globalise and strengthen its primary business
of entertainment audience research. The purchase of A.C. Nielsen Corp. in 2000
gave VNU undisputed dominance in tracking box-office sales, through A.C.
Nielsen's subsidiary Entertainment Data Inc., and in the global consumer
research business, where A.C. Nielsen has operations in over one hundred
countries. The acquisition further expanded VNU's surveillance network by
offering a 'single source of complete consumer insights' for the home video distributor and related trade and consumer media ('VNU and ACNielsen', 1999).
The initial alliance with A.C. Nielsen was formed to market VNU's VideoScan,
which provides home video distributors with video and DVD point-of-sale
tracking, and is often credited with boosting distributor acceptance of the DVD
format. A.C. Nielsen's surveillance of sales through discount mass merchandisers, drug stores and grocery stores, including information and analysis from its
trademarked consumer panel, was thus merged with VideoScan's records of
purchases from specialty retailers, direct mail and Internet. VideoScan is also

the dominant source of video industry information for *Billboard*, *Hollywood Reporter*, *Video Business*, *Video Week*, *New York Times*, *Los Angeles Times*, *Wall Street Journal* and other trade and consumer publications ('VNU and ACNielsen', 1999). VNU had previously integrated consumer surveillance with its trade magazines to sell information on sport fans and amateur athletes through one of its subsidiary holdings, Bill Communications (Bill's Sports Trend Info, a marketing research firm, tracks retail sporting goods sales and sells consumer data to subscribers and advertisers of Bill's *Sporting Goods Dealer* magazine).

The NRG story reveals that film marketing research is located in a much wider political economy of consumer surveillance, where the horizon stretches in line with the growing concentration and conglomeration in US and European entertainment industries. Even if VNU's 'bigger-is-better' idea does not eliminate the inherent problem of knowing the film audience, VNU helps to make Hollywood global by meeting the demand of entertainment conglomerates that must now imagine filmmaking within an integrated marketing concept, one that includes all the major exhibition windows (theatrical release, home video, pay-per-view TV, national cable and satellite television, network television, local cable and broadcast television and the Internet) plus recorded music and publishing, as well as tie-in merchandising and cross promotions with retailers, restaurants and any other entertainment or leisure industry promotion. In Malaysia, for example, US-style surveillance permits the continuation of US texts on prime-time television – they rate lower than domestic programmes, but the consumption pattern of their ruling-class fans is more powerful than the taste of ordinary viewers (Karthigesu, 1998: 50).

Finally, it is important to note that, at present, globalisation of audience research is still largely financed through massive surveillance of the US population. That is, while the large MNCs are globalising the consumer-surveillance business, most investment in film audience research remains focused on US filmgoers. This is, in part, an effect of the non-existent or, where they exist, shamefully pro-business privacy laws in the US, which pale when measured against the EU's more comprehensive protections against surveillance (Maxwell, 1999). The surveillance bias towards the US filmgoer also reflects the lack of business opportunities for film audience research firms outside the US. Audience research requires heavy investment that is hard to justify in small national film markets, and it is virtually non-existent in all but a few urban enclaves of the poor regions of Asia, Eastern Europe, Latin America and Africa. Consider that for most British films it is cost-effective simply to wait until a film opens in order to judge its commercial potential, given the comparatively small national audience (Andrews, 1998: 1). In contrast, the sheer size of the US filmgoing population guarantees a better return on investments in motion-picture audience research and consumer research generally. In this way, the US population functions as a valuable productive asset for the majors, as well as the market research MNCs like VNU, to the exclusion of other competitors. This is another instance where major distributors are able to exploit economies of scale to purchase and accumulate consumer information that most independent and non-US competitors cannot afford. Understanding these political and economic conditions helps explain why global consumer surveillance in general, and film audience research in particular, concentrate their spying on the US population.

Conclusion

> Our movies and TV programs are hospitably received by citizens around the world.
>
> (Jack Valenti, quoted in Gershon, 1997: 47)

If VNU is an indication of things to come, we can predict that consumer surveillance will follow the trend towards greater concentration of corporate control over the infrastructure of consumption. And, with its rapacious appetite for innovation of techniques for 'knowing' filmgoers, the industry's construct of audiences will continue to be ascendant, absorbing much of the depoliticised discourse of active audiences as well as a deracinated vision of the globe-trotting, deal-seeking citizen. Both make up people as marketplace citizens whose labours of interpretation, judgement, enjoyment and so on are exploited without much contest (so far) in the informational labour market created and regulated by consumer research in the service of global Hollywood. With this in mind, we draw attention again to integrated marketing that depends on research that tracks people's filmgoing, consumer tastes, television viewing, Internet use, financial information, people's whereabouts, behaviours and beliefs. These surveillance capabilities are poised to converge with recent technological innovations in digital telecommunication film and television delivery. They embody the DEM, but as a tool of control rather than critique. Whereas the state and critics see the audience as a dope in need of protection, marketers view it as a dope in need of exploitation. The result is a regime of surveillance that produces the GEM as a negative political reaction and the DEM as a negative psychic one. In each case, the audience is a drastically overextended signifier, onto which are projected fantasies of consumption.

TiVo and ReplayTV (the dead labour of active audiences?) are just beginning to experiment with new modes of real-time tracking of television viewing over the Internet (the living labour of audiences made even more productive for capital). The majors, for their part, are considering an electronic film format that can be digitally downloaded and screened. While forecasting the decline of traditional film projection is something of a cottage industry in itself, recent demonstrations in direct-to-theatre satellite delivery have convinced a number of Hollywood distributional arms to create executive departments to research and pursue this new technology. While distributors hope to save millions of dollars in print reproduction, the enormous cost of even partial conversion of traditional theatres, as well as the much greater problem of hackers breaking the encryption keys that are supposed to keep satellite delivery piracy-free, have Hollywood on a firm course to seek ever more complex methods of copyright control.

When digital film delivery arrives, filmgoers should expect the industry to alter images surreptitiously for digital product and commercial message placement, as sport fans exposed to digital inserts on televised sporting events already see. They will do this as long as the industry view of audiences as marketplace citizens is allowed to persist. In this scenario, filmgoers would view scenes with digitally placed brands, digitally altered retail signage and other 'brandable' features in the background that can be localised to fit viewing locations, targeting specific locales with commercial plugs for local retailers. The active audience member would walk out of the cinema and encounter a shop or brand that had just appeared in a film, and in marketers' dreams, that filmgoer will be positively disposed to buy something (of course, this will be touted as the voluntary action of an independent mind). Merchandising and tie-ins could be built around the flexibility of such digital delivery. The consumer surveillance industry is gathering the kind of geo-demographic information it needs to do this. Filmmakers like Lucas are experimenting with digital delivery systems.

As long as filmgoers' cultural citizenship is represented through the marketers' vision of audiences – and the franchise of one dollar, one vote – it is bound to happen. For those who question the influence of marketing on the movies, not to mention the commercialisation of everything, this forecast is appalling. The *next* question is whether marketing and audience-bearing discourses will continue to influence the way movies are made, and the answer has a lot to do with how we imagine the society we want to live in. This should be an abiding lesson for screen studies: the medium's promiscuity points every day and in every way towards the social and its inequalities. The screen is three things, all at once: a *recorder* of reality (the unstaged pro-filmic event); a *manufacturer* of reality (the staged and edited event); and *part of* reality (watching film as a social event on a Saturday night, a protest event over sexual, racial or religious stereotyping, or a site for being analysed for one's patterns of desire). The DEM and the GEM apply to both citizen and consumer – audience categories that are as real and purposive, unfortunately, as the people whose lives they purport to describe whilst drawing them into Hollywood's division of labour. The DEM and the GEM are probably impossible to demolish, so fixed are they at the centre of public, academic, media and governmental discourse. But they can at least be read for what they are – signs of activity in search of control, not sources of empirical truth.

Conclusion

At the end of 50 years journeying the American Motion Picture Industry stood on a mountaintop from which the beacon of its silver screen was sending rays of light and color and joy into every corner of the earth.

(Will Hays, 1938, quoted in Grantham, 2000: 1)

What's the point of saying no to America's nuclear ships when we've said yes, a thousand times yes, to the Trojan Horse of American Culture, dragging it throughout city gates into our very lounge-rooms. MGM is mightier than the CIA. . . . We are, all of us, little by little, becoming ventriloquial dolls for another society. We are losing our authenticity, our originality, and becoming echoes.

(*Australian Weekend Magazine*, quoted in Pendakur, 1990: 16–17)

The Washington Family, the large painting which Edward Savage completed in Philadelphia in 1796, aptly captured Washington's vision for the seat of empire. In it the family sits around a map of the federal city with the wide majestic Potomac River behind them. Washington rests his arm on the shoulder of young George Washington Parke Custis. The boy, symbolic of the next generation, rests his hand on the globe.

(Kenneth Bowling, 1991: 208)

While *How the Grinch Stole Christmas* (Ron Howard, 2000) dominated US theatres in late 2000, *flâneurs* in the Peoples' Republic of China could already buy dubbed or subtitled DVD versions of *Guijingling* for US$1.20 apiece – and pirated copies of the government's anti-corruption video, *Life and Death Choice*. Both discs were playable on technology made in state-owned factories. (Illegal use of the format became popular after pirated copies of *Titanic* outsold the more expensive legal ones (sales of 25 million versus 300,000) [Smith, 2000a].) The same week as the *Grinch*'s theft, Hollywood's Screen Actors Guild announced that members' earnings for 1999 had gone up by just 1.3 per cent on the previous year, despite the booming US economy and the extraordinary amounts paid to big stars (Kiefer, 2000). Across town, two other monetary deals were revealed. The MPAA released a study showing that copyright contributed more to the US economy in 1999 than any other industrial sector, with US$79.65 billion in overseas sales (McClintock, 2000a). And with copyright on its Mouse about to expire, Disney gave Trent Lott money for his re-election on the very day that the Republican Congressional leader and Klan fellow-traveller sponsored a Bill extending their control of the rodent by another twenty years (Bromley, 1999). A few months later, AOL-Time Warner was busy issuing cease-and-desist orders against young fans of the *Harry Potter* books around the world who had the gall to create Web pages without obtaining permission from the rights holders, who were looking forward to a profitable film about the young hero's gripping adventures (Ingram, 2001).

We shall have more on *Harry Potter* later. For now, let us say that, like the other snapshots above, it carries a clear message – globalisation's significance for the screen varies between concerns over American-dominated cultural flow, as per cultural imperialism, the international spread of capitalistic production and conglomerates, and attempts to govern the chaotic, splintered circulation of signs across cultures. Ownership is concentrated in a diminishing number of increasingly large corporations. What used to be nationally-dominated markets for terrestrial television have undergone vast changes. Companies like Disney are in a position to produce films, promote them across a variety of sub-sidiaries, screen them on an owned network, and generate television replicas – not to mention CDs, reading material, toys and branded apparel – and all with an eye to external profits (but they may cower in the face of Marguerite Duras' condemnation of EuroDisney as 'cultural Chernobyl') (McChesney, 1999: 4; Duras quoted in Van Maanen, 1992: 26). All of this is purposive, much of it is facilitated by (formally) democratically accountable politicians, and none of it is 'necessary'. It can be reversed or changed.

Of course, some theorists are sanguine about such developments, stressing the skill of audiences in negotiating texts, or offering multicultural business strat-egies, themselves a segment of US transnationalism extending its domain. Others focus on the direction of multinational finance: the Hollywood studios have recently been French-, Japanese-, Canadian- and Australian-owned, and are increasingly beholden to cross-cultural audiences for their success. But at the same time as this apparent diversity appears, the means of communication, association and political representation are converging (Jacka, 1992: 5, 2; Jame-son, 1991: xiv–xv; Reeves, 1993: 36, 62; Sreberny-Mohammadi, 1996: 3–8). Hollywood has embarked on a vigorous campaign of outspending its opposi-tion. Whereas the average cost of feature films in France, the UK, Australia and Italy barely rose between 1990 and 1997 (it remained well below US$10 million), the average cost of features in the US went from US$26 million in 1990 to US$39 million in 1996 and US$53 million in 1997. In 1999, Hollywood spent US$8.7 billion, a total far in excess of all other national cinemas combined (European Audiovisual Observatory, 1998; 'Film Production and Distribution', 2000).

Pollyannaish critics of cultural imperialism discourse should have been given especial pause on the cusp of the new century, as Hollywood exported its run-away NICL gaze to South-East Asia. Thai environmental and pro-democracy activists publicised the arrogant despoliation they experienced when Fox was making *The Beach* (Danny Boyle, 2000) in Maya Bay, part of Phi Phi Islands National Park. Natural scenery was bulldozed in late 1998 because it did not fit the producers' fantasy of a tropical idyll. They paid off the government with a donation to the Royal Forestry Department and a campaign with the Tourism Authority of Thailand to twin the film as a promotion for the country. Mean-while, the next monsoon saw the damaged sand dunes of the region collapse – natural defences against erosion had been destroyed by Hollywood bulldozers. All the while, director Boyle claimed that the film was 'raising environmental consciousness' among a local population allegedly 'behind' US levels of 'aware-ness' (Justice for Maya Bay International Alliance, 2000). Much of *Tomb Raider* (Simon West, 2001) was shot at Angkor Wat, Cambodian sandstone temple ruins dating from the ninth century. Four other Hollywood films went into pro-duction there soon afterwards. The producers sought new and cheap terrain (they pay just US$10,000 a day to film in a wonder of the world, with the money going to a petroleum company which inherited the preservation department's duties as part of privatisation; and the filmmakers had roads built for them by the military). The government sought a promotion for filmmaking in concert with Thailand (under the slogan 'two countries, one film locale' and 'Desti-nation Thailand') and a boost to tourism that showed the country as safe in its post-Khmer Rouge incarnation. Critics feared destruction of the country's ancient treasures by visitors and the association of the ruins with the hyper viol-ence of *Tomb Raider* (the state allowed foreigners to bear arms – normally against the law – in order to ensure that the actress Angelina Jolie felt safe) (Seno and Reap, 2001; Rosenberg, 2001; 'Movie Shoot', 2000; 'Tough Girl', 2000). Meanwhile, Korean activists, actors and directors were shaving their heads, protesting in the streets, and going on hunger strikes against their gov-ernment's deal with the US to cut screen quotas, likening the decision to the experience of the Japanese empire (Kim, 2000: 364–65).

Globalisation stands for something real, a sense from across time, space and nation that those very categories are in peril. (Our sense of the temporal is ques-tioned – think of the panic generated by the thought of computers dealing with the difference between 1900 and 2000.) Space, too, is problematised by the NICL, as jobs are undertaken by people on the basis of price and docility rather than locale. And nations are threatened by corporate control, as unelected, far-distant élites displace or instruct locally 'accountable' politicians. In each category, the cultural corollary is clear. Time is manipulated in concert with the interests of global capital, space is torn asunder, and traditional social bonds are compromised by ownership based on profit rather than township. At the

political, economic and class level, this can lead to 'social and economic fatal-
ism and chronic insecurity'. Democracies seem unable to deal with economic
forces (Held *et al.*, 1999: 1).

But counter-power is always at work. Textiles, shipping and agriculture
remain massively subsidised across the world. The US, supposedly a poster-
child for free trade and true competition, has hundreds of anti-dumping
measures aimed at blocking imports where prices have been 'unfairly' set, and
maintains a semi-secret deal with Japan to restrict steel sales, while the EU
remains firm on refusing to import genetically modified beef. The Seattle 1999
and Washington 2000 actions in opposition to 'Washington Consensus' hacks
illustrated as much. Environmentalists, trade unions and consumer groups
have problematised globalisation as defined by neo-liberal *nostra*. All of this
leads the *Economist*, a key business advocacy voice, to admit that 'Globalization
is not irreversible' ('Storm Over Globalization', 1999).

Bourdieu postulates a model of world culture that continues the bipolarity
of the Cold War, if without its political ramifications, military corollaries and
economic isolations. His vision of the struggle for world culture pits the United
States *contra* France – *laissez-faire* dogma juxtaposed against cultural nationalism. This Enlightenment conflict between anomic monads and collective
identities sets bourgeois individualism and collaborative unity against each
other, with reincarnations of the Depression and Sovietism hanging over each
model. Bourdieu calls for a pre-Marxist, Hegelian way through the debate, a
democratic mode that favours the state neither as an aid to capital accumulation nor as totalitarian, but as the expression of a popular will that
contemplates itself collectively rather than atomistically, and acts under the sign
of a general interest rather than singular egotism (Bourdieu, 1999: 20). That
struggle – of structure and agency, of capital and the state intricated in the production and symbolism of culture – requires analysis via political economy
mixed with cultural studies. The critical question for such work is this: in an
era of globalised film and television, the idea that audiovisual spaces should be
accountable to local viewers, as well as far-distant shareholders, is a powerful
one. But how much can be expected from citizenship and consumer ideals
when for the first time, trade between corporations exceeds that between states;
deregulation sees huge monopoly capitalists converging and collaborating;
screen texts are designed to transcend linguistic and other cultural boundaries;
textual diversity is a myth; cultural production is not independent of the state;
and finally, many of us live in societies that deny or limit our citizenship and
consumption claims? Does this mean that notions of citizenship and consumption are useless in discussing accountability, sovereignty and democracy
with regards to the culture industries?

Not exactly. Theorists such as George Yúdice (2000) and García-Canclini

(2001) have elaborated alternative models of citizenship and consumption that improve on standard left-wing critiques of cultural imperialism (watching US drama will turn rural people around the world into Idaho potato farmers) and invectives about socially responsible shopping (purchasing environmentally sound toilet paper and free-range chicken will transform the world, one roll/wing at a time). Yúdice argues that it may no longer be possible to speak of citizenship and democracy without also considering consumption. First World practices, such as juridical prosecution of discrimination in the private workplace, and practices from Latin America – for example the need to go beyond individual consumer choices in cultural politics to consider the collaboration of local groups, transnational businesses, financial institutions, media and non-governmental organisations – can combine. García-Canclini agrees, and although he acknowledges that the private takeover of state cultural functions has 'compounded the already existing problems of the inadequate development and instability of our democracies' (2001: 2) and threatens Latin American civil society, he also believes that it is necessary to expand notions of citizenship to include consumption of health, housing and education.

Yúdice and García-Canclini propose a regional federalism to promote a specifically Latin American media space, with the state setting quotas for Latin American productions in movie theatres, radio broadcasts and television programming, the creation of a Foundation for the Production and Distribution of Latin American media, and policies designed to strengthen Latin American economies and regulate foreign capital in order to foster a citizenship that promotes multiculturalism and democratises the relationship between the nation and the state (Yúdice, 1995).

García-Canclini (1996) criticises the widespread neo-liberal dismissal of the state as an inappropriate arbiter of regulation and control. He argues that the market and civil society are not the same thing, thus challenging tenets of neo-classical economics which assert that a free market best serves the interests of society at large. This does not mean a return to the critiques of left-wing cultural commentators that transnational culture perverts pure indigenous traditions. Indeed, his (1990) theories of hybridity preclude this kind of analysis. Nor does it elicit more aristocratic complaints that mass dissemination corrupts high art. Rather, it challenges neo-liberal policy-makers and authors such as Mario Vargas Llosa who assert that the free market finally allows peripherally produced cultural products such as Like Water for Chocolate (Alfonso Arau, 1992) to be disseminated around the world. García-Canclini asserts instead that without reviving nationalism, there must be a critical state intervention, one that recognises 'culture is too important to be relinquished exclusively to the competition among international markets' (1996: 155). Yúdice (2000) states that the creation of regional/continental trading blocs, organised with the intent of moderating US audiovisual dominance and providing space for local cultural expression outside national frameworks, must involve public-private partnerships, including the participation of non-governmental organisations, the state and industry.

This strategy to create an alternative media space diverges from the European model of pan-regional audiovisual culture in one fundamental way. It rejects the abiding logic of the EU's audiovisual cultural policy of privatisation and expansion of existing large industrial concerns. We saw in Chapter 3 how the 'Television Without Frontiers' directive deregulated national industries and fostered the rise of pan-European pay-TV conglomerates, fuelling Hollywood coffers at rates that far outpaced co-production treaty provisions. We also noted that while motion picture co-productions facilitated pan-European collaboration and distribution, they did so through exclusionary, art-house-centred boards that privileged artistic above-the-line talent without care for below-the-line labour standards or the openness of decision-making. Moreover, the existence of the NICL collapses the equation of the US with entertainment and Europe with education – the globalisation of cultural labour makes art cinema effectively a 'Euro-American' genre in terms of sweat, finance, marketing and management, not to mention that much of Hollywood itself is owned by foreigners (Lev, 1993). A seeming discontinuity with earlier concerns, when the EU had a primarily economic personality, is misleading: a notion of cultural sovereignty underpins concerns *vis-à-vis* the US, but so too does support for European monopoly capital and the larger states inside its own walls (Burgelman and Pauwels, 1992). There are, then, many good reasons to be sceptical about the model of European audiovisual space, so what can an alternative strategy of audiovisual space learn from it?

As the case of co-production attests, state provision is key to maintaining a diverse audiovisual culture through local, national and regional work. Perhaps the most productive state-capital alliance has been Canal Plus' proviso to spend 60 per cent on European works in exchange for its prominent position in the pay-TV market. This support has given France the strongest national film industry in Europe, which suggests that policy must amplify Europe's long history of broadcasting in the public interest, and extend this citizen-based philosophy from (what remain) public airwaves to the new media conduits of cable and satellite. With digital convergence of telephony and television, these conduits hold the potential to become new gateways of public expression, rather than freeways for Hollywood to take off in search of the NICL. This is of particular importance now, as European policy on convergence faces pressures from the US, the WTO and the OECD to liberalise policy. As one OECD representative suggests, 'there will be no need to have separate broadcasting and telecommunications regulators' under technological convergence. Because telecommunications policies on competition and foreign ownership are historically less restrictive than in broadcasting, it is important that legal reform quickly bring public interest and universal access rules to convergence policy initiatives (Harcourt, 1998: 442).

Recent mergers heighten urgency in these matters – 1999 mergers and acquisitions in Europe totaled US$1.3 trillion, a threefold increase since 1997. Much of this activity consisted of telecommunications mergers, such as the British firm Vodafone's hostile US$179 billion takeover of rival Mannesmann in 2000. Emerging global telecom conglomerates Vodafone, Vivendi and the Spanish Telefónica have been acquiring content producers to position themselves for televisual and telephonic convergence through the Internet (Hopewell, 2000). Behind the unleashing of market forces through privatisation and deregulation is the promise of a technological revolution and universal access to participatory expression. Yet as Shalini Venturelli has argued, liberalisation has not guaranteed the democratisation of expression as much as it has facilitated 'proprietary concentration' (1998: 56–58). Vivendi (Universal) holds stakes in the pan-European cable/satellite systems of Canal Plus (49 per cent) and BSkyB (25 per cent), and has an alliance with the world's largest wireless phone service, Vodafone AirTouch. This extends Vivendi's multi-access Internet portal Vizzavi to a potential 80 million subscribers. Unless the EU acts to stall this trend of convergence and concentration, there will be no place for public service policies such as the one that called on Canal Plus to support the national film industry (Goldsmith, 2000; James and Dawtrey, 2000).

There must be great care in ensuring that industry *compradores* do not overdetermine cultural policy. With a critical eye on the possibilities and limitations of the EU's model, García-Canclini (2001) asserts that the proposal of an audiovisual space is a good one for Latin America, because its particular way of being multicultural and modern is very different from both Europe and the US: Latin America prioritises solidarity over sectarianism. In this way, multiculturalism avoids separatism, which he states is the case in the US and Europe. Instead, there is a hybridity which precludes each fighting for his own; the Zapatistas in Chiapas, for example, link their regional and ethnic demands to the nation and to globalisation, mounting an inclusive critique of modernity that goes beyond the promotion of isolated local interests. García-Canclini attributes this to the hybrid ethnic and national identities in Latin America, which comprise a particularly uneven form of modernity that includes complicated mixtures of tradition, modernity and postmodernity and links the continent in a way that does not apply to Europe, because the former is almost entirely dominated by the Spanish language (with the notable but changing exception of Brazil). The organic unity of this language has been crucial, for example, in the pan-continental and global success of the *telenovela*, which sees production

sites, labour and intertextual references drawn from the entire continent, providing a precedent for a broader Latin American linkage in terms of both
personnel and cultural signification (Mato, 1999: 248–49; Mazziotti, 1996).

Because a resistive cultural policy depends on such organic linkages, it is
drawn into conflict with the chauvinism of national cultures and their border
wars. We have therefore pulled our theory of cultural imperialism away from
its historical attraction to the nation-state, which was resistive in its own
moment through the 1950s and 1960s. This dialectic took us back, in a sense,
to a more fundamental source of culture: work. As we urged in Chapter 1, cultural imperialism theory needs to be modified to account for its lost intellectual
cachet (noting that it has gained diplomatic and political adherents even as it
has lost academic fashionability). Our answer is to return to the person as
labourer, but not as an idealistic category of identity. We have installed a political and ethical regard for labour and its alienation into a model of citizenship
and consumer that allows us to question the role of states and markets in
extending or stemming the power of global Hollywood. Such a model of citizenship, we suggest, must deal with dedomiciled workers, with all the
dispossession entailed in that status. Citizenship assumes governmental policing of rights and responsibilities. Does this apply when a NICL is in operation,
and either the deregulation or the protection of media bourgeoisies seem to be
the only alternatives? To whom do you appeal as a person unhappy with the
silencing of your local dramatic tradition through television imports, but
demoralised by the representation of ethnic and sexual minorities or women
within so-called national screen drama or network news? We have seen first the
slow and now the quick dissolution of cultural protectionism on screen. That
hardly seems an effective place to struggle *vis-à-vis* citizenship, when such
effects of globalisation stem from a profound reconfiguration of the global
labour force. Efforts within the labour movement to overcome national chauvinism among its ranks will be crucial in this respect (Wasko, 1998: 183–86).

Audiences, too, are doing work. In contesting global Hollywood's command
over the NICL, and with it the conditions and possibilities of cultural labour
worldwide, we seek to articulate a materialist cultural policy on the same
ground of supra-nationalism proposed by García-Canclini and Yúdice. Such a
policy would extend to the consumer in order to comprehend the needs of any
number of constituencies currently excluded or marginalised from formal discussions of cultural trade, labour and consumption. Our policy would thereby
enact a different narrative of the filmgoing experience from the one that has
closed around the narrow institutional identity disciplined by intellectual
property, constituted in marketing narratives as an audience with tastes
amenable to market criteria, and unaware of the surveillance that surrounds it.

Policy that disarticulates intellectual property (IP) from corporate interests removes the cornerstone of Hollywood's global control over the resources for making and watching movies. Such policy begins with the practical problems that already weaken the corporate enclosure around intellectual property: (1) the prioritisation of copyright law alone fails to insure monopoly rights because it neglects the shift towards trademark law embraced by licence-based industries (like television); (2) copyright is far too difficult to enforce in so-called emerging markets; and (3) copyright has trouble working in new distributional arenas without seriously compromising user privacy. Further weaknesses can be found in the liberal foundation that already informs policy reform – whether to shore up progressive moral-rights provisions against corporate control or give corporations a human face. First, the issue of artistic livelihood is sustained only *accidentally* by copyright. More often than not, copyright involves the signing away of moral rights under work-for-hire doctrine. Second, copyright in its current evocation is tied to forms of legislation that grant legal personhood to corporations who become 'authors' in the act of contractual transfer. Finally, there is no equality in trade of IP because the slippery *Realpolitik* transfer of authorial moral-rights provisions privileges ownership-oriented regimes (which is what allowed the US, finally, to sign the Berne Convention). In sum, moral rights arguments work well within the narrow purview of tributary rights attached to the creative work (i.e., that it cannot be 'distorted' without approval from its author and that the authorship must always be attributed); however, by design, moral rights are incapable of negotiating the everyday ways in which IP relations are subject to the *commercial transfer* inherent in the 'right in the work'.

Perhaps what communications and cultural policy needs is a more nuanced approach to the issue of ownership. Rather than attend to issues of ownership at the level of production, why not begin with the act of *consumption*? Acts of consumption generate ownership in a myriad of ways. Taking advantage of limited rights attached to screen a copyrighted programme, you may screen Blockbuster videos within the confines of your own home, or in non-profit educational arenas. However, the rolling-back of first-sale rights (discussed in Chapter 4) creates digital property in the very act of consumption; this transitory act of ownership is used by the copyright industries as a warrant to install tracking technologies in your PC. Clearly, copyright cuts across the spatio-temporal parameters of ownership in specific ways.

Instead of endlessly recycling ownership ideals rooted in property, we suggest that cultural policy shift the debate to a recognition of bundles of consumer rights. Rather than protect sites of creation (rights to own) through the phantasmatic evocation of authorship under copyright law, policy might protect *rights to consume* (which are the key rights under fire in recent DMCA legislation). This would involve a thorough consideration of the public domain and fair use, not merely as byproducts designed in some way to compensate for the possible excesses of IP, but at a more fundamental level that ensures we have the rights to do things with texts, not simply the rights to sign them away in the act of creation (which is what common-law copyright does). A set of moral rights for the act of consumption (suggesting perhaps that we are libidinally connected to the acts of our consumption) rather than for the location of an originary act of creation might go a long way towards conceptualising the extension of fair use in the current informational environment. This re-tooling takes us away from fair use's traditional evocation as a form of subsidy given by copyright owners (see Ginsberg, 1997b), towards a form of subsidy to users, whose labour as audiences is exploited by market research that protects the results of their surveys – as IP, no less.

Since market research understands audiences as an untamed labour force that requires domestication, users might demand labour compensation in the form of an extension of fair use that keeps monopoly rights in check, rather than as simply an excuse for 'stealing'. In addition, user's rights would redeploy the public domain away from its conceptualisation as the maligned progeny of IP (Cain to the commercial imperative's Abel), which fences off discrete areas of knowledge from public use or serves as the public's toll for conferring private property rights in authorship. Instead, we might recognise that the public domain should be understood as 'a device that permits the rest of the system to work by leaving the raw materials of authorship available for others to use' (Litman, 1990: 968–69). In other words, the public domain must be the constitutive ground upon which creativity rests, rather than its remainder. This idea is at the heart of the open-source movement. To achieve this reorientation in US legal discourse, the Electronic Frontier Foundation (EFF) already funds ongoing legal challenges to the DMCA. By providing financial and strategic support to plaintiffs who deploy legal arguments based on the open-source movement in cases before the judicial court circuit, the EFF hope to counter the DMCA and other attempts to lock up intellectual property in corporate hands. One industry analyst worried that by 'forcing the government to defend the law over and over' the EFF poses a 'far more serious challenge in their battle to assert their intellectual property rights in cyberspace than a bunch of college kids swapping music via the Internet' (Sweeting, 2001).

Consider two further approaches to establish greater consumer control over copyright: usage as a speech act and as an act of labour. While 'US First Amendment jurisprudence has defined readers' rights only incidentally' (Cohen, 1996: 1003), there have been consistent claims for limiting copyright's power to interrupt the democratic imperatives of the public sphere through the constitutional guarantee of freedom of speech. Melvin Nimmer, for example, argued in 1970 that there existed a 'speech interest with respect to copyright', such that copy-right would be subject to violation if the act of copying sustained a 'unique contribution to an enlightened public dialogue' (1193, 1197). While he had in mind a scenario where copyrighted photographs of the My Lai massacre might be withheld from a critical public, Paul Goldstein (1970) used Howard Hughes' attempt to stop Random House from publishing a biography (he created a cor-porate façade that bought the copyrights to articles written about him) to claim that copyright infringement should be excused when supporting the general public interest.

Media and legal theorists on the left often equate the copy-related rights of information creators with forms of speech (see, for example, Braman 1998: 81) or maintain that copyright itself is a regulation of speech (Benkler, 1999: 446). Some suggest that copyright law pertain to acts of speech rather than property rights objectified in certain works (Rotstein, 1992: 739–42). Still others argue that the conflation of speech rights with property rights – even in its progress-ive modality – simply recapitulates the public/private and commons/commodity orthodoxies inscribed in IP law (Coombe, 1996: 239, 241, 247). What we are suggesting, however, is a reorientation of property rights (which undergird the NICL) towards labour rights. Such a fundamental move away from the politics of ownership to the politics of work recognises that, for fair use and the public domain to have any meaning, audience work will have to be recognised as a form of speech act. Julie Cohen (1998: 1038-39) notes that 'reading is intimately connected with speech', and is therefore amenable to con-stitutional protections. Hartley adds that reading as a form of media response is a practice akin to speech, in that it is 'a universal technology of communi-cation, while not an already-existing attribute of persons' (1996: 119, 66). We suggest that, like speech, reading deserves protection.

The equation of basic human rights with reading rights is more than just rhetorical majesty. Under the strict schedules of harmonisation posed by the American and Western European powerhouses at the WTO, Venturelli warns,

> communications rights and human rights as expressed in communication
> policy and social policy can be contested on the grounds that they act to
> constrain trade through a set of non-commercial public interest
> requirements whether in infrastructure or content.
>
> (Venturelli, 1997: 63)

Following free-speech precepts, communications policy must think itself out of traditional forms of IP rights, in order to protect forms of creativity that stimulate the 'production of media content at the fringes of the range of pref-erences, thus promoting equal access to diverging preferences and opinions in

society' (Van Cuilenburg, 1999: 204). But the DMCA curtails free-speech protection with anti-circumvention provisions that state consumers may not use
devices or services designed to by-pass copyright management systems (such
as watermarking). The only way in which corporate owners of copyrighted
products can regulate such possible infringements is to monitor the entire terrain of media consumption; as such, the anti-circumvention policies pose a
significant invasion of privacy as well as fair use. Cultural policy must deflate
the widespread corporate acceptance of rights-management software that
threatens significant sectors of use, and begin to 'contemplate built-in technological limits on copyright owners' monitoring capabilities' (Cohen, 1996: 988).
In arguing for technologically guaranteeing the anonymity of media users in
order to prevent a forced fixing of their audience practice within a prescribed
form of affiliative politics, Cohen notes:

> Reading is an intellectual association, pure and simple. As such, it is
> profoundly constitutive of identity as direct interpersonal association.
> There are reasons for according even stronger protection to reading,
> moreover. Interpersonal association and group affiliation are, by definition,
> voluntary expressions of a common purpose or interest.
>
> (Cohen, 1996: 1014)

To modify the mostly individualist language of these rights, cultural policy might draw from the 1996 report by UNESCO and the UN's World
Commission on Culture and Development. *Our Creative Diversity* notes that
one of the challenges in the wake of the GATT is maintaining a 'balance
between those countries that export copyright and those that import it'
(Pérez de Cuéllar, 1996: 244). Defining an intermediary sphere of IP rights
between individual authorial rights and the national/international public
domain, *Our Creative Diversity* suggests that certain cultures deserve IP
rights as *groups* (Pérez de Cuéllar, 1996). Not surprisingly, the protection of
collective authorship (specifically with regards to folklore) was not raised at
the January 1997 meeting of the WTO in Geneva, and when Third World
countries supported such protection at a joint UNESCO/WIPO meeting
later that year, the move was opposed by US and British delegates. As Kirster
Malm writes,

> when the US delegate said that since most of the folklore that was
> commercially exploited was US folklore, Third World countries would have
> to pay a lot of money to the US if an international convention should come
> about. The Indian lawyer, Mr. Purim, answered that that was already the
> case with existing conventions and by the way all US folklore except the

> Amerindian one was imported to the US from Europe and Africa. . . . Thus
> the money should go to the original owners of that folklore.
>
> (Malm, quoted in Smiers, 2000: 397)

A current case involving the shutting down of a collective form of modern folklore illustrates the powerful correlation of consumption and speech act – the
Harry Potter controversy, touched on earlier.

After the AOL-Time Warner aggression against fans and Website owners, the
latter engaged in a war of position. The formation of such sites as www.potter
war.org.uk and the cleverly named www.harrypotter-warnercansuemyarse.
co.uk was followed by the 'Defense Against the Dark Arts' (DADA) Project
(www.dprophet.com/dada/), which urged a boycott of *Harry Potter* merchandise and the film (though, interestingly, *not* the books). DADA suggested that
reparations be made to *Potter* fans by Warner Bros., 'whether this is in a substantial donation to UNICEF, or tickets to the premiere to the actual fans who
were threatened themselves; we'd like to see Warner Brothers come up with a
plan that shows how sorry they feel'. In rallying support for an upcoming con-
stitutional battle, DADA put the corporate policing actions this way:

> There are dark forces afoot, darker even than He-Who-Must-Not-Be-
> Named, because these dark forces are daring to take away something so
> basic, so human, that it's close to murder. They are taking away our
> freedom of speech, our freedom to express our thoughts, feelings and ideas,
> and they are taking away the fun of a magical book.

Although AOL-Time Warner has stopped sending the cease-and-desist letters
– no doubt swayed by the tremendous negative publicity their trademark protection generated – the *Potter* case is part of a long line of corporate policing
efforts that stretch from *Star Wars* Websites to *The Simpsons*, *Star Trek* and the
X-Files (see Tushnet, 1997). In connection with its licensing efforts, AOL-Time
Warner is applying and registering 2,000 trademarks connected to *Harry Potter* (Demarco, 2001: 4). Clearly, the corralling of words associated with the
novels has entailed a silencing of consumer speech.

In addition to the conceptualisation of consumption as a form of speech,
which is protected under most forms of democratic constitutional provision,
cultural policy must recognise that every act of consumption is an act of
authorship, or rather an act that hybridises the traditional parameters of singular gatekeeping authority. In other words, every act of authorship 'in any
medium is more akin to translation and recombination' than it is to a spurious
originary act (Litman, 1990: 966). We have already shown how IP law fails to
recognise collectively authored works like folklore, which are texts in constant

states of flux, secured only through the contexts of their use and the forms of life constituted by their meanings. Ironically, we can use the restrictive language of corporate-friendly initiatives to substantiate our claim for the labour of consumption. In Chapter 4, we discussed the US negotiating team's position at the 1996 WIPO conference, which called for an inherent reproduction in every act of digital transmission. In effect, this makes *all* users of digital media *writers* – as Pool puts it, 'to read a text stored in electronic memory, one displays it on the screen: one writes to read it' (quoted in Van der Merwe, 1999: 311).

In many ways, the idea of the labour of consumption ironically redeploys Lockean labour theory (which traditionally underpins the romantic idea of authorship) towards a socialist vision of property rights gained through the act of adding one's labour (Boyle, 1996: 57). Although such conceptualisations of labour have supported worker exploitation, since wages transfer the property right of labour to the employer, they have also prioritised the forms of *creative* labour that make the author's work his or her own. Conceiving of a more open public use as a kind of *symbolic* wage for users is one way of working through the dilemma of monopoly rights, even though it recapitulates the foundation of property-exchange as the root of media transactions.

We might look further, then. Borrowing from studies of subcultural practices, Aoki refers to 'audience recoding rights'. He notes that focusing on the dynamic and fluid nature of textuality (with its audiences equal partners in the creative act) might 'dilute the property-ness of interests protected by copyright'. Such an approach, focused on 'texts-as-speech-events, would begin allowing space for a judicial consideration of "recoded" cultural productions and enhanced respect for free speech values' (Aoki, 1993b: 826–27). While Aoki recognises that such a reconceptualisation might introduce commercial imperatives into the regulation of speech, understanding media consumption as a collaborative network of productive labour takes us part of the way towards a wider definition of 'fair use'.

Jane Ginsberg (1997a) has suggested that traditional forms of fair use privilege certain types of users and allow the redistribution of value enclosed by copyright to these users. Redirecting fair use towards *ordinary* users – (who are otherwise 'paedocratised' as dopes by both academic and governmental cultures for supposedly being incapable of either 'critical distance, scepticism or reason, or with being able to integrate, compare or triangulate media discourses with other elaborated in different institutional sites' (Hartley, 1996: 59) – would entail a recognition of the transient nature of reading rather than the fixed site of authorship. Fair use, as Wendy Gordon (1982: 1653) notes, has not often been extended to 'ordinary users', since 'the public interest served by second authors [creators of derivative works or specialised users using the stuff of public domain] are likely to be stronger than the interests served by ordinary consumers'. This prejudice recapitulates copyright's espousal of the author as a functional exclusionary principle that impedes the free circulation and recomposition of cultural production. Authorship provides the common terrain for laws that claim that lists of telephone numbers are not copyrightable by phone directory publishers – because there is no proof of 'sweat of the brow' labour (see *Feist Publications Inc. v. Rural Telephone Service Co.*, 499 US (1991)), and statutory protections of market research firms' computer databases as copyrightable 'literary works', with all the ownership benefits of authorship.

As technology, such as the 'trusted systems' and 'rights management tracking software' discussed in Chapter 4, begins to supplant copyright's traditional function (which includes a significant, if underdeveloped, evocation of fair use), legal manoeuvrability within the statutory sphere will become even more difficult: 'every single copy of a digital work would become its own tollbooth' (Benkler, 1999: 422). Of course, we will always have hackers, who will be the last guardians of an old system that recognises some forms of the public domain and private use.

'The tendency to undervalue the public domain', writes Boyle, 'is a worldwide phenomenon' (1996: 130). Public policy designed to control knowledge capital by monopoly rents instead of a public archive-based consensual access to knowledge represents, as Frow (2000) notes, a 'major erosion of the public domain'. While the public domain has traditionally signified as the abject detritus of non-copyrightable materials, its roots in European feudalism (as the true public commons, scarce land reserved for public use) mask the fact that 'knowledge actually increases when it is shared' (Frow, 2000: 182). Yochai Benkler calls for two policy proposals alongside free and open source-software strategies that might meaningfully sustain the public domain and resist its enclosure: 'identifying and sustaining a series of commons in the resources necessary for the production and exchange of information', and a 'shift in distributive policies from low cost or free reception to ubiquitous access to the facilities necessary for production and dissemination of information' (2000: 576). The market model theorised by Napster suggests a group of peer users exchanging information, and Internet-based users rights might be conceived of along a service-based approach based on the shared-resource market network. Bundling users into groups that share resources, rather than individuated consumers who consume in private singular acts, clearly threatens both the existence of copyright as well as the corporate distributional middlepeople who have mediated between traditional artists and consumers.

With digital commerce changing the way we consume by compressing the traditional space and time of services interaction (the gap into which distributional middlemen have staked their claim), a cultural policy that privileges reception as an *act of creative labour* can help fracture the authorial underpinnings of copyright, while at the same time encouraging the proliferation of responses to new aesthetic forms. To use John Perry Barlow's (n. d.) words, a politics of labour (which prioritises *doing*) rather than of objects (which favours *owning*), reconceptualises media interaction as conduct 'in a world made more of verbs than nouns'.

Our call for a labour theory of consumption that inverts the negative liberties granted by the NICL is based, in part, on the acts of surveillance performed on media users. We have shown, in Chapters 5 and 6, how spectators are alienated from their labour as subjects of market research. The labour of audiences, owned by market research and protected by corporate IP laws, deny the research subjects access to the very speech acts that constitute the labour of reception. Like the broadcast media it supports, market research structures the diversity of user activity into suspected or probable sorts of 'audience', wherein consumers *themselves* become the product.

Hollywood's marketers confront vexing and arbitrary connections between what they think people are, as members of a suspected audience, and the personal story people elaborate for themselves as filmgoers. In working through this contradiction, film marketing identifies some ways to build film attendance, but guesswork plays a big part in determining which ways, and constant monitoring of filmgoers works to improve the guesswork. An important ethical dilemma flows from this guesswork. Even though they regularly get it wrong, marketing must make up audiences into images that suit their client's needs, and to do this they must probe, analyse and interpret filmgoing habits. Absent in this process is an ethos of respect for filmgoing experiences that do not fit into pre-scripted versions of probable audience behaviour. Even when they shift responsibility to the sovereign consumer, marketers still rely on pre-scripted notions of who you are. Tracking this ethical problematic a bit further can help locate additional points of departure for innovative cultural policy.

Imagine an encounter in which marketers come face to face with the people they presume to know, rather than the usual pre-scripted and automated encounter of surveillance. Here the proxies of the corporate view of film and its audiences might have to acknowledge the unknowable, namely, an unruly, unpredictable filmgoer or an ineffable filmgoing experience. Such an encounter might expose the deficiency inside marketing's will to know how to predict audience behaviour. All marketers do is cast a statistical shadow of a made-up audience, nothing substantial. People might laugh at these corporate soothsayers and wonder how they can stand there without laughing at themselves. This encounter might also disclose how marketers make up audiences and call them to account for the elaborate deception covering their surveillance. Such an encounter would be full of sources for an ethical and political awakening. Yet it might also give marketers an opportunity to appeal to the moral authority that comes from either of two institutional sources: from their position as servants of a legitimate (for now) business operation or from the value-neutral protocols of their research technique. Perhaps a textual turn can help us imagine such an encounter.

At the beginning of *Magic Town* (William Wellman, 1947) news spreads that the 'Institute of Public Opinion', run by Lawrence 'Rip' Smith (Jimmy Stewart), is going out of business. A clerk scoffs: 'Gettin' opinions from the public; that's a screwy way to make a livin'.' 'Hold on', says a customer, 'lotsa guys clean up on it. Look at Gallup. You know, big corporations pay a lot of money to find out what you and I think.' 'They do?', says the befuddled clerk. We know they do, for in that moment Rip's luck changes as he reads a letter from an old army pal telling him of Grandview, a town where opinions mirrored the nation's perfectly across sex, income, political party and other demographic markers. 'I'm gonna make a million bucks on this', Rip exclaims.

The next morning, Rip steps off the train at Grandview. He poses as an insurance salesman from Hartford because 'people in that town can't know what we're doing there, so we gotta have a cover. Sooner or later they're gonna get self-conscious, and that's fatal.' As he gazes across the town square he rhapsodises: 'the moment Columbus first sighted land must have been just like this'. Rip motions toward one of the natives and comments:: 'I know all about him.' 'He's married, he has 1.7 children, out of his income he spends 11.2 for rent, 23.5 for food, 17.2 for clothing.' Rip's partner Ike interrupts. 'Poor guy', he grumbles. 'He's just a series of fractions. He oughtta stop acting like a human being.' In their view, he never had. Weeks pass. Rip wins the people's trust with his 'devotion to the basketball team' and his antic flirtations with Mary Peterman (Jane Wyman), the acting editor of the local newspaper. All the while Rip has secretly collected everyone's opinions and thoughts; only his partners and his old army pal know what he is doing.

Rip's personal involvement begins to threaten the research. Ike wonders if Rip is getting too close to Mary: 'Howdya like to kick this whole deal over?', Ike asks. Rip says he hasn't worked his whole life to 'kick it over' now – 'What kind of lame-brain do you think I am?' At the town dance, his army pal suggests that Rip 'must be having an awful tussle' with his conscience. 'Don't worry about my conscience', Rip snaps. Life is a rat race, he says, but at least he's out in front of it. Rip leaves the dance to phone Ike, who tells him that the survey results are perfect; they will become rich. Just then, Mary enters the front office worriedly looking for Rip, who left the dance upset. Looking around for him, she sees a sheet of tabulations alerting her to Rip's con game. The worm turns. Mary picks up the phone and hears Rip say: 'I'll handle the Peterman girl'.

Rip emerges from the back room and stands face to face with Mary, unwilling to let her act upon him as a catalyst for an ethical understanding of his actions:

'We had to work secretly,' he told her, adding coldly, 'Nobody's been hurt by it, have they?' He can't hear her heart break. Rip becomes increasingly self-right-eous as he tries to stop Mary from writing an article that would expose his deception to the people of Grandview. This is the limit point for him. 'You can't go around telling people they're special,' he says, 'not even these people. It's deadly.' Rip cannot see his mendacity as a form of violence. Instead, he passes the burden of killing the town to the messenger. What she kills, he implies, is the town's innocence – a pious judgement based on the moral authority of his social science. Mary stands for a competing ethical orientation, one that is open and solicitous without being pious and exploitative: her act of writing will only kill Rip's ability to exploit innocence. By removing the researcher's mask of friendship and solidarity, she creates the conditions for the town's ethical and political awakening.

At this point, the story of *Magic Town* closes around the representational authority inscribed in Rip's institutional identity – the social scientist would be proven right. Mary's article changes the town. Opinions 'are our chief export,' Grandview's mayor declares. 'We're through giving them away.' So they build opinion-collecting booths, each containing a reference library to ensure that people would say smart things. Journalists, tourists and house-hunters from the big city overrun the streets of the magic town; property values soar. Speculation in building projects for civic centres and schools multiply. Rip spends his remaining days in Grandview drunk and disorderly, never losing the occasion to tell Mary that she is to blame for turning Grandview into a circus. Eventu-ally, Rip leaves town, Grandview's self-made poll flops, and the town becomes a national joke. At the end, Rip returns, professes his love for Mary, and saves the town from itself. 'We murdered a town', Mary confesses after realising that Grandview could have lived as before had it not been given knowledge of Rip's scheme.

Magic Town introduces constituencies that can help us imagine features of cultural policy which reconfigure consumption and consumer surveillance for the new politics of citizenship suggested earlier by Yúdice. There are those who, by remaining innocent, become susceptible to the protocols of marketing research. As long as they are unaware that they are being surveilled, they serve as informational resources for the consumer surveillance industry. As such, their identities are interpreted and judged within a moral framework deter-mined by business and statistical research criteria. They 'live', to borrow from *Magic Town*'s lament, as long as they work for the research. As soon as they awaken to their conditions as subjects of surveillance, they are dead to the researchers.

In our view, this is a salutary death, for it creates new conditions of possibility for cultural policy. We can imagine, for instance, a policy that bans the exploitation of innocence through consumer surveillance. Full disclosure of all the sites of audience and consumer research would immediately offer a bit more freedom. The citizen is in the house of consumption. People could opt-in to the research, but in so doing they would already make it a much weaker form of surveillance. Given what we know about the expanding surveillance network that interlocks multiple sites of cultural consumption, this policy would have to have a wider remit. Imagine, then, that all point-of-sale tracking required the buyer's permission – no information about a CD, video or DVD purchase could be gathered or sold without consent. The burden of the added cost of disclosure would be carried by the retailer and marketer, as would the tax levy to pay for added costs of policing the legal use of personal information and punishment of commercial offenders, which together would probably be great enough to radically reduce the commercial incentive and severely limit the growth of the exposed surveillance system. In this context, current EU policy on personal data protection in global data trade would be instructive, in particular how it succeeds, and where it fails, in creating a mode of comprehending supra-national commitments to citizenship while accommodating the commercial logic of EU audiovisual policy, especially in defence of a right to know the surveyors, correct one's own data, and be informed when personal information is being extracted for consumer surveillance purposes (Maxwell, 1999).

Banning the exploitation of innocence is only a first step in this policy scenario. If people become aware of the extent of consumer surveillance, they might want to participate more fully in the resulting economy of display, forging a little entrepreneurial bridge between citizen, consumer and worker. People might want to start their own personal information business, as did the folks of Grandview, polling one another and selling the information themselves. Major studios have recently banded together with NRG and other marketers to demonise one such film opinion entrepreneur, Harry Knowles. It seems that Harry formed a network of people who infiltrate test screenings and then leak home-made reviews about the movie on his Website, ain't-it-cool-news.com (Lerner, 1999). Marketers complain that Harry corrupts the research process. But they may be angry because Harry is telling us to listen to his friends, not to the industry's version of audiences (Harry's own version of *Magic Town* statisticide). For this constituency of small-time marketers and survey researchers, a policy that assures them adequate resources to compete with large marketers and the state could become a feature of our policy. Of course, their ability to surveill their neighbours would come under the same scrutiny and ethical commitments applied to the larger firms: no secrets or deceptions, opt-in only rules and proportional tax levies.

Because such a small business policy encourages the socialisation of the economy of surveillance and display, it demands sharper inspection (see Maxwell, 1999). It would at a minimum necessitate a radical critique of the liberal principles underlying the rights conferred upon the owners of the proprietary information gathered through surveillance as well as the extremely limited freedoms of privacy protections based in the same property standards. This critique would have to test whether greater face-to-face determination of the line between public and private information would make an improvement over current practices of automated and detached surveillance encounters. Here, in theory, the heartbreak suffered by betrayal of a confidence or a friendship could be minimised; the human-scale marketers would hear and see the violence of their mendacity. But how does this theory of a little liberation from surveillance avoid recapitulation of governmentality and discipline in another, apparently more humane form (Maxwell, 1996a)? In practice, these marketers might still feel drawn to the moral authority embedded in their research technique or in the fees and instructions they receive from clients. Our policy has to strive to build in a principle of cooperation and solidarity that heartens the individual marketer to cultivate a greater ethical regard for personal information, minimising the draw of methodological purity or money. One such principle might derive from García Canclíni's proposal to socialise consumption to promote collaboration of constituencies across a number of social and cultural fields (already mentioned were health, housing and education, but we would add communication). The US offers audiences minimal protection of privacy by comparison with the EU, and Microsoft and others are lobbying fiercely to prevent democratic accountability of business practices via the usual strategy – let us take care of you by writing software and bundling it into your system. Their partners in US corporate self-regulation are mostly in accord, and the Republican Party never misses an opportunity to deride European safeguards (Simpson, 2001a; Sykes and Simpson, 2001; Simpson, 2001b; Bridis, 2001).

With the theoretical modifications and political and historical reminders from Chapter 1, we can also begin to articulate cultural policy from within the cultural imperialism critique. First, there is a need to preserve a local infrastructure that encourages public debate about national culture, regardless of whether this is done in the name of a regressive, liberatory or invented heritage – as a space for locally conducted and stimulated talk and disagreement on local concerns (Baker, 2000). In addition, attention must shift from an exclusive focus on textuality and national identity to the NICL, as we explore cultural mediation and customisation. It is clear that the contradictory nature of ideas-in-trade may not make for a docile cultural workforce, and that any policy we articulate will have to stand up against pressure from cultural MNCs for national cultural labour markets that conform to the NICL.

In rethinking the links of citizen-consumer-labour, our policy scenario would remove the conditions that lead marketers to deepen, and hide, their complicity with major distributors and their corporate parents. This would necessitate enfranchising the desires and needs of constituencies of filmmakers, filmgoers and others, reducing the representational authority of major distributors, large marketing firms, banks and studio marketing executives. We can imagine cultural workers seeking points of alliance with marketing, for example, to amplify the presence of labour in public discourse, to help bring attention to working conditions and the process of alienation, and to draw on marketing expertise to revitalise the relation between filmmaking and filmgoing. Such a policy converts the currently one-way surveillance of filmgoers into a mode of sociality that raises awareness of the differences between values invested by film workers in making movies and those values that people derive from the filmgoing experience. A greater ethical regard for each constituency's needs, values and desires could flow from this refunctioning of film marketing and its surveillance operations. It has the potential of fostering an end to differences between the institutional identities of producer and consumer, offering instead a vision of culture work as the interdependent efforts in production, distribution and consumption that bring value and meaning into the world. Such a policy would have to ensure some level of subsidy and legal freedom to collectively organise new institutions, both domestically and through international networks. It would also have to be alert to the problems confronted by new identities seeking to gain recognition as they come into being – in particular the resistance within and from settled constituencies within the NICL that might react to a perceived threat by silencing what has yet to be.

When the US Government (2000) offered the WTO a strategy for liberalising the screen, it actually proposed some limits on untrammeled commerce. This sop to critics was based on provisions in both the GATS and the GATT about 'measures necessary to protect public morals'. Hollywood showed a similar taste for dispensing fat-free human kindness milk when the studios won a case in the Mexican Supreme Court in March 2000 against a Federal Film Law provision that required subtitles rather than dubbing for feature imports, on the basis that this discriminated against the twenty million Mexicans who do not read because of age, sight or literacy issues (Tegel, 2000). This care of the audience takes us back to where we began in the Introduction and the moral panics and panaceas conjured up by silent-cinema critics, Depression-era Payne Fund sociologists and post-war ethnographers that grew into the positivistic reign of psychologists and communications scholars, via the DEM, and cultural mavens, via the GEM (discussed in Chapter 6).

Culture has a moral authority that is a terrain of struggle against neo-liberalism. It is ambivalent space for the left to occupy, given connections between 'public morals' and religion/superstition, oppression of women, racism, homophobia and limits to free expression. But it is also space to be grabbed, as per ethical debates that have ensued these past two years over the limits to patents and the availability of HIV/AIDS drugs at affordable prices. Ethical issues such as fair use, the surveillance of screen audiences, and fair trade comparability of wages for screen workers are all questions that should be raised under the rubric of morality. They alert us to the more sinister aspects of the 'Third Way', that polite amalgam of social conscience and pro-capitalist sentiment that moderates its redistributive conservatism with cultural liberalism and a commitment to the investment in human capital beloved of 'progressive' neo-liberals (Burbach, 2001: 148).

Global Hollywood has wrestled throughout with a variety of complex trends that inhibit our thinking of policy in appropriate ways. We have endeavoured to write for filmgoers whose identities rival the ones generated for and about them by global Hollywood. In so doing, we envisaged a filmgoer with capacious interests that take into account the ethical and political problems of the contemporary political economy of culture: the Americanisation of production, distribution and exhibition with its persistent vision of separate spheres of work and consumption; the bureaucratisation of national policy and the privatisation of global policy; the impact of deregulated markets, including television; the dominance of the 'Washington Consensus'; the spread of the NICL; the co-optation of resistive national cultural policy by bourgeoisies and Hollywood itself; the harmonisation of copyright under neo-liberal evangelism; the continued power of the US domestic audience as a marketing site; and the force of DEM/GEM logics of citizenship and consumption. Our critique of screen trade has also come up against the preeminence of exchange value defended by IP, a relation that disguises or displaces labour behind the fetishisms of text, interiority and authorship, even as in the US alone, 270,000 films are being 'pirated' each day (Valenti, 2001c).

In the Introduction, we posed two questions: is Hollywood global – and in what sense? And what are the implications of that dominance? Here are our answers. Yes, Hollywood *is* global, in that it sells its wares in every nation, through a global system of copyright, promotion and distribution that uses the NICL to minimise cost and maximise revenue. The implications are that we need to focus on the NICL and the global infrastructure of textual exchange in order to make world film and television more representative, inclusive and multiple in its sources and effects. Knowing more about how Hollywood 'works' might not exactly make us free, but it could provoke us to confront the NICL and imagine alternative, more salutary conditions and possibilities for our own cultural labour and for our brothers and sisters in the culture works everywhere.

In March 2001, *coup* beneficiary George Bush Minor announced his trade policy priorities. He favored trade liberalisation on the basis of three putative benefits that would accrue to 'the American people' (good of him to include Latin America and Canada in this). The first was increased job opportunities and income from exports. The second was 'freedom', because '[e]conomic freedom creates habits of liberty and habits of liberty create expectations of democracy'. The third was 'our nation's security' which had been threatened over the previous half century by 'hostile protectionism and national socialism' ('USTR 2001', 2001). We agree with Bush Minor. Exports should see income equitably distributed among the workers who have made goods and services that are in demand. Liberty and democracy should exist in workplace politics, both in the US and for its partners. And anti-worker corporate welfare and fascism must indeed be resisted. So the basics in terms of philosophical principles are there! The task now is to orient world trade away from its current distributional politics and towards an equitable share of wealth. In the planned expansion of NAFTA into the Free Trade Area of the Americas, the US persuaded other nations to permit AOL-Time Warner, Microsoft, IBM and others to sit at the table (Anderson, 2001). In keeping with Bush Minor's commitment to 'Americans', the corollary of encouraging business participation is ensuring labour representation as well.

In this lonely hour of the last instance, we return to that ambiguous figure, the Hollywood worker. When we consider the past, the present and projected future of California, and Los Angeles in particular, the amount of wealth created might give pause before lamenting the movement of jobs offshore:

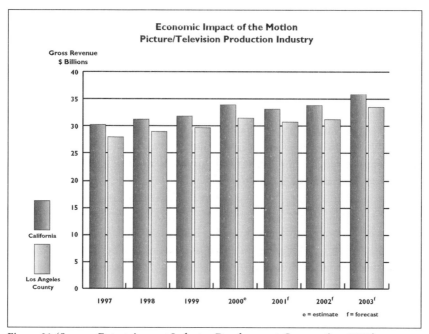

Figure 21 (Source: Entertainment Industry Development Corporation, 2001)

But these figures cloak both technical and experienced exploitation of workers. The stories below represent the labour utilised and then discarded, replaced by others elsewhere, that made up the substance of the nice, clean columns depicted in Figure 21.

In that spirit, we close with some words from disemployed people affected by the NICL:

Below-the-line workers speak out

> I have been a member of the I.A.T.S.E. Local 705 for the past 20 years. For 14 of those years I have also been a small business owner in the entertainment industry. I am supposed to be living the American Dream. Instead, after 20 years of hard work I am on the verge of living the American Nightmare. I hear about potential jobs all the time. Unfortunately, they are in Canada or Australia.
>
> Jean Rosone, IATSE Local 705

> My husband and I have worked in the film industry for over 20 years. We are now seriously considering closing our doors, losing our modest home and facing bankruptcy. It is infuriating for production after production to request bids from our company only to take the work out of the country.
>
> Jennifer E. Manus, Sticks and Stones Studio

> The film business is a driving economic force [in] California. The monies spent on filming filter down through our community creating jobs in related industries and providing sales and income tax revenues.
>
> Gary Jackson, President, Jackson Shrub Supply

> While we are small employers in the entertainment industry, we have already been forced to reduce our staff by 10 per cent and anticipate that further cuts of up to 25 per cent will be necessary in the near future if this problem is not addressed.
>
> Raymond Claridge, President, C.P. Enterprises

> In its first season back in California, *X-Files* spent $328,494.74 in rentals and expendables, and another $168,000.00 in manufacturing and graphics from our companies. Our company employs 95–125 people with salaries greatly varying. We can't afford to lose even one SHOW.
>
> Gregg H. Bilson, Jr., Executive VP/CFO , Independent Studio Services, Inc.

During the past 12 months, Omega experienced a significant drop in revenue. Moreover, first quarter 1999 figures are down 10 per cent from 1998. Normally studios have several feature films in production in the Spring. Currently we are working only on one feature in US production, and Omega is working closely with the set decorator to control costs.

Barry Pilchard, VP/General Manager, Omega Cinema Props

My business in the past year has seen a decrease of $500,000.00 in revenue resulting in layoffs and consideration of a permanent down sizing.

Frank Uchalik, President, ALPHA Medical Resources, Inc.

I lost three movies in four months with producers I have worked with for years. I only made $1800 in the first four months of 1999.

David Lewis, Director of Photography, age 53

For 24 years I have worked as a costume designer making between $80,000 and $120,000 in a good year. I have lost two jobs to Canada in the last year. I did a commercial for three days in January and that's the only work I've had since last March. We're scared of losing our home.

Betty Pecha Madden

I'm trying to stay afloat, but it's tough because of all the money I owe. What I'm finding is a lot of business going toward Canada and out of state. When I do sell something, I have to cut the price by 50–60 percent.

Jesse Hurtado, Owner, Prima Equipment (lighting business)

Source: Department of Commerce (2001: 13) (see also 'Runaway Production: an Opinion', 2000)

Hollywood is assuredly operating on a global scale. The impact may be visible on screen, but it is also felt at a bodily level by the labour that makes it happen.

References

Articles by title

'A Disquieting New Agenda for Trade'. (1994) *Economist*, 332, no. 7872: 55–56.
'A World View'. (1997) *Economist*, 29 November.
'Administration Settles Television Piracy Case'. (2001) Associated Press, 23 March.
'Africa's Hollywood'. (1997) *Economist*, 1 November.
'After GATT Pique, Pix Pax Promoted'. (1994) *Daily Variety*, 8 June: 1, 16.
'Americans Go On-line with Anti-Canuck Views'. (2001) *Toronto Star*, 14 February.
'Animation: The Challenge for Investors'. (2001) *Screen Digest*, www.screendigest.com/rep_animation.htm.
'Asia's Toonsville'. (1997) *Economist*, 22 February.
'Australia as a Film Location. Wallaby-wood'. (1998) *Economist*, 30 May.
' "Baywatch" Goes Out with the Tide'. (1999) *Economist*, 6 March: 39.
'B3M Fund Will Fight Piracy; Film Industry Unites to Spur Enforcement'. (2000) *Bangkok Post*, 27 December.
'Big Harry Deal! It's an Image Thing'. (2001) *Chicago Tribune*, 27 February.
'Canada Probes 2 Leading Exhibs'. (2000) *Hollywood Reporter*, 20 December.
'Canal Plus at 15: In the Big Leagues'. (1999) *Variety*, 28 June–11 July: 44.
'Chinese Film Industry to Go Global'. (2001) *China Daily*, 29 March.
'Chinese Film Producers Leery of Open Trade'. (2001) *Rotten Tomatoes*, www.rottentomatoes.com/news-1921 (22 January).
'Circulation of Audiovisual Works and Training of Professionals: Commission Adopts its Proposals for the MEDIA PLUS Programme (2001–2005)'. (1999) Commission of the European Communities RAPID, 14 December.
'Clarity, Bouillabaisse, Story Telling and a Tail-Wagging Dachshund. All Part of the Felicities of 1998'. (1999) MPA Press Release, 9 March.
'Columbia Pictures' *Stuart Little* Debuts With Major Event at Toy Fair '99'. (1999) *Business Wire*, 8 February.
'Commerce Secretary Mineta Releases Report on the Impact of the Migration of U.S. Film and Television Production'. (2001) US Department of Commerce Press Release, 18 January.

'Commission Report on the Results Obtained Under the Media II Programme (1996–2000) From 1.1.96–30.6.98'. (1998) European Commission.

'Congress to Address Runaway Production'. (2001) International Cinematographers Guild,www.cameraguild.com/news/global/congress_runaway.htm.

'Culture Wars'. (1998) *Economist*, 12 September.

'Defend Culture, Says ACTRA in Seattle for WTO Talks'. (1999) www.actra.com/news/.

'Déjà Vu'. (1994) *Film Journal*, 97, no. 6: 3.

'Disney Labor Abuses in China'. (1999) www.summersault.com/~agi/clr/alerts/disneysweatshopsinchina.html.

'Distribuidores Apuntan Oportunidad Negocio Cine en Español en USA'. (2000) *Efe News Services*, 22 June.

'Equifax Forms Alliance With VNU MIS Precision Marketing Group – Long Term Strategic Cross-Licensing Agreement Signed'. (2000) *Business Wire*, 15 May.

'España Promocionará Estreno de Coproducciones con Latinoamerica'. (2000) *Efe News Services*, 20 June.

'European Commissioner Wants More Film Exchange Within EU'. (1999) Agence France Presse, 16 December.

'Film Production and Distribution Trends: Shift in Balance Between US and the Rest of the World – Part 1'. (2000) *Screen Digest*, June.

'Film Production Soars in U.K'. (2001) *Rotten Tomatoes*, www.rottentomatoes.com/news-1926/ (23 January).

'Foreign Bums on Seats'. (1998) *Economist*, 15 August.

'Fracasa el Estreno Ultimo del Filme Disney en Español para Hispanos'. (2001) *Efe News Services*, 9 January.

'Full of Eastern Promise'. (2001) *Sunday Times*, 21 January.

'Global Finance: Time for a Redesign?' (1999) *Economist*, 30 January: 4-8 Survey Global Finance.

'Global Media Breakdown'. (2001) *Variety*, 19–25 February: 14.

'Hollywood Cashes Runaway Checks in Czech Republic'. (n. d.) International Cinematographers Guild, www.cameraguild.com/news/global/czech.htm.

'Hollywood Defends Itself Against Cultural Imperialism Charges'. (1998) Agence France Presse, 1 July.

'Hollywood Heads South of Border to Mexico'. (2000) *Jefferson City News Tribune*, 12 June.

'Hollywood on the Vltava'. (2001) *Economist*, 3 February: 65.

'Hollywood's Incredible Turkey Machine is as Prolific as Ever'. (1999) *National Post*, 17 March: C09.

'Home Alone in Europe'. (1997) *Economist*, 22 March.

'H'wood Buries Overseas Pix'. (1999) *Variety*, 25–31 January: 1, 90–91.

'iBeam and CinemaNow Partner to Stream Pay-Per-View Feature Films'. (2000) *Business Wire*, 9 November.

'IP Watch'. (1998) *IP Worldwide*, November/December.

'IP Watch'. (1999) *IP Worldwide*, January/February.

'Lerner'. (1999) 'Shadow Force: Hundreds Of Movies Have Been Reshaped as a Result of Work by Joseph Farrell's National Research Group'. *Los Angeles Times Magazine*, 7 November: 18.

'Movie Shoot Gives Shot in the Arm to Cambodia'. (2000) *Movie/TV News* us.imdb.com/SB?20001201 (1 December).

'MPA Appoints New Technology Officer'. (1999) MPA Press Release, 21 June.

'MPAA Continues Pirate Video Lab Assault'. (1995) MPAA Press Release, 29 November.

'MPAA Identifies Malaysia, Brazil as Problem Areas for Intellectual Property'. (2000) MPAA Press Release, 18 February.

'New Line Cinema Verifies Approximately 1.7 Million Downloads of Exclusive 'The Lord Of The Rings' Preview During 1st Day of Operation'. (2000) *PR Newswire*, 10 April.

'1999: Une Année de Cinéma dans le Monde'. (2000) *Eurodata TV*, www.euro datatv.com/news/2000/23.06.html.

'Not the Last Picture Show'. (1995) *Economist*, 2 December.

'Paramount Gets New Financing'. (1996) *New York Times*, 14 May: D11.

'Polish Leader Wants EU-wide Worker Movement'. (2000) *United Press International*, 19 December.

'Presidents of SAG, DGA, TV Academy to Join Edward James Almos, Other Actors, Politicians, Union Leaders and Thousands of Filmworkers at March and Rally in Hollywood on Sunday, Aug. 15'. (1999). *Business Wire*, 8 December.

'Principal Photography Under Way on New Regency's 'Made in America' for Distribution by Warner Bros'. (1992) *PR Newswire*, 18 May.

'Protecting America's Grandest Trade Prize'. (1998) MPAA Press Release, 10 September.

'Protecting America's Most Prized Export in the Digital World'. (1998) MPAA Press Release, 16 July.

'Quo Vadis'. (1996) MPAA Press Release, 23 January.

'Saving Hollywood'. (2001) *Los Angeles Daily News*, 9 January.

'Screens Without Frontiers'. (2000) http://webworld.unesco.org/screens/ html/ about.html.

'Shall We, Yawn, Go to a Film?' (1997) *Economist*, 1 February: 85–86.

'Solidarity With Striking SAG and AFTRA Members'. (2000) www.actra.com/ news/101900n.htm.

'Statement by Jack Valenti on the 9th Circuit Court of Appeals Ruling on Napster'. MPAA Press Release, 12 February.

'Statement of Jack Valenti, Chairman and CEO, MPA, Before the Committee on Ways and Means Subcommittee on Trade, Regarding US-China Trade Relations and the Possible Accession of China to the WTO'. (1999) MPAA Press Release, 8 June.

'Storm Over Globalisation'. (1999) *Economist*, 27 November: 15–16.

'Technology-Labor: New Opportunities for Developing Countries'. (1999) *Inter Press Service English News Wire*, 8 December.

'Telenovela de Caracol Vendida a Walt Disney Company'. (2001) *El Tiempo*, 25 January.

'Thailand Sees Insult to Monarchy as it Bans "Anna" '. (1999) *Wall Street Journal*, 29 December: B11.

'The G-Word'. (1997) *Financial Times*, 30 July: 15.

'The PolyGram Test'. (1998) *Economist*, 15 August.

'TiVo partners with Nielsen, ASI'. (2000) *Advertising Age*, 24 July: 2.

'Top 100 All-Time Domestic Grossers'. (1994) *Variety*, 17–23 October: M60.

'Tough Girl Lara Needs Armed Bodyguards'. (2000) *Movie/TV News*, http://us.imdb.com/WN?20001020 (20 October).

'Trade Barriers, Erected in Fear, Hurt U. S. Workers'. (1997) *USA Today*, 16 October: 10A.

'USTR 2001 Trade Policy Agenda and 2000 Annual Report'. (2001) *Office of the United States Trade Representative*, 6 March.

'Valenti Calls on Congress to Protect Copyright, Says Some Studios to be Online Within Six Months'. (2001) MPAA Press Release, 22 January.

'VNU and ACNielsen to Provide Complete Measurement of Pre-Recorded Video and DVD Sales'. (1999) *Business Wire*, 15 September.

'VNU'. (2000) Hoover's Company Profile Database – World Companies.

'VNU NV'. (2000) The Major Companies Database. Graham & Whiteside Ltd.

'Why Hollywood is Losing the Limelight'. (2001) *Financial Times*, 8 March: 24.

'With a Wild Surmise, Silent, Upon a Peak in Darien ..'. (1996) The Audiovisual Revolution in the Americas'. MPAA Press Release, 15 July.

'World Cinema: Poor Product Fails Multiplexes'. (2000) *Screen Digest*, September.

'You're Not in Kansas Any More: Hollywood'. (1995) *Economist*, 4 February.

Articles and books

Abel, Richard. (1999) *The Red Rooster Scare: Making Cinema American, 1900–1910*. Berkeley: University of California Press.

Acheson, Keith and Christopher Maule. (1989) 'Trade Policy Responses to New Technology in the Film and Television Industry'. *Journal of World Trade* 23, no. 2: 35–48.

224

GLOBAL HOLLYWOOD

Acheson, Keith and Christopher Maule. (1991) 'Shadows Behind the Scenes: Political Exchange and the Film Industry'. *Millennium Journal of International Studies* 20, no. 2: 287–307.

Acheson, Keith and Christopher Maule. (1994) 'International Regimes for Trade, Investment and Labour Mobility in the Cultural Industries'. *Canadian Journal of Communication* 19: 149–63.

Adler, M. (1985) 'Stardom and Talent'. *American Economic Review* 75, no. 1: 208–12.

Aiyer, V. Shankar. (2000) 'Film Marketing: Happy Endings'. *India Today*, 6 November: 78.

Aksoy, Asu and Kevin Robins. (1992) 'Hollywood for the Twenty-First Century: Global Competition for Critical Mass in Image Markets'. *Cambridge Journal of Economics* 16, no. 1: 1–22.

Alberge, Dalya and Dominic Kennedy. (1999) 'Lottery-funded Films Fail to Show a Profit'. *The Times*, 20 May: 36–37.

Albert, Steven. (1998) 'Movie Stars and the Distribution of Financially Successful Films in the Motion Picture Industry'. *Journal of Cultural Economics* 22, no. 4: 249–70.

Alexander, Garth. (2000) 'Cyber-raiders Attack'. *Sunday Times*, 1 August.

Allan, Blaine. (1988) 'The State of the State of the Art on TV'. *Queen's Quarterly* 95, no. 2: 318–29.

Allen, Donna, Ramona R. Rush, and Susan J. Kaufman, eds. (1996) *Women Transforming Communications: Global Intersections*. Thousand Oaks: Sage.

Allen, Jeanne Thomas. (1983) 'Copyright and Early Theater, Vaudeville, and Film Competition'. *Film Before Griffith*. Ed. John Fell. Berkeley: University of California Press.

Altman, Rick. (1998) 'Reusable Packaging: Generic Products and the Recycling Process'. *Refiguring American Film Genres: History and Theory*. Ed. Nick Browne. Berkeley: University of California Press.

American Academy of Pediatrics. (2001) *Media Matters*, www.aap.org/advocacy/ mediamatters.htm.

Amin, Samir. (1997) *Capitalism in the Age of Globalization*. London: Zed.

Amir, Hussein Y. (1999) 'American Programs on Egyptian Television'. *Images of the U.S. Around the World: A Multilateral Perspective*. Ed. Yahya R. Kamalipour. Albany: State University of New York Press. 319–34.

Amsden, Alice H. and Takashi Hikino. (1999) 'The Left and Globalization'. *Dissent* 46, no. 2: 7–9.

Anderson, Benedict. (1983) *Imagined Communities: Reflections on the Origin and Spread of Nationalism*. London: Verso.

Anderson, Kurt. (1993) 'No Tariff on Tom Cruise'. *Time*, 19 July: 67.

Anderson, Sarah. (2001) 'Peddling the E-Ticket to the Development Train'. *Corporate Watch*, www.corpwatch.org/trac/issues/net/sanderson.html (8 March).

Andrews, N. (1998) 'Roll Up! It's a Launch: Filming a Blockbuster is One Thing; Striking Gold is Another'. *Financial Times*, 3 January: 1

Aoki, Keith (1993a) 'Authors, Inventors, and Trademark Owners: Private Intellectual Property and the Public Domain. Part 1'. *Columbia-VLA Journal of Law and the Arts* 18: 1-73.

Aoki, Keith. (1993b) 'Adrift in the Intertext: Authorship and Audience 'Recoding' Rights: Comment on Robert H. Rotstein, 'Beyond Metaphor: Copyright Infringement and the Fiction of the Work'''. *Chicago-Kent Law Review* 68.

Aoki, Keith. (1996) 'Surveying Law and Borders: (Intellectual) Property and Sovereignty. Notes Towards a Cultural Geography of Authorship'. *Stanford Law Review* 48.

Armes, Roy. (1987) *Third World Film Making and the West*. Berkeley: University of California Press.

Arnheim, Rudolf. (1983) 'On Duplication'. *The Forger's Art: Forgery and the Philosophy of Art*. Ed. Denis Dutton. Berkeley: University of California Press.

Arthur, Charles. (2001) 'First Film Released for Rental over the Internet'. Independent Digital Ltd.

Association of Internet Professionals. (2000) 'Helping Our Members Succeed in Business', www.association.org/about.cfm.

Atkinson, G. (1997a) 'Capital and Labour in the Emerging Global Economy'. *Journal of Economic Issues* 31, no. 2: 385–91.

Atkinson, Lisa. (1997b) 'What's Entertainment? China's Entertainment Industry'. *China Business Review* 24, no. 2.

Austin, Bruce A. (1989) *Immediate Seating: A Look at Movie Audiences*. Belmont: Wadsworth.

Axtmann, Roland. (1993) 'Society, Globalization and the Comparative Method'. *History of the Human Sciences* 6, no. 2: 53–74.

Bacon, David. (1999) 'Is Free Trade Making Hollywood a Rustbelt?' *Labournet* www.labournet.org/x/copy-of-site/news/112399/01.html (19 November).

Bacon, David. (2000a) 'Globalization: Two Faces, Both Ugly'. *Dollars and Sense*, 1 March: 18–20, 40.

Bacon, David. (2000b) 'Can Workers Beat Globalisation?' www.focusweb.org/publications/2000/Can%20workers%20beat%20globalisation.htm.

Baker, C. Edwin. (2000) 'An Economic Critique of Free Trade in Media Products'. *North Carolina Law Review* 78: 1357–435.

Baker, Wayne E. and Robert R. Faulkner. (1991) 'Role as Resource in the Hollywood Film Industry'. *American Journal of Sociology* 97: 279–309.

Balio, Tino. (1993). *History of American Cinema, Volume Five: Grand Design: Hollywood as a Modern Business Enterprise, 1930–1939*, New York: Scribner.

Balio, Tino. (1998a) ' "A Major Presence in all the World's Important Markets": The Globalization of Hollywood in the 1990s'. *Contemporary Hollywood Cinema*. Ed. Steve Neale and Murray Smith. London: Routledge. 58–73.

Balio, Tino. (1998b) 'The Art Film Market in the New Hollywood'. *Hollywood and Europe: Economics, Culture, National Identity 1945–95*. Ed. Geoffrey Nowell-Smith and Steven Ricci. London: BFI. 63–73.

Bardach, Ann Louise. (2000) 'The Last Tycoon'. *Los Angeles Magazine* 4, no. 45: 74.

Barker, Ernest. (1927) *National Character and the Factors in its Formation*. London: Methuen.

Barker, Martin. (1993) 'Sex, Violence, and Videotape'. *Sight and Sound* 3, no. 5: 10–12.

Barlow, John Perry. 'The Economy of Mind on the Global Net'. (n.d.) www.eff.org/pub/Publications/John_Perry_Barlow/idea_economy.article.

Barrett, Amy. (2000) 'The Unkindest "Cut!" ' *New York Times Magazine*, 10 September: 22.

Barshefsky, Charlene. (1998) Testimony of the United States Trade Representative Before the House Appropriations Committee Subcommittee on Commerce, Justice, State, the Judiciary and Related Agencies, 31 March.

Barson, Steve. (2000) 'Cross-Border Trade with Mexico and the Prospect for Worker Solidarity: The Case of Mexico'. *Critical Sociology* 26, nos. 1–2: 13–35.

Bart, Peter. (2000) 'Will France's Hollywood Souffle Rise?' *Variety*, 19–25 June: 1, 4, 84.

Bates, James. (1993) 'Canal Plus Pulls Back'. *Los Angeles Times*, 21 February: D1.

Bates, James. (1998) 'Making Movies and Moving On'. *Los Angeles Times*, 19 January: 1.

Bates, James. (2000) 'Site Hopes to Put Profitable Spin on Hollywood Fame Game'. *Los Angeles Times*, 19 May: C1.

Bauman, Zygmunt. (1998) *Globalization: The Human Consequences*. New York: Columbia University Press.

Becker, Gary S. (1983) *Human Capital: A Theoretical and Empirical Analysis, With Special Reference to Education*, 2nd edn. Chicago University of Chicago Press.

Behar, Richard. (2000) 'Beijing's Phony War on Fakes'. *Fortune*, 30 October.

Bellah, Robert N., Richard Madsen, William M. Sullivan, Ann Swidler, and Steven M. Tipton. (1992) *The Good Society*. New York: Alfred A. Knopf.

Benhabib, Seyla. (1999) 'Citizens, Residents, and Aliens in a Changing World: Political Membership in the Global Era'. *Social Research* 66, no. 3: 709–44.

Benjamin, Walter. (1968) *Illuminations*. New York: Harcourt, Brace and World.

Benkler, Yochai. (1999) 'Free as the Air to Common Use: First Amendment Constraints on Enclosure of the Public Domain'. *New York University Law Review* 74.

Benkler, Yochai. (2000) 'VIACOM-CBS Merger: From Consumers to Users: Shifting the Deeper Structures of Regulation Towards Sustainable Commons and User Access'. *Federal Communications Law Journal* 52.

Bennett, Tony. (1990) *Outside Literature*. New York: Routledge.

Bennett, Tony. (1992) 'Putting Policy into Cultural Studies'. *Cultural Studies*. Ed. Lawrence Grossberg, Cary Nelson, and Paula Treichler. New York: Routledge.

Berkman, Meredith. (1992) 'Coming to America'. *Entertainment Weekly*, 14 October.

Berlingame, Jon. (2000) 'The Sound of Work Leaving LA'. *Los Angeles Times*, 23 July.

Berman, Nathaniel. (1992) 'Nationalism Legal and Linguistic: The Teachings of European Jurisprudence'. *New York University Journal of International Law and Politics* 24, no. 1: 1515–578.

Bettig, Ronald V. (1990) 'Extending the law of Intellectual Property: Hollywood's International Anti-Videotape Piracy Campaign'. *Journal of Communication Inquiry* 14, no. 2.

Bettig, Ronald V. (1996) *Copyrighting Culture: The Political Economy of Intellectual Property*. Boulder: Westview Press.

Bettig, Ronald V. (1997) 'The Enclosure of Cyberspace'. *Critical Studies in Mass Communication* 14: 138–57.

Binning, Cheryl. (1999a) 'Demand Outstrips Healthy Cash Injections'. *Playback*, 5 April: 23.

Binning, Cheryl. (1999b) 'NSI Launches Marketing Initiative'. *Playback*, 14 June: 2.

Bjork, Ulf Jonas. (2000) 'The U.S. Commerce Department Aids Hollywood Exports, 1921–1933'. *Historian* 62, no. 3: 575–87.

Blackstone, Erwin A. and Gary W. Bowman. (1999) 'Vertical Integration in Motion Pictures'. *Journal of Communication* 49, no. 1: 123–39.

Blankstein, Andrew. (2001) 'Company Town: Lawmaker Urges Stop to Runaway Production'. *Los Angeles Times*, 31 January.

Blumer, Herbert. (1933) *Movies and Conduct*. New York: Macmillan.

Blumer, Herbert and Philip M. Hauser. (1933) *Movies, Delinquency and Crime*. New York: Macmillan.

Bobo, Jacqueline. (1995) *Black Women as Cultural Readers*. New York: Columbia University Press.

Bodo, Carla. (2000) *The Film Industry in Italy: The Market and the State in the Nineties*. Report for the European Audiovisual Labouratory.

Boliek, Brooks. (2000) 'Bush's Haul from Hollywood Growing'. *Milwaukee Journal Sentinel*, 1 August: 6B.

Bono, Francesco. (1995) 'Cinecittà'. *UNESCO Courier*, 8 July: 68.

Bordwell, David, Kristin Thompson, and Janet Staiger. (1985) *The Classical Hollywood Cinema: Film Styles and Mode of Production to 1960*. New York: Routledge.

Bosch, Aurora and M. Fernanda del Rincón. (2000) 'Dreams in a Dictatorship: Hollywood and Franco's Spain, 1939–1956.' *'Here, There and Everywhere": The Foreign Politics of American Popular Culture'* Ed. Reinhold Wagnleitner and Elaine Tyler May. Hanover: University Press of New England. 100–15.

Bourdieu, Pierre. (1998) *On Television*. Trans. Priscilla Parkhurst Ferguson. New York: New Press.

Bourdieu, Pierre. (1999) 'The State, Economics and Sport'. Trans. Hugh Dauncey and Geoff Hare. *France and the 1998 World Cup: The National Impact of a World Sporting Event*. Ed. Hugh Dauncey and Geoff Hare. London: Frank Cass. 15–21.

Bowling, Kenneth. (1991) *The Creation of Washington, DC: The Idea and Location of the American Capital*. Fairfax: George Mason University Press.

Bowser, Eileen. (1990) *History of the American Cinema, Volume Two: The Transformation of Cinema, 1907–1915*. Berkeley: University of California Press.

Boyle, James. (1996) *Shamans, Software, and Spleens: Law and the Construction of the Information Society*. Cambridge, MA: Harvard University Press.

Braman, Sandra and Annabelle Sreberny-Mohammadi, eds. (1996) *Globalization, Communication and Transnational Civil Society*. Cresskill: Hampton Press.

Braman, Sandra. (1998) 'The Right to Create; Cultural Policy in the Fourth Stage of the Information Society'. *Gazette* 60, no. 1.

Braudy, Leo and Marshall Cohen. (1999) 'Preface'. *Film Theory and Criticism: Introductory Readings*, 5th edn. Ed. Leo Braudy and Marshall Cohen. New York: Oxford University Press. xv–xviii.

Brecher, Jeremy, Tim Costello, and Brendan Smith. (2000) *Globalization from Below: The Power of Solidarity*. Cambridge, MA: South End Press.

Bridis, Ted. (2001) 'Industry Studies Attack Web-Privacy Laws'. *Wall Street Journal*, 13 March: B6.

Briller, B. R. (1990) 'The Globalization of American TV'. *Television Quarterly* 24, no. 3: 71–79.

Brinsley, John. (1999) 'Hollywood's Obsession Over Runaway Production: Eyes Wide Shut'. *Los Angeles Business Journal* 21, no. 31: 1.

British Film Commission (n. d.). www.britfilmcom.co.uk/content/film ing/site.asp.

Broad, Dave. (1995a) 'Globalization and the Casual Labor Problem: History and Prospects'. *Social Justice* 22, no. 3: 67–91.

Broad, Dave. (1995b) 'Globalization Versus Labor'. *Monthly Review* 47: 20–32.

Brodesser, Claude and Charles Lyons. (2000) 'Pic Partners Do the Splits'. *Variety* 21–27 February: 1, 57.

Bromley, Carl. (1999) 'What Hollywood Wants from Uncle Sam'. *Nation*, 5 April: 28.

Bronfenbrenner, Kate. (2000) 'Raw Power: Plant Closing Threats and the Threat to Union Organizing'. *Multinational Monitor*, December: 24–29.

Brooks, David. (1994) 'Never for GATT'. *American Spectator* 27, no. 1: 34–37.

Browett, John and Richard Leaver. (1989) 'Shifts in the Global Capitalist Economy and the National Economic Domain'. *Australian Geographical Studies* 27, no. 1: 31–46.

Brown, Charles, ed. (1995) *Co-production International*. London: 21st Century Business Publications.

Brown, DeNeen L. (2000) 'Canada's New Role: Movie-War Villain'. *Washington Post*, 5 November: A33.

Bruce, David. (1996) *Scotland the Movie*. Edinburgh: Polygon.

Brush, Stephen B. and Doreen Stabinsky. (1996) V*aluing Local Knowledge: Indigenous People and Intellectual Property Rights*. Washington: Island Press.

Buchanan, Andrew and Stanley Reed. (1957) *Going to the Cinema*. London: Phoenix House.

Buck, Elizabeth B. (1992) 'Asia and the Global Film Industry'. *East West Film Journal* 6, no. 2: 116–33.

Buckingham, David. (1997) 'News Media, Political Socialization and Popular Citizenship: Towards a New Agenda'. *Critical Studies in Mass Communication* 14, no. 4: 344–66.

Burawoy, Michael, Joseph A. Blum, Sheba George, Zsuzsa Gille, Teresa Gowan, Lynne Haney, Maren Klawiter, Steven H. Lopez, Seán Ó Riain, and Millie Thayer. (2000) *Global Ethnography: Forces, Connections, and Imaginations in a Postmodern World*. Berkeley: University of California Press.

Burbach, Roger. (2001) *Globalization and Postmodern Politics: From Zapatistas to High-Tech Robber Barons*. London: Pluto Press.

Bureau of Labor Statistics. (2000a) *Career Guide to Industries 2000-01*.

Bureau of Labor Statistics. (2000b) *Occupational Outlook Handbook 2000*.

Burgelman, Jean-Claude and Caroline Pauwels. (1992) 'Audiovisual Policy and Cultural Identity in Small European States: The Challenge of a Unified Market'. *Media, Culture and Society* 14, no. 2: 169–83.

Butsch, Richard. (2000) *The Making of American Audiences: From Stage to Television, 1750–1990*. Cambridge: Cambridge University Press.

California Film Commission. (2000) www.filmcafirst.ca.gov.

Calkins, P. and M. Vézina. (1996) 'Transitional Paradigms to a New World Economic Order'. *International Journal of Social Economics* 23, nos. 10–11: 311–28.

Carson, Diane and Lester D. Friedman, eds. (1995) *Shared Differences: Multicultural Media and Practical Pedagogy*. Urbana: University of Illinois Press.

Carson, Diane, Linda Dittmar, and Janice R. Welsch, eds. (1994) *Multiple Voices in Feminist Film Criticism*. Minneapolis: University of Minnesota Press.

Carson, Tom. (1983) 'Homage to Catatonia'. *Village Voice*, 19 April: 58.

Carver, Benedict. (1998) 'Bridge Makes Novel Buys to Jumpstart Pic Production'. *Variety*, 9–15 February: 24.

Carver, Benedict. (1999a) 'Hollywood Tack: Grin and Share It'. *Variety*, 13–19 September: 1, 95.

Carver, Benedict. (1999b) 'Bel Air Nails US$225 Mil Bank Line'. *Variety*, 30 August–5 September: 12.

Chadha, Kalyani and Anandam Kavoori. (2000) 'Media Imperialism Revisited: Some Findings from the Asian Case'. *Media, Culture and Society* 22, no. 4: 415–32.

Chartrand, Harry Hillman. (1992) 'International Cultural Affairs: A Fourteen Country Survey'. *Journal of Arts Management, Law and Society* 22, no. 2: 134–54.

Chartrand, Harry Hillman. (1996) 'Intellectual Property Rights in the Postmodern World'. *Journal of Arts Management, Law and Society* 25, no. 4: 306–19.

Chidley, Joe. (2000) 'Hollywood's Welfare Bums'. *Canadian Business*, 3 April: 11–12.

Chinni, Christine L. (1997) 'Droit d'Auteur Versus the Economics of Copyright: Implications for the American Law of Accession to the Berne Convention'. *Copyright Law Symposium* 40.

Chmielewski, Dawn C. (2000) 'Movie Studios, Tech Firms Team Up to Bolster Copyright-Proof Technology'. *San Jose Mercury News*, 29 December.

Christopherson, Susan. (1996) 'Flexibility and Adaptation in Industrial Relations: The Exceptional Case of the U.S. Media Entertainment Industries'. *Under the Stars: Essays on Labor Relations in Arts and Entertainment*. Ed. L. S. Gray and R. L. Seeber. Ithaca: Cornell University Press. 86–112.

Christopherson, Susan and Michael Storper. (1986) 'The City as Studio; the World as Back Lot: The Impact of Vertical Disintegration on the Location of the Motion Picture Industry'. *Environment and Planning D: Society and Space* 4, no. 3: 305–20.

Christopherson, Susan and Michael Storper. (1989) 'The Effects of Flexible Specialization and Industrial Politics and the Labor Markets: The Motion Picture Industry'. *Industrial and Labor Relations Review* 42, no. 3: 331–47.

Chung, K. and R. Cox. (1994) 'A Stochastic Model of Superstardom: An Application of the Yule Distribution'. *Review of Economics and Statistics* 76, no. 4: 771–75.

Clark, Danae. (1995) *Negotiating Hollywood: The Cultural Politics of Actors' Labor.* Minneapolis: University of Minnesota Press.

Clark, Jon. (1997) 'Copyright Law and Work for Hire'. *Copyright Law Symposium* 40.

Cohen, Julie E. (1996) 'A Right to Read Anonymously: A Closer Look at "Copyright Management" in Cyberspace'. *Connecticut Law Review* 28.

Cohen, Robin. (1991) *Contested Domains: Debates in International Labor Studies.* London: Zed Books.

Cohen, Roger. (1994) 'Aux Armes! France Rallies to Battle Sly and T. Rex'. *New York Times* 2 January: H1, 22–3.

Coletti, Elisabetta Anna. (2000) ' "Made in Italy" Label Gains Celluloid Cachet'. *Christian Science Monitor*, 4 November.

Collins, Jim. (1992) 'Television and Postmodernism'. *Channels of Discourse, Reassembled: Television and Contemporary Criticism,* 2nd edn. Ed. Robert C. Allen. Chapel Hill: University of North Carolina Press. 327–53.

Collins, Richard. (1999) 'The European Union Audiovisual Policies of the U.K. and France'. *Television Broadcasting in Contemporary France and Britain.* Ed. Michael Scriven and Monia Lecompte. Oxford: Berghahn Books. 198–221.

Connell, David. (2000) 'Customs Clearance: Runaway Production Update'. *Cinematographer.com.* www.cinematographyworld.com/article/mainv/ 0,7220,114816,00.html (21 July).

Connelly, M. Patricia. (1996) 'Gender Matters: Global Restructuring and Adjustment'. *Social Politics* 3, 1: 12–13

Coombe, Rosemary. (1996) 'Innovation and the Information Environment: Left Out on the Information Highway'. *Oregon Law Review* 75.

Coombe, Rosemary J. (1998) *The Cultural Life of Intellectual Properties: Authorship, Appropriation, and the Law.* Durham: Duke University Press.

Cooper, Marc. (2000a) 'Runaway Shops'. *Nation*, 3 April: 28.

Cooper, Marc. (2000b) 'Acting for Justice'. *Nation*, 9 October: 7, 38.

Cornford, James and Kevin Robins. (1998) 'Beyond the Last Bastion: Industrial Restructuring and the Labor Force in the British Television Industry'. *Global Productions: Labor in the Making of the 'Information Society'.* Ed. Gerald Sussman and John A. Lent. Cresskill: Hampton Press. 191–212.

Costa-Gavras, Michael Eisner, Jack Lang, and Benjamin Barber. (1995) 'From Magic Kingdom to Media Empire'. *New Perspectives Quarterly* 12, no. 4: 4–17.

Council of Europe. (1992) 'European Convention on Cinematographic Coproduction'. The European Treaty Series no. 147. culture.coe.fr/ infocentre/txt/eng/econ147.html.

Council of Europe. (2000a) 'Report on the Activities of Eurimages in 1999'. Eurimages, 31 March.

Council of Europe. (2000b) 'Guide: Support for the Co-production of Full Length Feature Films, Animation and Documentaries'. Eurimages.

Cox, Dan. (1998) 'Canal+, Col Jump Bridge'. *Daily Variety*, 13 November: 4.

Cox, Kay. (2000) 'Gaul Systems Go; Asterix Theme Park is Stunning Success Story'. *Sunday Mail*, 25 June: 34–35.

Cox, Kevin R. (1997) 'Globalization and the Politics of Distribution: A Critical Assessment'. *Spaces of Globalization: Reasserting the Power of the Local*. Ed. Kevin R. Cox. New York: Guildford Press.

Crock, Stan, Dexter Roberts, Joyce Bernathan, Paul Magnusson, and Emily Thornton. (1997) 'America and China'. *Business Week*, 3 November.

Crofts, Stephen. (1998) 'Authorship and Hollywood'. *Oxford Guide to Film Studies*. Ed. John Hill and Pamela Church Gibson. Oxford: Oxford University Press. 310–24.

Cunningham, Stuart. (1992) *Framing Culture: Criticism and Policy in Australia*. Sydney: Allen and Unwin.

Cunningham, Stuart and Elizabeth Jacka. (1996) *Australian Television and International Mediascapes*. Melbourne: Cambridge University Press.

D'Alessandro, Anthony. (2000) 'The Top 125 Worldwide'. *Variety* 24–30 January: 22.

Danan, Martine. (1995) 'Marketing the Hollywood Blockbuster in France'. *Journal of Popular Film and Television* 23, no. 3: 131–40.

Dawtrey, Adam. (1994) 'Playing Hollywood's Game: Eurobucks Back Megabiz'. *Variety*, 7–13 March: 1, 75.

Dawtrey, Adam. (1997) 'Hollywood Muscle Pushes Brit Pix Blitz'. *Variety*, 11–17 August: 7, 9.

Dawtrey, Adam. (1998) 'Lottery Franchises Mark First Year'. *Variety*, 14–20 December: 74.

Dawtrey, Adam. (1999) 'U, Canal+ Working Jointly'. *Variety*, 17–21 May: 26.

Dawtrey, Adam and Liza Foreman. (2001) 'Biz Takes Pulse of Teuton Quake'. *Variety*, 5–11 March: 8, 12.

Dawtrey, Adam, Alison James, Liza Foreman, Ed Meza, David Rooney, and John Hopewell. (2000) 'Yanks Rank But Locals Tank'. *Variety*, 18–31 December: 1, 77–78.

De Bens, Els de Smaele and Hedwig de Smaele. (2001) 'The Inflow of American Television Fiction on European Broadcasting Channels Revisited'. *European Journal of Communication* 16, no. 1: 51–76.

De Grazia, Victoria. (1989) 'Mass Culture and Sovereignty: The American Challenge to European Cinemas 1920–1960'. *Journal of Modern History* 61, no. 1: 53–87.

De Los Reyes, Aurelio. (1996) 'El Gobierno Mexicano y las Películas Deni-grantes. 1920–1931'. *México Estados Unidos: Encuentros y Desencuentros en el Cine.* Ed. Ignacio Durán, Iván Trujillo, and Mónica Verea. Mexico: Universidad Nacional Autónoma de México. 23–35.

De Silva, I. (1998) 'Consumer Selection of Motion Pictures'. *The Motion Picture Mega-Industry.* Ed. Barry R. Litman. Boston: Allyn and Bacon. 144–71.

De Vany, Arthur S. and W. David Walls. (1996) 'Bose-Einstein Dynamics and Adaptive Contracting in the Motion Picture Industry'. *Economic Journal* 106, no. 439: 1493–514.

De Vany, Arthur S. and W. David Walls. (1997) 'The Market for Motion Pictures: Rank, Revenue, and Survival'. *Economic Inquiry* 35, no. 4: 783–97.

Demarco, Peter. (2001) 'Legal Wizards Crack Whip at Harry Potter Fan Sites'. *Daily News*, 22 February.

Demers, David. (1999) *Global Media: Menace or Messiah?* Cresskill: Hampton Press.

Denicola, Robert. (1999) 'Freedom to Copy'. *Yale Law Journal* 108.

Denzin, Norman. (1995) 'The Birth of the Cinematic, Surveillance Society'. *Current Perspectives in Social Theory* no. 15: 99–127.

Department of Commerce. (1997) *Commercial Opportunities in the Western Cape Film Industry.* Washington, D.C.

Department of Commerce. (2001) *The Migration of U.S. Film and Television Production.* Washington, D.C.

Diawara, Manthia. (1992) *African Cinema.* Bloomington: Indiana University Press.

Diawara, Manthia, ed. (1993) *Black American Cinema.* New York: Routledge.

Dicken, Peter. (1998) *Global Shift: Transforming the World Economy*, 3rd edn. New York: Guilford.

DiOrio, Carl. (2001) 'Exhibs: Glass Half Full'. *Variety*, 12–18 March: 9, 16.

Directors Guild of America. (2000) 'DGA Commends Action by Governor Gray Davis to Fight Runaway Production'. Press Release, 18 May.

Dobson, John. (1993) 'TNCs and the Corruption of GATT: Free Trade Versus Fair Trade'. *Journal of Business Ethics* 12, no. 7: 573–78.

Donahue, Ann. (2000) 'Confab's Focus Turns to Piracy'. *Variety*, 7–13 August.

Donnelly, Peter. (1996) 'The Local and the Global: Globalization in the Sociology of Sport'. *Journal of Sport and Social Issues* 20, no. 3: 239–57.

Downing, John H. (1996) *Internationalizing Media Theory: Transition, Power, Culture.* London: Sage.

Drake, William J. and Kalypso Nicolaïdis. (1992) 'Ideas, Interests, and Institutionalization: Trade in Services and the Uruguay Round'. *International Organization* 46, no. 1: 37–100.

Dreazen, Yochi J. (2000a) 'Old Labor Tries to Establish Role in New Economy'. *Wall Street Journal*, 15 August: B1, B10.

Dreazen, Yochi J. (2000b) 'Labor Unions Turn to Mergers in Pursuit of Growth'. *Wall Street Journal*, 9 September: A2, A6.

Duarte, Luiz Guilherme and S. Tamer Cavusgil. (1996) 'Internationalization of the Video Industry: Unresolved Policy and Regulatory Issues'. *Columbia Journal of World Business* 31, no. 3.

Duke, Paul F. (2000) 'House Vote Cracks China's Great Wall'. *Variety*, 29 May–4 June.

Dunkley, Cathy and Dana Harris. (2001) 'Foreign Sales Mavens See Their Empires Fade'. *Variety*, 15–21 January: 1, 103.

Dupagne, Michel and David Waterman. (1998) 'Determinants of U.S. Television Fiction Imports in Western Europe'. *Journal of Broadcasting and Electronic Media* 42, no. 2: 208–20.

Durie, John, Annika Pham, and Neil Watson. (2000) *Marketing and Selling Your Film Around the World: A Guide for Independent Filmmakers*. Los Angeles: Silman-James Press.

Durkheim, Émile. (1984) *The Division of Labor in Society*, trans. W. D. Halls. New York: Free Press.

Dyer, Richard. (1992) *Only Entertainment*. London: Routledge.

Eco, Umberto. (1972) 'Towards a Semiotic Inquiry into the Television Message'. Trans. Paola Splendore. *Working Papers in Cultural Studies* no. 3: 103-21.

Eco, Umberto. (1987) *Travels in Hyperreality: Essays*. Trans. William Weaver. London: Picador.

Edelman, Bernard. (1979) *Ownership of the Image: Elements for a Marxist Theory of Law*. Trans. Elizabeth Kingdom. London: Routledge and Kegan Paul.

Edmunds, Marlene. (2000a) 'Netherlands'. *Variety*, 15–21 May: 54.

Edmunds, Marlene. (2000b) 'Dutch Seek Subsidy Cut'. *Daily Variety*, 25 July: 18.

Eisner, Michael. (2000) 'Fostering Creativity'. *Vital Speeches* 66, no. 16.

Eller, Claudia. (1998) 'Producing Partners Step Aside for Spielberg with "Saving" Grace'. *Los Angeles Times*, 24 July: D1.

Eller, Claudia. (2000a) ' Spyglass Hopes for More Good "Sense" in Future Projects for the Record'. *Los Angeles Times*, 23 May: B1.

Eller, Claudia. (2000b) 'After Years of Trying, Canal Plus Set to be a Player'. *Los Angeles Times*, 20 June: C1.

Elley, Derek. (1999) 'Review: Asterix and Obelix vs. Caesar'. *Variety*, 1–7 February: 54.

Elliot, Stuart. (1999) 'The Hype is With Us'. *New York Times*, 14 May: C1.

Elliot, Stuart. (2000) 'Intelligex, a New Web Site, Moves into the New World of Online Market-Research Exchanges'. *New York Times*, 19 December: C7.

Endicott, R. C. (2000) 'Studios Soar to New Box-office Nirvana'. *Advertising Age*, 17 July: S12.

Entertainment Industry Development Corporation. (2001) 'Movies of the Week and Production Flight'. www.eidc.com/MOWwebLR.pdf.

European Audiovisual Observatory. (1998) *Statistical Yearbook 1998. Film, Television, Video and New Media in Europe*, Spain.

Evans, Peter. (1979) *Dependent Development: The Alliance of Local Capital in Brazil*. Princeton: Princeton University Press.

Everett, Michael. (1999) 'Unionists Chasing Daley and Gore on Trade Issue'. *Labornet*, www.labornet.org /news/123199/06.html.

Fabrikant, Geraldine. (2001) 'A U.S. Cable Baron Bets His Money Overseas'. *New York Times*, 26 March: 1, 14.

Falk, Richard. (1997) 'State of Siege: Will Globalization Win Out?' *International Affairs* 73, no. 1: 123–36.

Featherstone, Mike, ed. (1990) *Global Culture: Nationalism, Globalization and Modernity*. London: Sage.

Featherstone, Mike and Scott Lash. (1995) 'Globalization, Modernity, and the Spatialization of Social Theory: An Introduction'. *Global Modernities*. Ed. Mike Featherstone, Scott Lash, and Roland Robertson. London: Sage Publications. 1–24.

Feltes, N. N. (1994) 'International Copyright: Structuring "the Condition of Modernity" in British Publishing'. *The Construction of Authorship: Textual Appropriation in Law and Literature*. Ed. Martha Woodmansee and Peter Jaszi. Durham: Duke University Press.

Ferguson, Marjorie. (1992) 'The Mythology About Globalization'. *European Journal of Communication* 7, no. 1: 69–93.

Field, Heather. (2000) 'European Media Regulation: The Increasing Importance of the Supranational'. *Media International Australia* 95: 91–105.

Film and Television Action Committee. (1999) 'A Statement of Principles'. www.ftac.net/mission.html.

Finney, Angus. (1996) *The State of European Cinema: A New Dose of Reality*. London: Cassell.

Fitzgerald, Michael. (2000) 'Inside Sydney: Harboring Hollywood'. *Time International*, 31 July: 48.

Fitzpatrick, Liam. (1993) 'Does Asia Want My MTV? An Interview with Richard Li'. *Hemispheres* July: 21–3.

Foreman, Liza *et al.* (1999) 'H'Wood Buries Overseas Pix'. *Variety*, 25–31 January: 1.

Foucault, Michel. (1972) *The Archeology of Knowledge*. Trans. A.M. Sheridan Smith. New York: Pantheon.

Foucault, Michel. (1977) 'What is an Author?' *Language, Counter-Memory, Practice*, Ed. Donald F. Bouchard. Trans. Donald F. Bouchard and Sherry Simon. Ithaca: Cornell University Press.

Foucault, Michel. (1989) *Foucault Live (Interviews, 1966–84)*. Ed. Sylvère Lotringer. Trans. John Johnston. New York: Semiotext(e) Foreign Agents Series.

Foucault, Michel. (1991) *Remarks on Marx: Conversations With Duccio Trombadori*. Trans. J. R. Goldstein and J. Cascaito. New York: Semiotext(e).

Frater, Patrick. (2000) 'Eurowood'. *Screen International*, 4 June: 8–9.

Freeman, Carla. (2000) *High Tech and High Heels in the Global Economy: Women, Work, and Pink-Collar Identities in the Caribbean*. Durham: Duke Press.

Friedman, Wayne. (2000a) 'Chicken Plucks US$100 Mil for Media, Marketing Run'. *Advertising Age*, 19 June: 3.

Friedman, Wayne. (2000b) 'Hollywood Swings for Box Office Fences'. *Advertising Age*, 10 July: 24.

Friedman, Wayne. (2001) 'Studios Mull Ad Cuts for Local Papers'. *Advertising Age*, 8 January: 1.

Fröbel, Folke, Jürgen Heinrichs, and Otto Kreye. (1980) *The New International Division of Labour: Structural Unemployment in Industrialised Countries and Industrialisation in Developing Countries*. Trans. P. Burgess. Cambridge: Cambridge University Press; Paris: Éditions de la Maison des Sciences de l'Homme.

Frow, John. (1992) 'Cultural Markets and the Shape of Culture'. *Continental Shift: Globalisation and Culture*. Ed. Elizabeth Jacka. Sydney: Local Consumption, 1992. 7–24.

Frow, John. (1995) *Cultural Studies and Cultural Value*. Oxford: Clarendon Press.

Frow, John. (1997) *Time and Commodity Culture: Essays in Cultural Theory and Postmodernity*. Oxford: Clarendon Press.

Frow, John. (2000) 'Public Domain and the New World Order in Knowledge'. *Social Semiotics* 10, no. 2.

Frundt, Henry. (2000) 'Models of Cross-Border Organizing in Maquila Industries'. *Critical Sociology* 26, nos. 1–2: 36–55.

Fry, Andy. (1998) 'Major Players Backing New Euro Finance Shops'. *Daily Variety*, 27: Special Section 1.

Fry, Andy. (2001) 'Taking TV Deals Across Borders'. *Media Monitor*, 8 March: 41.

Fung, Richard. (1991) 'Looking for My Penis: The Eroticized Asian in Gay Video Porn'. *How do I Look? Queer Film and Video*. Ed. Bad Object-Choices. Seattle: Bay Press. 14–68.

Fuson, Brian. (1998) 'Valenti Hails $6.4 Bil B.O. but Fears "Fiscal Godzilla"'. *Hollywood Reporter*, 11 March.

Gaines, Jane. (1991) *Contested Culture: The Image, the Voice, and the Law.* Chapel Hill: University of North Carolina Press.

Galbraith, James K. (1999) 'The Crisis of Globalization'. *Dissent* 46, no. 3: 13–16.

Galetto, Mike and Jo Dallas. (2000) 'Sony's New Gameplan'. *Multichannel News International*, 1 November: 16.

Gandy, Oscar H., Jr. (1992a) 'The Political Economy Approach: A Critical Challenge'. *Journal of Media Economics* 5, no. 2: 23–42.

Gandy, Oscar H., Jr. (1992b) *The Political Economy of Personal Information.* Boulder: Westview Press.

Gandy, Oscar H., Jr. (1998) *Communication and Race: A Structural Perspective.* London: Arnold; New York: Oxford University Press.

Gandy, Oscar H., Jr. and Paula Matabane. (1989) 'Television and Social Perception Among African Americans and Hispanics'. *Handbook of International and Intercultural Information.* Ed. M. Asante and W. Gudykunst. Newbury Park: Sage. 318–48.

García-Canclini, Néstor. (1990) *Culturas Híbridas: Estrategias para Entrar y Salir de la Modernidad.* Mexico, D.F: Editorial Grijalbo.

García-Canclini, Néstor. (1996) 'North Americans or Latin Americans? The Redefinition of Mexican Identity and the Free Trade Agreements'. *Mass Media and Free Trade: NAFTA and the Culture Industries.* Ed. Emile D. McAnany and Kenton T. Wilkinson. Austin: University of Texas Press. 142–56.

García-Canclini, Néstor. (2001) *Consumers and Citizens: Multicultural Conflicts in the Process of Globalization.* Trans. George Yúdice. Minneapolis: University of Minnesota Press.

Gardels, Nathan. (1998) 'From Containment to Entertainment: The Rise of the Media-Industrial Complex'. *New Perspectives Quarterly* 15, no. 5: 2–3.

Garfinkel, Harold. (1992) *Studies in Ethnomethodology.* Cambridge: Polity Press.

Gasher, Mike. (1995) 'The Audiovisual Locations Industry in Canada: Considering British Columbia as Hollywood North'. *Canadian Journal of Communication* 20, no. 2.

Gaudreault, André. (1990) 'The Infringement of Copyright Laws and Its Effects (1900–1906)'. *Early Cinema: Space, Frame, Narrative.* Ed. Thomas Elsaesser. London: BFI.

Gentile, Gary. (2001) 'Report Released on Runaway Films'. Associated Press, 19 January.

Gerbner, George. (1994) 'Unesco in the U.S. Press'. *The Global Media Debate: Its Rise, Fall, and Renewal.* Ed. George Gerbner, Hamid Mowlana, and Kaarle Nordenstreng. Norwood: Ablex. 111–21.

Gerbner, George, Hamid Mowlana, and Kaarle Nordenstreng. (1994) 'Preface'. *The Global Media Debate: Its Rise, Fall, and Renewal*. Ed. George Gerbner, Hamid Mowlana, and Kaarle Nordenstreng. Norwood: Ablex. ix–xii.

Gershon, Richard A. (1997) *The Transnational Media Corporation: Global Messages and Free Market Competition*. Mahwah: Lawrence Erlbaum.

Gever, Martha, John Greyson, and Pratibha Parmar, eds. (1993) *Queer Looks: Perspectives on Lesbian and Gay Film and Video*. New York: Routledge.

Gibbons, Fiachra. (2000) 'Tax Could Make Film Industry a Sleepy Hollow'. *Guardian*, 7 February.

Gibson-Graham, J. K. (1996-97) 'Querying Globalization'. *Rethinking Marxism* 9, no. 1: 1–27.

Gimbel, Mark. (1998) 'Some Thoughts on the Implications of Trusted Systems for Intellectual Property Law'. *Stanford Law Review* 50.

Ginsberg, Jane, and Pierre Sirinelli. (1991) 'Authors and Exploitations in International Private Law: The French Supreme Court and the Huston Film Colorization Controversy'. *Columbia-VLA Journal of Law and the Arts* 15, no. 2.

Ginsberg, Jane C. (1997a) 'Authors and Users in Copyright'. *Journal of the Copyright Society USA* 45.

Ginsberg, Jane C. (1997b) 'Copyright, Common Law, and *Sui Generis* Protection of Databases in the United States and Abroad'. *University of Cincinnati Law Review* 66.

Gitlin, Todd. (1983) *Inside Prime Time*. New York: Pantheon Books.

Gitlin, Todd. (1997) 'The Anti-Political Populism of Cultural Studies'. *Cultural Studies in Question*. Ed. Marjorie Ferguson and Peter Golding. London: Sage. 25–38.

Gittler, Robert J. and Markus Scheuer. (1998) 'Low Unemployment in the Czech Republic: "Miracle" or "Mirage"?' *Monthly Labor Review* 121, no. 8: 31–37.

Goldberg, Jonathan Evan. (1995) 'Now That the Future Has Arrived, Maybe the Law Should Take a Look: Multimedia Technology and its Interaction With the Fair Use Doctrine'. *American University Law Review* 44.

Golden, Peter. (1998) 'Trolling the Net; Digimarc's Watermarking Technology'. *Electronic Business* 24, no. 9.

Golding, Peter and Phil Harris. (1997) 'Introduction'. *Beyond Cultural Imperialism: Globalization, Communication and the New International Order*. Ed. Peter Golding and Phil Harris. London: Sage. 1–9.

Goldman, Michael. (2000) 'The Politics of Post: Lobbying Congress for HD Relief'. *Millimeter*, 1 May.

Goldsmith, Jill. (2000) 'U Gets New Modus: Vivendi: Gauls Invade Fraternity of Media Behemoths'. *Variety*, 19–25 June: 1, 84.

Goldstein, Adam O., Rachel A. Sobel, and Glen R. Newman. (1999) 'Tobacco and Alcohol Use in G-Rated Children's Animated Films'. *Journal of the American Medical Association* 28, no. 12: 1131–36.

Goldstein, Paul. (1970) 'Copyright and the First Amendment'. *Columbia Law Review* 70.

Goldstein, Paul. (1994) *Copyright's Highway: The Law and Lore of Copyright from Gutenberg to the Celestial Jukebox.* New York: Hill and Wang.

Golodner, Jack. (1994) 'The Downside of Protectionism'. *New York Times*, 27 February: H6.

Gordon, Wendy. (1982) 'Fair Use as Market Failure: A Structural and Economic Analysis of the Betamax Case and its Predecessors'. *Columbia Law Review* 82.

Gould, Ellen. (2001) 'The 2001 GATS Negotiations: The Political Challenge Ahead'. www.thealliancefordemocracy.org.

Graham, Jefferson. (2001a) 'Next Napsters Wait in the Wings: As Music-Swap Site Goes Legit, Users Threaten to Quit'. *USA Today*, 8 February.

Graham, Jefferson. (2001b) 'Video on Demand Has Come Into View'. *USA Today*, 22 March.

Grainge, Paul. (1999) 'Reclaiming Heritage: Colourization, Culture Wars and the Politics of Nostalgia'. *Cultural Studies* 13, no. 4.

Gramsci, Antonio. (1978) *Selections from the Prison Notebooks.* Ed. and trans. Quintin Hoare and Geoffrey Nowell-Smith. New York: International Publishers.

Grantham, Bill. (1998) 'America the Menace: France's Feud with Hollywood'. *World Policy Journal* 15, no. 2: 58–66.

Grantham, Bill. (2000) *'Some Big Bourgeois Brothel': Contexts for France's Culture Wars With France.* Luton: University of Luton Press.

Gray, L. and R. Seeber. (1996a) 'The Industry and the Unions: An Overview'. *Under the Stars: Essays on Labor Relations in Arts and Entertainment.* Ed. L. S. Gray and R. L. Seeber. Ithaca: Cornell University Press. 15–49.

Gray, L. and R. Seeber. (1996b) 'Introduction'. *Under the Stars: Essays on Labor Relations in Arts and Entertainment.* Ed. L. S. Gray and R. L. Seeber. Ithaca: Cornell University Press. 1–13.

Greenhouse, Steven. (1999a) 'Unions Need Not Apply'. *New York Times*, 26 July: C1, C14.

Greenhouse, Steven. (1999b) 'The Most Innovative Figure in Silicon Valley? Maybe This Labor Organiser'. *New York Times*, 14 November: 32.

Greider, William. (2000) 'It's Time to Go on the Offensive. Here's How'. *Globalize This! The Battle Against the World Trade Organization and Corporate Rule.* Ed. Kevin Danaher and Roger Burbach. Monroe: Common Courage Press. 143-57.

Grey, Rodney de C. (1990) *Concepts of Trade Diplomacy and Trade in Services*. Hemel Hempstead: Harvester Wheatsheaf.

Grossberg, Lawrence. (1997) *Bringing it all Back Home: Essays on Cultural Studies*. Durham: Duke University Press.

Groves, Don. (1992) ' "1492" Sinks in Italy, Cruises in Germany'. *Daily Variety*, 9 October: 14.

Groves, Don. (1994) 'O'seas B. O. Power Saluted at Confab'. *Variety* 356, no. 4: 18.

Groves, Don. (1999) 'A Major Force O'seas'. *Variety*, 12–18 April: 9.

Groves, Don. (2000a) 'Trade Push May Crack Great Wall for US Pix'. *Variety*, 15–21 May.

Groves, Don. (2000b) 'Boffo B.O. Bucks Foreign Coin Ills'. *Variety*, 18–31 December: 9, 74.

Groves, Don. (2000c) 'CineAsia Basks in Rebound'. *Variety*, 20–26 November: 45.

Groves, Don. (2001a) 'China Sez it Can't Handle 20 U.S. Pix'. *Variety*, 12–18 March: 20.

Groves, Don. (2001a) 'Foreign Exchange Flattens H Wood'. *Variety*, 2–8 April: 7, 45.

Groves, Don and Anthony D'Alessandro. (2001) 'H'W'D Frets Over Foreign Aid'. *Variety*, 12–18 February: 1, 77.

Groves, Don and Mark Woods. (1999a) 'Co-production Battle Lines Set'. *Variety*, 8 August: 28.

Groves, Don and Mark Woods. (1999b) 'Oz Tinkers with Co-production Rules'. *Variety*, 5 September: 159.

Grumiau, Samuel. (1998) 'Behind the Scenes With the Show-Business Trade Unions'. *Trade Union World*, 9 January.

Grumiau, Samuel. (2000) 'The Hollywood Union'. *Trade Union World*, 2 November.

Guback, Thomas H. (1969) *The International Film Industry: Western Europe and America Since 1945*. Bloomington: Indiana University Press.

Guback, Thomas H. (1974) 'Cultural Identity and Film in the European Economic Community'. *Cinema Journal* 14, no. 1: 2–17.

Guback, Thomas H. (1984) 'International Circulation of U. S. Theatrical Films and Television Programming'. *World Communications: A Handbook*. Ed. George Gerbner and Marsha Siefert. New York: Longman. 153–63.

Guback, Thomas H. (1985) 'Hollywood's International Markets'. *The American Film Industry*. Ed. Tino Balio. Madison: University of Wisconsin Press.

Guback, Thomas H. (1987) 'Government Support to the Film Industry in the United States'. *Current Research in Film: Audiences, Economics and Law Vol. 3*. Ed. Bruce A. Austin. Norwood: Ablex. 88–104.

Gubernick, Lisa and Joel Millman. (1994) 'El Sur is the Promised Land'. *Forbes* 153, no. 7: 94–95.

Guider, Elizabeth. (1999) 'Sony Ups its Local Payoff'. *Variety*, 26 July–1 August: 23.

Guider, Elizabeth. (2000a) 'Report Sees US$10 Bil B.O. Decade Rise'. *Variety*, 14–20 February: 20.

Guider, Elizabeth. (2000b) 'Mutual Pacts O'Seas on Pix'. *Daily Variety*, 9 May: 4.

Guider, Elizabeth. (2001) 'Majors' Local TV Push'. *Variety*, 22–28 January: 53, 60.

Gumbel, Andrew. (2001) 'Short Shrift for Unions in Amazon's Silicon Jungle'. *Independent*, 3 February.

Guttridge, Peter. (1996) 'Our Green and Profitable Land'. *Independent*, 11 July: 8–9.

Hainsworth, Paul. (1994) 'Politics, Culture and Cinema in the New Europe'. *Border Crossing: Film in Ireland, Britain and Europe*. Ed. John Hill, Martin McLoone, and Paul Hainsworth. Belfast: Institute of Irish Studies in Association with the University of Ulster and the British Film Institute. 8–33.

Hall, Stuart and Paddy Whannell. (1965) *The Popular Arts*. New York: Pantheon.

Hall, Stuart. (1980) 'Encoding/Decoding'. *Culture, Media, Language*. Ed. Stuart Hall, Dorothy Hobson, Andrew Lowe, and Paul Willis. London: Hutchinson. 128–39.

Hamelink, Cees. (1990) 'Information Imbalance: Core and Periphery'. *Questioning the Media: A Critical Introduction*. Ed. John H. Downing, Ali Mohammadi, and Annabelle Sreberny-Mohammadi. Newbury Park: Sage.

Hamelink, Cees. (2001) 'Remember Herbert Schiller: Our Common Efforts'. *Television and New Media* 2, no. 1: 11–16.

Hames, Peter. (2000) 'Czech Cinema: From State Industry to Competition'. *Canadian Slavonic Papers* 42, no. 1: 63–85.

Hamilton, Annette. (1992) 'The Mediascape of Modern Southeast Asia'. *Screen* 33, no. 1: 81–92.

Hancock, David. (1998) 'Global Film Production', paper prepared for EURO-MEI Venice Conference, 29–30 August.

Hancock, David. (1999) *Film Production in Europe: A Comparative Study of Film Production Costs in Five European Territories France-Germany-Italy-Spain-UK*. European Audiovisual Laboratory.

Hanrahan, John. (2000) 'Studios Busy With all Aspects of Production'. *Variety*, 4–10 December: 58.

Hansen, Miriam. (1994) *Babel and Babylon: Spectatorship in American Silent Film*. Cambridge, MA: Harvard University Press.

Harcourt, Alison. (1998) 'The European Commission and the Regulation of the
   Media Industry'. *Cardozo Arts and Entertainment Law Journal* 16: 425–49.
Harding, James. (2000) 'Angst for the Blue Angels of German Film Neuer Markt
   Backers Who Poured Money Into Hollywood are Now Rushing for the Exits'.
   Financial Times, 30 November: 25.
Harley, John Eugene. (1940). *World-wide Influences of the Cinema: A Study of
   Official Censorship and the International Cultural Aspects of Motion Pictures.*
   Los Angeles: University of Southern California Press.
Harmon, Amy. (2000) 'Free Speech Rights for Computer Code'. *New York Times*,
   31 July: C1.
Harrington, C. Lee and Denise D. Bielby. (1995) *Soap Fans: Pursuing Pleasure
   and Making Meaning in Everyday Life.* Philadelphia: Temple University Press.
Hartley, John. (1987) 'Invisible Fictions: Television Audiences, Paedocracy,
   Pleasure'. *Textual Practice* 1, no. 2: 121–38.
Hartley, John. (1996) *Popular Reality: Journalism, Modernity, Popular Culture.*
   London: Arnold.
Harvey, David. (1999) *The Limits to Capital*, 2nd edn. London: Verso.
Haug, W. F. (1986) *Critique of Commodity Aesthetics: Appearance, Sexuality and
   Advertising in Capitalist Society.* Trans. Robert Bock. Cambridge: Polity Press.
Hay, James. (1987) *Popular Film Culture in Fascist Italy: The Passing of the Rex.*
   Bloomington: Indiana University Press.
Hayes, Dade. (2000) 'Global Release Sked Tightens'. *Variety*, 19–25 June.
Hayes, Dade. (2001) 'Late Rally Lifts Wilted Wickets'. *Variety*, 8–14 January: 9,
   16.
Hays, Will. (1931) Speech, 12 May, J. Walter Thompson Collection, Duke Uni-
   versity, Creative Staff Meeting File, Monday Evening Meetings.
Hayward, Susan. (1993) 'State, Culture and the Cinema: Jack Lang's Strategies
   for the French Film Industry'. *Screen* 34, no. 4: 382–91.
Hearon, Fanning. (1938) 'The Motion-Picture Program and Policy of the
   United States Government'. *Journal of Educational Sociology* 12, no. 3: 147–62.
Heilemann, John. (1994) 'Feeling for the Future: A Survey of Television'. *Econ-
   omist* 330, no. 7850: Survey 1–18.
Hejma, Ondrej. (2000) 'Quality Filmmakers Turn to Prague When They Can't
   Afford Hollywood'. *Columbian*, 22 September: Weekend.
Held, David, Anthony McGrew, David Goldblatt, and Jonathan Perraton.
   (1999) *Global Transformations: Politics, Economics and Culture.* Stanford:
   Stanford University Press.
Hellen, Nicholas. (1999) 'Labour Cuts Film Funding for Flops'. *Sunday Times*,
   7 November.
Herman, K. (2000) 'Screen Test'. *Chain Leader* 5, no. 2: 48.

Herod, A. (1997) 'Labor as an Agent of Globalization and as a Global Agent'. *Globalization: Reasserting the Power of the Local*. Ed. K. R. Cox. New York: Guilford Press. 167–200.

Herskovitz, Jon. (1998) 'Bridging Culture Gap'. *Variety*, 18–24 May: 47.

Hettrick, Scott (2001) 'Tarzan Puts Grinch in Vidlock'. *Variety*, 8–14 January: 1, 79.

Higgott, Richard. (1999) 'Economics, Politics, and (International) Political Economy: The Need for a Balanced Diet in an Era of Globalisation'. *New Political Economy* 4, no. 1: 23–36.

Higson, Andrew and Richard Maltby. (1999) ' "Film Europe" and "Film America": An Introduction'. *'Film Europe' and 'Film America': Cinema, Commerce and Cultural Exchange*. Ed. Andrew Higson and Richard Maltby. Exeter: University of Exeter Press. 1–31.

Hill, John. (1994a) 'The Future of European Cinema: The Economics and Culture of Pan-European Strategies'. *Border Crossing: Film in Ireland, Britain and Europe*. Ed. John Hill, Martin McLoone and Paul Hainsworth. Belfast: Institute of Irish Studies in association with the University of Ulster and the British Film Institute. 53–80.

Hill, John. (1994b) 'Introduction'. *Border Crossing: Film in Ireland, Britain and Europe*. Ed. John Hill, Martin McLoone, and Paul Hainsworth. Belfast: Institute of Irish Studies in association with the University of Ulster and the British Film Institute. 1–7.

Hill, John. (1999) *British Cinema in the 1980s: Issues and Themes*. Oxford: Clarendon Press.

Hill, John and Martin McLoone, eds. (n.d.) *Big Picture Small Screen: The Relations Between Film and Television*. Luton: University of Luton Press/John Libbey Media.

Hill, John, Martin McLoone, and Paul Hainsworth, eds. (1994) *Border Crossing: Film in Ireland, Britain and Europe*. Belfast: Institute of Irish Studies in association with the University of Ulster and the British Film Institute.

Hills, Jill. (1994) 'Dependency Theory and its Relevance Today: International Institutions in Telecommunications and Structural Power'. *Review of International Studies* 20, no. 2: 169–86.

Himpele, Jeffrey D. (1996) 'Film Distribution as Media: Mapping Difference in the Bolivian Cinemascape'. *Visual Anthropology Review* 12, no. 1: 47–66.

Hindes, Andrew. (1998a) 'US Co-pros Play Well in Japan'. *Variety*, 18–24 May: 52.

Hindes, Andrew. (1998b) 'Mandalay Pacts with C+P'. *Variety*, 21–27 September: 26.

Hindley, B. (1999) 'A Bogey and its Myths'. *Times Literary Supplement*, 22 January: 28.

Hirst, Paul. (1997) 'The Global Economy – Myths and Realities'. *International Affairs* 73, no. 3: 409–25.

Hirst, Paul and G. Thompson. (1996) *Globalization in Question: The International Economy and the Possibilities of Governance*. Cambridge: Polity Press.

Hiscock, John. (1998) 'Hollywood Backs British Film Drive'. *Daily Telegraph*, 24 July: 19.

Hobsbawm, Eric. (1998) 'The Nation and Globalization'. *Constellations* 5, no. 1: 1–9.

Hoekman, Bernard M. and Michel M. Kostecki. (1995) *The Political Economy of the World Trading System: From GATT to WTO*. Oxford: Oxford University Press.

Holley, David. (2000) 'Prague: AKA "Hollywood East"'. *Bergen Record*, 27 August.

Hollows, J. and M. Jancovich. (1995) 'Popular Film and Cultural Distinctions'. *Approaches to Popular Film*. Ed. J. Hollows and M. Jancovich. Manchester: Manchester University Press. 1–14.

Holmlund, C. and C. Fuchs, eds. (1997) *Between the Sheets, in the Streets: Queer, Lesbian, Gay Documentary*. Minneapolis: University of Minnesota Press.

Hook, Janet. (2000) 'Film Industry Lobbies for China Trade Bill'. *Los Angeles Times*, 23 May.

Hopewell, John. (2000) 'Deregulation Causes Euro Takeovers to Triple'. *Variety*, 15–21 May: 58.

Hopewell, John. (2001) 'Das Werk Takes Street into Spain'. *Variety*, 12–18 February: 22.

Hoppenstand, Gary. (1998) 'Hollywood and the Business of Making Movies: The Relationship between Film Content and Economic Factors'. *The Motion Picture Mega-Industry*. Ed. Barry R. Litman. Boston: Allyn and Bacon. 222–42.

Horowitz, M. (1997) 'How to Make a Blockbuster'. *New York Times Magazine*, 16 November: 140.

Hoskins, Colin, Stuart McFadyen, and Adam Finn. (1997) *Global Television and Film: An Introduction to the Economics of the Business*. Oxford: Clarendon Press.

Howard, Andrew. (1995) 'Global Capital and Labor Internationalism in Comparative Historical Perspective: A Marxist Analysis'. *Sociological Inquiry* 65, nos. 3–4: 365–94.

Hozic, Aida A. (1999) 'Uncle Sam Goes to Siliwood: Of Landscapes, Spielberg and Hegemony'. *Review of International Political Economy* 6, no. 3: 289–312.

Hughes, Steve and Rorden Wilkinson. (1998) 'International Labour Standards and World Trade: No Role for the World Trade Organization?' *New Political Economy* 3, no. 3: 375–89.

Husband, Warren. (1994) 'Resurrecting Hollywood's Golden Age: Balancing the Rights of Film Owners, Artistic Authors and Consumers'. *Columbia-VLA Journal of Law and the Arts* 17, no. 3.

Hutchinson, John. (1999) 'Re-interpreting Cultural Nationalism'. *Australian Journal of Politics and History* 45, no. 3: 392–407.

I'Anson-Sparks, Justin. (2000) 'Hollywood Goes Even Further East'. *Independent*, 3 August.

Idato, Michael. (1999) 'Mission Not Impossible: We Could be Tinseltown'. *Daily Telegraph*, 5 May.

Ingram, Mike. (2001) 'AOL-Time Warner Threatens Children Running Harry Potter Fan Sites'. *World Socialist Web Site*, www.wsws.org/articles/2001/feb2001/pott-f28_prn.shtml (28 February).

International Labour Office. (1999) *Key Indicators of the Labour Market*, 1999. Geneva.

International Labour Office. (2000a) *Sectoral Activites Programme: Media; Culture; Graphical*. Geneva.

International Labour Office. (2000b) *Symposium on Information Technologies in the Media and Entertainment Industries: Their Impact on Employment, Working Conditions and Labour-Management Relations*. 28 February–3 March. Geneva.

International Monetary Fund. (2000) *Globalization: Threat or Opportunity*. www.imf.org/external/np/exr/ib/2000/041200.htm.

Jacka, Elizabeth. (1992) 'Introduction'. *Continental Shift: Globalisation and Culture*. Ed. Elizabeth Jacka. Sydney: Local Consumption.

Jäckel, Anne. (1996) 'European Co-production Strategies: The Case of France and Britain'. *Film Policy*. Ed. Albert Moran. London: Routledge. 85–97.

Jäckel, Anne. (1999) 'Broadcasters' Involvement in Cinematographic Co-productions'. *Television Broadcasting in Contemporary France and Britain*. Ed. Michael Scriven and Monia Lecompte. Oxford: Berghahn Books. 175–97.

Jacob, Preminda. (1998) 'Media Spectacles: The Production and Reception of Tamil Cinema Advertisements'. *Visual Anthropology* 11, no. 4: 287–322.

James, Alison. (2000) 'Canal Plus Shares its Bonbons with Ovitz'. *Variety*, 10–16 July: 7.

James, Alison and Adam Dawtrey. (2000) 'Oui are the World'. *Variety*, 19–25 June: 1, 85.

James, Nick. (2001) 'In Bed With the Film Council'. *Sight and Sound* 11 no. 1: 14–17.

Jameson, Fredric. (1996) 'Five Theses on Actually Existing Marxism'. *Monthly Review* 47, no. 11: 1–10.

Jameson, Fredric. (2000) 'Globalization and Political Strategy'. *New Left Review* 4 (second series) July–August: 49–68.

Jarvie, Ian. (1998) 'Free Trade as Cultural Threat: American Film and TV Exports in the Post-war Period'. *Hollywood and Europe: Economics, Culture, National Identity: 1945–95*. Ed. Geoffrey Nowell-Smith and Steven Ricci. London: BFI. 34–46.

Jaszi, Peter and Martha Woodmansee. (1996) 'The Ethical Reaches of Authorship'. *South Atlantic Quarterly* 95, no. 4.

Jauss, Hans Robert. (1982) *Toward an Aesthetic of Reception*. Trans. T. Bahti. Minneapolis: University of Minnesota Press.

Jeancolas, Jean-Pierre. (1998) 'From the Blum-Byrnes Agreement to the GATT Affair'. *Hollywood and Europe: Economics, Culture, National Identity: 1945-95*. Ed. Geoffrey Nowell-Smith and Steven Ricci. London: BFI. 47–60.

Johnson, Greg. (2000) 'Can Settlement Lure Runaway Production Home?' *Los Angeles Times*, 24 October.

Joseph, May. (1995) 'Diaspora, New Hybrid Identities, and the Performance of Citizenship'. *Women and Performance* 7, nos. 2–8, no. 1: 3–13.

Jury, Louise. (1996) 'Mission Possible: Red Tape Cut to Boost Film Industry'. *Independent*, 4 July: 3.

Justice for Maya Bay International Alliance. (2000) 'No to Hollywood's "The Beach"! Boycott the Bulldozer Movie.'

Kakabadse, Mario. (1995) 'The WTO and the Commodification of Cultural Products: Implications for Asia'. *Media Asia* 22, no. 2: 71–77.

Kanter, L. (1999) 'Dutch Publishing Firm Colonizes U.S.: Nielsen Deal Caps VNU's Buying Spree'. *Crain's New York Business*, 23 August: 1.

Karthigesu, R. (1998) 'Transborder Television in Malaysia'. *TV Without Borders: Asia Speaks Out*. Ed. Anura Goonasekera and Paul S.N. Lee. Singapore: Asian Media Information and Communication Centre. 38–77.

Katz, Elihu. (1990) 'A Propos des médias et de leurs effets'. *Technologies et Symboliques de la Communication*. Ed. L. Sfez and G. Coutlée. Grenoble: Presses Universitaires de Grenoble.

Kehr, Dave. (1999) 'Planet Hollywood Indeed'. *New York Times*, 2 May: 23, 33.

Kellner, Douglas. (1990) *Television and the Crisis of Democracy*. Boulder: Westview Press.

Kempster, Norman. (2001) 'Federal Study Backs Claims of Lost Movie Jobs'. *Los Angeles Times*, 20 January.

Kendall, David E., Joel M. Litvin, Kevin T. Baine, and Dennis M. Black. (2000) *Amicus Curiae* for MPAA et al. Napster v. A&M Records et al. Appeal nos. 00–16401 and 00–16403 US Court of Appeals for the Ninth Circuit.

Kenny, Jim and Elena Pernia. (1998) 'The Filipino's Window on the World: Viewing Foreign Television in the Philippines'. *TV Without Borders: Asia Speaks Out*. Ed. Anura Goonasekera and Paul S.N. Lee. Singapore: Asian Media Information and Communication Centre. 78–140.

Kessler, Kirsten L. (1995) 'Protecting Free Trade in Audiovisual Entertainment: A Proposal for Counteracting the European Union's Trade Barriers to the U.S. Entertainment Industry's Exports'. *Law and Policy in International Business* 26, no. 2: 563–611.

Keynes, John Maynard. (1957) *The General Theory of Employment Interest and Money*. London: Macmillan; New York: St. Martin's Press.

Kiefer, Peter. (2000) 'Screen Actors Guild Members See Slight Rise in Income – Except Those in TV Who Take Home Less'. *Inside.Com*, 11 December.

Kim, Carolyn Hyun-Kyung. (2000) 'Building the Korean Film Industry's Competitiveness'. *Pacific Rim Law and Policy Journal* 9: 353–77.

King, John. (1989) *Magical Reels: A History of Cinema in Latin America*. London: Verso.

Kirby, Carrie. (2000) 'Hollywood Attacks Digital Movie Piracy'. *San Francisco Chronicle*, 21 July: F1.

Kirkland, Bruce and Claire Buckley. (2001) 'Hollywood vs. Hollywood North'. *Ottawa Sun*, 18 February: S6.

Kirschbaum, Erik. (2001) 'German Thriving Centre for European Film'. *Reuters*, 16 February.

Kissinger, Henry. (1999) Globalization and World Order. Independent Newspapers Annual Lecture, Trinity College Dublin, 12 October.

Klady, L. (1994) 'Gallup Rolls Pic Poll: Film Research Unit to Challenge Dominant NRG'. *Daily Variety*, 21 March: 1.

Klady, L. (1996) 'Moviegoers Stump Science: Despite Reams of Data, Trackers Still Can't Predict Pic's Fate'. *Daily Variety*, 23 August: 3.

Klady, L. (1997) 'Why Can't Johnny Track?' *Variety*, 19–25 May: 7.

Klady, L. (1998) 'More B.O. Oracles Take up Trackin''. *Variety*, 19–25 October: 9.

Kozul-Wright, R. and R. Rowthorn. (1998) 'Spoilt for Choice? Transnational Corporations and the Geography of International Production'. *Oxford Review of Economic Policy* 14, no. 2: 74–92.

KPMG. (1996) *Film Financing and Television Programming: A Taxation Guide*. KPMG. Amsterdam.

Kracauer, Siegfried. (1949) 'National Types as Hollywood Presents Them'. *Public Opinion Quarterly* 13, no. 1: 53–72.

Krosnar, Katka, Adam Piore, and Stefan Theil. (2001) 'Take One: Prague'. *Newsweek International*, 19 March: 40.

Kuhn, Michael. (1998) 'How Can Europe Benefit from the Digital Revolution?' Presentation to the European Audiovisual Conference, Birmingham, 6–8 April.

Kuhn, Raymond and James Stanyer. (1999) 'Television and the State'. *Television Broadcasting in Contemporary France and Britain*. Ed. Michael Scriven and Monia Lecomte. Oxford: Berghahn Books. 2–15.

Kurz, Otto. (1967) *Fakes*. New York: Dover.

LaFranchi, Howard. (1999) 'Mexifilms vs. Mickey Mouse'. *Christian Science Monitor*, 5 January.

Lagny, Michéle. (1992) 'Popular Taste: The Peplum'. *Popular European Cinema*. Ed. Richard Dyer and Ginette Vincendeau. London: Routledge. 163–80.

Lai, Edwin L.C. (1998) 'International Intellectual Property Protection and the Rate of Product Innovation'. *Journal of Development Economics* 55.

Lall, Chander. (1999) 'New Rulings Bolster Copyrights in India'. *IP Worldwide*, May–June.

Landers, Jim. (2000) 'A Tempest Abroad: Other Countries Can be Over-whelmed by American Cultural Exports Such as Music, Movies and Food'. *Dallas Morning News*, 12 November: 1J.

Landler, Mark. (2001) 'A Glut of Cable TV in India'. *New York Times*, 23 March: C1, C12.

Lang, Tim and Colin Hines. (1993) *The New Protectionism: Protecting the Future Against Free Trade*. New York: New Press.

Lange, Andre. (1998) 'Andrew Says Local Financing is Reducing the Number of European Co-productions'. *Screen International*, 5 June: 11.

Latour, Bruno. (1993) *We Have Never Been Modern*. Trans. C. Porter. Cambridge, Mass.: Harvard University Press.

Laurance, Jeremy. (2001) 'The Habit Hollywood Just Can't Stub Out'. *Independent*, 5 January.

Lauzen, Martha M. and David M. Dozier. (1999) 'The Role of Women on Screen and Behind the Scenes in the Television and Film Industries: Review of a Program of Research'. *Journal of Communication Inquiry* 23, no. 4: 355–73.

Lears, T. J. Jackson. (1983) 'From Salvation to Self-realization: Advertising and the Therapeutic Roots of the Consumer Culture, 1880–1930'. *The Culture of Consumption: Critical Essays in American History, 1880–1980*. Ed. Richard Wightman Fox and T. J. Jackson Lears. New York: Pantheon. 1–38.

Leets, Laura, Gavin de Becker, and Howard Giles. (1995) 'Fans: Exploring Expressed Motivations for Contacting Celebrities'. *Journal of Language and Social Psychology* 14, nos. 1–2: 102–23.

Leff, Lisa. (2000) 'The Past is Prologue'. *Los Angeles Times Magazine*, 29 October.

Le Heron, Richard, Ian Cooper, Martine Perry, and David Hayward. (1997) 'Commodity System Governance: A New Zealand Discourse'. *Uneven Development: Global and Local Processes*. Ed. M. Taylor and S. Conti. Aldershot: Avebury. 81–100.

Lent, John A. (1998) 'The Animation Industry and its Offshore Factories'. *Global Productions: Labor in the Making of the 'Information Society'*. Ed. Gerald Sussman and John A. Lent. Cresskill: Hampton Press. 239–54.

Lev, Peter. (1993) *The Euro-American Cinema*. Austin: University of Texas Press.

Levinson, Mark. (1999) 'Who's in Charge Here?' *Dissent* 46, no. 4: 21–23.

Levy, Emmanuel. (1989) 'The Democratic Elite: America's Movie Stars'. *Qualitative Sociology* 12, no. 1: 29–54.

Lewis, Gerry. (2001) 'Think Local When Going Global'. *Variety*, 26 February–4 March: 7.

Lewis, Justin. (1991) *The Ideological Octopus: An Exploration of Television and its Audience*. New York: Routledge.

Lexington. (1999) 'Pokémania v Globophobia'. *Economist*, 20 November: 36.

Light, Julie. (1994) 'Cooperation and Compromise: Co-production and Public Service Broadcasting'. *Screen* 35, no.1: 78–90.

Lindsay, Vachel. (1970) *The Art of the Moving Picture*. New York: Liveright.

Litman, Barry R. (1998) *The Motion Picture Mega-industry*. Boston: Allyn and Bacon.

Litman, Barry R. and Hoekyun Ahn. (1998) 'Predicting Financial Success of Motion Pictures: The Early '90s Experience'. *The Motion Picture Megaindustry*. Barry R. Litman. Boston: Allyn and Bacon. 172–97.

Litman, Jessica. (1990) 'The Public Domain'. *Emory Law Journal* 39.

Loeb, Hamilton. (2000) 'The Management and Resolution of Cross-border Disputes as Canada/U.S. Enter the 21st Century. Telecommunications and Culture: Transborder Freedom of Information or Cultural Identity?' *Canada-United States Law Journal* 26: 303–12.

London Economics. (1992) *The Competitive Position of the European and US Film Industries*. Report for the Media Business School (an initiative of the MEDIA programme of the European Community, London).

Long, Doris E. (1998) 'China's IP Reforms Show Little Success'. *IP Worldwide* November–December.

López, Ana M. (2000) 'Facing up to Hollywood'. *Reinventing Film Studies*. Ed. Christine Gledhill and Linda Williams. London: Arnold. 419–37.

Lowry, Brian. (2000) 'Greetings from Vancouver'. *Los Angeles Times*, 1 October.

Lukk, T. (1997) *Movie Marketing: Opening the Picture and Giving it Legs*. Los Angeles: Silman-James Press.

Lumiere Data Base on Admissions of Films Released in Europe. (n. d.) 'Methodol-ogy – Limitations of the *Lumiere* Database'. lumiere.obs.coe.int/web/sources/EN/metho.html.

Lury, Celia. (1993) *Cultural Rights: Technology, Legality and Personality.* New York: Routledge.

Lyman, Eric J. (2000) 'Hollywood Goes to Rome'. *Adageglobal,* December.

Machan, Dyan. (1997) 'Mr. Valenti Goes to Washington'. *Forbes,* 1 December.

Mackenzie, Drew. (2000) 'Mel's Making a Monkey of Me'. *Mirror,* 2 December: 3.

Madigan, Nick. (1999a) 'Prod'n Headed North'. *Variety,* 28 June–11 July: 12.

Madigan, Nick. (1999b) 'Runaways Inspire Taxing Questions'. *Variety,* 23–29 August: 7.

Madigan, Nick. (1999c) 'Flight or Fight? Industry Gears Up to Keep Produc-tion in Area'. *Variety,* 22–28 November: L3–4.

Madigan, Nick. (2000) 'Surviving the Odds'. *Variety,* 13–19 November: 43–44, 46, 50.

Magder, Ted. (1998) 'Franchising the Candy Store: Split-run Magazines and a New International Regime for Trade in Culture'. *Canadian-American Public Policy* no. 34: 1–66.

Mahendra, Sunanda. (1996) 'A Note on Television in Sri Lanka'. *Contemporary Television: Eastern Perspectives.* Ed. David French and Michael Richards. New Delhi: Sage. 221–27.

Major, Wade. (1997) 'Hollywood's Asian Strategy'. *Transpacific* 68 (March).

Malcolm, Paul. (2000) 'Below the (Color) Line'. *LA Weekly,* 20–26 October.

Mallet, James. (2001) 'Lights, Cameras … But No Action'. *Observer,* 25 March.

Mann, Charles C. (2000) 'The Heavenly Jukebox: Efforts to Obtain Control Access to Sound Recordings from the Internet'. *Atlantic Monthly,* 1 Septem-ber.

Mann, Michael. (1993) 'Nation-States in Europe and Other Continents: Diver-sifying, Developing, Not Dying'. *Daedalus* 122, no. 3: 115–40.

Manvell, Roger. (1950) *Film.* Harmondsworth: Penguin.

Marshall, Don D. (1996) 'Understanding Late-Twentieth-Century Capitalism: Reassessing the Globalization Theme'. *Government and Opposition* 31, no. 2: 193–215.

Martin, Judith N. and Thomas K. Nakayama. (2000) *Intercultural Communi-cation in Contexts,* 2nd edn. London: Mayfield Publishing.

Martin, Reed. (1995) 'The French Film Industry: A Crisis of Art and Com-merce'. *Columbia Journal of World Business* 30: 6–17.

Martin, Reed. (2000) 'The Casting Accent is on Foreign Appeal'. *USA Today,* 13 December.

Martín-Barbero, Jesus. (1993) *Communication, Culture, and Hegemony: From the Media to Mediations*. London: Sage Publications.

Marvasti, A. (1994) 'International Trade in Cultural Goods: A Cross-sectional Analysis'. *Journal of Cultural Economics* 18, no. 2: 135–48.

Marvasti, A. (2000) 'Motion Pictures Industry: Economies of Scale and Trade'. *International Journal of the Economics of Business* 7, no. 1: 99–115.

Marx, Karl. (1906) *Capital: A Critique of Political Economy*. Trans. Samuel Moore and Edward Aveling. Ed. Frederick Engels. New York: Modern Library.

Masur, Richard and Jack Shea. (1999) 'Letter to the Editor'. *Los Angeles Business Journal*.

Mathews, Anna Wilde. (2001) 'Studios Have Their Own Movies-on-Demand Plans'. *Wall Street Journal*, 29 January: B1.

Mato, Daniel. (1999) 'Telenovelas: Transnacionalización de la Industria y Transformación del Género'. *Las Industrias Culturales en la Integracion Latinoamericana*. Ed. Néstor García-Canclini and Carlos J. Moneta. Mexico, D. F.: Grijalbo. 245–82.

Mattelart, Armand. (1979) *Multinational Corporations and the Control of Culture: The Ideological Apparatuses of Imperialism*. Trans. Michael Chanan. Brighton: Harvester Press; Atlantic Highlands: Humanities Press.

Mattelart, Armand and Michèle Mattelart. (1992) *Rethinking Media Theory: Signposts and New Directions*. Trans. James A. Cohen and Marina Urquidi. Minneapolis: University of Minnesota Press.

Mattelart, Armand and Michèle Mattelart. (1998) *Theories of Communication: A Short Introduction*. Trans. Susan Gruenheck Taponier and James A. Cohen. London: Sage.

Mattelart, Armand, Xavier Delcourt, and Michèle Mattelart. (1988) 'International Image Markets'. *Global Television*. Ed. Cynthia Schneider and Brian Wallis. New York: Wedge Press; Cambridge, MA.: MIT Press. 13–33.

Mattelart, Michèle. (1986) 'Women and the Cultural Industries'. Trans. Keith Reader. *Media, Culture and Society: A Critical Reader*. Ed. Richard Collins. London: Sage. 63–81.

Maxwell, Richard. (1996a) 'Ethics and Identity in Global Market Research'. *Cultural Studies* 10, no. 2: 218–36.

Maxwell, Richard. (1996b) 'Out of Kindness and Into Difference: The Value of Global Market Research'. *Media, Culture and Society* 18, no. 1.

Maxwell, Richard. (1999) 'The Marketplace Citizen and the Political Economy of Data Trade in the European Union'. *Journal of International Communication* 6, no. 1.

Maxwell, Richard, ed. (2001) *Culture Works*. Minneapolis: University of Minnesota Press.

Mayer, Gerald M. (1947) 'American Motion Pictures in World Trade'. *Annals of the American Academy of Political and Social Science* no. 254: 31–36.

Mayer, J. P. (1946) *Sociology of Film: Studies and Documents*. London: Faber and Faber.

Mayrhofer, Debra. (1994) 'Media Briefs'. *Media Information Australia* no. 74: 126–42.

Mazziotti, Nora. (1996) *La Industria de la Telenovela: La Producción de Ficción en América Latina*. Buenos Aires: Paidós.

McCann, Paul. (1998) 'Hollywood Film-makers Desert UK'. *Independent*, 14 August: 7.

McChesney, Robert W. (1999) *Rich Media, Poor Democracy: Communication Politics in Dubious Times*. New York: New Press.

McClintock, Pamela. (2000a) 'Valenti Touts Value of Copyright Biz'. *Variety Extra*, 13 December. www.variety.com.

McClintock, Pamela. (2000b) 'Treaty Trips, Falls: US–Euro Rift Thwarts Thesp Film Royalty Accord'. *Daily Variety*, 21 December: 7.

McColley, Carolyn. (1997) 'Limitations on Moral Rights in French "Droit d'Auteur"'. *Copyright Law Symposium* 41.

McDonald, Kevin. (1999) 'How Would You Like Your Television: With or Without Borders and With or Without Culture – A New Approach to Media Regulation in the European Union'. *Fordham International Law Journal* 22: 1991–2031.

McHoul, Alec and Tom O'Regan. (1992) 'Towards a Paralogics of Textual Technologies: Batman, Glasnost and Relativism in Cultural Studies'. *Southern Review* 25, no. 1: 5–26.

McMichael, Philip. (1996) *Development and Social Change: A Global Perspective*. Thousand Oaks: Pine Forge.

McMichael, Philip. (2000a) *Development and Social Change: A Global Perspective*, 2nd edn. Thousand Oaks: Pine Forge.

McMichael, Philip. (2000b) 'Globalisation: Trend or Project?' *Global Political Economy: Contemporary Theories*. Ed. R. Palan. London: Routledge.

McNary, Dave. (2001) 'Guild by Association'. *EV*, February: 3.

Meils, Cathy. (1998) 'Prague Studio Steels for Future'. *Variety*, 22–28 June: 46.

Meils, Cathy. (2000a) 'More Pix Say "Czech, Please"'. *Variety*, 1–7 May: 88.

Meils, Cathy. (2000b) 'Milk and Honey Cuts in With *Blade 2* Prod'n'. *Daily Variety*, 28 November: 38.

Meils, Cathy. (2000c) 'Czech it Out: Studio Biz Good, Sale is On'. *Daily Variety*, 22 December: 8.

Menon, Vinay. (2001) 'Foreign Filming Makes Gains in T.O.'. *Toronto Star*, 7 February.

Michael, Ian. (1999) 'Pirates in Space'. *The Times*, 19 June.

Michaels, Eric. (1990) 'A Model of Teleported Texts (With Reference to Aboriginal Television)'. *Continuum* 3, no. 2.

Miège, Bernard. (1989) *The Capitalization of Cultural Production*. Trans. J. Hay, N. Garnham, and UNESCO. New York: International General.

Milkman, Ruth. (2000) 'Immigrant Organizing and the New Labor Movement in Los Angeles'. *Critical Sociology* 26, nos. 1–2: 59–81.

Millea, Michael. (1997) 'Czech Privatisation: The Case of Fimove Studio Barrandov'. *Journal of International Affairs* 50, no. 2: 489–505.

Miller, Daniel. (1987) *Material Culture and Mass Consumption*. Oxford: Blackwell.

Miller, J. D. B. (1981) *The World of States: Connected Essays*. London: Croom Helm.

Miller, J. D. B. (1984) 'The Sovereign State and its Future'. *International Journal* 39, no. 2: 284–301.

Miller, Toby. (1990) 'Mission Impossible and the New International Division of Labour'. *Metro* no. 82: 21–28.

Miller, Toby. (1996) 'The Crime of Monsieur Lange: GATT, the Screen and the New International Division of Cultural Labour'. *Film Policy: International, National and Regional Perspectives*. Ed. Albert Moran. London: Routledge. 72–84.

Miller, Toby. (1998a) *Technologies of Truth: Cultural Citizenship and the Popular Media*. Minneapolis: University of Minnesota Press.

Miller, Toby. (1998b) 'Hollywood and the World'. *The Oxford Guide to Film Studies*. Ed. John Hill and Pamela Church Gibson. Oxford: Oxford University Press. 371–81.

Mingo, J. (1997) 'Postal Imperialism'. *New York Times Magazine*, 16 February: 36–37.

Minnesota Film Board. (2000) www.mnfilm.org.

Mittell, Jason. (2000) 'The Cultural Power of an Anti-television Metaphor: Questioning the "Plug-In Drug" and a TV-free America'. *Television and New Media* 1, no. 2: 215–38.

Mittelman, James H. (1995) 'Rethinking the International Division of Labour in the Context of Globalisation'. *Third World Quarterly* 16, no. 2: 273–95.

Miyoshi, Masao. (1993) 'A Borderless World? From Colonialism to Transnationalism and the Decline of the Nation-State'. *Critical Inquiry* 19.

Moerk, Christian. (2000) 'Studios See Leaner, Greener Times'. *Variety*, 10–16 January: 9, 30.

Mohammadi, Ali, ed. (1997) *International Communication and Globalization*. London: Sage.

Mokhiber, Russell and Robert Weissman. (1999) 'The Globalization Horror Picture Show'. *Focus on the Corporation*. lists.essential.org/corp-focus/msg00036.html.

Monitor. (1999) *U.S. Runaway Film and Television Production Study Report*.

Moore, Schuyler M. (2000) *The Biz: The Basic Business, Legal and Financial Aspects of the Film Industry*. Los Angeles: Silman-James Press.

Moran, Albert. (1996) 'Terms for a Reader'. *Film Policy*. Ed. Albert Moran. London: Routledge.

Moran, Albert. (1998) *Copycat TV: Globalisation, Program Formats and Cultural Identity*. Luton: University of Luton Press.

Morris, Meaghan. (1990) 'Banality in Cultural Studies'. *Logics of Television: Essays in Cultural Criticism*. Ed. Patricia Mellencamp. Bloomington: Indiana University Press; London: BFI. 14–43.

Motion Picture Association of America. (2001) *2000 US Economic Review*. Los Angeles.

Mowlana, Hamid. (1993) 'Toward a NWICO for the Twenty-first Century?' *Journal of International Affairs* 47, no. 1: 59–72.

Mowlana, Hamid. (1996) *Global Communication in Transition: End of Diversity?* Newbury Park: Sage.

MPA-LA (2000) The Motion Picture Association-America Latina. www.mpaa.org/mpa-al/default.asp.

Munck, Ronaldo. (2000) 'Labour and Globalisation: Results and Prospects'. *Work, Employment and Society* 14, no. 2: 385–93.

Murdoch, Rupert. (1998) Presentation Prepared for the European Audiovisual Conference, Birmingham, 6–8 April.

Murdock, Graham. (1995) 'Across the Great Divide: Cultural Analysis and the Condition of Democracy'. *Critical Studies in Mass Communication* 12, no. 1: 89–95.

Murdock, Graham. (1996) 'Trading Places: The Cultural Economy of Co-productions'. *European Co-productions in Television and Film*. Ed. Sofia Blind and Gerd Hallenberger. Heidelberg: Universitätsverlag C. Winter. 103–14.

Murphy, David G. (1997) 'The Entrepreneurial Role of Organised Labour in the British Columbia Motion Picture Industry'. *Industrial Relations* 52, no. 3: 531–54.

Murray, Alan. (1999) 'The American Century: Is it Going or Coming?' *Wall Street Journal*, 27 December: 1.

Muscio, Giuliana. (2000) 'Invasion and Counterattack: Italian and American Film Relations in the Postwar Period'. *'Here, There and Everywhere': The Foreign Politics of American Popular Culture*. Ed. Reinhold Wagnleitner and Elaine Tyler May. Hanover: University Press of New England. 116–31.

Nader, Ralph. (1999) 'Introduction'. *The WTO: Five Years of Reasons to Resist Corporate Globalization*. Lori Wallach and Michelle Sforza. New York: Seven Stories Press. 6–12.

Nain, Zaharom. (1996) 'The Impact of the International Marketplace on the Organization of Malaysian Television'. *Contemporary Television: Eastern Perspectives*. Ed. David French and Michael Richards. New Delhi: Sage. 157–80.

Nairn, Tom. (1993) 'Internationalism and the Second Coming'. *Daedalus* 122, no. 3: 155–70.

Nakayama, Thomas K. (1994) 'Show/down Time: "Race", Gender, Sexuality, and Popular Culture'. *Critical Studies in Mass Communication* 11: 162–79.

Nakayama, Thomas K. (1997) 'Dis/orienting Identities'. *Our Voices*, 2nd edn. Ed. A. González, M. Houston, and V. Chen. Los Angeles: Roxbury. 14-20.

Nakayama, Thomas K. and R. L. Krizek. (1995) 'Whiteness: A Strategic Rhetoric'. *Quarterly Journal of Speech* 81: 291–309.

Nakayama, Thomas K. and Judith N. Martin, eds. (1999) *Whiteness: The Communication of Social Identity*. Thousand Oaks: Sage.

Natale, Richard. (2000) 'Year In Review: Hollywood – What Really Lies Beneath?' *Los Angeles Times*, 24 December.

Nayyar, Deepak. (1988) 'The Political Economy of International Trade in Services'. *Cambridge Journal of Economics* 12: 279–98.

Neale, Steve. (1995) 'Questions of Genre'. *Film Genre: A Reader II*. Ed. Barry Keith Grant. Austin: University of Texas Press. 159–83.

Negrine, R. and S. Papathanassopoulos. (1990) *Internationalisation of Television*. London: Pinter Publishers.

Nelson, Randy A., Michael R. Donihue, Donald M. Waldman, and Calbraith Wheaton. (2001) 'What's an Oscar Worth?' *Economic Inquiry* 39, no. 1: 1–16.

New York City Office of Film, Theatre and Broadcasting. (2000) www.ci.nyc.ny.cs/html/filmcom.

Newcomb, Horace. (1996) *Mass Media and Free Trade: NAFTA and the Cultural Industries*. Ed. Emile G. McAnany and Kenton T. Wilkinson. Austin: University of Texas Press.

Newman, Matthew and Michael M. Phillips. (2000) 'WTO Says U.S. Copyright Law Violates Global Trade Rules on Musical Rights'. *Wall Street Journal*, 8 June: A6.

Nimmer, Melvin. (1970) 'Does Copyright Abridge the First Amendment Guarantees of Free Speech and the Press?' *UCLA Law Review* 17.

Noam, Eli M. (1993) 'Media Americanization, National Culture, and Forces of Integration'. *The International Market in Film and Television Programmes*. Ed. Eli M. Noam and Joel C. Millonzi. Norwood: Ablex. 41–58.

Norman, Neil. (2000) 'Controversy as Gilliam's Film Gets 2m Lottery Boost'. *Variety*, 25 April: 7.

Nowell-Smith, Geoffrey. (1998) 'Introduction'. *Hollywood and Europe: Economics, Culture, National Identity: 1945–95*. Ed. Geoffrey Nowell-Smith and Steven Ricci. London: BFI. 1–18.

Nowell-Smith, Geoffrey, James Hay, and Gianni Volpi. (1996) *The Companion to Italian Cinema*. London: Cassell/BFI.

Nussbaum, Bruce. (1991) 'The Worldwide Web Steve Ross is Weaving'. *Business Week*, 13 May: 82.

O'Brien, Robert. (2000a) 'The Difficult Birth of a Global Labour Movement'. *Review of International Political Economy* 7, no. 3: 514–23.

O'Brien, Robert. (2000b) 'Workers and World Order: The Tentative Transformation of the International Union Movement'. *Review of International Studies* 26, no. 4: 533–55.

O'Connor, Pamela L. (2001) 'Tracking a Suspect On an Online Trail'. *New York Times*, 8 January: C4.

O'Donnell, Hugh. (1999) *Good Times, Bad Times: Soap Operas and Society in Western Europe*. London: Leicester University Press.

O'Regan, Tom. (1992) 'Too Popular by Far: On Hollywood's International Reputation'. *Continuum* 5, no. 2: 302–51.

O'Regan, Tom. (1993) '(Mis)taking Policy: Notes on the Cultural Policy Debate'. *Australian Cultural Studies: A Reader*. Ed. John Frow and Meaghan Morris. Urbana: University of Illinois Press.

O'Shea, Alan. (1989) 'Television as Culture: Not Just Texts and Readers'. *Media, Culture and Society* 11, no. 3: 373–79.

Office of the United States Trade Representative. (2001a) *The President's 2000 Annual Report on the Trade Agreements Program*. Washington.

Office of the United States Trade Representative. (2001b) *The FTAA and Labor Issues*. Washington.

Office of the United States Trade Representative. (2001c) *WTO Services – U.S. Negotiating Proposals*. Washington.

Oh, Errol. (2000) 'Change in Tack'. *Malaysian Business*, 16 March.

Ollman, Bertell. (2000) 'What is Political Science? What Should it Be?' *New Political Science* 22, no. 4: 553–62.

Olson, Scott Robert. (1999) *Hollywood Planet: Global Media and the Competitive Advantage of Narrative Transparency*. Mahwah: Lawrence Erlbaum.

Olson, Scott Robert. (2000) 'Hollywood Goes Global'. *World and I* 16, no. 2: 263–75.

Orwall, Bruce. (1999) 'Studios Try to Hush Box-offices Guesses'. *Wall Street Journal* 25 October: 16.

Orwall, Bruce. (2000) 'Can Grinch Steal Christmas Abroad?' *Wall Street Journal*, 16 November: B1, B4.

Orwall, Bruce. (2001) 'Ticket to Nowhere'. *Wall Street Journal*, 26 March: R15.

Owens-Ibie, Nosa. (2000) 'Programmed for Domination: U.S. Television Broadcasting and its Effects on Nigerian Culture'. *'Here, There and Everywhere': The Foreign Politics of American Popular Culture*. Ed. Reinhold Wagnleitner and Elaine Tyler May. Hanover: University Press of New England. 132–46.

Palley, Thomas I. (1999) 'Toward a New International Economic Order'. *Dissent* 46, no. 2: 48–52.

Palmer, Michael. (1999) 'Multimedia Multinationals: Canal Plus and Reuters'. *Television Broadcasting in Contemporary France and Britain*. Ed. Michael Scriven and Monia Lecomte. Oxford: Berghahn Books. 140–67.

Park, Robert S. (1943) 'Education and the Cultural Crisis'. *American Journal of Sociology* 48, no. 6: 728–36.

Parker, Richard A. (1991) 'The Guise of the Propagandist: Governmental Classification of Foreign Political Films'. *Current Research in Film: Audiences, Economics and Law Vol. 5*. Ed. Bruce A. Austin. Norwood: Ablex. 135–46.

Parkes, Christopher. (1995) 'Carolco Bought by Murdock for US$50m'. *Financial Times*, 13 November: 23.

Parkin, Frank. (1971) *Class Inequality and Political Order*. London: Magibbon and Kee.

Peers, Martin. (2001) 'Video on Demand Arrives – Sort Of'. *Wall Street Journal*, 29 January: B1, B10.

Pendakur, Manjunath. (1990) *Canadian Dreams and American Control*. Toronto: Garamond.

Pendakur, Manjunath. (1998) 'Hollywood North: Film and TV Production in Canada'. *Global Productions: Labor in the Making of the 'Information Society'*. Ed. Gerald Sussman and John A. Lent. Cresskill: Hampton Press. 213–38.

Peres, Shimon and Pollack, Sydney. (1998) 'Out of Hollywood'. *New Perspectives Quarterly* 15, no. 5: 9–12.

Pérez de Cuéllar, J. (1996) *Our Creative Diversity: Report of the World Commission on Culture and Development*. Paris: UNESCO.

Perlmutter, Shira. (1998) 'Future Directions in International Copyright'. *Cardozo Arts and Entertainment Law Journal* 16, nos. 2–3.

Peters, Anne K. (1974) 'Aspiring Hollywood Actresses: A Sociological Perspective'. *Varieties of Work Experience*. Ed. P. L. Stewart and M. G. Cantor. Cambridge, Mass.: Schenkman.

Peters, Anne K. and Muriel G. Cantor. (1982) 'Screen Acting as Work'. *Individuals in Mass Media Organisations: Creativity and Constraint*. Ed. James S. Ettema and D. Charles Whitney. Beverly Hills: Sage. 53–68.

Peterson, V. S. (1996) 'The Politics of Identification in the Context of Globalization'. *Women's Studies International Forum* 19, nos. 1–2: 5–15.

Petras, James. (2000) 'Estados Unidos: Una Democracia en Venta'. *El Mundo*, 31 August: 4.

Petroski, Henry (1999). *The Book on the Bookshelf*. New York: Alfred A. Knopf.

Pfister, Bonnie. (2000) 'Movie May Help Hurt Mexican Village'. *San Diego Union-Tribune*, 31 May.

Pham, Alex. (2000) 'Technology and Innovation'. *Boston Globe*, 30 November: C1.

Polan, Dana. (1996) 'Globalism's Localisms'. *Global/Local: Cultural Production and the Transnational Imaginary*. Ed. Rob Wilson and Wimal Dissanayake. Durham: Duke University Press. 255–83.

Pool, Ithiel de Sola (1983) *Technologies of Freedom*. Cambridge, Mass.: Harvard University Press.

Porter, Eduardo. (2000) 'Hispanic Actors Await End of Strike'. *Wall Street Journal*, 22 September: B3.

Porter, Michael. (1990) *The Competitive Advantage of Nations*. New York: Free Press.

Porter, Michael F. (1998) 'Clusters and the New Economics of Competition'. *Harvard Business Review*, November–December: 77–90.

Porter, Vincent. (1978) 'Film Copyright: Film Culture'. *Screen* 19, no. 1.

Postrel, Virginia. (1999) 'The Pleasures of Persuasion'. *Wall Street Journal*, 2 August.

Powdermaker, Hortense. (1950) *Hollywood: The Dream Factory: An Anthropologist Looks at the Movie-makers*. Boston: Little, Brown and Company.

Preston, Morag. (2001) 'My Life as a Dot.com Dog at Amazon'. *Independent*, 5 March.

Primo, Alex Fernando Teixeira. (1999) 'The Paradoxical Brazilian Views Concerning American Media Products'. *Images of the U.S. Around the World: A Multilateral Perspective*. Ed. Yahya R. Kamalipour. Albany: State University of New York Press. 179–95

Purnell, Sonia. (1999) 'The Pathe to 33m. Pounds'. *Daily Mail*, 11 February: 17.

Puttnam, David, with Neil Watson. (1998) *Movies and Money*. New York: Alfred A. Knopf.

Pye, Lucian W. (1965) 'Introduction: Political Culture and Political Development'. *Political Culture and Political Development*. Ed. Lucian W. Pye and Sidney Verba. Princeton: Princeton UP. 3–26.

Quester, George H. (1990) *The International Politics of Television*. Lexington, Mass.: Lexington.

Raco, Mike. (1999) 'Competition, Collaboration and the New Industrial Districts: Examining the Institutional Turn in Local Economic Development'. *Urban Studies*, May: 951–70.

Raghavan, Chakravarthi. (1990) *Recolonization, GATT, the Uruguay Round and the Third World*. London and Penang: Zed Books/Third World Network.

Ramsaye, Terry. (1947) 'The Rise and Place of the Motion Picture'. *Annals of the American Academy of Political and Social Science* no. 254: 1–11.

Raphael, Chad. (2001) 'The Web'. *Culture Works: The Political Economy of Culture*. Ed. Richard Maxwell. Minneapolis: University of Minnesota Press.

Rawsthorn, Alice. (1997) 'Return of the Blockbuster Moviemakers'. *Financial Times*, 6 May: 18

Rawsthorn, Alice. (1999) 'Canal Plus in Film Link With Universal'. *Financial Times*, 14 May: 33.

Reeves, Geoffrey. (1993) *Communications and the 'Third World'*. London: Routledge.

Regourd, Serge. (1999) 'Two Conflicting Notions of Audiovisual Liberalisation'. *Television Broadcasting in Contemporary France and Britain*. Ed. Michael Scriven and Monia Lecomte. Oxford: Berghahn Books. 29–45.

Reich, Robert. (1999) 'Brain Trusts'. *New York Times Book Review*, 19 December: 10.

Rettig, Ellen. (1998) 'Lights, Camera, Tax Incentives?' *Indianapolis Business Journal*, 28 September: 3.

Richard, Julie. (2000) 'U.S. Projects Bolster Blighty's Studio, Post Facilities'. *Variety*, 11–17 December: 55–56.

Ricketson, Sam. (1987) *The Berne Convention for the Protection of Literary and Artistic Works: 1886–1986*. London: Centre for Commercial Law Studies.

Riding, Alan. (1999) 'French Comic Book Heroes Battle Hollywood's Hordes'. *New York Times*, 10 February: E2.

Ries, Al and Jack Trout. (1981) *Positioning: The Battle for Your Mind*. New York: McGraw Hill.

Riley, Michael. (1999) 'Producers Find Magic in Mexico'. *Houston Chronicle*, 3 December.

Roach, Colleen. (1997) 'Cultural Imperialism and Resistance in Media Theory and Literary Theory'. *Media, Culture and Society* 19, no. 1: 47–66.

Robins, Kevin and John Cornford. (1992) 'What is "Flexible" About Independent Producers?' *Screen* 33, no. 2: 190–200.

Robinson, Jim. (2000) 'Reel Renaissance'. *Business Mexico* 10, no. 4: 51–55.

Robinson, W. I. (1996) 'Globalization: Nine Theses of our Epoch'. *Race and Class* 38, no. 2: 13–31.

Robles, Alfredo C. (1994) *French Theories of Regulation and Conceptions of the International Division of Labour*. New York: St. Martin's Press.

Rockett, Kevin, Kevin Gibbons and John Hill. (1998) *Cinema and Ireland*. Syracuse: Syracuse University Press.

Rockwell, John. (1994) 'The New Colossus: American Culture as Power Export'. *New York Times*, 30 January: H1, H30.

Roddick, Nick. (1994) 'A Hard Sell: The State of Documentary Film Marketing'. *Dox* no. 2: 30–32.

Rose, Marla Matzer. (2001a) 'Film Industry Profile'. *Business.Com*, www.business.com.

Rose, Marla Matzer. (2001b) 'Television Industry Profile'. *Business.Com*, www.business.com.

Rosen, S. (1981) 'The Economics of Superstars'. *American Economic Review* 71, no. 5: 845–57.

Rosenberg, Scott. (2001) 'Thailand Puts Arm Around H'w'd'. *Variety*, 12–18 February: 22.

Ross, Bob and Kevin Walker. (2000) 'Hollywood on the Bay'. *Tampa Tribune*, 10 October: 1.

Ross, Murray. (1947) 'Labor Relations in Hollywood'. *Annals of the American Academy of Political and Social Science* no. 254: 58–64.

Ross, Robert and Kent Trachte. (1990) *Global Capitalism: The New Leviathan*. Albany: State University of New York Press.

Rothkopf, David. (1997) 'In Praise of Cultural Imperialism'. *Foreign Policy* 107: 38–53.

Rotstein, Robert H. (1992) 'Beyond Metaphor: Copyright Infringement and the Fiction of the Work'. *Chicago-Kent Law Review* 68.

RSVP Film Studios. (n. d.) 'Why Shoot in the Philippines'. www.rsvpfilm.com/shoot.htm.

Ryall, Tom. (1998) 'Genre and Hollywood'. *The Oxford Guide to Film Studies*. Ed. John Hill and Pamela Church Gibson. Oxford: Oxford University Press. 327–38.

Ryan, James. (1999) 'Action Heats Up in Film Biz War'. *Toronto Sun*, 29 August: 50.

Sabin, Rob. (2000) 'The Movies' Digital Future is in Sight and It Works'. *New York Times*, 26 November: B1.

Salokannel, Marjut. (1997) *Ownership of Rights in Audiovisual Productions*. Boston: Kluwer Law International.

Sama, Emmanuel. (1996) 'African Films are Foreigners in Their Own Countries'. *African Experiences of Cinema*. Ed. Imruh Bakari and Mbye B. Cham. London: BFI. 148–56.

Samuelson, Pamela. (1996) 'The Copyright Grab'. *Wired* (January).

Samuelson, Pamela. (1997) 'The Digital Agenda of the World Intellectual Property Organization (Principal Paper): The US Digital Agenda at the WIPO'. *Virginia Journal of International Law* 37.

Samuelson, Pamela. (1999) 'Intellectual Property and the Digital Economy: Why the Anti-circumvention Regulations Need to Be Revised'. *Berkeley Technology Law Journal* 14.

Sanai, Darius. (1999) 'Taking a Leaf Out of Hollywood's Book – British Filmmakers Need to Learn that Great Quality Doesn't Guarantee Box-office Success'. *Independent*, 30 March: 12.

Sankowski, Edward. (1992) 'Ethics, Art and Museums'. *Journal of Aesthetic Education* 26, no. 3: 1–15.

Sardar, Ziauddin. (1998) 'Hollywood Postmodernism: The New Imperialism'. *New Perspectives Quarterly* 15, no. 5: 23–32.

Sartre, Jean-Paul. (1990) *What is Literature?* London: Routledge.

Saunders, David. (1990) 'Copyright, Obscenity and Literary History'. *ELH* 57, no. 2 (Summer): 431–44.

Saunders, David. (1992) *Authorship and Copyright*. London: Routledge.

Saunders, David and Ian Hunter. (1991) 'Lessons from the Literary: How to Historicize Authorship'. *Critical Inquiry* 17 (Spring).

Schaeffer, R. K. (1997) *Understanding Globalization: The Social Consequences of Political, Economic, and Environmental Change*. Lanham: Rowman and Littlefield.

Schatz, Thomas. (1988) *The Genius of the System: Hollywood Filmmaking in the Studio Era*. New York: Pantheon.

Schiller, Dan. (1996) *Theorizing Communication: A History*. New York: Oxford University Press.

Schiller, Herbert I. (1974) *Mind Managers*. Boston: Beacon Press.

Schiller, Herbert I. (1976) *Communication and Cultural Domination*. New York: International Arts and Sciences Press.

Schiller, Herbert I. (1989) *Culture Inc.: The Corporate Takeover of Public Expression*. Oxford: Oxford University Press.

Schlesinger, Philip. (1991) *Media, State and Nation: Political Violence and Collective Identities*. London: Sage.

Schultz, Clifford J. and Bill Saporito. (1996) 'Protecting Intellectual Property: Strategies and Recommendations to Deter Counterfeiting and Brand Piracy in Global Markets'. *Columbia Journal of World Business* 31, no. 1.

Schwab, S. (1994) 'Television in the 90's: Revolution or Confusion?' Tenth Joseph I. Lubin Memorial Lecture. 1 March. New York University.

Scott, Allen J. (1998a) 'From Silicon Valley to Hollywood: Growth and Development of the Multimedia Industry in California'. *Regional Innovation Systems: The Role of Governances in a Globalized World*. Ed. Hans-Joachim Braczyk, Philip Cooke, and Martin Heidenreich. London: UCL Press. 136–62.

Scott, Allen J. (1998b) 'Multimedia and Digital Visual Effects: An Emerging Local Labor Market'. *Monthly Labor Review* 121, no. 3: 30–38.

Screen Actors Guild. (2000) 'The Guild's Efforts to Address Runaway Film and Television Production'. www.sag.org/runaway/sagaddresses.html.

Segrave, Kerry. (1997) *American Films Abroad: Hollywood's Domination of the World's Movie Screens from the 1890s to the Present.* Jefferson: McFarland.

Seiter, Ellen. (1999) *Television and New Media Audiences.* Oxford: Clarendon Press.

Sen, Krishna. (1994) *Indonesian Cinema: Framing the New Order.* London: Zed.

Seno, Alexandra A. and Siem Reap. (2001) 'Lights, Camera – Tourists!' *Asia week,* 2 March: 38.

Sergeant, Jean-Claude. (1999) 'Cable Television'. *Television Broadcasting in Contemporary France and Britain.* Ed. Michael Scriven and Monia Lecompte. Oxford: Berghahn Books. 107–19.

Sewell, James P. (1974) 'UNESCO: Pluralism Rampant'. ' *The Anatomy of Influence: Decision Making in International Organization.* Ed. Robert W. Cox and Harold K. Jacobson. New Haven: Yale University Press. 139–74.

Seyoum, Belay. (1996) 'The Impact of Intellectual Property Rights on Foreign Direct Investment'. *Columbia Journal of World Business* 31, no. 1.

Shatilla, Christopher Andrew. (1996) *Reaching a Global Audience: The Economic Geography of Toronto's Film and TV Industry.* MA thesis, Queen's University at Kingston, Canada.

Shohat, Ella and Robert Stam. (1994) *Unthinking Eurocentrism: Multiculturalism and the Media.* New York: Routledge.

Short, David. (1996) 'Pearson Resists Pressure for a Focus on Television'. *European,* 21 March: 24.

Short, David. (1997) 'Batman and Robbing'. *European,* 31 July: 28–29.

Simonet, T. (1980) *Regression Analysis of Prior Experience of Key Production Personnel as Predictors of Revenue from High Grossing Motion Pictures in American Release.* New York: Arno Press.

Simpson, Glenn R. (2001a) 'The Battle Over Web Privacy'. *Wall Street Journal,* 21 March: B1, B4.

Simpson, Glenn R. (2001b) 'U.S. Officials Criticise Rules on EU Privacy'. *Wall Street Journal,* 27 March: B7.

Sinclair, John. (1999) *Latin American Television: A Global View.* Oxford: Oxford University Press.

Sinclair, John, Elizabeth Jacka, and Stuart Cunningham, eds. (1996) *New Patterns in Global Television: Peripheral Vision.* Oxford: Oxford University Press.

Sinclair, Scott. (2000) GATS: *How the World Trade Organization's New 'Services' Negotiations Threaten Democracy.* Canadian Centre for Policy Alternatives.

Sjolander, Claire Turner. (1992–3) 'Unilateralism and Multilateralism: The United States and the Negotiation of the GATS'. *International Journal* 48, no. 1: 52–79.

Smiers, Joost. (2000) 'The Abolition of Copyright: Better for Artists, Third World Countries and the Public Domain'. *Gazette* 62, no. 5.

Smith, Adam. (1970) *The Wealth of Nations Books I–III*. Ed. A. Skinner. Harmondsworth: Penguin.

Smith, Anthony D. (1990) 'The Supersession of Nationalism?' *International Journal of Comparative Sociology* 31, nos. 1–2: 1–31.

Smith, Anthony D. (1996) 'LSE Centennial Lecture: The Resurgence of Nationalism? Myth and Memory in the Renewal of Nations'. *British Journal of Sociology* 47, no. 4: 575–98.

Smith, Craig S. (2000a) 'Copyright Pirates Strike at Beijing'. *International Herald Tribune*, 6 October: 6.

Smith, Craig S. (2000b) 'Tale of Piracy: How the Chinese Stole the Grinch'. *New York Times*, 12 December.

Smith, Craig S. (2000c) 'Turnabout: China's Copyright Pirates Steal the Grinch'. *International Herald Tribune*, 13 December: 20.

Smithsimon, Greg. (1999) 'Transnational Labor Organizing: Opportunities and Obstacles for Unions Challenging Multinational Corporations'. *Socialist Review* 27, nos. 3–4: 65–93.

Smoodin, Eric. (1993) *Animating Culture: Hollywood Cartoons from the Sound Era*. New Brunswick: Rutgers University Press.

Snider, Mike. (2001) 'No Copying, No Trading? No Kidding: Copyright Fight Might Narrow Our Options'. *USA Today*, 6 March.

Sobel, Lionel S. (1995) 'Back from the Public Domain'. *Entertainment Law Reporter* 17, no. 3.

Soriano, Csar G. (2001) 'Top 3 Prove Hard to Cast Out'. *USA Today* 23 January.

Sorlin, Pierre. (1991) *European Cinemas, European Societies 1939–1990*. London: Routledge.

Sreenivasan, Sreenath. (1997) 'What is a Hit Film? Moviefone May Know'. *New York Times*, 2 June: D9.

Staiger, Janet. (1983) 'Combination and Litigation: Structures of US Film Distribution, 1986–1917'. *Cinema Journal* 23, no. 2.

Stalker, Peter. (2000) *Workers Without Frontiers: The Impact of Globalization on International Migration*. Boulder: Lynne Reinner.

Stam, Robert. (1989) *Subversive Pleasures: Bakhtin, Cultural Criticism and Film*. Baltimore: The Johns Hopkins University Press.

Stanbery, Jennifer. (2001) 'Hollywood Envy? Europe's Films Struggle to Compete'. *Reuters*, 9 February.

Steinbock, Dan. (1995) *Triumph and Erosion in the American Media and Entertainment Industries*. Westport: Quorum.

Stern, Andy. (1994a) 'Film/TV Future Tops Confab Agenda'. *Variety*, 27 June–3 July: 39.

Stern, Andy. (1994b) 'Valenti Denies Euro TV Crisis'. *Daily Variety*, 23 June: 1, 17.

Stern, Andy. (1999) 'Reding Plans More Green for Distrib'n'. *Variety*, 1–7 November: 18.

Stern, Andy. (1999–2000) 'EC Funnels $355 Mil to Boost Pix'. *Variety*, 20 December–2 January: 20.

Stern, Christopher. (1998) 'US Ideas Top Export Biz'. *Variety*, 11–17 May.

Sterngold, James. (1996) 'Debacle on the High Seas'. *New York Times,* 31 March: 1.

Stevens, Tracy, ed. (2000) *International Motion Picture Almanac*, 71st. edn. La Jolla: Quigley.

Stevenson, Richard W. (1994) 'Lights! Camera! Europe!' *New York Times*, 6 February: 1, 6.

Stevis, Dimitris and Terry Boswell. (1997) 'Labour: From National Resistance to International Politics'. *New Political Science* 2, no. 1: 93–104.

Stokes, Bruce. (1999) 'Lights! Camera! More Inaction'. *National Journal*, July: 2106.

Storper, Michael. (1989) 'The Transition to Flexible Specialisation in the U.S. Film Industry: External Economies, the Division of Labour, and the Crossing of Industrial Divides'. *Cambridge Journal of Economics* 13: 273–305.

Storper, Michael. (1993) 'Flexible Specialisation in Hollywood: A Response to Aksoy and Robins'. *Cambridge Journal of Economics* 17, no. 4: 479–84.

Storper, Michael and Susan Christopherson. (1987) 'Flexible Specialization and Regional Industry Agglomerations: The Case of the U. S. Motion Industry'. *Annals of the Association of American Geographers* 77, no. 1: 104–17.

Strange, Susan. (1995a) 'The Defective State'. *Daedalus* 124, no. 2: 55–74.

Strange, Susan. (1995b) 'The Limits of Politics'. *Government and Opposition* 30, no. 3: 291–311.

Streeter, Thomas. (1996) *Selling the Air: A Critique of the Policy of Commercial Broadcasting in the United States*. Chicago: University of Chicago Press.

Streif, Tilman. (2000) 'Movies are Next Battle Zone in War Over Digital Copyrights'. *Deutsche-Presse-Agentur*, 25 July.

Stringer, Robin. (2001) 'Lottery's £92m For Film Flops'. *Evening Standard*, 2 January: 1.

Stroud, Michael. (1999) 'Valley to Lose Film Jobs?' *Wired News* www.wired.com/news/culture/0,1284,20443,00.html (26 June).

Sullivan, Jeanne English. (1996) 'Copyright for Visual Art in the Digital Age: A Modern Adventure in Wonderland'. *Journal of Arts Management, Law and Society* 26, no. 1.

Sullivan, Maureen. (1999) 'H.K. Mulls Harsher Piracy Fines'. *Daily Variety*, 25 February: 10.

Sussman, Gerald and John A. Lent, eds. (1998) *Global Productions: Labour in the Making of the 'Information Society'*. Cresskill: Hampton Press.

Sutter, Mary. (1998a) 'Viva Mexico! – Hollywood Heads South of the Border'. *Kempos*, 21–27 December: 1, 4–5.

Sutter, Mary. (1998b) 'Woman on Top in a Macho Man's Union'. *Kempos*, 21–27 December: 8.

Svetkey, Benjamin. (1994) 'Why Movie Ratings Don't Work'. *Entertainment Weekly* no. 250: 26–33.

Swanson, Tim. (2000) 'Writers Reboot'. *Variety*, 31 July–6 August.

Sweeting, Paul. (2001) 'The Movie and Music Industries Have Good Reason to Feel Picked On'. *Video Business*, 12 March: 12.

Swift, Brent. (1999) 'Film and Television Action Committee Past and Present'. www.ftac.net/about.html.

Swyngedouw, Erik. (1997) 'Neither Global Nor Local: "Glocalization" and the Politics of Scale'. *Spaces of Globalization: Reasserting the Power of the Local*. Ed. Kevin R. Cox. New York: The Guilford Press. 137–66.

Sykes, Jason and Glenn R. Simpson. (2001) 'Some Big Sites Back P3P Plan; Others Wait'. *Wall Street Journal*, 21 March: B1, B4.

Talcin, Marsha. (n. d.) 'Many Film Productions Hopping the Northern Border'. *Showbiz Industry Digest,* www.showbizdigest.com.

Tanzer, Andrew. (1998) 'Tech-Savvy Pirates'. *Forbes*, 7 July.

Tartaglione, Nancy. (2000) 'The Final Vote: Canal Plus Shareholders Approve Vivendi-Universal Merger'. *[Inside]* 8 December: 17.

Taylor, Paul. (1998) *Responding to the Shock of the New: Trade, Technology and the Changing Production Axis in Film, Television and New Media*. Ph.D. dissertation, University of Washington.

Taylor, Paul W. (1995) 'Co-productions – Content and Change: International Television in the Americas'. *Canadian Journal of Communication* 20: 411–16.

Teeple, G. (1995) *Globalization and the Decline of Social Reform*. New Jersey: Humanities Press.

Tegel, Simeon. (2000) 'Hollywood Gets Last Word in Mexican Dubs'. *Variety*, 13 March.

Tegel, Simeon. (2001) 'Sand and Stardust'. *Business Mexico*, 1 February.

Theiler, Tobias. (1999) 'Viewers into Europeans?: How the European Union Tried to Europeanize the Audiovisual Sector, and Why it Failed'. *Canadian Journal of Communication* 24, no. 4: 557–87.

Thomas, Pradip. (1999) 'Trading the Nation: Multilateral Negotiations and the Fate of Communications in India'. *Gazette* 61, nos. 3–4.

Thompson, E.P. (1975) *Whigs and Hunters: The Origins of the Black Act*. New York: Pantheon.

Thompson, Kristin. (1985) *Exporting Entertainment: America in the World Film Market 1907–1934*. London: BFI.

Thompson, Paul and Chris Smith. (1999) 'Beyond the Capitalist Labor Process: Workplace Change, the State and Globalisation'. *Critical Sociology* 24, no. 3: 193–215.

Throsby, David. (2001) 'Defining the Artistic Experience: The Australian Experience'. *Poetics* 28: 255–71.

Ting Yu, Liza Hamm, Fran Brennan, Michelle Caruso, Alison Gee, Jennifer Longley, and York Member. (2000) 'Czech, Please!' *People*, 9 October: 26.

Tomkins, R. (2000) 'Taylor Nelson Buys into Internet Trends Group'. *Financial Times*, 13 March: 24.

Tomlinson, John. (1991) *Cultural Imperialism: A Critical Introduction*. Baltimore: The Johns Hopkins University Press.

Toto, Dominic. (2000) 'Job Growth in Television: Cable Versus Broadcast, 1958–99'. *Monthly Labor Review* 123, no. 8: 3–14.

Townson, Don. (1999) 'H'wood Techs Migrate North'. *Variety*, 23–29 August: 9.

Tracy, James F. (1999) 'Whistle While You Work: The Disney Company and the Global Division of Labor'. *Journal of Communication Inquiry* 23, no. 4: 374–89.

Tricot, Agnès. (2000) 'Screens Without Frontiers': Project to Establish a Database for Television Programs for Use of the Public Television Channels of Developing Countries'. UNESCO/URTI.

Truffaut, François with Helen G. Scott. (1967) *Hitchcock*. New York: Touchstone.

Tunstall, Jeremy. (1981) *The Media are American: Anglo-American Media in the World*. London: Constable.

Tunstall, Jeremy and David Machin. (1999) *The Anglo-American Media Connection*. Oxford: Oxford University Press.

Turner, Graeme. (1988) *Film as Social Practice*. London: Routledge.

Tushnet, Rebecca. (1997) 'Legal Fictions: Copyright, Fan Fiction and a New Common Law'. *Loyola of Los Angeles Entertainment Law Journal* 17.

Tyner, James A. (1998) 'Asian Labor Recruitment and the World Wide Web'. *Professional Geographer* 50, no. 3: 331–44.

Ukadike, Nwachukwu Frank. (1994) *Black African Cinema*. Berkeley: University of California Press.

Ulff-Moller, Jens. (1999) 'Hollywood's "Foreign War": The Effect of National Commercial Policy on the Emergence of the American Film Hegemony in France, 1920–1929'. *'Film Europe' and 'Film America': Cinema, Commerce and*

Cultural Exchange. Ed. Andrew Higson and Richard Maltby. Exeter: University of Exeter Press. 181–206.

UNDP. (1999) *Human Development Report.*

UNESCO. (2000a) *Cinema: A Survey on National Cinematography.* www.unesco.org/culture/industries/cinema/html_eng/trade.shtm.UNESCO (2000b) *Statistics,* unescostat.unesco.org/statsen/Statistics/yearbook/tables/CultAndCom/Table_IV_12_America.html.

Ungureit, Heinz. (1991) 'Le Groupement Européen de Production: Rassembler les Forces du Service Public …'. *Dossiers de l'Audiovisuel* no. 35.

United Nations Development Programme. (1999) *Human Development Report.* Oxford: Oxford University Press.

United States Government. (2000) 'Communication from the United States: Audiovisual and Related Services'. World Trade Organization. Council for Trade in Services Special Session. S/CSS/W/21, 18 December.

Ursell, Gillian. (2000) 'Television Production: Issues of Exploitation, Commodification and Subjectivity in UK Television Labour Markets'. *Media, Culture and Society* 22, no. 6: 805–25.

US Government Working Group on Electronic Commerce. (1998) 'First Annual Report'. www.ecommerce.gov.

USIA. (1997) '1997 National Trade Estimate Report – European Union'. M2 Press Wire.

Valenti, Jack. (1993) 'Expanding Competition in the International Market – An Industry Perspective'. *The International Market in Film and Television Programs.* Ed. Eli M. Noam and Joel C. Millonzi. Norwood: Ablex. 147–50.

Valenti, Jack. (1998a) 'Collapse of the Common Wisdom: How Movies Beat the Competition! A Recounting of a Very Good Year'. MPA Press Release, 10 March.

Valenti, Jack. (1998b) 'Cinema Renaissance – "it's Morning in Britain" – By Jack Valenti'. MPA Press Release, 16 June.

Valenti, Jack. (2000a) 'Valenti Announces Formation of Committee in Support of China Trade'. MPA Press Release, 9 February.

Valenti, Jack. (2000b) 'There's No Free Hollywood'. *New York Times,* 21 June: A23.

Valenti, Jack. (2001a) 'Copyright and Creativity – The Jewel in America's Crown'. Address to the International Trademark Association, Santa Monica, 22 January.

Valenti, Jack. (2001b) 'Opinion: Copyright and Creativity'. *Newsweek,* 19 March.

Valenti, Jack. (2001c) 'Traveling that Sweet Road that Leads to Success', Sho-West, Las Vegas, Nevada, 6 March.

Valentine, John. (1997) 'Global Sport and Canadian Content: The *Sports Illustrated* Controversy'. *Journal of Sport and Social Issues* 21, no. 3: 239–59.

Van Camp, Julie. (1994) 'Creating Works of Art from Works of Art: The Problem of Derivative Works'. *Journal of Arts Management, Law and Society* 24, no. 3.

Van Cuilenburg, Jan. (1999) 'On Competition, Access and Diversity in Media, Old and New: Some Remarks for Communications Policy in the Information Age'. *New Media and Society* 1, no. 2.

Van der Merwe, Dana. (1999) 'The Dematerialization of Print and the Fate of Copyright'. *International Review of Law Computers* 13, no. 3.

Van Elteren, Mel. (1996a) 'Conceptualizing the Impact of US Popular Culture Globally'. *Journal of Popular Culture* 30, no. 1: 47–89.

Van Elteren, Mel. (1996b) 'GATT and Beyond: World Trade, the Arts and American Popular Culture in Western Europe'. *Journal of American Culture* 19, no. 3: 59–73.

Vasey, Ruth. (1992) 'Foreign Parts: Hollywood's Global Distribution and the Representation of Ethnicity'. *American Quarterly* 44, no. 4: 617–42.

Vasey, Ruth. (1997) *The World According to Hollywood, 1918–1939*. Madison: University of Wisconsin Press.

Venturelli, Shalini. (1997) 'Prospects for Human Rights in the Political and Regulatory Design of the Information Society'. *Media and Politics in Transition: Cultural Identity in the Age of Globalization*. Eds. Jan Servaes and Rico Lie. Leuven and Amersfoort: Acco.

Venturelli, Shalini. (1998) 'Cultural Rights and World Trade Agreements in the Information Society'. *Gazette* 60, no. 1: 47–76.

Veronis Suhler Media Merchant Bank. (2000) *Communications Industry Forecast*, 14th edn. New York.

Verrier, Richard. (2000) 'Disney's Big Ideas: Company is a Magnet for Accusations of Intellectual Thefts'. *Orlando Sentinel*, 2 August: H1.

VerSteeg, Jac Wilder. (2000) 'A Wild West – With No Sheriffs'. *Palm Beach Post*, 19 September.

Vogel, Harold L. (1998) *Entertainment Industry Economics: A Guide for Financial Analysis*, 4th edn. Cambridge: Cambridge University Press.

Wagnleitner, Reinhold and Elaine Tyler May. (2000) 'Here, There, and Everywhere: Introduction'. *'Here, There and Everywhere': The Foreign Politics of American Popular Culture*. Ed. Reinhold Wagnleitner and Elaine Tyler May. Hanover: University Press of New England. 1–13.

Walker, Alexander. (1999) 'Adding Insult to Injury'. *Evening Standard*, 9 February: 46.

Walker, Alexander. (2000) 'The Split Screen'. *Evening Standard*, 5 October: 31.

Wallace, W. Timothy, Alan Seigerman, and Morris B. Holbrook. (1993) 'The Role of Actors and Actresses in the Success of Films: How Much is a Movie Star Worth?' *Journal of Cultural Economics* 17, no. 1: 1–27.

Wallerstein, Immanuel. (1989) 'Culture as the Ideological Battleground of the Modern World-System'. *Hitotsubashi Journal of Social Studies* 21, no. 1: 5–22.

Wallerstein, Immanuel. (2000) 'Introduction'. *Review* 23, no. 1: 1–13.

Wanger, Walter. (1939) '120,000 American Ambassadors'. *Foreign Affairs* 18, no. 1: 45–59.

Wanger, Walter. (1950) 'Donald Duck and Diplomacy'. *Public Opinion Quarterly* 14, no. 3: 443–52.

Wasko, Janet. (1982) *Movies and Money: Financing the American Film Industry.* Norwood: Ablex.

Wasko, Janet. (1994) *Hollywood in the Information Age: Beyond the Silver Screen.* Cambridge: Polity Press.

Wasko, Janet. (1998) 'Challenges to Hollywood's Labor Force in the 1990s'. *Global Productions: Labor in the Making of the 'Information Society'.* Ed. Gerald Sussman and John A. Lent. Cresskill: Hampton Press. 173–89.

Wasser, Frederick. (1995) 'Is Hollywood America? The Trans-nationalization of the American Film Industry'. *Critical Studies in Mass Communication* 12, no. 4: 423–37.

Waterman, David and Krishna P. Jayakar. (2000) 'The Competitive Balance of the Italian and American Film Industries'. *European Journal of Communication* 15, no. 4: 501–28.

Waters, Dan. (1999) 'Throwing Cash at Movieland'. *Sacramento Bee*, 23 April.

Waxman, Sharon. (1999) 'Location, Location: Hollywood Loses Films to Cheaper Climes'. *Washington Post*, 25 June: C1.

Wedell, George. (1994) 'Prospects for Television in Europe'. *Government and Opposition* 29, no. 3: 315–31.

Weil, Lynn (1998) 'Italian Film Biz Slumping'. *NPR Morning Edition*, 5 May.

Weinraub, Bernard. (1993) 'Directors Battle Over GATT's Final Cut and Print'. *New York Times*, 12 December: L24.

Welch, L. S. and R. Luostarinen. (1988) 'Internationalization: Evolution of a Concept'. *Journal of General Management* 14, no. 2: 34–55.

Weller, Jerry. (1999) Congressional Testimony, 5 August.

Weller, Jerry. (2000) Congressional Testimony, 27 October.

Wenders, Wim. (1991) *The Logic of Images: Essays and Conversations.* Trans. Michael Hofmann. London: Faber and Faber.

West, Stephen. (1991) 'Universal to Make Films With European Pay-TV Firm'. *Los Angeles Times*, 15 July: D2.

Wheeler, Mark. (2000) 'Research Note: "The Undeclared War" Part II'. *European Journal of Communication* 15, no. 2: 253–62.

Whitaker, Barbara. (2000). 'Private Sector; Trading on Hollywood's Future'. *New York Times*, 29 October.

White, Jerry. (2001) 'Union Membership in US at Lowest Level in 60 Years'. *World Socialist Web Site.* www.wsws.org (26 February).

Wildman, Steven S. and Stephen E. Siwek. (1993) 'The Economics of Trade in Recorded Media Products in a Multilingual World: Implications for National Media Policies'. *The International Market in Film and Television Programs.* Ed. Eli M. Noam and Joel C. Millonzi. Norwood: Ablex. 13–40.

Willens, M. (2000) 'Putting Films to the Test, Every Time'. *New York Times*, 25 June: 11, 20.

Williams, Michael. (1994) 'The Future Speaks English'. *Variety*, 12–18 December: 57.

Williams, Michael. (1997) 'Canal+, Pathe in Pic Pact'. *Variety*, 2–8 June: 9.

Williams, Michael. (1999) 'US Pix Get French Kiss'. *Variety*, 15 21 November: 1.

Williams, Raymond. (1989) *The Politics of Modernism: Against the New Conformists.* London: Verso.

Williams-Jones, Michael. (2001) 'Global Biz Requires Global Expertise'. *Variety*, 19–25 February: 7.

Willman, David and Alan Citron. (1992) 'Carolco Pictures Pins Hopes For Rescue on its "Universal Soldier"'. *Los Angeles Times*, 10 July: D1.

Winslow, George. (2001) 'Hollywood Wired'. *Multichannel News International*, 1 January.

Wolf, Michael J. (1999) *The Entertainment Economy: How Mega-Media Forces are Transforming Our Lives.* New York: Random House.

Woodmansee, Martha. (1984) 'The Genius and the Copyright: Economic and Legal Conditions of the Emergence of the "Author"'. *Eighteenth Century Studies* 17: 425–48.

Woods, Mark. (1999a) 'That Championship Season'. *Variety*, 11–17 January: 9, 16.

Woods, Mark. (1999b) 'Foreign Pix Bring Life to Biz'. *Variety*, 3–9 May: 37, 44, 46, 59.

Woods, Mark. (2000) 'More Players Split O'Seas Pie'. *Variety*, 10–16 January: 9–10.

Woolf, Marie. (1998) 'Why the Next English Patient Will be British'. *Independent On Sunday*, 20 December: 9.

World Trade Organization. (1998) 'Audiovisual Services: Background Note by the Secretariat'. S/C/W/40 of 15 June.

World Trade Organization. (2000) 'Growth Rate of World Merchandise Trade Expected to Double in 2000, According to Latest Report by WTO Secretariat'. www.wto.org/english/news_e/pres00_e/pr200_e.htm.

World Trade Organization. (2001) 'Overview of the State-of-Play of WTO Disputes.'

Worth, Sol. (1981). *Studying Visual Communication*. Ed. Larry Gross. Philadelphia: University of Pennsylvania Press.

Wuliger, Deborah. (2000) Posting on Citizens' Media Watch. forum. oneworld.net:8080/~mediachannel/read?2619,358 (6 December).

Wyatt, Justin. (1994) *High Concept: Movies and Marketing in Hollywood*. Austin: University of Texas Press.

Younge, Gary. (2000) 'The Big Picture'. *Guardian*, 26 July.

Yúdice, George. (1995) 'Civil Society, Consumption, and Governmentality in an Age of Global Restructuring: An Introduction'. *Social Text* no. 45: 1–27.

Yúdice, George. (2000) 'The Creation of a Latin American Cultural Space'. Presentation to the Crossroads in Cultural Studies Conference, Birmingham, 21–25 June.

Zecchinelli, Cecilia. (1994) 'Gaps Seen for EU TV Meet'. *Daily Variety*, 26 June: 13.

Zolberg, Vera. (1995) 'Museum Culture and GATT'. *Journal of Arts Management, Law and Society* 25, no. 1: 5–16.

Zollars, C. L. and M. G. Cantor. (1993). 'The Sociology of Culture Producing Occupations: Discussion and Synthesis'. *Current Research on Occupations and Professions*. 8: 1–29.

Zwick, Steve. (2000) 'Top Marks for Hollywood German Film Production Companies are Pouring into Big U.S. Movies – with Mixed Results'. *Time International*, 16 October: 58.

Index